P
Classical Social Tl

MW00565275

"Royce's skillful analysis focuses on questions of continuing significance (modernity, individualism, democracy, and socialism). He provides clear and concise overviews of Marx, Weber, and Durkheim, effectively defining and explaining key ideas, outlining points of connection, and developing the comparisons among the three theorists. Without losing his own clear voice, Royce writes with close attention to, and frequent citations from, primary texts. This will resonate with students who are simultaneously reading the primary texts and will give students for whom this is their only exposure to Marx, Weber, and Durkheim a taste of the theorists' language. A clear and compelling—and beautifully written—introduction to the classic social theorists."

—Cheryl Laz, University of Southern Maine

"In *Classical Social Theory and Modern Society*, Edward Royce provides a unique thematic approach to the founding fathers of classical sociology by presenting their ideas in an accessible and informative dialogue with each other. Offering a clear, succinct, and comprehensive outline of the main positions in the canon around the most significant themes of modernity, the book skillfully guides the reader through a wide range of complicated issues and critical debates surrounding classical social theory."

—Kaan Agartan, Framingham State University

"One might have thought that there is little that could productively be added to the secondary literature on the classics of social theory, but this book shows otherwise. A refreshing contribution, Royce's work contains many insights: it is written in a lucid and lively style and will, I am confident, be very well received in the community of social theorists."

—Jeff Coulter, Boston University

"Royce's masterful survey of the ideas and sociological vision of Marx, Durkheim, and Weber is unique in dealing with these three thinkers as political public intellectuals and sociologists, while also remaining grounded in meticulous close readings of the texts. Grounding the sociological classics in the intellectual and cultural context of their times, Royce allows their insights to speak to us again on the big questions of democracy, individualism, freedom, and equality that are all too relevant in today's world in turmoil, change, and crisis. Students will find the prose and organization easy to follow, and professors and students will be both stimulated by Royce's insights and impressed by his scholarly care."

—Neil McLaughlin, McMaster University

Classical Social Theory and Modern Society

Marx, Durkheim, Weber

Edward Royce

ROWMAN & LITTLEFIELD
Lanham • Boulder • New York • London

Published by Rowman & Littlefield
A wholly owned subsidiary of
The Rowman & Littlefield Publishing Group, Inc.
4501 Forbes Boulevard, Suite 200, Lanham, Maryland 20706
www.rowman.com

Unit A, Whitacre Mews, 26-34 Stannary Street, London SE11 4AB,
United Kingdom

British Library Cataloguing in Publication Information Available

Library of Congress Cataloging-in-Publication Data
Royce, Edward Cary.
Classical social theory and modern society : Marx, Durkheim, Weber / Edward Royce.
pages cm
Includes bibliographical references and index.
ISBN 978-1-4422-4322-4 (cloth : alk. paper) — ISBN 978-1-4422-4323-1 (pbk. : alk.
paper) — ISBN 978-1-4422-4324-8 (electronic)
1. Sociology—History. 2. Social sciences—Philosophy. 3. Marx, Karl, 1818–1883. 4.
Durkheim, Emile, 1858–1917. 5. Weber, Max, 1864–1920. I. Title.
HM435.R69 2015
301—dc23
2014039782

Printed in the United States of America

Brief Contents

Detailed Contents

Acknowledgments

A number of people read all or part of this book at various stages of its development. I greatly appreciate their feedback and am grateful for all the time and effort they devoted to this project. In particular, I would like to thank Doug Amy, Rick Eckstein, Ashley Kistler, Susan Libby, Shannon Mariotti, Julia Maskivker, Matt Nichter, Eric Schutz, Clair Strom, Tom Wartenberg, and Larry Van Sickle. Three originally anonymous reviewers for Rowman & Littlefield who have kindly allowed me to acknowledge them by name—Jeff Coulter (Boston College), Susan Roxburgh (Kent State University), and Kaan Agartan (Framingham State University)—also provided thoughtful and constructive recommendations for revision. I used early drafts of chapters from this book in my teaching over the past three years, and I would very much like to thank my social theory students for their comments and criticisms. I also received valuable feedback on parts of this manuscript from students taught by Rick Eckstein and Shannon Mariotti. Thanks to Kathryn Tracy as well for providing me with a great place to write over the past three summers. Sarah Stanton was extremely helpful and supportive in shepherding this book through the review and publication process. I would like to thank her along with Kathryn Knigge and all the other fine people at Rowman & Littlefield.

Chapter One

Introduction

Classical sociological theory arose in the nineteenth century as an effort to comprehend the ongoing transition from traditional feudal society to modern industrial society. The three figures I focus on in this book—Karl Marx (1818–1883), Emile Durkheim (1858–1917), and Max Weber (1864–1920) —are commonly regarded as the foremost representatives of this "classical tradition." They are of course not the only significant contributors to the development of sociological theory or to the emergence of sociology as an academic discipline. I concentrate on this trio rather than the larger group of sociology founders for several reasons: a strong personal interest in their work, a preference for depth over breadth, the intelligence and originality of their diagnoses of the modern condition, and their undeniably prominent status in the pantheon of social theory. Marx, Durkheim, and Weber remain remarkably influential even in the twenty-first century. Their writings, revealing divergent viewpoints, permit thought-provoking contrasts and comparisons. And their work is a particularly rich resource for reflecting on one's own intellectual assumptions and political commitments. By no means do these three give us the final word on anything, but they are essential reading if we wish to understand sociological theory and make sense of the modern world. [1]

The purpose of this book is to present an accessible introduction to the writings of Marx, Durkheim, and Weber, but one that is also deeply immersed in the primary source material. I have not set out to offer a critique of these three theorists; or to consider how their ideas might be revised and updated for application in the contemporary era; or to document how their thinking is expressed, extended, or abandoned in the practice of present-day sociology. These are worthy issues certainly, but they require that one already possess a reasonably faithful understanding of classical sociology. This is where I hope to make a contribution. With a student audience in mind, my aim is to describe as clearly, sympathetically, and in as much detail as feasible what Marx, Durkheim, and Weber each have to tell us about the nature of modern society and explain how they differ in their interpretations of modernity's perils and prospects. Along the way, I discuss some of their strengths and weaknesses, insights and blind spots, but for the most part I leave it up to readers to assess the relative merit of their work and ponder what of value they have to say to us today.

CLASSICAL SOCIOLOGY AND THE GREAT TRANSFORMATION

Sociology originated in the midst of what economic historian Karl Polanyi called the "great transformation." Located primarily in Western Europe during the eighteenth and nineteenth centuries, varying in timing and effect from one country to another, this transformation culminated in the demise of the pre-modern world and the rise of the modern world. Though Polanyi's primary interest was the expansion of the market economy, the period of European history he wrote about was shaped by a profound triple revolution—an intellectual and cultural revolution: the Enlightenment; a social and political revolution: the French Revolution of 1789; and an economic revolution: the rise of capitalism and the subsequent process of industrialization. These three intertwined revolutions, preceded by the Renaissance and the Reformation, radically altered the European landscape. They gave rise to new worldviews and aspirations, new attitudes and orientations, new political and economic institutions, and new forms of social organization and patterns of living; they set into motion new social forces, new developmental dynamics, and new social movements; and they brought new problems and new possibilities onto the historical stage. As one indicator of the dramatic changes occurring during this "age of revolution," consider the following list of words, all of which became part of the common vocabulary or acquired their modern meaning during this period: industry, factory, working class, middle class, capitalism, socialism, communism, liberal, conservative, scientist, engineer, utilitarian, journalism, economic crisis, pauperism, strike, ideology, intellectual, humanitarian, statistics, bureaucracy, commercialism, masses, unemployment, and sociology.[2]

The issues raised by the advent of modernity are no less relevant today than in the era of classical sociology. The cultural, political, and economic revolutions that gave birth to modern society are, in fact, still ongoing and deeply contested. On the cultural front, for example, we see this in the persistence of traditional values and beliefs, the continued resistance to the process of secularization, and the enduring conflict between science and religion. On the political front, in the sometimes life-and-death struggles around the world—the developed nations included—for human rights, individual freedoms, and democratic institutions. And on the economic front, in the worldwide expansion of capitalism, whose fate is nowadays decidedly uncertain given the threat of global warming, the depletion of oil reserves, and the precarious state of the world economy. It is an open question whether these revolutions will lose momentum or continue to shape the course of history and what consequences will ultimately result from their unfolding.

In what follows, to fill in some of the historical context, I present a highly abbreviated overview of the Enlightenment, the French Revolution, and the Industrial Revolution. My purpose here is a limited one: to explain briefly what was revolutionary about each of these revolutions, familiarize readers with the period of transition from traditional society to modern society, and shed some light on the historical setting in which Marx, Durkheim, and Weber found themselves.

The Enlightenment

Historian Peter Gay dates the period of the Enlightenment from approximately 1689 (the English Revolution and the birth of Montesquieu) to 1789 (the outbreak of the French Revolution). The leading figures of the Enlightenment include, among others: from France—Voltaire (1694–1778), Jean-Jacques Rousseau (1712–1778), Denis Diderot (1713–1748), Jean d'Alembert (1717–1783), Anne Robert Jacques Turgot (1727–1781), and the Marquis de Condorcet (1743–1794); from Scotland—David Hume (1711–1776), Adam Smith (1723–1790), and Adam Ferguson (1723–1816); from England—John Locke (1632–1704); and from Germany—Immanuel Kant (1724–1804). This was a diverse group. But as writers and scholars living during a period described by Kant as the "age of criticism," they did share a certain family resemblance in their intellectual and political convictions. Whatever their country of origin, Gay declares, the Enlightenment philosophers had at least one thing in common: they were all "lyrical in their single-minded praise of criticism" and uncompromising in their opposition to the "cancer of superstitions," the "gloom of accepted nonsense," and the "citadel of unreason."[3]

The philosophers of the Enlightenment—the *"philosophes"* as they were called in France—were deeply committed to the idea of an empirical science. A reliable understanding of the world, they insisted, could only be attained through experience, observation, and experimentation. By endorsing the scientific method and asserting the superiority of an empirical approach to the acquisition of knowledge, the Enlightenment took aim at the authority of traditional beliefs and customary ways of thought. And by proposing that worldly problems be examined from a scientific and critical standpoint, the *philosophes* also placed themselves in opposition to the religious establishment. Though not necessarily anti-religious, they were hostile to the religious dogmatism propagated by the Catholic Church. By putting faith ahead of reason, the scriptures ahead of science, the Church, they maintained, was responsible for the perpetuation of ignorance, superstition, fanaticism, and all the evils these entailed. The *philosophes*, by contrast, adopting a distinctly modern frame of mind, promoted a secular and scientific worldview.[4]

The central premise of the Enlightenment was faith in the power of reason, not only as an instrument for understanding the world, but for bettering the world as well. The *philosophes* were "practical social reformers," seeking knowledge "above all for the sake of its utility." They were confident that the findings of science could be employed to improve the human condition. As Peter Hamilton explains, they believed that through the application of scientific knowledge, "social institutions could be created that would make men happier and free them from cruelty, injustice, and despotism." This vision implied a conception of the world as malleable, capable of being rearranged to align more closely with the dictates of reason and the requirements of human welfare. And with science on the march, already yielding remarkable accomplishments, the *philosophes* were cautiously optimistic. They did not necessarily believe that progress was inevitable, but they did see it as possible, and perhaps even likely.[5]

The *philosophes* were social critics, targeting the chicanery, abuses, and tyranny of the clergy and the nobility, and they were advocates for a more rational and humane society. But they were not political radicals. They did not seek to incite rebellion on the part of the masses or to overthrow the existing social order. The Enlightenment was revolutionary nevertheless. It contributed to the creation of a new and modern secular mentality where the future, no longer shackled to the past, was seen as an open-ended point of reference, a "realm of unrealized possibilities." In their defense of science and reason, their denunciation of religious orthodoxy, and their anticipation of a better world, the *philosophes* launched an anti-traditionalist cultural revolution.[6]

The French Revolution

Prior to the 1789 revolution, France was an absolute monarchy, with the king—Louis XVI since 1774—wielding power unconstrained by any constitutional restrictions. The population over whom the king ruled was divided into three "orders" or "estates," each itself internally stratified. The *first estate*, consisting of the clergy, was based in the Catholic Church. The *second estate* comprised the nobility, many of whom were large landholders who also held important positions within the Church, the army, and the government. Everyone else, more than 90 percent of the population, fell into the *third estate*. This large group, the common people, included the middle and working classes as well as the peasantry who made up the vast majority of the population. Fueled by economic distress and political discontent, the French Revolution, to put it simply, involved the revolt of the third estate against the traditional privileges and entitlements of the first and second estates and ultimately against the hereditary monarchy itself.[7]

The revolution originated during a period of prolonged economic crisis and political paralysis. The central problem was the unmanageable debt that had accumulated from court expenses, costly military ventures, and tax exemptions for the privileged. On May 5, 1789, in a last-ditch attempt to forge an acceptable compromise and avert bankruptcy, Louis XVI reluctantly, and for the first time in nearly two centuries, convened the Estates General, a political body consisting of representatives from each of the three orders. But since each order was allotted one vote, the third estate found itself outgunned by the more or less united forces of the clergy and the nobility. With a "riotous people" standing behind them, the deputies of the third estate refused to go along with such a patently unjust arrangement. After several weeks of deadlock, and in defiance of the king, they elected to proceed unilaterally, renouncing the Estates General in favor of a "National Assembly." This flanking maneuver, creating something approximating a people's parliament, empowered representatives to vote as individuals, counted by head, rather than as members of an estate. The commoners were thus able to assert their majority status, undermining the veto power of the privileged orders. Historian William Doyle refers to this as the "founding act of the French Revolution."[8]

With the establishment of the National Assembly, sovereign power in France was effectively transferred from the monarchy to the nation itself. Meanwhile, amid the ensuing political turmoil, armed troops under the command of the king began converging on Paris and Versailles. Outraged at this response and fearing a counter-revolutionary plot, ordinary people, already agitated by rising bread prices, took to the streets in open rebellion. On July 14, 1789, they demonstrated their opposition to royal authority in historic fashion by storming the Bastille, a prison fortress in Paris. A potent measure of popular power, the destruction of the Bastille ignited an outbreak of anti-aristocratic insurrection throughout the country. Less than a month later, the National Assembly, scaling down the authority of the Church and repudiating noble privileges, announced the abolition of the "feudal regime." Shortly thereafter, as a preliminary to the formation of a new constitution, the Assembly issued the "Declaration of the Rights of Man and Citizen." In the first of seventeen decrees, this declaration famously proclaimed that "Men are born and remain free and equal in rights." As Jack Censor and Lynn Hunt observe, with this document "the *subjects* of the monarch became participating *citizens*."[9]

Thanks partly to the presence of a lively press and the increasing importance of public opinion, the French Revolution was a truly popular revolt. It brought the masses of ordinary people into the political arena as never before. Not just objects of history, they became subjects of history as well, agents of social change. Stirring the imagination and fears of people throughout the western world, the year 1789 witnessed an extraordinary phenomenon: a population rising up and transforming what was previously assumed to be the natural order of things. As Robert Darnton observes, in this historical moment the people of France "experienced reality as something that could be destroyed and reconstructed, and they faced seemingly limitless possibilities, both for good and for evil." Following closely on the heels of the Enlightenment, the French Revolution dramatically affirmed the *philosophes'* belief in the malleability of the world.[10]

The French Revolution pitted the common people, including many well-to-do members of the emerging middle class, against the monarchy, the nobility, and the clergy. It was a revolt against royal despotism, hereditary privilege, and economic oppression and a revolt in the name of democratic government, political equality, and human rights. In the decade following the formation of the National Assembly, however, the revolution foundered as France became embroiled in wars abroad and violent factional battles at home. In 1799, the period of the French Revolution came to an end as General Napoleon Bonaparte assumed power in a coup d'état, proclaiming himself emperor in 1804. For the next seventy years, through several regime changes, France remained in the grip of authoritarian rule. Though not successful in realizing the ideals of liberty, equality, and fraternity, the French Revolution, like the Enlightenment, was a modernizing force and a decisive turning point in western history. It went a long way toward dismantling and delegitimizing the despotic order of the ancien régime. It promulgated the idea of popular sovereignty, a powerful "new principle of political legitimacy." And it left an inspiring and world-changing legacy in the form of enduring and deeply felt democratic and egalitarian aspirations. [11]

The Industrial Revolution

The Industrial Revolution, with machine labor gradually replacing hand labor, originated in Great Britain in the late 1700s and then spread to Western Europe and the United States. This revolution was predicated on the prior development of a market economy, including a market for labor, and the expansion of opportunities for international trade. The emergence of Britain as the "workshop of the world" in the first decades of the nineteenth century depended on the availability of domestic and overseas markets, both to keep producers supplied with raw materials and to ensure a sufficient demand for the growing output of industrial goods. In this respect, given its supremacy as a colonial power and London's status as the epicenter of world finance, eighteenth-century Britain was primed for economic takeoff. [12]

For most economic historians, the Industrial Revolution proper began with the introduction of new technologies, particularly in the textile, iron, and mining industries. The spinning mule (for making cotton products), the steam engine, and numerous other inventions from the 1760s onward, by mechanizing the process of production, greatly accelerated the productivity of labor and the pace of economic growth. More fundamentally, however, the Industrial Revolution initiated an outpouring of *continuous* scientific and technological innovation and *continuous* improvement in the methods of production. Once the process of industrialization got under way, Eric Hobsbawm writes, "change became the norm." [13]

The development of machine production was a big part of the story, but the Industrial Revolution was not just a technological revolution. It was also, and more importantly, a social revolution. It resulted in the dissolution of a traditional way of life and a radical transformation in the basic organization and workings of society. Prior to the 1800s, to take one important example, people lived a predominantly rural existence, earning a living as agricultural laborers, often with the family as the basic unit of production. As the process of industrialization took hold, in combination with a rapidly growing population, the rural society of the pre-modern world gave way to the increasingly urban society of the modern world. The migration from the countryside into cities and towns represented a momentous change in the circumstances of people's lives. The newly arrived city dweller encountered a harsh and alien social environment: crowded and unsanitary housing, air and water pollution, inadequate public facilities and services, unfamiliar and oppressive working conditions, and urban social relationships of a characteristically impersonal and market-mediated form. In the transition from the traditional agrarian economy to modern industrial capitalism, the social dimension of change, and the many hardships people experienced along the way, was at least as important as the technological dimension. In a well-known passage, Karl Polanyi, referring to this mixture of progress and tragedy, captures the central contradiction of the great transformation. "At the heart of the Industrial Revolution of the eighteenth century," he states, "there was an almost miraculous improvement in the tools of production, which was accompanied by a catastrophic dislocation of the lives of the common people."[14]

Among the most consequential developments accompanying the process of industrialization was the creation of the modern industrial workplace—the factory. The rise of the factory system thoroughly transformed the conditions of labor and the lives of working people. The emergence of factory production created a division between work life and family life, separating the public sphere of the workplace from the private sphere of the household. It centralized the process of production, gathering workers under the same roof, placing them under the direct supervision of their employers, and thereby enabling capitalists to more effectively control and monitor the labor process. It turned thousands of women and children, presumed to be less expensive and more docile, into industrial laborers working under brutal circumstances. It facilitated the expansion of the specialized division of labor, increasing economic efficiency but also confining workers to a repetitive and monotonous routine. And by tying workers to the pace of the machinery and the "tyranny of the clock," the factory system, in violation of "pre-industrial rhythms of work," imposed a new and more intensive form of labor discipline. In countless ways, due especially to the appearance of the factory, "the industrial world of 1850," Maxine Berg and Pat Hudson emphasize, "was vastly different for most workers from that of 1750."[15]

As the industrial economy displaced the agrarian economy, wealth in the form of landed property declined in importance relative to wealth in the form of industrial capital (e.g., buildings, factories, and machinery). Over time, correspondingly, the capitalist unseated the landowner as the dominant economic power in society. Meanwhile, at the other end of the class structure, a modern industrial proletariat came into existence. This population of market-dependent wage laborers, torn from a traditional way of life, did not accommodate to the new world of industrial capitalism without opposition, and they continued to resist the advance of capitalism throughout the nineteenth century. Workers in England, for example, with particular intensity during the 1830s and 1840s, struggled to win political and economic rights, including the right to vote, the right to form labor unions, and the right to strike. The era of the Industrial Revolution was not just a period of technological innovation; it was also a period of bitter class conflict, with waves of working-class protest and political agitation throughout the first half of the 1800s. The Industrial Revolution resulted in the triumph of modern capitalism, but on the other side it also gave birth to capitalism's chief adversary: the modern socialist movement.[16]

* * *

Anthony Giddens describes sociology as the "study of modernity." A "shorthand term for modern society or industrial civilization," the concept of modernity, Giddens maintains, embraces three essential characteristics. As should be obvious, these characteristics correspond respectively to the three revolutions discussed above. First, "a certain set of attitudes toward the world, including the idea of the world as open to transformation by human intervention." Second, "a certain range of political institutions, including the nation-state and mass democracy." And third, "a complex of economic institutions, especially industrial production and a market economy." The combined force of the Enlightenment, the French Revolution, and the Industrial Revolution paved the way for the emergence of the modern western world. These three revolutions also set the agenda for the nascent discipline of sociology—an academic field conceived with the purpose of investigating the development of modern society.[17]

CLASSICAL SOCIOLOGY AND MODERN SOCIETY

Classical sociology is a phenomenon of modernity itself, an outgrowth of the very development it set out to study. And the "theme of modernity," as Gerard Delanty notes, is the "great unifying motif" of classical sociology. That the topic of modernity captured the attention of nineteenth-century intellectuals is not surprising. They could hardly ignore the fact of a new world springing up around them. The scope of social change during this age of revolution was so far reaching that for many observers, both at the time and in retrospect, the passage from the pre-modern era to the modern era represented a fundamental rupture or discontinuity in the human experience. This great transformation, so profound in its implications, gave sociological theory its reason for existence.[18]

Another development during this historical period, though not quite as earthshaking, also proved pivotal to the emergence of sociology: the discovery of the idea of the "social" or "society." In the wake of the social transformations accompanying modernity, intellectuals began looking at the life of humanity through a new lens. They came to recognize the existence of society as a supra-individual entity, a distinct phenomenon having its own "specific characteristics, its constraints and its variables." From this premise, furthermore, it was only a short step to the conclusion that individuals themselves were products of society. The idea of the social, which Durkheim famously ratified by introducing the concept of "social facts," gave sociologists their unique vantage point. While economics focused on the market and political theory of the state, sociology took up the study of social life itself, handing down to us a new terminology: social organization, social structure, social institutions, social change, social action, and social order. Sociological theory adopted as its subject matter not simply *modernity*, but modern *society*.[19]

Marx, Durkheim, and Weber: Theorists of Modernity

Because they are considered the founding fathers of sociology, Marx, Durkheim, and Weber form a natural trio of sorts. We study their work to inform ourselves about the history and development of sociological theory, to learn what it means to think sociologically, to gain some appreciation for the sociological enterprise and the practice of social research, to acquaint ourselves with different perspectives and schools of thought within the discipline, and to acquire the background knowledge necessary to understand current issues and controversies in the field.

But there is another reason to read Marx, Durkheim, and Weber. They are also among the foremost theorists of modernity. The classical sociologists resided in what is generally regarded as the "birthplace" of modern society, Western Europe, and they were witnesses to that birth as well. They were, as Philip Abrahms states, among the "first generation of human beings ever to have experienced within the span of their own lifetime socially induced social change of a totally transformative nature." They lived during an era of great social change, and one that portended even greater changes to come. Marx, Durkheim, and Weber are still interesting in part because they were firsthand observers of the passage from the pre-modern world to the modern world, and because they were among the first intellectuals to make use of the tools of empirical science to comprehend this passage. Their "sociology remains relevant, indeed indispensable" today, furthermore, because the world they studied is arguably still the world we currently live in, a *modern* world now gone global—as Randall Collins observes, a world that in the twenty-first century is "pretty much everyone's world."[20]

As theorists of modernity, Marx, Durkheim, and Weber each pursued a similar set of questions: what are the origins and defining characteristics of the new capitalist or industrial society, how does it differ from the traditional society of the past, through what processes did the transition from the pre-modern world to the modern world come about, what are the driving forces and developmental tendencies of the emergent industrial society, what is the fate of the individual in the modern age, what new problems and dangers does the era of modernity pose, what does the future hold, and how might we best respond to the radically new circumstances of modern social life? These and related issues concerning the nature of modernity were central to the lifework of these three theorists. Marx, Durkheim, and Weber were founders of sociology, but more importantly they were theorists of modernity.

Marx, Durkheim, and Weber: Defenders of Modernity

Marx, Durkheim, and Weber each applied the principles of science inherited from the Enlightenment to examine the origins, characteristics, and dynamics of modern society. Beyond being *theorists* of modernity, however, they were also *defenders* of modernity, vehemently opposed to the reactionary currents of their day. Unlike many of their contemporaries, they sided with the forces of change. They neither regretted the demise of traditional society nor dreaded the rise of modern society.

Even while documenting its horrific human costs, Marx welcomed the rise of modern industry, believing it held out the promise of human liberation. And despite being among its most severe critics, he regarded the development of capitalism as a "civilizing influence." It not only uprooted a moribund feudal order with its archaic institutional and ideological trappings, but it also accelerated the growth of society's productive forces, in the process accomplishing "wonders far surpassing Egyptian pyramids, Roman aqueducts, and Gothic cathedrals." By relentlessly increasing human productive power, capitalism, Marx claimed, was a historically progressive force, creating the objective conditions necessary for the realization of a socialist future. In contrast to the nostalgic critics of the modern economic order who hoped vainly to return to some "bygone form of society," Marx's outlook was thoroughly forward looking.[21]

The same was true of Durkheim. "Steeped in the spirit of the Third Republic," he waged constant battle against those forces hoping to stifle the process of modernization, reaffirm the authority of traditional values, and restore some version of the old regime. In opposition to this "reactionary school," Durkheim denied that the solutions appropriate to the past could be counted on to alleviate the problems of the present. Instead, he embraced the "republican ethos" and the modern ideals of democracy, science, and secularism. Going on the offense against modernity's anti-liberal critics, he applied the sociological method to make an empirically grounded case in support of industrialization, individualism, intellectualism, and egalitarianism. Durkheim, like Marx, was a champion of modernity.[22]

While viewing modern society with more trepidation than either Marx or Durkheim, Weber too was anything but an anti-modernist. Indeed, he saved his most savage criticisms for romantics aspiring to resurrect aristocratic traditions and literary figures writing in celebration of feudal values and hereditary privileges. Averse to the rigors of economic modernization, this backward-looking social stratum longed for "a more 'easy-going' way of life as an ideal for the future." Weber denounced these "spokesmen for economic stagnation," fearing they would hinder Germany's entry into the industrial world and jeopardize its economic future. At the same time, concerned about the prospects for individual freedom, he acknowledged the inherently constraining features of modern capitalist society. For Weber, however, like Marx and Durkheim, it was neither desirable nor possible to turn back the hands of time. The only question was how individuals might live an autonomous and meaningful life within the framework of the modern economic order.[23]

Marx, Durkheim, and Weber: Critics of Modernity

Marx, Durkheim, and Weber applauded the achievements of modern society and fought to extend the process of modernization in directions they deemed desirable. They were defenders of modernity. But they were also critics of modernity. They drew attention to the hazards, dilemmas, and ailments of modern social life, and in fact they regarded the Western European world of their day as being in a state of crisis. In response, they each set forth a diagnosis of their time, unveiling the contradictions, pathologies, and irrationalities of the modern era. No matter how thoroughgoing and critical their interrogation of the modern condition, at no point however did they ever relinquish their commitment to the idea of a modern society.

Though they each undertook a critical analysis of the modern world, Marx, Durkheim, and Weber differed in what they saw as the central problems of modern society, how they interpreted those problems, and the remedies they proposed. Marx drew attention to the oppression of the working class, the dehumanizing conditions of labor, and the crisis-prone nature of the capitalist economic system. Durkheim bemoaned the absence of a moral framework governing modern economic life, a circumstance resulting in the loosening of social bonds, the malady of egoism, and the perpetuation of injustice. Emphasizing the bureaucratization and rationalization of society, Weber worried that modern institutions would come to form an "iron cage," undermining individual autonomy and social dynamism. I discuss their diagnoses of the modern condition more fully in chapters 5 and 6, but the point worth making for now is that while Marx, Durkheim, and Weber defended modernity in principle, they were also sharply critical of the modern era in which they lived.[24]

Marx, Durkheim, and Weber: Public Intellectuals

Marx, Durkheim, and Weber each embraced the identity of scientist, they were each devoted to the scientific enterprise, and they each amassed an impressive body of social science scholarship. In their scientific endeavors, however, they also each thought of themselves as serving other, extra-scientific purposes, political purposes broadly speaking. Their goal was not merely to add to the stock of scientific knowledge but to effect social change. Through the force of their writings and speeches, they sought to educate and enlighten, demystify and debunk; they sought to alter public consciousness and win converts to their causes. What is obviously true for Marx—that he intended not only to interpret the world but to change it as well—is equally true for Durkheim and Weber.

None of the three fit the mold of the cloistered academic, cut off from real life and absorbed in esoteric research. They were in fact what are today sometimes called "public intellectuals" or "public sociologists." Not only did they address audiences beyond the scholarly community, but their writings were also "informed by a 'public' concern," by a "caring for public things." Their aim was not primarily to fill gaps in scientific knowledge or solve intellectual puzzles—though they certainly contributed to both of these ends. More fundamentally, however, in the tradition of what Sheldon Wolin calls "epic" theory, they directed their attention toward real-world issues, for example, the alienation of labor for Marx, the malaise of modern society for Durkheim, and the routinization of social life for Weber. Their writings addressed problems "created by actual events or states in the world" rather than "problems related to deficiencies in theoretical knowledge." They were motivated by practical concerns, by the social and political issues of their day, rather than by purely academic, intellectual, or scientific concerns. They were, in other words, inspired by "problems-in-the-world" rather than "problems-in-a-theory."[25]

Nor were they content to observe from the sidelines, simply recording the vast changes occurring around them. Their writings were often of a political and value-laden nature—interventions *in* the world as much as investigations *of* the world. And they took sides as well, defending some ways of responding to the modern condition while denouncing others. Without abandoning their commitment to science, Marx, Durkheim, and Weber each sought to utilize their intellectual capital for political purposes and to deploy their ideas in such a way as to make a practical difference.

THE PLAN OF THE BOOK

For the purposes of this book, I treat Marx, Durkheim, and Weber not primarily as founders of sociology or as sociological theorists narrowly conceived, but as sociologically minded theorists of modernity and as proponents of politically charged worldviews. Perhaps more so than other such books, I focus not only on their specifically sociological writings, but on their political writings as well and on the political and normative dimension of their sociological writings. Looking at these three social theorists in this light inevitably brings to the forefront the differences among them, not only in their intellectual assumptions and analyses, but also in their political values and commitments. This approach draws attention to what is in any case a central component of their scholarly work—its critical and evaluative examination of the modern world. My strategy in sum is to compare Marx, Durkheim, and Weber on the common ground of their practice as politically engaged sociologists, each with a distinctive interpretation of and reaction to the emergence and evolution of modern society, and each determined not just to understand the world or even "to change men's views of the world," but "to change the world itself."[26]

As theorists of modernity and practically minded public intellectuals, Marx, Durkheim, and Weber challenge us to think about the workings of society, the fate of the individual, and the trajectory of social change. Along with this, however, their writings are also an invaluable resource for critically contemplating our own political orientations and worldviews. The work of these three theorists is compelling. It provokes us to take stock—to reassess who we are, what we believe, and where we stand. This book is designed to encourage readers to wrestle with the contrasting viewpoints of Marx, Durkheim, and Weber. It invites readers—in dialogue with classical sociology— to take a position, to argue one side or another. Sociological theory, when read from this vantage point, is "a crucial basis for reflection on social life" and for the thoughtful reappraisal of our own political identities, convictions, and practices. It is, in this respect, not merely a "tool for sociologists," but a tool for citizens as well. This, certainly, is one good reason for continuing to read the work of Marx, Durkheim, and Weber.[27]

This book is divided into two parts, plus this introductory chapter and a short concluding chapter. In part I, consisting of chapters 2 through 4—the "overview" chapters—I introduce readers to the writings of Marx, Durkheim, and Weber, respectively. These chapters summarize the key ideas of these three theorists, with an emphasis on their thinking about the origins, nature, and destiny of the modern world. In chapter 2, I discuss Marx's materialist perspective, his critical analysis of the capitalist system of production, and his conception of how the development of capitalism sets the stage for the rise of socialism. In chapter 3, I concentrate on Durkheim's elaboration of a distinctly sociological methodology and his effort on this basis to develop a theory of modernity and an interpretation of the relationship between the individual and society. In chapter 4, I focus on Weber's view of modernization as a process of rationalization, examining the implications of this process through his writings on social action, modern capitalism, rational-legal authority, bureaucratic administration, western science, and the disenchantment of the world.

In part II, consisting of chapters 5 through 8—the "thematic" chapters—I discuss the thinking of Marx, Durkheim, and Weber on four topics central to their analyses of modernity: the pathologies of modern society, the predicament of the individual, the state and democracy, and socialism versus capitalism. I single out these specific themes for several reasons, all of which relate to the larger objectives of this book. (1) More than any other concerns, these four, I believe, best serve to illuminate Marx, Durkheim, and Weber's respective theories of modern society. (2) At the same time these topics mutually inform one another, combining to produce a coherent narrative, with each theme facilitating a deeper understanding of the other three. (3) Marx, Durkheim, and Weber have a lot to say about these four topics—which bear directly on problems critical to their work as a whole—and what they have to say goes to the heart of who they are as social and political theorists. (4) These themes are also well suited to exploring both the sociological dimension and the political dimension of these theorists' writings and for examining the interplay in their work between sociological analysis and political argument. (5) What is especially important about these four themes, furthermore, is that they reveal with particular clarity the chief differences among Marx, Durkheim, and Weber in their analyses of modernity, their responses to the modern condition, and their thoughts about the future. (6) Because they raise enduring questions with considerable contemporary relevance, these topics also have great potential for provoking readers' interest and prompting readers to reflect critically on their own conceptions of the nature and problems of modern life.

While I do not have a single template for the overview chapters, the thematic chapters are organized identically. They each begin with a short introduction to the theme under consideration followed by four segments: one each on Marx, Durkheim, and Weber and a concluding segment that explicitly compares the three of them. With this combination of juxtaposition and comparison, the thematic chapters offer a close reading of Marx, Durkheim, and Weber on four issues that are at the core of their conceptions of modern society, while at the same time exploring the differences among the three in their diagnoses of the modern condition.

The segments on Marx, Durkheim, and Weber in the thematic chapters are more or less stand-alone. It is necessary to read the overview chapter for any one theorist before moving on to the thematic segments on that theorist. But it is possible to read all the segments of any one theorist before turning to any of the segments of the other two. This allows for some flexibility in how the book might be used for pedagogical purposes. One can, of course, read the book in the order in which it is written. This approach has the advantage of bringing the contrasting viewpoints of Marx, Durkheim, and Weber to the forefront throughout. Or one can read the Marx overview chapter followed by all the Marx segments, move on in the same manner to Durkheim and Weber, and then conclude by turning to the comparison segments. This approach—examining each theorist in sequence rather than in tandem—is more in line with the typical format of a course on classical sociological theory. Even then, however, more so than a conventionally organized book, the thematic focus of chapters 5 through 8 should draw readers' attention to the differences among Marx, Durkheim, and Weber in their analyses of modern society.

Part I

Overview

Chapter Two

Karl Marx (1818–1883)

Readers new to Marx might be surprised to discover that nowhere in his writings does he present a detailed blueprint of a socialist or communist utopia. There is no theory of socialism in Marx's work if by this one means a well-defined vision of the post-capitalist world. Some of his predecessors—Henri de Saint-Simon, Charles Fourier, and Robert Owen—were not so reluctant to offer up depictions of the *good society*. Marx admired these so-called utopian socialists, praising their critical view of the modern condition, but his embrace of the revolutionary cause took him down a different path: "We do not dogmatically anticipate the world, but only want to find the new world through criticism of the old one." The chief task, he declared, was not to construct fanciful models of the future, but to work toward a new society through the *"ruthless criticism of all that exists."* This is precisely what we find in Marx: a comprehensive critique of *capitalist* society, not an elaborate plan for a *socialist* society. Rather than trying to influence the thinking of the working class and its allies by painting a beautiful picture of the socialist future, he sought instead to expose the ugly reality of the capitalist present. [1]

While Marx prepared no instruction manual for building a socialist society, he was not entirely silent about what a working-class revolution might bring. As a participant and leader in many of the radical organizations of his day, he could hardly avoid talking about the goals of the socialist movement, and he often defended some conceptions of socialism while denouncing others. And though he refused to go into detail about how a socialist society might be organized, he did set forth some general principles. For example, he envisioned a socialism where every individual would be able to develop freely and fully all of his or her capabilities, where the system of production would serve the goal of fulfilling human needs rather than maximizing profit, where "all the burdens of society" would not fall on one class and its advantages monopolized by another, and where society's resources would be distributed "from each according to his abilities, to each according to his needs." These principles tell us something about his hopes for a socialist society, but just as much they tell us something about his antipathy toward capitalist society. Marx's writings affirm the need to move beyond capitalism more than they delineate the particulars of any future socialism. At the same time, however, by exposing the failings of capitalism, Marx does point us in the direction of what a socialist alternative might entail. In any case, it is fair to say that for Marx we can only comprehend the meaning, possibility, and necessity of a socialist society by grasping the inner workings of the capitalist economic system.[2]

Marx's standing as one of the most important social theorists of modern times rests on his analysis of the capitalist mode of production. In an era where capitalism has attained global dominance, his work, though an outgrowth of the nineteenth century, remains highly relevant. And whatever one might think about the likelihood of a socialist future, Marx's writings will continue to be relevant as along as capitalism persists. His critique of the capitalist system, particularly in the U.S. context, deserves careful consideration, not only because it might help us understand the current state of American society, but also because it is usefully provocative. He challenges many of the taken-for-granted beliefs a typical American is likely to have about the society in which we live. For this reason alone—whether we end up deciding we are with Marx or against him—he is worth taking seriously. It is important however that we evaluate Marx on his own terms, not according to our inherited preconceptions about communism, but on the basis of what he actually has to say about capitalism.

This chapter provides an overview of some of Marx's most important concepts, ideas, and arguments. It is intended to serve as an introduction to his work while at the same time setting the stage for later chapters which will delve into certain key issues more deeply. In the first section of this chapter, focusing on his general theoretical framework, I discuss Marx's materialist conception of society, history, and politics. In the second section, turning to the heart of the matter, I provide an overview of Marx's critique of capitalism, a topic I explore in greater detail in the thematic chapters. In the third section, I consider Marx's analysis of how the development of capitalism prepares the way for the rise of socialism.

HISTORICAL MATERIALISM

From what vantage point can we best comprehend the nature of society, the dynamics of social change, the trajectory of human history, and the lineaments of the future? There are many possibilities. Some theorists give priority to the realm of politics. Proponents of this perspective believe that political institutions, political processes, and government policy decisions are the pivotal factors determining the quality of social life, the functioning of society, and the course of history. Cultural forces receive top billing for others. From this standpoint, the character, operation, and developmental tendencies of a society are assumed primarily to be an expression of its dominant values, beliefs, and ideals. For Marx, however, economics matters most, not politics or culture. This premise—the primacy of the economic—is the core idea of his materialistic perspective. By *economic* he means specifically the organization of productive activity, how people come together to satisfy their needs for food, shelter, and clothing. Marx calls this economic assemblage the "mode of production." This concept occupies a central place in his theory, reflecting the materialist conviction that production is the "basis of all social life" and "all real history."[3]

Marx developed this materialist outlook through a critique of the philosophical idealism of G. W. F. Hegel and post-Hegelian German philosophy. He faults idealism for dwelling entirely in the "realm of pure thought," spinning out philosophical generalities, but refraining from studying the "actual world" itself. Marx proposes a more down-to-earth procedure, starting out from "real individuals, their activity and the material conditions under which they live." He shifts the focus from abstract speculation to concrete analysis, from philosophy and metaphysics to economics and history. This materialist approach, putting the economic system center stage, is premised on what Marx takes to be a fundamental fact of social existence. As human beings we make our lives and express ourselves through *labor*, through our collective interaction with nature. Our survival requires we grow crops, unearth minerals, construct buildings, and manufacture goods. Unlike non-human animals, Marx observes, we must consciously *produce* our "means of subsistence." In the study of human history, therefore, the process of production is the appropriate starting point.[4]

The purpose of this section is to familiarize readers with the logic of Marx's materialist perspective. In three separate subsections I discuss in turn his materialist conception of society, his materialist conception of history, and the political lessons these imply.[5]

Marx's Materialist Conception of Society

For Marx, the defining feature of society, putting its mark on all other facets of social life, is its economic setup—its *mode of production*. Though his usage is not always consistent, this concept generally denotes a discernible economic order, one defined by the manner in which humans mobilize the labor necessary to fulfill their basic needs. How this system of production is organized, as with human needs themselves, changes over time. Several different modes of production have appeared throughout history, including slavery, feudalism, and capitalism. More precisely, using Marx's technical terminology, a mode of production is characterized by a specific combination of "forces of production" and "relations of production." Forces of production consist of two factors: (1) "means of production," including land, tools, machinery, and raw materials, and (2) "labor power," varying in productivity according to the skills, expertise, and technical know-how of the workforce. In the process of production, we thus see workers with the assistance of assorted implements expending physical and mental energy to shape raw materials into finished goods.[6]

The forces of production are set in motion by the relations of production—the social framework within which economic activity is carried out. The process of production for Marx, bringing economics and sociology together, is not merely a *technical* process; it is a *social* process, one presupposing a definite system of social organization. This social framework is constituted by property or ownership relations, meaning the pattern of control over means of production and labor power—how these are put to work, under what conditions, subject to whose authority, and for what purposes. The relations of production in effect stipulate the rules of the economic game—who has what rights, powers, and privileges. These social relations, Marx emphasizes, vary from one kind of economic system to another. The social framework specific to capitalism, for example, differs from that of slavery or feudalism; and the status of a wage worker, correspondingly, differs from that of a slave or a serf.

The relations of production, the underpinning of Marx's theory of class, are bound up with the distribution of economic power, more specifically the power of some to avail themselves of the labor of others. Marx typically envisions this economic structure in the form of a two-class system: (1) a minority class of owners, the dominant class, which monopolizes land, factories, and other means of production, and (2) a majority class of producers, the subordinate class, the mass of people who actually perform society's work and produce its goods. With slavery, we have masters and slaves; with feudalism, lords and serfs; with capitalism, the bourgeoisie (capitalist class) and the proletariat (working class). In each case, the dominant class lives off the unpaid or surplus labor of the subordinate class—the former enriching itself at the expense of the latter. The unique feature, the "innermost secret," of each of these modes of production is the configuration of power through which this unpaid surplus labor is extracted from the direct producers. Despite their differences, however, all class societies are systems of exploitation. One class, by virtue of its control over society's productive assets, is empowered to profit from the labor of another class. Whether under slavery, feudalism, or capitalism, the dominant class and the subordinate class thus confront one another with opposing economic interests, each pitted against the other. The inherent antagonism built into the relations of production is what gives history the quality of being "the history of class struggles."[7]

Marx singles out the mode of production because it is essential to the reproduction of humanity's physical existence. Beyond its obvious economic import, however, the mode of production has broader ramifications. It shapes the entire configuration of a society, engendering a "definite *mode of life*." And because it is the framework within which individuals inhabit their economic world and exercise their productive faculties, it shapes the character and qualities of human beings as well. What individuals are, Marx asserts, depends on the material conditions of production, on "*what* they produce and *how* they produce." In transforming the natural world through labor, individuals also transform themselves, changing their own nature, developing "new powers and ideas, new modes of intercourse, new needs and new language."[8]

The system of production generates an entire mode of life also through the influence it exerts on society's political, legal, cultural, and intellectual characteristics. In making this argument, Marx employs his well-known substructure-superstructure imagery. The relations of production, he states, form "the economic structure" or "real foundation" of society. On the basis of this economic structure, partly due to the power of the dominant class, there arises a corresponding "legal and political superstructure" and "forms of social consciousness." The cultural beliefs and social institutions making up the superstructure, according to Marx, including the state itself, typically function to stabilize the relations of production, promote the interests of the dominant class, and lend political and intellectual support to the existing economic system. In combination with his conception of the interplay between forces and relations of production, this substructure-superstructure model is the centerpiece of Marx's theory of how societies are put together and how they operate.[9]

In proposing this materialist theory, Marx underlines the point that politics and law, beliefs and ideas, all bear the indelible imprint of the prevailing mode of production. The organization of society's economic activity, he contends, "conditions the general process of social, political and intellectual life" as well as "legal relations" and "political forms." These superstructural phenomena, which we otherwise might regard as having a completely independent existence, are part of the larger mode of life formed from the relations of production. They cannot be fully understood on their own terms, therefore, but must be interpreted in light of the underlying economic structure. Marx's materialist perspective thus alerts us to the deeper realities often concealed by the surface appearances of everyday life.[10]

Marx applies the same materialist analysis to the realm of thoughts and ideas. The consciousness of individuals, he insists, is a "social product." The social conditions of people's existence give rise to "an entire superstructure of distinct and peculiarly formed sentiments, illusions, modes of thought and views of life." Our moral ideals, religious beliefs, and ideological convictions also grow out of our material circumstances and our real-life economic activities. In the very act of production, Marx explains, individuals produce not only "linens and silks," but also "*ideas, categories.*" For Marx, in sum, once again underlining the contrast between idealism and materialism, "it is not consciousness that determines life, but life that determines consciousness."[11]

This substructure-superstructure argument does not mean we can simply reduce social consciousness to economic conditions, nor does it imply that thoughts and ideas have no reality of their own. For Marx, to be sure, the economic substructure influences the political and cultural superstructure more profoundly than the reverse. Economic forces weigh more heavily than non-economic forces. Indeed, this premise is an essential element of his materialist perspective. This does not entail any simple-minded economic determinism, however. In claiming economics matters *most*, Marx is not saying *only* economics matters. Nor is he proposing that economics explains everything. But he does suggest that we cannot fully comprehend the characteristics and workings of society and the lives of individuals unless we focus first and foremost on the complex of social relations, practices, and institutions making up that society's mode of production. The United States from this standpoint, drawing attention to its distinctive economic system, is thus best thought of as a *capitalist* society, not a *democratic* society, a *consumer* society, a *Judeo-Christian* society, or even a *modern* society. In sum, what distinguishes Marx's materialist conception of society from alternative theoretical perspectives is the importance he ascribes to the system of economic production and its class relations.[12]

Marx's Materialist Conception of History

With Marx's materialist theory of history, we turn from a depiction of society at a single point in time to an analysis of the dynamics of epochal social change. And just as he presents an *economic* conception of society, so too does he advance an *economic* interpretation of history. For Marx "the history of humanity" is not a story of great men, or great ideas, or "spectacular political events," or the unfolding of human consciousness. Instead, he declares, the "true focus and theatre of all history" is economic life: industry and exchange, property ownership and productive forces, commerce and consumption, the division of labor and class struggle.[13]

There is considerable controversy surrounding the details of Marx's theory of history, with textual evidence supporting competing interpretations. To gain some entrée into his theory, ignoring for the time being the tangled debates setting one version of Marx against another, I take as my primary point of departure what is generally regarded as the canonical statement of the materialist conception of history: Marx's 1859 preface to *A Contribution to the Critique of Political Economy*. This is a useful summary, but running less than two pages in length and written under the threat of punitive censorship laws, it by no means exhausts or perfectly reflects his thinking about the subject. The preface represents an important, perhaps even the dominant, strand of Marx's theorizing about history. Elsewhere in his writings, however, he presents a less deterministic view of social change, giving more attention to human agency, class struggles, and political strategies, thus bringing historical contingency more fully into the picture. In later chapters I devote more attention to this other side of Marx, but for now, as an introduction to his materialist conception of history, I present a brief four-part overview of his argument as laid out particularly in his preface.[14]

First, there is, according to Marx, a strong historical tendency, driven by the requirements of human survival along with advances in science and technology, for the forces of production to develop, to increase in power over time. Each generation inherits the productive forces amassed by its predecessors, building on these in turn and further augmenting society's productive capacity. This fact—the continuous accumulation of productive forces—endows human history with a certain coherence or meaningfulness; it is not simply a random string of events. Indeed, despite the horrific exploitation and suffering he documents in his analysis of capitalism, Marx can be counted among those theorists who perceive a progressive movement in history. Though, in contrast to the philosophers of the French Enlightenment for whom progress meant the liberation of humanity from false ideas, a passage from ignorance to wisdom, for Marx progress takes the form of increasing economic productivity and the evolution of modes of production.[15]

Second, just as Marx posits a correspondence between the economic substructure and the political and cultural superstructure, so too does he envision an analogous correspondence between the forces of production and the relations of production. As the introduction of new methods of production transforms the labor process and increases productivity, the social relations of production are likewise altered. Advances in technology cause shifts in the class structure and in the larger social framework of society. "In acquiring new productive forces men change their mode of production; and in changing their mode of production, in changing the way of earning their living, they change all their social relations." So, Marx concludes, in a passage notable for its technological determinist slant, "the handmill gives you society with the feudal lord; the steam-mill, society with the industrial capitalist."[16]

Third, as society's productive forces develop, Marx argues, they eventually "come into conflict with the existing relations of production," which "fetter" or inhibit the continued growth and full utilization of society's productive capacity. The social framework of the economic system, its class structure, becomes a barrier to further economic progress. This "antagonism between the productive powers, and the social relations of our epoch," Marx observes, referring to the capitalism of his day, is "a fact, palpable, overwhelming, and not to be controverted." As evidence, he cites the contradiction between "modern industry and science on the one hand," whose development would seem to hold out great promise for the advancement of human welfare, and "modern misery and dissolution on the other hand." Marx's basic argument here is that at a certain point the relations of production are unable to accommodate the potential built up by the forces of production, and this circumstance creates pressure for a fundamental change in the economic structure of society.[17]

Fourth, once it reaches a crisis point, Marx argues, the contradiction between the forces and relations of production inaugurates "an era of social revolution." This is eventually resolved by the destruction of the old economic structure along with its "whole immense superstructure" and its replacement by a new mode of production suitable for the continued growth of the forces of production. Human history, propelled by the accumulation of productive forces, is thus for Marx a story of how one mode of production develops, matures, stagnates, and eventually gives way to another, more advanced mode of production. In this, the standard or orthodox version of Marx's materialist conception of history, there is an imperative, presumably rooted in some concept of human rationality, for an economic system which has become an obstruction to the continued development of the forces of production to be replaced by one capable of promoting the further growth of human productivity.[18]

Marx's Practical Materialism

In the *German Ideology* Marx ridicules those who imagine liberation to consist of nothing more than a "mental act," a mere change of consciousness. People, he reminds us, are not oppressed by false conceptions of the world, but by the "real existing world" itself, by historically given economic and political conditions. In opposition to the idealism of German philosophy, Marx refers to communists like himself as "practical materialists." The goal of such materialists is one of "revolutionising the existing world," not simply freeing people from wrongheaded ideas but "practically coming to grips with and changing the things found in existence." The true political mission is not so much to alter thinking—that will come in the course of political struggle—but rather to abolish oppressive conditions in a "practical, objective way."[19]

Marx's critique of religion provides a useful illustration of the logic of this practical materialism. Religion, Marx famously states, is "the *opium* of the people"; it performs an ideological function. By banishing the desire for a better world into an imaginary afterlife, it encourages acceptance of even the most unpleasant status quo. But unlike many critics, Marx does not simply condemn religion, expose it as a delusion, or denounce it for purveying falsehoods. Indeed, he suggests there is something authentic about religious belief. It testifies to a definite reality and gives voice to a legitimate demand. The truth of religion lies in its acknowledgment of the inhumanity of earthly existence. "*Religious* suffering," Marx says, "is at the same time an *expression* of real suffering and a *protest* against real suffering. Religion is the sigh of the oppressed creature, the sentiment of a heartless world, and the soul of soulless conditions." To attack religion on its own terms is misguided; it is merely a symptom, an understandable response to a more fundamental problem, namely, the sorry state of the "real existing world." The truly pressing task is a practical one: to combat suffering by rebelling against a "heartless world." Thus in contrast to many of his philosophical contemporaries who believed the critique of religion to be the essence of true criticism, Marx proposes a more practical, materialist approach: to replace the "criticism of heaven" with "the criticism of earth." The purpose of this earthly, practical criticism is to eradicate the need for religious illusions by overthrowing "*all those conditions* in which man is an abased, enslaved, abandoned, contemptible being." For Marx the practical point is not simply to alter consciousness or shatter illusions, but to transform the real world itself.[20]

Marx's materialist perspective suggests a twofold political message. First, it implies that true human liberation and real improvement in the welfare of humanity can be achieved only by overturning the economic structure of society, by changing the material circumstances of people's lives. From this perspective, the ultimate source of poverty, joblessness, oppressive work, environmental decay, meaningless lives, and other social problems is not false ideas, debased values, corrupt politicians, or individual pathologies. The root cause of these troubles derives instead from the workings of the economic system, from the structure and dynamics of capitalism itself. For example, under the capitalist system, Marx argues, unemployment is a normal condition, necessary to maintain a downward pressure on wages and sustain profitable production. Only by abandoning capitalism in favor of socialism, he claims, can we ever hope to provide a meaningful work life for everyone or to resolve many of the other seemingly intractable problems we face in the modern world.

Marx's practical materialism also suggests that the economic structure of society cannot be changed through a mere "effort of *will*." "People make their own history," Marx says, "but they do not make it just as they please; they do not make it under circumstances chosen by themselves, but under circumstances directly encountered, given and transmitted from the past."

We cannot simply wish a new world into existence; what is desirable is not always immediately feasible. Whether a social revolution is possible or not depends on historical circumstances, on the "realities of the situation." To be successful, it requires an appropriate level of economic development. Serfdom, for example, cannot be abolished without improvements in agricultural production, and socialism cannot replace capitalism without a substantial increase in society's productive forces. The problems we encounter are handed down to us by history, but we are also dependent on history to provide us with the resources and opportunities for overcoming those problems.[21]

THE CAPITALIST MODE OF PRODUCTION

While his materialist perspective offers guidelines for understanding the "history of humanity," Marx's primary interest was the new world of capitalist industry. The bulk of his writings, including his most important work, *Capital*, is devoted to the critical analysis of the capitalist mode of production. For anyone serious about coming to terms with Marx, this must be the primary focus. My purpose in this section, building a foundation for later chapters, is to provide an overview of Marx's theory of capitalism, in the process summarizing his thinking about the origins, nature, functioning, and destiny of the capitalist economic system.[22]

Capitalist Commodity Production

Human survival requires the production of goods capable of satisfying needs. We grow food to eat, sew clothes to wear, and write books to educate and entertain. Marx calls these useful things "use-values." When produced as commodities, when goods are destined for sale or exchange rather than personal consumption, they acquire a dual character. They not only possess use-value; they are also the bearers of "exchange-value." A commodity's exchange-value takes the form of a quantitative equivalence, the proportion a use-value of one kind is traded for a use-value of another kind. In a barter economy, for example, a dozen salmon might be exchanged for one chicken or two knives or three blankets. These ratios, arising from ongoing transactions among buyers and sellers, designate the exchange-value of a commodity, meaning how much at that particular time and place one commodity is worth relative to other commodities.[23]

The production and exchange of commodities existed prior to the rise of capitalism. In pre-capitalist economies, as in the previous example, one commodity might be exchanged directly for another, fish for fowl. Where money or some monetary equivalent such as gold is used as a medium of exchange, the process remains essentially the same. One commodity (C) is sold for money (M) which in turn is used to purchase another commodity (C). Marx refers to this cycle of exchange, C-M-C, as the "simple circulation of commodities." For example, we might imagine family farmers selling whatever agricultural goods they produce beyond what they need for immediate consumption and spending the money they receive to purchase building materials, farm implements, clothing, and other necessities they do not produce for themselves. With capitalist commodity production, this simple circuit of exchange is inverted. Money is used to purchase commodities, which, after some refashioning, are subsequently sold for even more money: M-C-M'. By introducing this contrast between the pre-capitalist circuit of commodity exchange, C-M-C, and the capitalist circuit, M-C-M', Marx sheds light on some of the unique properties of the capitalist mode of production.[24]

With the simple circulation of commodities, money is spent to satisfy needs: "selling in order to buy." With the capitalist circulation of commodities, money is invested to accumulate more money: "buying in order to sell." The goals of these two circuits of exchange differ: consumption in the first case, profit in the second. Different goals yield different dynamics. The process of circulation under simple commodity production is episodic and contingent because the circuit ends once a need is satisfied and begins again only when a new need arises. With capitalism, however, because the aim is profit maximization rather than personal consumption, the process of circulation is interminable, a perpetual cycle of exchange, a "constantly renewed movement." Capitalists, in response to the imperatives of competition, are the driving force of this process. Their objective, which endows capitalism with its uniquely restless, insatiable quality, is not the production of use-values, Marx insists, nor profit "on any single transaction," but rather the "unceasing movement of profit making."[25]

Capitalism is a "generalized" system of commodity production where nearly everything we consume takes the form of a commodity, where every product is produced for sale, and where every sale is a moment in the endless pursuit of profit. The purpose of a capitalist business enterprise is not to make useful products. Its purpose is to make money. The food we eat, the clothes we wear, and the movies we watch are produced as commodities.

And though they may sate our hunger, warm our bodies, and engage our imaginations, these useful qualities are incidental to the ultimate aim of their production. What spurs the capitalist into action, Marx says, is not the "enjoyment of use-values," but the "augmentation of exchange-values," not the fulfillment of human needs but the accumulation of wealth. Goods are produced only because they can be sold for a profit, and the prospect of reaping a profit is the decisive motivation for their production. This reality, where production relates to profit as a means to an end, has not always been the norm. In the pre-modern world, Marx states, "the human being appears as the aim of production," but with the rise of capitalism, this relationship is turned upside down: "production appears as the aim of mankind and wealth as the aim of production."[26]

The Labor Theory of Value

The presence of commodity production raises an obvious question: what regulates the proportions in which commodities are exchanged for one another? How is it possible to weigh heterogeneous commodities with heterogeneous use-values on the same scale? Why is a car more costly than a bicycle and a bicycle more costly than a skateboard? There must be something all commodities have in common, Marx reasons, by reference to which their relative worth, their exchange-value, is calculated. The one property they all share, he argues, rendering even apples and oranges comparable, is that they are products of human labor. More precisely, they are products of *abstract* human labor. By this Marx means labor in general measured in units of time, ignoring the specific operations that differentiate one kind of work (e.g., tailoring) from another (e.g., carpentry). Where exchange-values are concerned, what matters is not the character or content of the labor invested in them, but its duration. By this yardstick, even though commodities as use-values differ from one another qualitatively, they can be made commensurable and appraised quantitatively according to the average labor time necessary for their production. This line of thinking leads Marx to adopt a labor theory of value. The *"relative values of commodities,"* he states, are "determined by the *respective quantities or amounts of labour, worked up, realized, fixed in them.*" Some commodities require more labor to produce than others and are thus more valuable. It takes more time to make a bicycle than a skateboard and even more to make a car. This explains why a car is worth more than a bicycle and a bicycle more than a skateboard.[27]

Marx's argument is a little more complicated than this. The value of a commodity, he explains, is not determined by the *actual* quantity of labor expended in its production. If this were the case, a skateboard made by a lazy and incompetent worker, because it would consume more labor time, would have greater value than one constructed by a highly proficient expert. What counts in determining the value of a commodity, rather, is the quantity of "socially necessary labour-time" required for its production. By this he means the labor time necessary under normal conditions "and with the average degree of skill and intensity of labour prevalent in that society." This value, furthermore, includes not only *direct* labor, the labor of the skateboard makers themselves, but also the *indirect* labor used up in producing the machinery and tools and in acquiring the raw materials necessary for fabricating the final product. In sum, then, the simplified essence of Marx's labor theory of value is this: commodities exchange according to the average labor time needed to produce them under normal conditions of production.[28]

Because of the ups and downs of the market, the actual purchase price of a commodity, Marx acknowledges, is sometimes more and sometimes less than its value. But over the long run the equilibrating dynamics of supply and demand tend to bring about a correspondence between market price and real value. Marx insists, however, that market forces do not *determine* the value of a commodity. A commodity does not have a particular value because of the price it yields in the market; instead, it yields a particular price in the market because it has a certain value. The laws of supply and demand "regulate nothing but the temporary *fluctuations* of market prices. They will explain to you why the market price of a commodity rises above or sinks below its *value*, but they can never account for that value itself." For Marx, *that value*, to repeat, derives from "the expenditure of human labour in general."[29]

Primitive Accumulation

While capitalism is a system of commodity production, the exchange of commodities is only a prerequisite. The more essential condition necessary for the development of capitalism is the appearance of a capitalist class on the one side and a working class on the other, the former owning the means of production and the latter having only their ability to work. How does it happen that these two classes—a property-owning minority and a property-less majority—come to encounter one another? "One thing . . . is clear," Marx says: "nature does not produce on the one hand owners of money or commodities, and on the other hand men possessing nothing but their own labour-power." So then what are the origins of capitalist class relations? This takes us to what Marx, borrowing from Adam Smith, calls "primitive accumulation."[30]

Treating England as his main example, Marx uses the term primitive (or original) accumulation to refer to the historical process that, beginning in the fifteenth century, undermines the feudal order and creates "the fundamental conditions of capitalist production." This process culminates in the formation of the capitalist class structure. On the one hand, a nascent capitalist class emerges from the ranks of wealthy merchant traders and moneylenders. They initially enter the world of capitalist production by establishing manufacturing industries along the periphery of the feudal economy. Once taking root, "capitalist private property" spreads like a virus, absorbing the "individual private property" of independent artisans and small-scale producers. The "dwarf-like property of the many" is thereby transformed into the "giant property of the few," with the means of production becoming increasingly concentrated in the hands of an emergent capitalist class. In response to new economic pressures and new opportunities for making money, partly emanating from colonialism, slavery, and the expansion of world trade, even much of the countryside is gradually converted into capitalist agriculture. Ultimately, the capitalist "knights of industry" displace the feudal "knights of the sword" as the dominant class, consolidating the reign of capital.[31]

On the other hand, meanwhile, accompanying the ascendancy of the capitalist class, a modern working class also appears on the scene as feudal agricultural workers, peasants or serfs, are transformed into dependent wage laborers. This is a bloody and brutal historical process, Marx claims, where "conquest, enslavement, robbery, murder, in short, force, play the greatest part." Through a combination of violent evictions and legislative edicts, including the enclosure acts, the peasant population is forcibly removed from the land to which it previously had customary rights. With "private property" for individual gain supplanting "communal property" for common use, peasants are deprived of their traditional means of subsistence. No longer able to earn a living off the land, this dispossessed mass, "dragged from their accustomed mode of life," is then thrown into the labor market and subjected to the brutal regimen of the new capitalist workplace. Just as state power is deployed to force peasants off the land, so too does it serve to bolster the new wage-labor system. To maintain a steady supply of compliant workers, legislators enact laws against vagrancy, making joblessness a crime punishable by

imprisonment. Through such measures, Marx argues, summing up the immediate pre-history of capitalism, agricultural workers are "first forcibly expro-
priated from the soil, driven from their homes, turned into vagabonds, and
then whipped, branded, tortured by grotesquely terroristic laws into accepting the discipline necessary for the system of wage-labour."[32]

The historical process of primitive accumulation is the central element of
Marx's analysis of the transition from traditional society to modern society,
from feudalism to capitalism. The most significant outcome of this process is
the birth of a new class of "free workers." Free in a "double sense." First,
unlike either slaves or serfs, they are the sole proprietors of their own persons, free to dispose of their capacity for labor however they wish. Second,
owning neither land nor tools, they are free of all possession in any means of
production. Having no independent way to secure a livelihood, no resources
other than their bodies and minds, nothing to offer but their ability to labor,
these "free workers," as Marx ironically puts it, are "compelled to sell themselves voluntarily." They are free insofar as they do not belong to "*this or
that*" capitalist, Marx says, but since they must hire themselves out to someone or starve, they do belong to *one or another* capitalist. They are free to tell
their boss to "take this job and shove it," but in the end they will just have to
find a new boss, "same as the old boss." The consequence of workers being
dependent on the labor market to earn a living is that labor power itself—the
ability to work—becomes a commodity. This development marks the rise of
the capitalist mode of production.[33]

Marx's discussion of primitive accumulation illustrates three important
features of his conception of capitalism. First, it underlines the historically
specific nature of the capitalist mode of production, demonstrating how capitalism, far from being "an eternal and *natural* . . . form of production," arose
on the basis of definite historical conditions. Second, it shows that capitalism
requires a market for labor, where human labor power is bought and sold like
any other commodity. Third, it reveals the centrality of the capital–labor
relationship in the operation of the capitalist economic system.[34]

Labor Power: A Most Peculiar Commodity

Under capitalism, labor power is a commodity, "no more, no less" than
sugar, the "former measured by the clock, the latter by the scales." But as
Marx states repeatedly, labor power, the human capacity to work, is a "peculiar" commodity, and this peculiarity goes to the heart of his critique of the
capitalist mode of production. Compared to other commodities, as I will

explain more fully in the pages to follow, labor power is unique in at least five respects. First, the determination of the value of labor power differs from that of other commodities because it depends on society's level of development and cultural standards. Second, though it is bought and sold in the market, capitalists do not *produce* labor power and therefore do not control its supply in the same manner as they do for other commodities. Third, capitalists consume labor power by extracting as much labor effort as possible from often resistant workers, and this process, rife with conflict, is unlike that entailed by the consumption of other goods. Fourth, labor power is a particularly special commodity, and uniquely valuable from the standpoint of the capitalist class, because it is capable of producing surplus value. Finally, labor power is a peculiar commodity also because it is an attribute of sentient human beings. [35]

The value of labor power, as with any other commodity, is determined by the quantity of socially necessary labor required for its production, in this case meaning the maintenance of the worker. This includes the labor time necessary to produce an adequate means of subsistence, for example, food, clothing, housing, and transportation; to acquire the requisite levels of education and training; and to raise a family and a future generation of workers. Under normal conditions, in other words, the wages workers receive must be sufficient to keep them fit enough to return to work every day, enable them to perform their jobs satisfactorily, and ensure over time a steady stream of replacement workers. [36]

In contrast to other commodities, however, Marx argues, the determination of the value of labor power incorporates a "historical and moral element." Beyond guaranteeing the sheer physical existence of workers, the social subsistence wage must be sufficient to provide them with a standard of living appropriate for the society in which they reside. What workers need to survive and reproduce themselves from day to day and generation to generation, Marx observes, depends on "the level of civilization attained by a country" and on socially given "habits and expectations." The laboring population must subsist not just at any level, but at a level in conformity with the general conditions of society and the "traditional standard of life." Just to get by, to live a normal life, in modern capitalist societies, for example, workers need automobiles, telephones, access to computers, and much else. The value of the necessities for maintaining and reproducing labor power is, Marx says, a "variable magnitude," changing with the times. [37]

The Industrial Reserve Army

There is, according to Marx, another difference between labor power and other commodities. Market forces ensure that the price of the typical commodity fluctuates around its value. If certain goods are sold above their value, generating surplus profit, capitalists will shift production to those goods, increasing their supply and driving down their price. And if certain goods are sold below their value, capitalists will reduce production of those goods, decreasing their supply and driving up their price. No similar market mechanism operates with respect to labor power, as capitalists cannot produce workers the way they produce breakfast cereal and electronic equipment.

Since the law of supply and demand does not apply in the usual manner, what mechanism ensures that the price of labor power remains roughly equal to its value? Why are workers typically unable to obtain more than a social subsistence wage? The answer to this question is found in what Marx refers to as "the industrial reserve army," the surplus population of the unemployed. The existence of a large pool of jobless workers, desperate for employment, inhibits workers with jobs, desperate to remain employed, from demanding higher pay. A substantial supply of unemployed workers, potentially in competition for the jobs of the employed, keeps wages from rising above their value. Periods of strong economic growth may exert an upward pressure on wages, however, as the unemployed are increasingly absorbed into the labor force. But this improvement in the standard of living of workers is only temporary; indeed, it is typically a "harbinger of crisis." If rising wages put a squeeze on profits, capitalists will respond by cutting back investment or substituting machinery for labor, in either case replenishing the surplus population, resulting in a renewed downward pressure on wages and restoring conditions for profitable growth. "The great beauty of capitalist production," Marx says, is that it "constantly reproduces the wage-labourer as a wage-labourer, but also always produces a relative surplus population of wage-labourers in proportion to the accumulation of capital." The very logic of capitalism both requires and ensures the division of the working class into two segments, one unable to work enough and the other forced to work too much. This circumstance keeps wages low enough to maintain profitability while also securing the essential condition necessary for the perpetuation of the system: "the social dependence of the worker on the capitalist."[38]

The Hidden Abode of Production

So far we have learned among other things that for Marx capitalism is a system of generalized commodity production where goods are produced to be sold for profit; where labor power itself is a commodity, albeit a most peculiar one; and where capitalists and "free workers" meet in the market as buyers and sellers of the uniquely human capacity to create value. All this is but a prelude, however. To really understand the inner logic of capitalism, as Marx sees it, we have to follow him as he ushers us out of the bustling sphere of circulation, "where everything takes place on the surface and in full view of everyone," and leads us on a tour deep inside the "hidden abode of production." In contrast to the mainstream economics of his day, and even more noticeably ours, Marx's analysis of capitalism shifts the primary focus from the sphere of exchange to the sphere of production, from market dynamics to the labor process. By focusing attention on what transpires within the workplace, moreover, Marx puts the spotlight on the capital-labor relationship at its most revealing point, while also exposing the awful working conditions typically experienced by wage laborers.[39]

The universe of commodity exchange, Marx says, appears to be "a very Eden of the innate rights of man." When we enter the market, so it seems, we are all equal before the law and free to make whatever choices we want. It is not unusual, in fact, to hear people describe capitalism in just this way—as a free market system. But what happens once market transactions are completed, once buyers of labor power ready themselves to consume their newly purchased product, once capitalists and workers assemble together within the factory? This is the terrain Marx sets out to explore. What he finds is anything but a Garden of Eden. His purpose in taking us on this journey is not simply to chart unknown territory or even to disclose the unsavory innards of the capitalist system. He turns to the process of production for a more fundamental reason. Only by looking at what goes on inside the workplace, he claims, can we uncover the "secret of profit-making." This is the big issue Marx proposes to tackle: where does profit come from?[40]

The Consumption of Labor Power

What capitalists buy from workers in the market is labor power, a potential, a capacity for labor. But what they really want is the labor itself, and even more they want the commodities that labor produces, and even more than that they want the profit realized from the sale of those commodities. It is a rocky road from purchase to sale, however. The first step for capitalists is to procure the use-value of labor power. They do this, as in the case of any other commodity, by consuming it. Just as a banana is consumed by eating it and a jacket by wearing it, labor power is consumed by putting it to work. But the consumption of labor power, this peculiar commodity, raises unique practical problems. To the misfortune of capitalists, labor power, unlike bananas and jackets, comes embodied in living persons who may not always be willing to relinquish their precious commodity on the terms dictated by employers. It is one thing to peel a banana or don a jacket, and something quite different to extract labor from thinking and feeling human beings.

While the purchase of labor power takes place in the market, its consumption, the real "appropriation of someone else's living labour," takes place in the "actual production process." This is one reason Marx's analysis of capitalism accords priority to the sphere of production over the sphere of exchange—we witness only the overture in the market; the main performance is staged in the workplace. And as the economic action shifts from the marketplace to the workplace, the "unavoidable antagonism" between capitalists and workers comes to the surface. Capitalists have the edge, however, not only because workers are dependent on them to earn a living, but also because the rules of the economic game favor capitalist property owners over propertyless wage laborers. In return for their promise to pay a wage, capitalists acquire ownership of workers' labor power for a stipulated period of time. This, Marx emphasizes, confers invaluable prerogatives—the "rights of property." First, capitalists have the right to command workers under their authority and to control how their labor power is utilized; they are free to dictate the conditions of work. Second, capitalists possess a proprietary right to the products of workers' labor; they are free to claim those products as their own and sell them on the market for a profit. Capitalism is not a neutral instrument for carrying out economic activities. It is, Marx reveals, a system of power, with the capitalist class, by virtue of owning the means of production, enjoying unique privileges denied to the working class.[41]

Workers pay a heavy price when they hire themselves out to capitalists. They are compelled to cede control over both their labor power and the products of their labor. At the same time they are also asked to surrender what Marx regards as their most human quality: the capacity to labor freely according to their own purposes and designs. The capitalist system of production is predicated on what he refers to in his early writings as the "alienation" of labor. I discuss this topic more fully in chapter 5.

The Secret of Profit Making

Why do capitalists go to all the trouble of purchasing and consuming labor power? The answer is obvious: they expect to make a profit. To uncover the secret of this profit making, Marx begins by taking us back to the capitalist circuit of exchange, M-C-M'. Capitalists invest one sum of money at the beginning of this circuit and withdraw a larger sum at its end. Marx calls this increment "surplus value." This finds its way into the pocket of the capitalist in the "mystified form" of profit. So where, he asks, does this surplus value or profit come from? He rejects the view that profit arises from capitalists selling commodities at a price higher than their value. What this ignores, which is no less true for capitalists than for everyone else, is that every seller is also a buyer and every buyer also a seller. If profit originated in the process of exchange, by selling commodities at inflated prices or by "capitalist A" screwing "capitalist B," then any gain on one side of the transaction would be a loss on the other, and in the aggregate there would be no surplus value. Marx recognizes that individual cases of profiting through price gouging do occur. But in general, he argues, capitalists buy commodities at their value, including the commodity labor power, and sell commodities at their value. And yet, mysteriously, "with all the charms of something created out of nothing," at the end of the process the capitalist receives "more value from circulation than he threw into it at the beginning."[42]

The exchange of commodities does not itself, Marx asserts, create value. Profit is only *realized* through the sale of commodities in the market; it is *produced* in the process of production. To follow Marx's thinking here we need to consider more closely his analysis of what goes on in the interval between M and M'. Capitalists purchase two sorts of commodities with their original investment: means of production, including machinery and raw materials, and labor power. These commodities are consumed within the production process. Aided by whatever instruments of labor are necessary, workers fashion raw materials into a new commodity to be sold in the market. The value of the raw materials, machinery, and other materiel used up in producing the final product is transferred to the new commodity. The cost of shoes, for example, includes the value of the tools and leather used up in their manufacture. Marx's key point here is that while machinery *imparts* value, equivalent to its depreciation, it does not *create* value. Because the value of this part of capital remains the same throughout the process of production, Marx refers to it as "constant capital." Labor power, on the other hand, "both reproduces the equivalent of its own value and produces an excess." Because it possesses this value-creating property, Marx calls the capital advanced for the purchase of labor power "variable capital." The human labor expended in the production of the final product thus takes two distinct forms: first, the past or dead labor congealed in the means of production and passed along to the new commodity; and second, living labor, "labour-power in action," which preserves the existing value of the original capital outlay and adds new value as well.[43]

But this still does not answer the key question: what is it about living labor that enables it to produce this surplus value? Marx's explanation is the cornerstone of his theory of capitalism. Workers are paid according to their value, he states, but there is a difference between *the value of labor power*— that is, the cost required for the reproduction of the worker—and *the value labor power creates*. The wealth workers produce, in other words, is greater than the wealth needed to sustain them. This is the secret of profit making. A fair day's work produces more than the equivalent of a fair day's pay. Workers, Marx argues, are not cheated (at least not according to capitalist rules of the game); they are paid the full value of their *labor power*. But they are *not* paid the full value of their *labor*; they are not paid the equivalent of what they produce. After all, where is the gain for capitalists if they give their workers $100 a day and all they get back in return is $100 worth of labor? The reality, Marx explains, and "a piece of good luck" for capitalists, is that in purchasing labor power they gain command of workers' capacity to labor for a period of time in excess of what is necessary for workers to produce the equivalent of their social subsistence wage.[44]

To gain a better understanding of this argument, imagine a working day of ten hours. In one part of that day, say five hours, workers produce the value of their labor power, the value of their means of subsistence. This is paid to them in the form of wages. Marx calls this portion of the working day "necessary labour-time." If they worked on their own rather than for a capitalist, workers would be able to provision themselves by laboring just five hours each day, leaving the other nineteen hours to do as they pleased. But since they have sold their labor power for a ten-hour period, they are obliged to continue working an additional five hours for the benefit of the capitalist. Marx underlines this key point: "The fact that half a day's labour is necessary to keep the worker alive during 24 hours does not in any way prevent him from working a whole day." Marx calls this second portion of the working day "surplus labour-time." It is from this surplus or unpaid labor that capitalists derive their profit. They pay each worker $100 per day, equal to the value of his or her labor power, and at the end of the day they get back from the labor of each worker not only the equivalent of that sum, recouping their initial investment, but an additional $100 of surplus value. This, Marx claims, is the secret of profit making: capitalists have at their "disposal a definite quantity of the unpaid labour of other people."[45]

The Exploitation of Labor

There is, for Marx, another more pointed way of describing the secret of profit making: the capitalist class appropriates surplus value through the *exploitation* of the working class. To say workers are exploited means they are forced to perform unpaid labor. Force enters the picture because workers, lacking access to means of production and needing to earn a living, have little alternative but to hire themselves out to capitalists. This situation enables capitalists to profit from the surplus labor of workers. And no matter how much this "might appear as the result of free contractual agreement," Marx declares, "by its very nature [it] always remains forced labour." In this respect, he suggests, capitalism is similar to slavery, though while slaves are compelled by law, "free workers" are driven by their circumstances to voluntarily perform unpaid labor.[46]

"The driving motive and determining purpose" of the capitalist system, Marx states, is "the greatest possible production of surplus-value, hence the greatest possible exploitation of labour-power." The *rate* of exploitation is the ratio of surplus labor to necessary labor. Surplus labor, remember, is the unpaid labor appropriated by the capitalist, and necessary labor is the labor required to cover the cost of workers' means of subsistence. Capitalists increase the rate of exploitation whenever they manage to increase the portion of the working day devoted to surplus labor rather than necessary labor. The more workers are forced to perform unpaid labor, the higher the rate of exploitation and the greater the surplus value received by capitalists.[47]

One strategy for increasing surplus value, which over the history of capitalism has provoked repeated conflict between the capitalist class and the working class, is to prolong the working day, lengthening it, say, from ten hours to twelve hours. Assuming five hours are required for necessary labor, capitalists thereby increase surplus-labor time from five to seven hours. Marx calls this the production of "absolute surplus-value." A second possibility, the more common way of augmenting surplus value once capitalism matures, is to shorten the portion of the working day devoted to necessary-labor time. Marx calls this the production of "relative surplus value." This is achieved by increasing the productivity of labor, particularly in industries producing means of subsistence, thereby lowering the value of labor power. If the equivalent of workers' maintenance costs can be produced in three hours instead of five, this increases surplus-labor time in a ten-hour day from five hours to seven.[48]

Time is money. With surplus labor originating from surplus-labor time, this adage applies nowhere better than in the capitalist production process. Workers, compelled to sell their labor power in the marketplace, are then drafted into the army of wage laborers under capitalist command and subjected to the "barrack-like discipline" of the workplace. Under the authority of managerial "officers," the working-class army is divided into two ranks, privates and sergeants, the first laboring away in the trenches, the second serving as foremen and overseers. The latter perform an essential supervisory role, keeping a watchful eye on the troops, maintaining labor discipline, ensuring the efficient operation of the production process, and making certain no labor power is wasted. The use of machinery in the workplace also facilitates the exploitation of labor by diminishing workers' discretion in the labor process and by tying them to "the uniform and unceasing motion of an automaton."[49]

With workers winning legislative battles to limit the length of the working day, employers' main recourse for increasing the rate of exploitation is the intensification of labor. By reengineering and speeding up the labor process and closely supervising the workforce, they strive to consume labor power as efficiently as possible, to increase the "quantity of labor" by filling up "the pores of the working day." Capitalists are at war against time. In "its insatiable appetite for surplus labour," Marx says, capital "usurps the time for growth, development and healthy maintenance of the body. It steals the time required for the consumption of fresh air and sunlight. It haggles over the meal-times, where possible incorporating them into the production process itself." Having a legal claim on workers' time, capitalists demand "the greatest possible daily expenditure of labour-power, no matter how diseased, compulsory and painful it may be." Capitalism, Marx concludes, surpasses all other systems of production "in its energy and its quality of unbounded and ruthless activity."[50]

Capitalist Contradictions and Crisis Tendencies

The very dynamic of capitalism, by continuously adding to the mass of people forced to sell their labor power, "reproduces and perpetuates the conditions under which the worker is exploited." In passages such as this Marx makes it seem as though capitalism resembles a perpetual motion machine, a self-sustaining system capable of enduring into perpetuity. But the reality, he makes clear, is quite different. First, even as it reproduces itself, capitalism never stays the same; it is always changing and expanding. Second, even as it persists, capitalism is inherently crisis prone, susceptible to periodic breakdowns. And third, from the standpoint of workers, exposed daily to the vagaries of the market and the despotism of the workplace, the malfunctioning of capitalism is a normal experience. Marx's economic writings are meant not only to inform us about how capitalism works, but also how it fails to work.[51]

Capitalists, in response to the "coercive laws of competition," are constantly pressured to increase efficiency and productivity. As one capitalist cheapens the costs of production by introducing labor-saving technologies, others are compelled to follow suit. But as they vie to outperform each other by improving the methods of production, the unintended result is a long-term decline in the overall rate of profit. The cause of this tendency, according to Marx, attesting to the self-destructive nature of the system, is the very technological prowess unleashed by capitalism. As machinery is increasingly substituted for labor in the process of production, as technology is called upon to do more and more of the work, the amount of living labor time embodied in commodities shrinks. But since living labor, or "variable capital," is the source of profit, the inner logic of capitalist development engenders a "progressive tendency for the general rate of profit to fall." This is only a *tendency*, Marx stresses, as it may be offset by various "counteracting factors," but it nevertheless presents a potential threat to the sustainability of the system.[52]

When the decline in the rate of profit becomes sufficiently serious, an economic crisis erupts. Less profitable industries are forced out of business, investment and production are curtailed, unemployment increases, and the industrial reserve army grows. Such crises exhibit a predictable pattern. "Feverish production," stimulated by the never-ending quest for profit, causes a "glut on the market" followed by a "contraction of the market," culminating in "over-production, crisis and stagnation," with devastating effects on workers' employment prospects and living conditions. The eventual effect of such "regularly recurring catastrophes"—by causing the destruction of less productive enterprises and the decline of wages—is to restore, at least temporarily, the conditions for profitable investment. "Stagnation in production,"

Marx states, "prepares the ground for a later expansion of production. . . . And so we go round the whole circle once again." But as this boom-and-bust cycle continues, he explains, crises become progressively more frequent and severe, not only hindering capitalism's ability to recover, but also threatening its "violent overthrow."[53]

The survival of capitalism is dependent on growing profits, and this requires the extraction of more and more surplus value and the production of more and more goods. Once this "first act" is completed, however, once surplus value is produced in the workplace, a "second act" begins. Capitalists now set off into the marketplace loaded down with their newly minted commodities in search of buyers. But there is no guarantee they will be able to sell all their goods or realize the full value of their commodities in the market. Indeed, this is a chronic problem because the vast majority of people in capitalist society are workers, having the resources to purchase only a small portion of what they produce; capitalists' spending on means of production and luxuries may be insufficient to pick up the slack. Workers are essential to the functioning of capitalism both as sellers of labor power and as buyers of commodities. But in a system where production is for profit, they are hindered in their capacity as buyers because as sellers their wages must be kept to a minimum.[54]

Capitalism is susceptible to crises, Marx argues, because of its unlimited ambition, its need for unceasing expansion and endless profit making. This imperative—"Accumulate, accumulate!"—inevitably comes into conflict with the limits imposed by "the poverty and restricted consumption of the masses." The crisis tendencies of capitalism are thus internal to the system itself. They are not simply contingent products of exogenous shocks, faulty economic policies, or other avoidable mishaps and malpractices; they result from the normal workings of the system. Capitalism is vulnerable to breakdown because of its intrinsically contradictory nature. It tends toward unlimited expansion in the production of surplus value, while its ability to realize surplus value through the sale of commodities in the market runs up against the inherent limitations on consumption. In short, capitalism is impelled to create far more productive capacity than can be profitably set into motion and to produce far more goods than consumers have the wherewithal to buy. The system inevitably gives rise to an apparent "absurdity—the epidemic of over-production," characterized by the familiar sight of idle factories, unsold goods, and jobless workers.[55]

Capitalism, Marx argues, is prone toward *"over-production,"* but at the same time it is also prone toward *"under-production."* From the standpoint of profitability, the system produces too much, resulting in periods of stagnation. But from the standpoint of human requirements—that is, what people need to live a decent life rather than what they can afford to buy—the system produces too little. Capitalists cease production when it is no longer profitable, regardless of whether or not people are sufficiently supplied with food, shelter, and clothing. The real problem with capitalism, Marx concludes, is not that it produces too many goods, but that it produces too few goods "to satisfy the mass of the population in an adequate and human way." This reveals the central contradiction of capitalism as a mode of production and the source of its perplexing irrationality: its purpose "is not the satisfaction of needs but the production of profit."[56]

* * *

Marx's analysis of the capitalist economic system has many distinguishing qualities. The most important perhaps is that he examines capitalism from the standpoint of the working class. He draws attention to the disparity between the vast riches on display in capitalist society and the relative impoverishment of the worker. But he is not primarily concerned with the living conditions of the working class, and certainly not with their style of life. The most significant fact about workers for Marx, not least because it is decisive for grasping the inner logic of capitalism, is that they are *workers*. They are compelled to sell their labor power in the market, transfer control over their labor time and its products to their employers, and perform unpaid work for the benefit of the capitalist class. In particular, Marx's analysis of capitalism is unique for its emphasis on the circumstances and experiences of workers within the workplace, the "hidden abode of production"; its focus on the alienation and exploitation of the working class; and its unveiling of the inherent antagonism and ongoing conflict—"now hidden, now open"—between the bourgeoisie and the proletariat. In today's capitalist society, while we are treated to minute-by-minute updates on the stock market, the world of work is perhaps even more concealed from view than it was in the nineteenth century, and even workers themselves remain largely invisible. In daring to pry open the doors of the workplace and take a look at what capitalism means for the lives of those who perform the real labor in society, Marx may still have a great deal to teach us.[57]

CAPITALIST DEVELOPMENT AND SOCIALIST REVOLUTION

Capitalism for Marx is the bridge between past and future. It puts an end to the old pre-capitalist world, it accelerates the growth of the modern industrial world, and it opens the door to a new post-capitalist world. Though he is one of its most severe critics, Marx views capitalism as playing a historically progressive role, unwittingly preparing the way for the socialist society of the future. Because it stimulates the expansion of the forces of production, increasing society's productive powers by leaps and bounds, capitalism makes socialism objectively possible. Because it undergoes periodic breakdowns and recurring crises, exposing its inefficiency and wastefulness as a system of production, capitalism calls forth a constituency for socialism. Because it "squanders human beings," accumulating misery in the same proportion as it accumulates wealth, capitalism invests socialism with the quality of a moral imperative. And because it produces its own "grave-diggers" in the form of a class-conscious proletariat, capitalism makes socialism politically feasible. Capitalism develops and reproduces itself in such a way, Marx suggests, that socialism appears not only desirable but practical, and if not inevitable, as he sometimes proclaims, at least possible.[58]

As noted at the beginning of this chapter, Marx has no theory of socialism understood as a detailed plan for the future. But he does propose a theory of socialism in a different sense, as an account of how a socialist movement arises from the contradictions of capitalism. This exemplifies one of the unique features of Marx's perspective. In contrast to other more romantic and backward-looking theorists who fought to restrain the advance of capitalism and who imagined socialism as the restoration of some idealized pre-capitalist past, Marx's standpoint is distinctly forward looking. He envisions socialism as a society of the future, emerging on the far side of capitalism, building on the latter's technological accomplishments.

In this, the third and final section of the chapter, I provide a brief summary of Marx's thinking about the transition from capitalism to socialism (a topic I discuss further in chapter 8). I focus on three interrelated issues: Marx's conception of capitalism as a modernizing force, his argument that capitalism creates the objective conditions necessary for socialism, and his analysis of how the dynamics of capitalism lead to the formation of a revolutionary working class.[59]

Capitalism as a Modernizing Force

Capitalism is a revolutionary system, overturning the traditional feudal order and replacing it with a profoundly new and qualitatively different type of society. As Marx and Engels describe it in the opening pages of the *Communist Manifesto*, once the capitalist mode of production is up and running, it is an utterly transformative force, sweeping away the old world and imposing an altogether new world. The capitalist revolution brings forth the modern bourgeoisie, the wealthy leaders of vast industrial armies; the modern proletariat, a mass of wage laborers distributed "among the machinery as so many cogs"; the modern state, responsible for "managing the common affairs" of the capitalist class; modern industry, an economic behemoth with giant machine-based factories displacing small-scale manufacture; and modern science and technology, harnessing human knowledge to the imperative of profit making. Wherever this capitalist revolution touches ground, it uproots traditional manners and mores, "turning all natural relations into money relations," leaving standing no bonds between people other than "naked self-interest."[60]

As industrial capitalism spreads, "enormous cities" appear in its wake, and the urban population multiplies, completing the "victory of town over country" and ending the "idiocy" of rural life. While transforming the internal demographics of the nation, capitalism also extends its reach globally, revolutionizing transportation and communications technologies and bringing the entire world under its influence. It creates a world market and a "world history," increasing the "inter-dependency of nations," giving "a cosmopolitan character to production and consumption," and drawing even "the most barbarian nations into civilization." Driven ceaselessly to expand, Marx declares, modern capitalism forges a new world "after its own image," forcing all other countries to "adopt the bourgeois mode of production." And as it succeeds in establishing itself around the globe, industrial capitalism also generates "new conditions of oppression" and "new forms of struggle."[61]

What is perhaps most revolutionary about modern industrial capitalism is its inherently dynamic quality. Unlike all previous modes of production which are "essentially conservative," capitalism is always developing, always introducing new technologies, and always looking for new ways to intensify the productivity of labor. It survives only by continuously transforming the system of production, though in the process adding to the distress of the working class. The capitalist system, Marx says, "does away with all repose, all fixity and all security as far as the worker's life-situation is concerned." In the *Communist Manifesto*, he and Engels make the same point, asserting that what distinguishes the capitalist epoch from all others is the constant "revolutionizing of production," the "uninterrupted disturbance of all social conditions," and the experience of "everlasting uncertainty and agitation." The modern capitalist world is one of permanent change, where "all that is solid melts into air."[62]

The Historical Mission of Capitalism

The capitalist revolution destroys the pre-capitalist world, spreads modern industry far and wide, and brings humanity to the threshold of a new epoch. It exerts a "civilizing influence," propelling history forward by burying a decrepit past with its "old ways of life" and by making it possible for the modern world to advance to a higher stage of development. Capitalism's "historical mission," Marx argues, and its singular contribution to civilization, is the powerful impetus it gives to the growth of human productive power. Through the application of science and technology and the intensification of labor, capitalism vastly increases society's productive capacity. With the bourgeoisie at the helm, Marx says, capitalism in just a single century "has created more massive and more colossal productive forces than have all preceding generations together."[63]

Because of its intrinsic nature, however, capitalism, Marx argues, is incapable of realizing the potential human benefits accruing from increasing productivity. The purpose of capitalism is not the cultivation of the person, but the appropriation of profit. And the governing motive of this system, likewise, is not to increase the free time at the disposal of the individual, but just the contrary, to increase the surplus-labor time at the disposal of the capitalist. The capitalist mode of production is premised on the exploitation of labor, and for this reason it cannot deliver on the promise of a good society. Capitalism develops the productive forces to such a degree that a society of abundance is possible; but while it produces great riches for the few, even the basic needs of the many go unfulfilled. Capitalism promotes a level of productivity sufficiently high to reduce substantially the time people must spend performing unpleasant labor; but here again, while a small minority enjoys a life of leisure, the mass of wage laborers, when they are lucky enough to find jobs at all, face a lifetime of overwork. Capitalism also produces a constant outpouring of scientific advances and technological achievements; but because its accomplishments must above all else satisfy the principle of profitability, they only incidentally function for the common good. Insofar as it contributes to the development of society's forces of production, capitalism is a historically progressive system. But because it is systemically unable to translate its tremendous potential into a more humane society—most importantly by freeing people from the burden of alienated labor—it eventually outlives its usefulness. What was once a civilizing force becomes a barrier to further progress. When this point is reached, Marx claims, the time is ripe for capitalism to be replaced by socialism. [64]

By compelling human beings to "produce for production's sake," Marx states, capitalism creates the "material conditions of production which alone can form the real basis of a higher form of society, a society in which the full and free development of every individual forms the ruling principle." This ideal is possible only in a society where the problem of scarcity has been overcome and where every individual is at liberty to exercise their creative abilities. The indispensable prerequisite of socialism, therefore, is the reduction of necessary labor time, for only by shortening the working day and enlarging the "realm of freedom" will individuals have the opportunity to realize their human potential. This explains why for Marx capitalism's role in augmenting the forces of production is so essential; it is, he says, the "necessary practical premise" of socialism. Without the productive power built up by capitalism, instead of enabling the free development of the individual, a revolution would achieve only a form of "crude communism" where "want is merely made general." Capitalism is important for Marx because it creates the productive forces necessary for a socialist society. The historical mission of socialism in turn is to liberate society's productive powers from the shackles of capitalist relations of production, placing them under the "joint control of the producers," and thus freeing society's productive potential to serve the goal of human self-realization. [65]

The Formation of a Revolutionary Working Class

As capitalism develops, large-scale industry emerges, the forces of production grow, and the means of production are increasingly centralized. These conditions, according to Marx, establish the economic foundations that make a socialist society possible. The historical destiny of the working class, he argues, is to translate that possibility into a reality. Marx's theory of how socialism arises from the dynamics of capitalism thus includes two distinct elements: on the objective side, the development of the "material conditions" necessary for a higher stage of society and, on the subjective side, the development of a revolutionary proletariat. These two elements appear hand in hand, Marx argues, as the growth of industrial capitalism itself lays the groundwork for the formation of a class-conscious proletariat and for the eventual "revolt of the working class."[66]

Capitalism, Marx maintains, produces "its own grave-diggers" in the form of the modern proletariat. This outcome results in part because the conditions of the working class tend to deteriorate over time, a circumstance made even more certain by the outbreak of periodic crises. It is not necessarily the case that workers' standard of living declines over the long run, though relative to that of the capitalist class this too is likely. But whether their "payment is high or low," Marx contends, the situation of workers—as wage laborers—grows worse. The more that capitalists increase the exploitation and productivity of labor, as they are compelled to do by competitive forces, the more that work becomes increasingly monotonous and repulsive. The worker is distorted into "a fragment of a man," reduced to "an appendage of a machine," and subjected to a dehumanizing workplace despotism. As capitalism matures, "the mass of misery, oppression, slavery, degradation and exploitation grows." The process of industrialization, Marx suggests, by heightening workers' experience of alienation and exploitation, fuels their opposition to the capitalist system and supplies the motivation for a socialist revolution.[67]

With the development of modern industry, furthermore, the working-class population grows in numbers and is brought together in large-scale factories and urban centers. The divisions among workers diminish as their life circumstances become more uniform, with machinery obliterating "all distinctions of labour," and as their wages are reduced "to the same low level." In this manner capitalism contributes to the formation among the working class of a common situation. This in turn leads workers to recognize their common interests and to develop a common class consciousness. It also facilitates their ability to organize themselves as a class. As they become more unified and as they achieve a higher level of class awareness, workers cease competing among themselves and begin carrying "on general competition with the capitalist" instead. "The advance of industry, whose involuntary promoter is the bourgeoisie," Marx states, "replaces the isolation of the labourers, due to competition, by their revolutionary combination, due to association." With the aid of "improved means of communication," furthermore, local working-class struggles are transformed into national struggles. Thus conflicts between individual workers and individual capitalists take on "more and more the character of collisions between two classes." As this conflict escalates, the mass of workers "becomes united, and constitutes itself as a class for itself. The interests it defends become class interests." The very logic of capitalist development, Marx claims, by both motivating and empowering the working class, transforms an exploited mass into an agent of socialist revolution.[68]

On the surface, Marx's argument does not seem implausible. But clearly his expectation that capitalism would give rise to a class-conscious and revolutionary proletariat has not been borne out, or at least not yet. More than a century and a quarter after Marx's death, no advanced capitalist nation has experienced anything approaching a successful socialist revolution, nor does this seem likely in the near future. Partly this is tied in complicated ways to changes since Marx's day in the nature of capitalism. To cite just a few examples: the appearance of gigantic multinational corporations; the rise of the welfare state and the extension of citizenship rights; the appearance of a pervasive mass media industry and a culture of consumerism; the shift from manufacturing industries to service industries; and the emergence of new social movements focused on issues of gender, race, nationality, sexual identity, the environment, and many other causes. None of this means that Marx has been proven wrong, however, or that his analysis of the capitalist mode of production is no longer relevant. As Eric Hobsbawm points out, Marx's "prediction" of a working-class revolution was "read into his analysis" of capitalist development, "but did not derive from it." The absence of a socialist future on the horizon therefore cannot be taken as a refutation of Marx's critique of capitalism. The basic question we are left with, one pursued by numerous scholars, Marxist and non-Marxist alike, is this: Can Marx's analysis be revised to account for the surprising persistence and changing nature of capitalism without abandoning its fundamental premises, without ceasing to be a "Marxist" theory?[69]

Chapter Three

Emile Durkheim (1858–1917)

Marx was a revolutionary, Durkheim an academic. Marx was deeply involved in the political struggles of his day; Durkheim remained aloof from the unseemly world of partisan politics. Marx dedicated his life to the cause of socialism; Durkheim devoted his to establishing the discipline of sociology. Both wrote manifestos, Marx calling upon the workers of the world to unite and Durkheim, in *The Rules of Sociological Method*, advocating on behalf of a science of society. Though they followed divergent paths, Marx and Durkheim did share one common objective: to understand the world for the purpose of changing it. Despite his disdain for normal politics, Durkheim, no less than Marx, had a political agenda. Indeed, according to Robert Alun Jones, Durkheim's "entire social science," from his basic terminology to his choice of topics, "was a deeply political act."[1]

Durkheim, like Marx, wrote against the backdrop of the "dual revolution": the French Revolution of 1789 and the Industrial Revolution, originating in England in the late 1700s. Both figured prominently in his work. But the French Revolution, partly due to its embattled and uncertain legacy in his home country, had a particularly strong influence on his thinking about modern society. The Revolution inaugurated a process of social and political modernization that even a century later remained incomplete, precarious, and deeply contested. This was the historical setting of Durkheim's sociology. At issue was the very future of the nation. Would France revert to the prerevolutionary past or would it embrace the modern era by institutionalizing the principles of 1789: liberty, equality, and fraternity?[2]

Though largely successful in destroying the old order (the ancien régime), the Revolution, Durkheim lamented, "built nothing new" to take its place. This instability persisted for decades, with one regime change after another. Throughout much of the nineteenth century, France remained in the grip of political upheaval and social conflict. This state of national crisis reached a boiling point during Durkheim's teen years with two dramatic events: France's devastating defeat in the Franco-Prussian War in 1871, and in that same year the brutal suppression of the Paris Commune, a short-lived insurgent government formed by Parisian workers. In the midst of these debacles, the Third Republic was established, giving hope to proponents of a democratic, liberal, secular society.[3]

By the turn of the century, Durkheim had become the "high priest," the "semiofficial ideologist" of this new political regime. In support of the Third Republic and in service to the goal of national regeneration, he took up intellectual arms against both the reactionary forces of the right and the revolutionary forces of the left. In opposition to the Church, the aristocracy, and other conservative champions of the traditional order, Durkheim mounted a defense of modernity. And in opposition to the socialist demand for a total remaking of society, he urged gradual, evolutionary, non-violent reform. Durkheim's sociology, including his most scholarly writings, is thoroughly imbued with political significance. His was a distinctly political project: to comprehend the crisis of modern society and, through the instrument of sociology, to provide scientific guidance for achieving a stable and just social order.[4]

This chapter provides an overview of Durkheim's analysis of modern society and his contribution to the development of sociology. As with the previous chapter on Marx, my purpose here is to familiarize readers with some of Durkheim's key ideas and prepare the way for the later thematic chapters. In the first of four sections, I consider Durkheim's conception of sociology and the sociological method, drawing primarily on *The Rules of Sociological Method* (1895; second edition, 1901). In the second section, focusing on his first book, *The Division of Labor in Society* (1893; second edition, 1901), I discuss his perspective on the origins and nature of modern society. While continuing to explore his theory of modernity, in the third section I turn to Durkheim's book *On Suicide* (1897). In the fourth section, touching on some of the issues raised in *The Elementary Forms of Religious Life* (1912) and in his writings on education, I conclude by addressing one of the themes most central to Durkheim's sociology: the relationship between the individual and society.

THE SOCIOLOGICAL ENTERPRISE

In his methodological writings and in much of the rest of his work as well, Durkheim's chief objective was to legitimate the discipline of sociology, not only in the eyes of the scientific community, but also in the larger court of public opinion. In pursuit of this goal, he delineated a distinct subject matter for sociology, the vital though hitherto "unknown world" of "social facts." He set forth the rules of the sociological method, proposing a scientific, empirically minded sociology in contrast to the more philosophical approach of his predecessors, Henri de Saint-Simon and Auguste Comte. He made a case for the practical value of sociology, insisting that the new science of society had a critical role to play in remedying the ills of the modern world. And he suggested that sociology—with its unique blend of subject matter, empirical method, and practical relevance—not only differed from other academic disciplines, but was in many respects superior to these, particularly in its ability to comprehend the modern condition and promote the cause of national restoration.[5]

The Domain of Sociology

To be considered a genuine science, sociology needs its own subject matter, "a definite field to explore." For Durkheim, sociology's particular object of study, distinguishing it from biology, psychology, philosophy, and the other sciences, is the realm of social facts. This realm includes a diverse array of social realities—from religious beliefs, legal codes, and moral rules to pedagogical practices, architectural styles, and political and economic institutions. To say such phenomena are *social* means they compose a definite collective reality; they originate from and are characteristic of the group rather than the individual. This quality requires that social facts be studied *sociologically*. To say they are *factual* means they have an objective reality outside the mind of the individual; they possess a nature of their own, no less substantial than phenomena in the physical world. This quality requires that social facts be studied *scientifically*.[6]

Durkheim singles out three defining characteristics of social facts: externality, constraint, and generality. Facts having these characteristics are expressly social phenomena, meaning in particular they cannot be ascribed to individual intentions, desires, or motivations. Because they "do not have their immediate and determining cause in the nature of individuals," such facts are explicable only from the standpoint of the sociological perspective.[7]

Externality. Social facts are ways of thinking and acting that exist prior to and "outside the consciousness of the individual." We are born into a world consisting of already formed and often long-standing social institutions, cultural ideals, and customary practices. As members of society, we communicate in the language of our culture; we fulfill the obligations associated with our roles as mothers and fathers, students and teachers; we obey laws and adhere to social conventions; and we subscribe to prevailing values and beliefs. While we do all these things more or less freely, the norms governing our behavior, the doctrines eliciting our allegiance, and the institutional settings within which we conduct our collective affairs are not expressions of our will or design. They are *social facts*, collective realities. They exist external to us as individuals, products of our historical heritage and social milieu. We can understand neither their nature nor their causes "by searching within ourselves."[8]

Constraint. Social facts, in addition to being external to the individual, possess a "compelling and coercive power." They impose themselves on the individual from the outside, "like moulds into which we are forced to cast our actions." We are thus constrained by the obligatory power of public opinion, religious beliefs, moral rules, and legal precepts; by the sanctity of traditional ways of thinking and acting; and by currents of collective emotion, as when carried along by the frenzy of a crowd. Society, by virtue of its "moral authority," forces us to submit to "rules of action and thought that we have neither made nor wanted" and "subjects us to all sorts of restraints, privations, and sacrifices." But though we are continuously pushed and pulled by the power of social forces, we typically fail to recognize their coercive influence, falsely imagining ourselves to be perfectly free agents. We internalize the demands of society, we become habituated to conventions learned as children, we conform routinely to social pressures, and we generally perceive legal codes and social institutions as deserving of respect. The constraining power of social facts becomes apparent, sometimes painfully so, only when we deviate from prescribed ways of thinking and acting. We face imprisonment for breaking laws, job loss for violating professional codes of conduct, ridicule for defying social norms, and ostracism for espousing unconventional ideas. The constraining power of social facts, made forcefully apparent in the application of punishments and penalties, attests not only to the reality of society, but also to the influence it exerts over the life of the individual.[9]

Generality. Social facts also have the characteristic of being general within a group. Durkheim underscores a difficult point here. Social facts are not collective phenomena because they are widespread; they are widespread because they are collective phenomena. The generality of a social fact, a particular moral rule or cultural belief, for example, is not the result of it being embraced independently by a multitude of individuals. A social fact, rather, has the quality of generality because it is "a condition of the group" more or less replicated in each of its members. Consider for example the widespread antipathy toward socialist ideas in the United States. It is not as though millions of Americans, each on their own weighing socialism's pros and cons, happened to arrive at a similarly negative view. This hostility is social in origin, embedded in deeply rooted cultural traditions, periodically reaffirmed in the public discourse, and passed along from one generation to the next through the process of socialization. The generality of such social facts is a concomitant of their constraining power. As socially approved ways of thinking and acting, they are general because they exercise a powerful influence over people's behavior and beliefs. In sum, according to Durkheim, a social fact "is in each part because it is in the whole," not in the whole because it is in each part.[10]

By drawing attention to the external, coercive power of social facts, Durkheim proposes a conception of society not only as a "reality *sui generis*" and a distinct object of knowledge, but as something superior to and even dominating the individual. He explicitly challenges the commonsense view that individuals are the "completely autonomous" authors of their own lives. Individuals, for Durkheim, are necessarily social beings; they are persons in their own right, certainly, but products of society nevertheless and subject to social forces beyond their immediate control.[11]

The *Social* Nature of Social Facts

Durkheim admits that individuals are the only "active forces" in the social world. But in his effort to establish the discipline of sociology, he asks us to accept the supra-individual reality of society. How does he resolve this seeming paradox? What reasoning leads him to believe that *society* even exists as anything more than a collection of individuals? How does he justify his claim that social facts have a reality of their own, irreducible to psychological or biological facts? To account for the existence of social facts, Durkheim proposes an analogy. Just as chemical elements interact to create new phenomena with their own unique properties—as for example when hydrogen and oxygen combine to produce water—so too do individuals, "by uniting, by acting and reacting on one another, by fusing, give birth to a new reality." When bound together in groups, individuals form distinctly collective ways of feeling, thinking, and living. They develop a language, a worldview, and a moral code, along with diverse institutional practices covering everything from the socialization of children to the organization of production. These are social as opposed to individual facts. They derive from human association, not human nature. They originate from the life of the group, not the mind of the individual. Society for Durkheim is more than the sum of the individuals who make it up, and the qualities of society are likewise different from the qualities of its constituent members. The "system" formed by individual relationships, he says, "represents a specific reality which has its own characteristics." This distinctly social reality, an outgrowth of human interaction, is the particular subject matter of sociology. [12]

Durkheim's concept of social facts, by affirming a collective reality external to the consciousness of individuals, is meant to legitimate the independent status of sociology, to show that it is not simply a "corollary of individual psychology." These two disciplines, Durkheim argues, have as their subject matter entirely different factual domains, different realities. Psychology is concerned with phenomena internal to the individual, "individual representations," the minds and thoughts of persons. Sociology, by contrast, is concerned with phenomena external to the individual, "collective representations," including for example culturally specific myths, morals, and manners. These social phenomena, which make up the "collective consciousness," are fundamentally different from the "states of the individual consciousness," just as the "mentality of groups is not that of individuals." For this reason, he claims, sociology and psychology are radically distinct from one another. Taking this argument a step further, Durkheim asserts the priority of sociology over psychology. Social life, he says, does not derive from the attributes of individuals; on the contrary, the attributes of individuals derive from social life. The beliefs and values of individuals, for example, are more or less only a variation on the beliefs and values of the groups to which they belong. Thus even psychological facts are subject to sociological analysis, since for the most part they are "only the prolongation of social facts within the individual consciousness." [13]

The *Factual* Nature of Social Facts

Besides being *social* in nature, the phenomena making up the domain of sociology also have the quality of being *factual*. They possess an independent reality. Though not always directly observable, they nevertheless exist in the external world, not merely in our heads. Like other scientific disciplines, sociology studies "things." In referring to social facts as things, Durkheim means they are not simply ideas. While an idea can be known "from the inside," through introspection, a thing is an "object of knowledge." It can be known only "from the outside," through observation and description, comparison and classification. To know a *thing* requires empirical investigation, getting outside of our minds and methodically examining the real world itself. Thus Durkheim, determined to place the discipline on solid scientific footing, arrives at the fundamental rule of sociology: *"consider social facts as things."*[14]

When Durkheim proposes that social facts be treated as things, he rejects the "dualist prejudice," the tendency to regard human beings and human societies as "outside of nature" and off limits as objects of scientific analysis. Along with this, he also calls upon social scientists to adopt a "certain attitude of mind." To avoid tainting their findings, he advises, sociologists must set aside their prior beliefs and approach their subject matter as though they know nothing about it. Only on this basis, on the presumption of ignorance, will sociologists be sufficiently receptive to the facts and open to discovery. To treat social facts as things means proceeding in a true spirit of inquiry, prepared to learn from observation and experimentation. This requires sociologists to rid their minds of preconceptions, attend only to the facts in themselves, and allow their conclusions to follow their empirical research wherever this might lead.[15]

By drawing attention to the factual nature of social facts, Durkheim, as I explain below, distinguishes sociology not only from psychology, but from common sense and philosophy as well. His thinking about social facts also leads him to propose a new program to reorient and reinvigorate the discipline, to steer it along a more genuinely scientific track.

Sociology versus Common Sense

As an inevitable concomitant of our normal, everyday existence, we cannot help but form ideas about such things as politics and economics, morality and law, education and marriage. These ideas may be useful in giving us a sense of meaning and guiding our daily conduct. But they lack scientific validity, and even worse they hinder us from comprehending the true nature of the world. Our everyday conceptions, Durkheim asserts, "are as a veil interposed between the things and ourselves." We are thus led to mistake our preconceptions for realities, our ideas for facts. When we reflect upon our social surroundings, it is not the phenomena in themselves we ponder, but an "imagined world," the world as filtered through "traditional prejudices," "accepted opinions," and taken-for-granted ideas. [16]

Sociology can achieve the status of a science, Durkheim insists, only through the mindful, arduous, and sustained practice of emancipating itself from everyday notions. Ordinary consciousness, a product of uncritical reflection, gives us concepts that are only "fleeting and subjective." Sociology needs to strike out in a new direction, to make a clean break with common sense by treating social facts as things. This means guarding against "first impressions," familiar modes of thought, and conventional ideas. To avoid the corrupting influence of everyday opinions and beliefs and to gain access to the facts in themselves, sociology should take sense perceptions, not ordinary concepts, as its point of departure, and it should proceed inductively, inferring from "things to ideas," not from "ideas to things." A scientific sociology is thus the enemy of conventional wisdom. With its commitment to systematic observation, the sociological perspective, he asserts, "should cause us to see things in a different way from the ordinary man." Sociology in Durkheim's view occupies a privileged epistemological position, at odds with and superior to lay knowledge. [17]

Sociology versus Philosophy

Sociology differs from psychology in its subject matter, social versus individual facts, collective as opposed to individual representations. There is, however, considerable substantive overlap between sociology and philosophy. Both disciplines for example have an interest in forms of political organization and moral principles. Philosophy, because it first began contemplating "things of a social order," might even be considered sociology's chief predecessor. Nevertheless, Durkheim argues, the contrast between sociology and philosophy is fundamental, perhaps even more so than that between sociology and psychology. Though they share some of the same concerns, sociology and philosophy are diametrically opposed in their methods, objectives, and views of society.

Philosophy, in Durkheim's interpretation, confines itself to purely *conceptual* analysis, armchair ruminations on the essential nature or idea of the individual, religion, the state, and morality, for example. Sociology follows a different path, *empirical* research—the scientific investigation of political, economic, religious, and moral facts as they exist in the real world. While philosophy proceeds deductively, constructing systems of thought based on *a priori* principles or assumptions about human nature, sociology's method is inductive, building up generalizations through the accumulation of specialized studies. Ultimately, these two disciplines arrive at their conclusions through radically different procedures: contemplation and conjecture for philosophy, observation and experimentation for sociology.[18]

The purposes of sociology and philosophy also differ. As with any science, the aim of sociology is "to offer us as true an image of nature as possible." The aim of philosophy, Durkheim states, referring to Plato and Aristotle, is quite different: "to confront our imagination with the idea of a perfect society, a model to be imitated." In contrast to sociology, philosophy is prescriptive rather than factual, normative rather than empirical. Philosophy does not seek to describe how things are or explain how they got that way, but rather to tell us how things ought to be. Consider the phenomenon of democracy. The objective of philosophy is not to reveal the history, preconditions, or characteristics of actually existing political systems, but rather to construct an image of the democratic ideal. Philosophy, unlike sociology, is thus directed toward the future—what might be wished for—not the past or the present. The purpose of sociology, in contrast, just as with the natural sciences, is to *know* reality, to reveal the facts about society and to discover its underlying laws.[19]

Sociology and philosophy also differ in their conceptions of society. When philosophers set forth economic, political, or moral ideals, they tacitly assume that society can be reordered to conform to theoretically contrived models. Philosophy, Durkheim argues, presupposes a view of society as nothing more than a human artifact, capable of being altered at will, fitted to human designs and desires. For philosophy, society is a purely human creation, like a piece of art, free to be assembled and reassembled according to deliberate plans. Durkheim rejects this assumption, insisting instead that society is a "natural fact," "subject to necessary laws." It has its own nature, he argues, deriving from its inner makeup, from the characteristics of group life. The social order can be modified, of course, and Durkheim himself proposes many reforms for the European nations of his day. But society is not infinite-

ly malleable. It can be changed only within the impersonal constraints imposed by its historical "conditions of existence." Society, he says, is not the
sort of thing that can be set up however we want it to be.[20]

Sociology as a Specialized Science

By demarcating the realm of social facts, Durkheim establishes a subject
matter for sociology. By proposing that social facts be treated as things, he
establishes a method for sociology. On this basis, he certifies sociology's
credentials, distinguishing it from common sense and competing academic
fields, particularly psychology and philosophy. But his purpose is not just to
legitimate the discipline. He is also intent on transforming the practice of
sociology, reorienting the sociological enterprise, and guiding it in a more
fruitful direction.

   In surveying the field of sociology and reflecting on the foundational
contributions of Auguste Comte and Herbert Spencer, Durkheim depicts a
discipline still in its youth. He credits his predecessors for envisioning a
science of society, but faults them for failing to follow through on that vision.
While in theory they correctly formulate sociology's program, in practice,
juggling concepts rather than studying facts, they seem less like sociologists
than philosophers. Comte, for example, rather than comparing and classify-
ing the many varieties of human society, took as his object of study a pure
fiction, society in general. This penchant for abstraction and speculation,
Durkheim laments, has left sociology in an empirically underdeveloped state.
It lacks basic information about even the most common social phenomena,
including religion, law, and the family. Because it has barely begun the
laborious task of systematic empirical investigation, sociology, even worse,
is in the sad state of not even knowing what it does not know.[21]

   The problem, according to Durkheim, is that sociology at this early stage
of its development is still inclined toward "metaphysical reflection," "sys-
tem-building," and "philosophical syntheses." Rather than addressing care-
fully defined issues of limited scope amenable to scientific study, sociologists are given to bold pronouncements and "brilliant generalities." Rather
than fulfilling the pressing need for "regular information," sociologists dog-
matize about social issues. Rather than getting down to the hard work of
undertaking specialized studies, sociologists offer up only a "metaphysic of
the social sciences."[22]

   To realize its potential as a genuine science of society, Durkheim argues,
sociology needs to relinquish its youthful enthusiasm for philosophical judg-

ments and grand theories. More to the point, he admonishes, the time has come for sociology "to end the era of generalities" and commence the "era of specialization." Sociologists can improve their knowledge of the world and advance the discipline only by focusing their research on "restricted questions" and "groups of facts clearly circumscribed." The most effective way for sociology to prove its scientific mettle is to undertake specialized studies in delimited areas, including morality, economics, law, and religion. A science truly exists, Durkheim says, "only when it has been divided and subdivided." Specialization, by facilitating the practice of treating social facts as things, is the cure for what ails the discipline of sociology. Through specialization, "science comes closer to things which are themselves specialized."[23]

Explaining Social Facts

Sociology is a "distinct and autonomous science," separate from psychology in particular, because it has its own unique subject matter, social facts, but also because it offers "exclusively sociological" explanations for social phenomena. Durkheim develops this argument, setting forth the "rules for the explanation of social facts," by working through two distinctions: first, between causal explanation and functional analysis and second, between individualistic explanations and sociological explanations.[24]

The aim of causal explanation is to discover the origins of social phenomena, how social facts under consideration came to be the way they are. Functional analysis, by contrast, seeks to understand the roles social phenomena play or the purposes they serve. The first looks to causes, the second to effects. For example, in studying the educational system, sociologists might, on the one hand, trace its pattern of development to determine how it evolved into its present form. On the other hand, they might also investigate the functioning of this system, the results it produces. The problem, Durkheim observes, is that sociologists sometimes confuse these two, falsely believing they have accounted for the existence of some phenomenon by identifying the functions it performs. But as he correctly points out, "to demonstrate the utility of a fact does not explain its origins, nor how it is what it is." The system of compulsory mass education in the United States, to take one example, functions to provide adult supervision for children, thus freeing parents to participate in the labor force, This, however, does not explain how or why this particular system was established in the first place. To identify the functions of social phenomena is an important feature of the sociological method, and it might even help explain why certain phenomena *persist*, but this form of analysis should not be confused with or substitute for causal explanation. Durkheim thus proposes the following rule: *"Therefore when one undertakes to explain a social phenomenon the efficient cause which produces it and the function it fulfills must be investigated separately."*[25]

Durkheim also insists that causal explanations in sociology take a genuinely sociological form. He rejects emphatically those explanations, essentially individualistic or psychological in nature, that attribute social phenomena to the desires, purposes, and needs of individuals. In criticizing individualistic explanations, Durkheim makes several points. First, the social world we currently occupy is not our creation, he points out. The institutions that nowadays govern our lives have been "handed down to us already fashioned by previous generations." Second, individuals do sometimes contribute to the emergence of new social phenomena—new laws, new norms, and new ideas. This would seem to be clearly so in the case of charismatic leaders, scientific pioneers, and innovative artists. But even when individuals step forward as historical actors, Durkheim claims, they remain unaware of how their efforts have been aided by the initiatives of others or abetted by social conditions. The outcomes of human actions, he insists, cannot be traced back to the aims of particular individuals. Third, social change inevitably results from a complex chain of collective action stretching from past to present; no particular individual plays anything more than an "infinitesimally small part" in shaping the course of history. Durkheim does not wish to deny individual agency, and at the very least he acknowledges that human actions might either "hasten or retard" the process of social evolution. Nevertheless, he stresses the deficiency of theories that ignore the causal power of social forces and purport to explain social phenomena by reference only to the intentions of individuals.[26]

The *"content* of social life," Durkheim says, underlining his objection to psychological explanations, cannot be explained "by states of the individual consciousness." Indeed, he asserts, "every time a social phenomenon is directly explained by a psychological phenomenon, we may rest assured that the explanation is false." Social phenomena must always be explained by reference to other social phenomena, meaning, more specifically, "the constitution of the inner social environment." Social facts, according to Durkheim, are products of the collective reality arising from patterns of human association, and in recognition of their social origins, the explanation of social facts must also be truly social. He thus proposes the following rule: *"The deter-*

mining cause of a social fact must be sought among antecedent social facts and not among the states of the individual consciousness."[27]

Durkheim's sociology, in sum, assumes that the life of the individual is dependent on the nature of society, on its inner constitution. We live the way we live because our society is the way it is, not because of our innate qualities as individuals. The job of sociology, as he conceives it, is to dig beneath the "surface of social life," where everything appears to originate from the intentions and actions of individuals, and disclose the underlying social forces at work, those "impersonal, hidden forces that move individuals and collectivities." These "deeper causes" are essentially sociological. They have to do with how individuals are grouped together, not individuals taken singly, but individuals in their associations with others.[28]

The Normal and the Pathological

Many philosophers and social scientists, including Max Weber, maintain that while science is capable of answering empirical questions, it is not equipped to answer evaluative questions. It can inform us about what *is*, but not about what *ought* to be. Science discloses facts and discovers relations of cause and effect, but it cannot tell us how we should live our lives or how we should organize our collective affairs. For Durkheim, the implications of this position are distressing. "What good is it to strive after a knowledge of reality," he wonders, "if the knowledge we acquire cannot serve us in our lives?" If sociology were "merely speculative," he declares, if it had no practical relevance, it would hardly be worth pursuing. Indeed, he was partly motivated to set forth the rules of the sociological method precisely to make sociology a more effective instrument of social reform.[29]

Challenging the conception of science as a value-neutral enterprise, Durkheim sets out to find some empirical means through which sociology—without reverting to ideology or political partisanship—might differentiate between what is *good* and what is *bad*. For a model of how to proceed, he turns to the field of medicine. The sociologist studying society, he proposes, in roughly the same manner as a physician examining the human body, can discriminate between health and sickness, between the "normal" and the "pathological." Assuming that health is good and sickness bad, this gives sociology an objective "reference point" for separating out what is desirable from what is undesirable, thus enabling the discipline to "throw light on practical matters while remaining true to its own method."[30]

The question remains, however, by what yardstick can the normal, healthy, and good be distinguished from the pathological, sick, and bad? Durkheim proposes two criteria—which I refer to respectively as the "generality" criterion and the "consistency" criterion. First, a social fact is normal, he states, if it is found in all or most societies of a similar type. In the current era, for example, individualism, occupational specialization, and moral diversity, because they are all prevalent in industrial societies, are normal and therefore healthy phenomena. This generality criterion is not always revealing, however. For instance, some social facts, for example, the institution of inheritance, though present across all modern societies, are nevertheless pathological. They endure only through "blind habit," as out-of-date relics from an earlier stage of development. What is general therefore is not always normal. This leads Durkheim to posit a second criterion: a social fact is normal, he argues, only if it accords with the immanent logic of society, with its essential "conditions of existence." By this consistency criterion, inheritance, despite being general, is an abnormal phenomenon because it is at odds with modernity's characteristically meritocratic and egalitarian foundations. For Durkheim, in sum, based on these two criteria, any particular social fact is judged pathological if, for societies of a given type, it is either exceptional or anachronistic.[31]

Durkheim relies mainly on the consistency criterion in distinguishing between the normal and the pathological. He evaluates the appropriateness of social facts according to whether or not they are in harmony with the fundamental, if sometimes only nascent, conditions of the modern world. If certain moral notions or institutional practices are in agreement with society's defining principles, if they fulfill social needs and serve useful functions, they are judged normal; and if not, they are judged pathological. This procedure, because it rests on an "objective standard," enables the sociologist to make "*reasoned* evaluations" of social facts and to offer informed recommendations for social reform. Sociology, for example, is thus able to identify phenomena that are present in modern society but should not be (e.g., anti-Semitism, exploitive labor contracts, barriers to equal opportunity) or are not fully present in modern society but should be (e.g., corporate organizations, rules of conduct in the business world, respect for science and reason). For Durkheim, the practical value of sociology derives from its ability to direct human action toward ends whose desirability is grounded in the facts themselves, thus transforming the art of politics into an "extension of science." Guided by the findings of sociology, accordingly, "the duty of the statesman," he says, "is no longer to propel societies violently towards an ideal which appears attractive to him. His role is rather that of the doctor: he forestalls the outbreak of sickness by maintaining good hygiene, or when it does break out, seeks to cure it." For Durkheim, sociology is to society what the physician is to the patient.[32]

MODERN SOCIETY: SPECIALIZATION AND SOLIDARITY

Durkheim presents his most sustained analysis of modern life in his first book, *The Division of Labor*. Laying the foundation for everything to follow, this work is essential for understanding his thinking about the origins, troubles, and future of modern society. Looking to the past to interpret the present, Durkheim examines the unique features of the modern world by comparing it to the pre-modern world of a distant era. He proceeds by contrasting the most elementary forms of social life, with simple hordes and tribal groups at the lower end of the evolutionary continuum, to more advanced forms of social organization, with the most developed being the industrial society of the present. On the basis of this comparison, Durkheim identifies the salient characteristics of modern society, offers a provocative diagnosis of the modern condition, and at the same time defends modernity against the backward-looking proponents of traditionalism.[33]

I begin this section by discussing Durkheim's description of the social structure of pre-modern and modern society, followed by a brief summary of his theory of the transition from the first to the second. Then, turning to the heart of his analysis, I explore more fully his elaboration of the contrast between these two social types. In separate subsections I focus on three interrelated differences between the pre-modern world and the modern world: (1) the "collective consciousness" is strong in the first and weak in the second; (2) legal rules take a "repressive" form in the first and a "restitutive" form in the second; and (3) social order is achieved through "mechanical" solidarity in the first and "organic" solidarity in the second.

Segmentary Society and Organized Society

Pre-modern and modern societies constitute two polar social types according to Durkheim, each with its own distinct social structure, each "put together" in its own unique way. The first—described as "segmentary," "unorganized," or "amorphous"—exhibits only rudimentary differentiation, meaning very little specialization of roles and functions. The basic elements making up such societies—whether individuals, families, or larger units—resemble one another. They all occupy similar social positions, participate in similar social activities, perform similar economic tasks, and live similar lives. This social type is formed through replication, yielding a collection of largely identical and interchangeable individuals, each capable of subsisting independent of the other. In its most elementary form, a segmentary society consists "of an absolutely homogenous mass" of indistinguishable parts.[34]

The second social type, modern "organized" society, is characterized by an advanced division of labor. This more complex type of society consists of a system of interlocking institutions—including the family, schools, the legal apparatus, and political and economic structures—each playing a "special role." The individual members of this system are likewise highly differentiated. They each occupy a niche in an immense division of labor, engaged in their own specialized spheres of activity and dependent on the many other occupants of complementary positions. In pre-modern societies, where most people's circumstances are similar, what they have in common is far greater than what distinguishes them. In modern industrial societies, where individuals are dispersed throughout a highly diversified occupational system, people's differences stand out more than their resemblances.[35]

The contrast between the social structure of segmentary societies and organized societies is roughly analogous to the difference between bowling and baseball. In a bowling alley, everyone has their own identical lane, each adjacent to the other; everyone is engaged in the same activity; and everyone is self-subsistent, each participating apart from neighboring bowlers. If someone abandons their alley, nothing changes for anyone else. Baseball is different. Assembled together on the same field, every player is assigned their own position, each different from yet joined to the other. If one or more players choose to leave, the game cannot continue and the play of everyone else is disrupted. In bowling, as in segmentary societies, because everyone does the same thing, they are independent of each other. In baseball, as in organized societies, because everyone plays different but complementary roles, they are dependent on each other. In pre-modern societies people are alike but not interdependent, while in modern societies people are interdependent but not alike.

The Origins of the Division of Labor

To account for the transition from pre-modern society to modern society, Durkheim proposes a theory of social evolution. Built on the premise that the process of modernization is essentially a process of differentiation, this theory purports to reveal the underlying causes of the division of labor. Following his methodological rulebook, Durkheim's explanation for this development, which he considers the defining feature of modern society, is emphatically sociological. He dismisses all "individualistic and psychological" explanations, rejecting in particular the idea that the division of labor arose in response to the desire of individuals to increase productivity and thereby enhance human happiness and well-being. Durkheim takes a radically different approach. If society changes, he argues, this is not because change is willed by individuals; "it is because the environment changes." To discover the origins of the division of labor, therefore, he looks for causal forces located in the social environment. Only through this method, he claims, can we determine how the sustainability of the pre-modern, segmentary type of society was undermined and how this precipitated the rise of the modern, organized type of society.[36]

The basic segments of pre-modern society are all alike, as we have seen, and they function independently of each other. This simple social order ceases to be viable when the level of contact and interaction among these previously separate units reaches a certain threshold. Durkheim refers to this "drawing together" of individuals as "dynamic or moral density." Increasing dynamic density weakens the segmentary structure. It puts people and groups in closer proximity to one another, multiplies points of contact, and aggravates rivalry over scarce resources and opportunities. Population growth, the formation of towns, and improved means of transportation and communication, by fueling the proliferation of "intra-social relationships," all contribute to higher levels of dynamic density.[37]

But why should increasing population size, concentration, and interaction cause people to specialize? Through what process or mechanism does dynamic density necessitate the growth of the division of labor, and under what conditions does this occur? Durkheim's answer is that dynamic density makes the struggle for existence more "strenuous." Where all individuals earn their livelihood in the same manner—for example, by eking out a living as farmers in a finite territory—an increase in their numbers and relationships is bound to cause a heightened level of conflict. The resulting intensification of competition, with weaker competitors driven from the field, impels indi-

viduals, as a matter of survival, to find some new way of earning a livelihood. The division of labor develops as individuals endeavor to find a way to
sustain themselves under increasingly arduous social circumstances. By enabling people to take up new and different occupations, each complementing
the other, the advent of specialization represents a peaceful means for moderating the struggle for existence. Thanks to the division of labor, individuals
are not compelled to enter into a war of all against all. They can each work in
their own differentiated occupational spheres—farmer, shoemaker, baker,
and tailor, coexisting in harmony side by side.[38]

The Collective Consciousness

As the pre-modern social type gives way to the modern social type, the state
of the collective consciousness undergoes a corresponding transformation.
Durkheim defines the collective consciousness as the "totality of beliefs and
sentiments common to the average members of a society." The stronger the
collective consciousness, the more similar individuals are in their values and
beliefs. In the pre-modern world the collective consciousness is an all-embracing social force. It is high in *volume*, enveloping the entirety of the
consciousness of individuals, impressing itself on nearly every facet of their
lives. It is high in *intensity*, exerting a powerful effect on people's thinking
and behavior, forcefully steering them in a "collective direction." It is high in
rigidity, consisting of well-defined rules of conduct, leaving little room for
individual interpretation or discretion. And it is high in *religious content*,
investing shared values and ideas with divine authority. In pre-modern society, where the group is preeminent, the "individual consciousness is almost
indistinct from the collective consciousness." There is nearly perfect consensus: "every consciousness beats as one."[39]

   With the development of the division of labor, the lives of individuals
become more varied. In the differentiated society of the modern era, a single
uniform set of beliefs, sentiments, and feelings to which everyone is expected to subscribe is no longer feasible. In response to increasing diversity
in people's circumstances and experiences, the collective consciousness
weakens, diminishing in volume, intensity, and rigidity. It becomes more
general, flexible, and abstract, loosening society's hold on the individual and
permitting greater freedom of thought and action. Rather than imparting
detailed and binding instructions for how people should live their lives, it
conveys only broad guidelines. In the United States, for example, the dominant culture promotes the ideal of the work ethic, but does not prescribe

specific occupations, leaving it up to individuals to chart their own career paths.[40]

The collective consciousness in the pre-modern world thoroughly absorbs the individual, demanding that everyone be alike, each an echo of the common psychic life. In its weakened modern state however, there is space for "the free development of individual variations." The individual consciousness is partially liberated from the collective consciousness. Indeed, because the rules of conduct in what remains of the collective consciousness are no longer so strict and clear cut, because they require interpretation and translation, individuals are not just allowed to think for themselves; they are forced to. In the pre-modern era, conformity is a moral rule, and individuals are expected to give unquestioned obedience to the authority of tradition. In the modern era, autonomy is a moral rule, and individuals are expected to make good use of their intelligence and "reflective thinking." The process of modernization entails not only specialization, but also its inevitable accompaniment, individuation.[41]

The modern sensibility, Durkheim asserts, converges on one particularly important article of "common faith": the belief in the dignity and value of the individual. In this one area, the collective consciousness, though altered in content, becomes stronger. The sanctity of the individual is at the heart of the modern collective consciousness. Despite their diversity in other respects, individuals in the modern world feel a shared moral obligation to respect the humanity of other people. Indeed, the individual today is "the object of a sort of religion"—hence Durkheim sometimes speaks of the "cult of the individual." With the development of the division of labor, Durkheim argues, individualism itself becomes a unifying moral rule and a "rallying-point" for the modern mind.[42]

Repressive Law and Restitutive Law

The types of laws that prevail derive from the organization of social life, so as societies evolve from the simple to the complex, a change necessarily occurs in the composition of legal rules. In the pre-modern era, with its strong collective consciousness, the legal code consists mainly of "penal" laws with "repressive" sanctions. In the modern era, with its advanced division of labor, the legal code consists mainly of "co-operative" laws with "restitutive" sanctions. Durkheim relies on the "visible symbol" of law as an empirical indicator of the type of social solidarity prevalent in any particular society.[43]

The legal system in the pre-modern world is diffusely organized. It operates through the informal agency of society as a whole rather than through the authority of specialized institutions. It intrudes in people's lives when they deviate from the beliefs and sentiments making up the collective consciousness. Transgressions of this kind constitute an affront to the authority of society, an assault by the individual on the group. Including everything from murder to blasphemy, such violations fall under the jurisdiction of *penal law*, they are considered *crimes*, and they are subject to *repressive sanctions*, ranging from banishment to dismemberment to execution. The function of punishment in such cases, Durkheim argues, is less to exact vengeance on the guilty than to reaffirm the authority of tradition and secure the continued compliance of the innocent. Legal intervention serves the purpose of bolstering the collective consciousness, thereby contributing to the continued cohesion of society.[44]

In the modern world, with its differentiated social structure and weak collective consciousness, the scope of law increases to encompass a multitude of non-criminal matters. What Durkheim refers to broadly as cooperative law becomes the dominant form, with penal law reduced to a proportionately small fraction of the legal code. Cooperative law includes, for example, legal rules governing the rights and duties of husbands and wives, creditors and debtors, and producers and consumers, as well as laws pertaining to property ownership, inheritance, bankruptcies, and contracts of all kinds. The modern legal system enters into people's lives primarily when there is a breakdown in the normal workings of things (e.g., the failure of a business or a marriage); a violation of rights and obligations (e.g., citizens denied the right to vote or individuals subjected to discrimination); or uncertainty about how to resolve a conflict (e.g., a child custody case or a contract dispute). The infringement of cooperative law, unlike penal law, does not usually constitute crime; and though wrongful parties are sometimes ordered to pay compensation, they are not typically branded with negative stigmas or exposed to repressive sanctions such as imprisonment. The modern legal system is designed less to quash deviance than to achieve restitution, less to punish criminals than to restore the orderly functioning of social life. Restitutive law, in contrast to repressive law, Durkheim argues, serves the purpose of managing cooperative relations and enabling individuals and institutions to "work together in a regular fashion."[45]

Repressive and restitutive laws both function to maintain social stability: the first by ensuring that individuals follow the dictates of the collective consciousness, the second by ensuring that the specialized functions in society relate in a coordinated manner. By punishing criminals, repressive law promotes social conformity; by specifying and enforcing rights and duties, restitutive law promotes social harmony. Both types of law reinforce the ties that bind individuals together. But while penal law strengthens those ties stemming from a "commonality of beliefs and sentiments," cooperative law strengthens those ties stemming from people's participation in the specialized division of labor.[46]

Mechanical Solidarity and Organic Solidarity

Durkheim, as we have seen, identifies two opposing social types. The first— pre-modern society—is characterized by an undifferentiated social structure, a strong collective consciousness, a homogeneous population, and a legal code consisting primarily of penal laws with repressive sanctions. The second—modern society—is characterized by a highly differentiated social structure, a weak collective consciousness, a heterogeneous population, and a legal code consisting primarily of cooperative laws with restitutive sanctions. This dichotomy goes even deeper. The process of social evolution, Durkheim insists, is simultaneously a process of "moral evolution." The contrast between these two social types extends to the moral rules and bonds of social solidarity characteristic of each. This is the crux of Durkheim's argument. Pre-modern and modern society differ in the glue that holds them together, "mechanical solidarity" for the first and "organic solidarity" for the second.[47]

In the pre-modern era, social solidarity derives from people's resemblances. Individuals form a cohesive community because they live similar lives and think similar thoughts. The collective consciousness is the fundamental basis of this type of social solidarity. When individuals threaten this sacred order, when they deviate from shared values, beliefs, and practices, they face the wrath of a punitive penal system. The strength of the collective consciousness and the continuity of society are ultimately dependent on the coercive power of repressive sanctions. This kind of solidarity, which Durkheim calls "mechanical," requires the complete suppression of individuality. Where mechanical solidarity prevails, the individual "does not belong to himself; he is literally a thing at the disposal of society." The moral order of the pre-modern world is strong "only if the individual is weak."[48]

One might think that a common culture, a system of shared values, beliefs, and traditions, is the only *possible* basis of social order. This is precisely the assumption Durkheim challenges. His central objective is to refute the supposition that social solidarity requires a strong collective consciousness, that it can *only* take the form of mechanical solidarity. He asks us to consider the possibility of an alternative form of social solidarity, one he believes is unique to the modern era, "organic solidarity." Indeed, he argues, rather than collapsing into anarchy as many feared, modern society is destined to give rise to a new social order even more cohesive than that found in the pre-modern world. Unlike mechanical solidarity, however, which draws its strength from the collective consciousness, organic solidarity arises from the division of labor itself. In modern society, characterized by diversity rather than uniformity, people are connected to one another by virtue of their differences, not their resemblances. Social cohesion is achieved through cooperation rather than consensus, through restitutive law rather than repressive law, and through regulation rather than coercion.[49]

Here we see the striking originality of Durkheim's contribution. He shifts the focus from the *economic* significance of the division of labor to its *moral* significance. Specialization increases economic productivity, but more importantly it engenders social solidarity. As with the collective consciousness of the pre-modern era, though in an entirely different manner, the division of labor binds people to one another. It ties individuals together in a web of interdependencies, placing them in a dense network of cooperative relations and joining them in a "lasting way" through the creation of "a whole system of rights and duties." As modern individuals, playing our specialized roles, we each contribute only a minuscule part to the overall functioning of society. We are dependent for our very survival on a multitude of others playing their specialized roles. We count on them just as they count on us. Despite the rise of individualism, the modern person is anything but self-sufficient. Because we are each minor components of a complex and differentiated social organism, we are more dependent on each other than ever before. This is what gives the division of labor its cohesive power and moral force. It links individuals "to one another who would otherwise be independent; instead of developing separately, they concert their efforts." It obliges people to work together for a common purpose, like players on an athletic team or musicians in an orchestra, implicating them in something larger than themselves. In the process it stimulates feelings of dependency, obligation, and solidarity. The division of labor, according to Durkheim, thus serves an essential moral function: it "forces man to take account of other people, to regulate his actions by something other than the promptings of his own egoism."[50]

* * *

Durkheim wrote *The Division of Labor* during a period of profound social change. The old pre-modern world in the European societies of his day was dying out, and the new modern world was still in its infancy. The resulting turmoil and uncertainty provoked a sense of crisis. For conservative critics the advent of modernity itself was the problem. The pressure of modernizing forces—industrialization, secularization, and individualism—threatened the stabilizing power of traditional institutions and worldviews. From this perspective, modern society was no society at all; it was a recipe for chaos. The only possible recourse, the only way to maintain social order, was to restore the old regime.

Durkheim's concept of organic solidarity gave him leverage to dispute this fundamentally reactionary perspective. If the division of labor itself produces a new and specifically modern form of social solidarity, as he claims, then there is no need to return to the traditions of the past. Modernity can have its cake and eat it too. It can have diversity *and* stability, individualism *and* order, autonomy *and* morality. The process of modernization undermines the old social order, but it creates a new and qualitatively different social order in its place, one in which individuals are both more independent and more closely bound to society. [51]

While defending modernity against its conservative critics, Durkheim nevertheless agrees that modern society is in a state of crisis. The development of the division of labor, *under normal conditions*, produces organic solidarity. But at the present time, he admits, modern society has deviated from its "natural course," resulting in a pathological condition. This is an "exceptional" circumstance, he insists; it is not due to the inherent nature of modernity itself. The problem, rather, is that modern society is in a transitional state, not yet fully developed, still experiencing the pangs of an extraordinarily rapid and difficult birth. The solution to this crisis, he urges, is to press on, to go forward not backward. In chapter 5, I will consider this topic more fully, discussing in greater detail Durkheim's diagnosis of the modern condition, his reflections on the crisis of modernity, and his analysis of the "abnormal forms of the division of labor." [52]

SOCIOLOGY, SUICIDE, AND MODERNITY

With the publication of his third book, *On Suicide*, Durkheim continued his quest to legitimate the discipline of sociology and establish its scientific credentials. The topic of suicide, which on the surface would seem to be anything but a social phenomenon, presented him with a challenging opportunity to further substantiate the existence of a realm of distinctly social facts and to apply and illustrate the methodological principles set forth in *The Rules*. With *Suicide* he also resumed his exploration of key themes from earlier writings, including the problem of social solidarity and the relationship between the individual and society. Beyond all this, however, Durkheim had an even more far-reaching agenda. The study of suicide, he promised, would also serve a more practical purpose. It would shed light on "the causes of the general contemporary maladjustment being undergone by European societies" and suggest "remedies which may relieve it."[53]

As with crime or any other form of deviance, Durkheim explains, a certain amount of suicide is to be expected in any society. While such "normal" cases are tragic for those affected, they do not constitute a social problem properly speaking. The rate of suicide throughout much of Europe in the nineteenth century was on the rise, however, reaching levels that could only imply the existence of a "pathological state." Along with many of his contemporaries, Durkheim looked upon the high incidence of suicide as yet another symptom of social dissolution, a product of the wrenching changes occurring with the emergence and rapid development of industrial society. "What we see in the rising tide of voluntary deaths is . . . a state of crisis and upheaval which cannot continue without danger." Durkheim took up the study of suicide to demonstrate not only the explanatory value of sociology, but its diagnostic and practical value as well.[54]

The Social Rate of Suicide

Suicide would seem to be a purely personal act, originating from psychological factors and precipitating events in the life of the individual, a family crisis or an economic setback, for example. If this were the case, the study of suicide would fall outside the province of sociology. Durkheim concedes, in fact, that individual instances of suicide are best understood using the tools of psychology. But while single cases constitute psychological facts, the *rate* of suicide—the proportion of "voluntary deaths" for a particular population during a specified time period—is a uniquely social phenomenon.[55]

Durkheim provides evidence on this issue by examining the data on suicide rates for European nations. He underlines two key findings. First, the
incidence of suicide, though rising in some cases in later years, remains fairly
constant over time for any particular country. Second, the rate of suicide
varies substantially from one country to another, with some exhibiting consistently higher rates and others consistently lower rates. Each country, the
statistics reveal, appears to have its own "particular disposition towards suicide." The propensity for suicide also varies according to the characteristics
of groups within society, differing by gender, religion, family status, and
occupational position. Some groups—for example, men compared to women
and Protestants compared to Catholics and Jews—have a greater "collective
tendency" toward suicide than others. Whether at the level of society or the
group, this "social rate of suicide," he emphasizes, is a specifically sociological phenomenon. Because the incidence of suicide is relatively stable and
because it varies systematically from group to group, it cannot be accounted
for by psychological causes. The rate of suicide, Durkheim concludes, is a
product of social forces external to the individual; it can only be explained by
the collective characteristics or "moral constitution" of people's immediate
social environment.[56]

Durkheim's strategy for studying suicide is eminently sociological. He
focuses not on "the individual as individual, with his motives and ideas," but
rather directs our attention to "the states of the different social milieux . . .
according to which suicide varies." Suicides are the acts of individuals, of
course, but their personal circumstances, experiences, and motives cannot
explain the patterns exhibited by the *rate* of suicide. Individual factors are
not irrelevant, Durkheim acknowledges, but their influence is always condi-
tioned—suppressed under some circumstances, heightened under others—by
the properties of the social environment.[57]

The Social Types of Suicide

Durkheim wrestles with the problem of how to determine the different types
of suicide and how individual cases might be classified according to these
types. The lack of adequate information on victims precludes sorting suicides
by their observable characteristics, so he identifies the "social types of suicide" according to the conditions presumed to cause them. He posits four
types of suicide: altruistic, fatalistic, egoistic, and anomic. These are *social*
types. They designate varieties of abnormal social environments, not varieties of troubled individuals. Each type refers to a social milieu where there is

an imbalance in the relationship between the individual and the group. Individuals experiencing unhappiness or adversity in such abnormal circumstances are more likely to opt for suicide than would be the case under
normal conditions. The result, with this being one indicator of a pathological
social state, is a higher than typical rate of suicide.[58]

The relationship between the individual and society is unhealthy, according to Durkheim, whenever the presence of the group in the life of the
individual is felt either too strongly or too weakly. He measures this group
presence across two dimensions: integration and regulation. While integration depends on people being attached to social groups, regulation depends
on people being subject to social control. Regarding integration, a healthy
social environment exists where individuals have a life in common with
others, where they are active participants in the social world and oriented to
collective goals and ideals. Regarding regulation, a healthy social environment exists where the passions and desires of individuals have attainable
outlets and clearly defined limits such that people experience congruity between their aspirations and their resources, between what they want and what
they are able to get.[59]

A stable and harmonious social order requires that individuals be well
integrated into society and subject to authoritative social regulation. Too
much or too little of either creates a situation where individuals are unduly
vulnerable to suicide. This proposition is the basis of Durkheim's four types.
Altruistic suicide stems from excessive integration, fatalistic suicide from
excessive regulation, egoistic suicide from insufficient integration, and
anomic suicide from insufficient regulation. These social types, to repeat,
denote pathological social environments. Since social conditions tend to express themselves psychologically, "penetrating the minds of individuals,"
these pathological environments, Durkheim argues, give rise to certain abnormal psychological types as well. In his discussion of each form of suicide,
therefore, Durkheim not only describes their social causes but also their
corresponding individual manifestations. In what follows I consider in turn
each of Durkheim's four types of suicide, giving more attention to the two
types most prevalent in modern society, egoistic suicide and anomic suicide.[60]

Altruistic Suicide

Altruistic suicide is characteristic of a social environment, mainly found
among "primitive peoples" and "inferior societies," where the life of the

individual is subordinated to the life of the group. In such pre-modern conditions, marked by insufficient individuation or excessive integration, individuals as such are of little importance. They derive their sense of worth entirely from their membership and participation in the group. Being "tightly dependent" on society and "absorbed in the group," they have no meaningful life apart from their service to the collective and their fulfillment of social duties and responsibilities.[61]

Durkheim cites three examples of altruistic suicide: infirm or aging men nearing the end of their lives as productive members of society, newly widowed women, and servants following the death of their masters. In each of these cases the bonds connecting individuals to social roles and purposes are severed, leaving them without a place in society; and since they lack value as persons in their own right, they no longer have a reason for existence. In this circumstance, suicide is a social imperative, "obligatory altruistic suicide," or at least encouraged by society, "optional altruistic suicide." Victims, in response to "public opinion," take their own lives because they are expected to, because it is their duty. When they kill themselves, they are not renouncing society but submitting to it.[62]

Durkheim finds one modern milieu also conducive to altruistic suicide: the army. In the military setting, as in more traditional societies, individuation is unusually low and integration unusually high. Individuals in the armed forces, where a strong collective ethos prevails, are subject to a regimen of sacrifice and obedience and are expected to subordinate their individual interests to those of the group. The suicide rate for soldiers, predictably, is consistently higher than for civilians. More generally, however, Durkheim claims, in modern industrial societies where "the individual personality becomes increasingly free from the collective personality," altruistic suicide is rare.[63]

Fatalistic Suicide

Fatalistic suicide is characteristic of a social environment where people's "future is pitilessly confined" and their passions "violently constrained by an oppressive discipline." In such circumstances, marked by excessive regulation, the individual, subject to an intolerable "physical or moral despotism," lives a life bereft of possibilities. While altruistic suicide results from a situation where people experience a feeling of uselessness, fatalistic suicide results from a situation where people experience a feeling of hopelessness. As examples of this type, he cites the suicide of slaves, men who marry too

young, and married women without children. Unfortunately, Durkheim relegates this type of suicide to a brief footnote. As we will see in a later chapter,
however, contrary to his claim that it is only of "historical interest," Durkheim's own analysis suggests that the conditions associated with fatalistic
suicide are not foreign to modern society.[64]

Egoistic Suicide

Egoistic suicide, the opposite of altruistic suicide, arises from a social environment characterized by insufficient integration or "exaggerated individuation." This abnormal state signifies the impoverishment of communal life
and collective involvement. Individuals are only loosely affiliated with
groups, disengaged from social activities, and detached from collective
ideals. They are disposed to act on their personal interests at the expense of
their social obligations, give priority to individual goals over communal purposes, and abide by their own consciences as opposed to social norms. Lacking strong social ties and a supportive network of relatives, friends, and
associates, modern individuals—isolated, withdrawn, and left to their own
devices—commonly experience depression, melancholy, apathy, and sadness. The excessive individualism from which they suffer, Durkheim asserts,
is the primary cause of the high rate of suicide in modern society. When
individuals are poorly integrated into the group, "the link that attaches man to
life is loosened." Primed by a "state of society" that "has made him an easy
prey for suicide," the individual yields to the "slightest adversity."[65]

Durkheim explores the social causes of egoistic suicide by examining
three different "societies": religious society, domestic society, and political
society. First, the rate of suicide, he finds, is higher among Protestants than
either Catholics or Jews. Protestantism is a more individualistic religion,
allowing for greater "freedom of inquiry," and it includes fewer "common
beliefs and practices," leaving ample room for the individual to be "the
author of his own belief." Catholicism, on the other hand, comes "ready-
made," consisting of a well-established "collective *credo*" supported by an
authoritative priestly hierarchy. Protestantism is "a less firmly integrated
Church than the Catholic one," and because they benefit less from a cohesive
religious community, Durkheim concludes, Protestants have a higher rate of
suicide.[66]

Second, the suicide rate is lower for people with children, and the larger
the family, the stronger the effect. As compared to the childless, parents have
tighter social bonds, close and highly affective ties to others, and a more

active social life. The family environment keeps individuals in a state of healthy dependency, stimulates sentiments of mutuality, and unites individuals around common goals. By restraining the impulse toward self-involvement, marriage with children is "a powerful preservative against suicide."[67]

Third, the incidence of egoistic suicide varies also with the state of political society. The rate of suicide, Durkheim observes, declines during "major political upheavals," "electoral crises," and national wars. These events "sharpen collective feelings" and concentrate people's "activities toward a single end," thus fostering heightened levels of social integration. Political events of this sort arouse people's nationalistic sentiments, "oblige men to cling together in order to confront a common danger," and inspire them to think less about themselves as individuals and more about their communities.[68] .

Anomic Suicide

Anomic suicide, the opposite of fatalistic suicide, prevails in a social environment where individuals are subject to insufficient regulation, where there is no moderating force restraining their desires and ambitions. As with egoistic suicide, anomic suicide occurs when the influence of society is too weakly present in the life of the individual. Durkheim's premise is that human aspirations are insatiable; no matter how much we get, we always want more. Our desires, if left unregulated, are incapable of being quenched. The goals we seek continually recede before us, dooming us to perpetual disappointment. To achieve a happy and healthy existence, humans need well-defined limits to rein in their otherwise infinite appetites. In the absence of an authoritative moral framework specifying the kind of life they can reasonably hope for, the ends they can realistically pursue, and the needs they can legitimately expect to satisfy, people will never be "content with their lot." In this anomic condition, individuals experience a constant state of agitation, irritation, and exasperation.[69]

Durkheim identifies two types of anomie, economic and conjugal, and, correspondingly, two forms of anomic suicide, one stemming from an unhealthy economic environment, the other from an unhealthy domestic environment. Economic anomie occurs during periods of dramatic economic change, whether in the form of rapidly rising economic hardship ("regressive" anomie) or rapidly rising economic prosperity ("progressive" anomie). In either case, Durkheim reports, the rate of suicide goes up. A sudden economic transformation, whether boom or bust, upsets the balance in people's lives, creating a disjunction between normative expectations and economic circumstances. Overnight successes, with more money in their pockets than they know what to do with, find it difficult to cope with their new status, as do newly unemployed workers unable to provide adequately for their families. Both experience a circumstance where they are no longer adjusted to their situation, where old expectations and rules of conduct cease to apply and new ones have yet to take hold. They are in a state of anomie—rootless, unsettled, and disoriented—cut loose from normative moorings and thus susceptible to suicide. [70]

The proximate cause of conjugal anomie is the weakening of the matrimonial bond and, correspondingly, the weakening of the restraining power of marriage on people's passions and desires. Because the marital relationship benefits the mental health of husbands more than wives, Durkheim argues, the destabilization of marriage is more harmful to men than to women. Men are more in need of the constraints marriage provides, and women are more in need of freedom, thus the adverse effects of this anomic condition vary by gender. Durkheim finds, accordingly, that conjugal anomie increases the rate of suicide for men but not for women. The ultimate cause of this anomic state, Durkheim asserts, is the institution of divorce, which impairs the solidity of the marital union and reduces the "moral calm and tranquility" that husbands would otherwise enjoy. In support of this, he finds that husbands "in countries where the number of divorces is high" are "less immune to suicide than in those where marriage is indissoluble." In sum, where divorce is permitted "by laws and customs," the "matrimonial rule" is weakened, marriage is reduced to "an enfeebled form of itself," and married men are more prone to taking their own lives. [71]

* * *

In modern society, Durkheim argues, with its powerful currents of individualism and turbulent industrial economy, egoism and anomie are chronic problems. They are, he says, "two different aspects of a single social state," one in which the life of the individual is detached from the life of society. For Durkheim, the rising rate of suicide is "an index of the inadequate effectiveness of social bonds." Such bonds serve two essential moral purposes. By providing "attachment to social groups," social bonds furnish the individual with "socially given ideals and purposes," thus warding off the threat of egoism. By providing a "spirit of discipline," social bonds regulate the individual's "desires and aspirations," thus warding off the threat of anomie. Egoism and anomie register in somewhat different ways the unhealthy relationship between the individual and society in the modern world. Suicides of both an egoistic and anomic type are symptoms of a common disease, the "yearning for the infinite." "In the first, thought, turning too much in on itself, finds itself without any object, while in the second, passion, no longer acknowledging any limits, is deprived of its goal. The first loses himself in the infinity of dreams and the second in the infinity of desire."[72]

THE INDIVIDUAL AND SOCIETY

The relationship between the individual and society is a central theme in all four of Durkheim's major books—*The Division of Labor*, *The Rules of Sociological Method*, *On Suicide*, and *The Elementary Forms*. To conclude this introductory chapter, looking ahead to the thematic chapters that follow, I continue to explore his view of the individual, society, and their relationship. Drawing especially on *The Elementary Forms* and his writings on education, I focus specifically on his theory of human nature, his conception of society as a civilizing force and sacred object, and his analysis of the role of education in the formation of the modern individual.

Civilization and Humanity

The innate predispositions of human beings are "vague" and "very malleable," according to Durkheim. There is no fixed human nature, no one single way of being human. Whether looking back into the past or across to other societies, we see that people "are not always and everywhere the same." Diversity is the rule. Human nature exhibits "amazing flexibility and fecundity." How people see the world and how they conduct themselves vary greatly over time and from place to place, as do their moral beliefs. These facts attest to the power of the social environment to shape even the most fundamental qualities of individuals and their lives.[73]

For Durkheim, the attributes we typically ascribe to human nature originate from society. Human beings are social products. And since societies themselves evolve, humans are also products of history. We "can discover what makes up man" only through historical analysis, he claims, "since it is only in the course of history that he is formed." The proper starting point for sociology, accordingly, is not some abstract conception of human nature, but society, and only through the study of society, in all its variety, can we hope to gain an accurate picture of the individual. Humanity, Durkheim asserts, clarifying the task of sociology, is "for us less a point of departure than a point of arrival."[74]

Because human beings do not enter the world ready-made, they have to be formed. This is the job of society. Indeed, according to Durkheim, the individual "gets the best part of himself from society." Take away what society bestows—"language, sciences, art, and moral beliefs"—and "nothing is left but an animal." We owe all of our civilized qualities to society, he reminds us. "We speak a language we did not create; we use instruments we did not invent; we claim rights we did not establish." We assimilate from society all our beliefs, values, and norms, everything that makes us civilized human beings. "Man is man," Durkheim says, "only because he lives in society."[75]

God and Society

As individuals, we are dependent on society, we live our lives under its protective umbrella, we submit to its rules of conduct, and we derive our very humanity from society. It would seem, in fact, that society has precisely the qualities of mystery, transcendence, and supremacy believers attribute to their deities. Society, no less than god, is a powerful entity, a superior being, a moral force, and an object of reverence.

Durkheim pursues this line of thinking in *The Elementary Forms*, a study of Australian totemism which he considers among the most primitive religious systems. I will not attempt to summarize Durkheim's complex analysis, but I do want to underline two particularly important points he emphasizes in this book. First, religion, Durkheim insists, though not based on fact, cannot be dismissed as a "vast error," an "inexplicable hallucination," or a mere delusion. It expresses something real. There is a truth to religion, though this truth is not what believers think it is. The task for sociology is to unravel the mystery of religion, to "reach beneath" the literal content of religious symbols, sensations, and experiences for the purpose of grasping the deeper social reality to which they correspond.[76]

This takes us to Durkheim's second point. The deeper reality underlying religion, he says, is society itself. "The idea of society" is the "soul of religion." Or to put it otherwise, god and society "are one and the same." People's lives are indeed shaped by forces beyond their control and comprehension, just as religion would have us think, but these forces are social, not supernatural. When the faithful proclaim their belief in a higher power, they are not mistaken, he declares. "That power exists, and it is society." For Durkheim, the moral authority attributed to religion is not some mystical or misconceived illusion. It emanates from a genuine social reality; it is nothing other "than the feeling that the collectivity inspires in its members."[77]

Homo Duplex

In his later writings, introducing the concept of "homo duplex," Durkheim formulates his theory of human nature more precisely, giving greater recognition to the conflict between the instincts of the individual and the demands of society. He presents this view in *The Elementary Forms* declaring that "man is a double." On the one hand, there is the "individual" or "physical" being, rooted in the bodily organism. On the other hand, at a higher "intellectual and moral realm," there is the "social" or "spiritual" being. This duality of human nature, "homo duplex," is a variation on what Durkheim regards as a universal distinction between the body and the soul, the profane and the sacred. The soul, in opposition to the body, represents the "spark of the divinity" within the individual. Originating from the presence of society, "that unique source of all that is sacred," this is the part of us that is larger than ourselves, the "divine substance" that moves us to embrace moral ideals and to subordinate our private interests to the common good. The soul, symbolizing the social nature of the individual, speaks to us through the authoritative voice of our moral conscience. And when believers proclaim the immortality of the soul, they are in fact attesting to a definite reality: the individual dies, but society lives on.[78]

The individual being and the social being are antagonistic forces, constantly at war with one another. Oriented inward, the individual being is driven by bodily appetites, egoistic impulses, and private interests. Oriented outward, the social being is guided by collective sentiments, moral rules, and social ideals. The physical being, acting on sensual inclinations, serves purely amoral, personal ends. The spiritual being, attaching us to something larger than ourselves and pulling us in a "social direction," serves moral, impersonal ends.[79]

The same duality is evident in our thought processes. The individual being experiences the world through unmediated sensations, purely personal and incommunicable impressions of color, sound, and taste. The social being, operating at a higher level of intelligence, experiences the world through concepts, socially given "categories of thought." These "collective representations," originally religious in nature, are the heritage of humanity, "the product of an immense cooperation" extending across space and time. Such concepts, the building blocks of shared language and shared ideas, are the "supreme instrument of all intellectual exchange." Through concepts, individuals are able to participate in a common cognitive world. A "man who did not think with concepts," Durkheim asserts, "would not be a man, for he would not be a social being."[80]

Durkheim's concept of homo duplex posits a social being superimposed over an individual being. The moral authority of society is brought to bear, curbing the anti-social and egoistic tendencies of individuals, causing them to take account of something other than their own personal interests. We are not destined to obey the dictates of an amoral human nature, Durkheim argues. As social beings, we are able to transcend our egoistic interests and biological urges. By virtue of our membership in society, we are capable of morality and reason.[81]

Moral Education and the Formation of the Social Being

Durkheim's theory of human nature implies a notion of human beings as malleable. This is a fortunate circumstance, as civilization is possible, he believes, much like Sigmund Freud, *only* on the condition that society intervenes to transform the physical being into a social being. In modern industrial society, this task, performed in an earlier era by the family, is the primary responsibility of the school system.

There is a revealing difference, Durkheim observes, between the education of human beings and the training of non-human animals. The latter, following their instincts, experience a natural course of development, becoming as adults what they were already fated to be at the moment of their conception. For animals, the maturation process is one in which they realize their essential and inborn nature. For humans, with society substituting for instinct, things are different. Assuming the process of socialization functions properly, as humans pass from infancy to childhood to adulthood, they experience a "second gestation," becoming something qualitatively distinct from what they were at birth.[82]

For Durkheim, accordingly, and in opposition to a common strand of pedagogical theory, the purpose of human education is not to perfect "our individual natures" or develop our latent potentialities. The role of education is not cultivation but conversion. Its objective is not to nurture pre-existing qualities, but to create a new person, a social being. This is no easy undertaking, as there is a great gulf between the individual being and the social being, "between the child's point of departure and the goal toward which he must be led." Bridging this gulf is all the more difficult because the social being does not lie dormant, ready to be awoken, within the "native make-up" of the newly born child. Humans, Durkheim says, are not naturally "inclined to submit to political authority, to respect a moral discipline, to dedicate himself, to be self-sacrificing." The social being, far from arising spontaneously, comes into existence only through the purposeful sublimation of the amoral tendencies of the individual being. "To the egoistic and asocial being that has just been born," Durkheim states, society "must, as rapidly as possible, add another, capable of leading a moral and social life." This is the "work of education": to create "in man a new being," not "as nature has made him, but as the society wishes him to be."[83]

Society, for Durkheim, is a powerful force, a sacred object standing apart from the individuals who make it up. But just as society is not reducible to the individual, neither is the individual reducible to society, and the more advanced the society, the more this is true. The individual is nothing without society, but each individual is a social being in his or her own particular way. Society does not impose itself on individuals with precisely the same effect; it does not produce a perfectly uniform population. In the process of socialization, we "individualize" the beliefs and practices of our society, modifying them according to our circumstances and experiences, giving them "our own personal stamp." While each individual consciousness embodies the beliefs and values of society, it does so "from its own point of view and in its own manner." Even the "most essential aspects of morality," Durkheim acknowledges, "are seen differently by different people." However much we are social beings, we each express our social nature uniquely.[84]

But even as we individualize collective sentiments, these remain the province of society and as such retain their sanctity. They speak to us in our own individual "tone" or "accent," but nevertheless they "command us," they "impose respect on us," and they "represent something within us that is superior to us." The sacred authority of collective ideals, for Durkheim, is not diminished because individuals put their "own mark on them."[85]

Chapter Four

Max Weber (1864–1920)

Like Marx and Durkheim, Weber is a theorist of modernity. We find in his writings an analysis of the origins and nature of the modern western world, a probing diagnosis of the dilemmas and pathologies of modern life, and an examination of the predicament of the individual in the industrial era. Also like Marx and Durkheim, Weber's objective is not just to understand the modern condition, but to consider how we might respond to it as well. As a politically engaged public intellectual, he "stood on the threshold between politics and science all his life," Wolfgang Mommsen observes, and he endeavored "to be of service to both at the same time." Weber too wanted to change the world.[1]

For Marx, as we have seen, the transition from traditional to modern society consists mainly of a transformation in economic structures and class relations, with the capitalist mode of production displacing the feudal mode of production. For Durkheim, the passage from the pre-modern era to the modern era, propelled by the growth of the division of labor, is conceived primarily as a change in the nature of social stability, from mechanical solidarity to organic solidarity. Weber too underlines the contrast between modern society and traditional society. What separates the present from the past in his theory is the peculiar "rationality" of the modern world. For Weber, the process of modernization is essentially a process of "rationalization." The defining characteristics of the modern age emerge from this rationalizing process: the "immense cosmos" of the capitalist economic system, an impersonal and pervasive bureaucratic apparatus, a world rendered meaningless and disenchanted by modern science, an increasingly fragmented and conflict-ridden culture, and a new "type of *human being*," the modern vocational person. The process of rationalization poses threats unique to the modern era, Weber maintains, but it also opens up new possibilities for individual freedom. In the next section I begin a chapter-long effort to shed light on Weber's theory of modernity and his concept of rationalization.[2]

THE RATIONALIZATION THEME

There is some debate among scholars about the "thematic unity" or "central question" of Weber's work, leaving us with conflicting interpretations of where his main contributions lie and why he is important. But in most of the varied readings of Weber, the theme of rationality, rationalism, or rationalization is prominent. He affirms the importance of this theme in the "Author's Introduction" to his collected writings on religion where he singles out the "specific and peculiar rationalism of Western culture" as his main object of study. In his research on the ethics of the world religions as well, his primary interest is the phenomenon of "economic rationalism." The concept of rationality is also the focal point of his analysis of the origins, characteristics, and trajectory of modern capitalism. Elsewhere, he identifies the problem of explaining the rationalization of "European and American social and economic life" as being among the "chief tasks" of the socio-cultural sciences.[3]

Rationalization, Gianfranco Poggi states, is for Weber "the master process of modernity." But precisely what this process entails is difficult to pin down. Weber admits as much, warning that rationalization has "many possible meanings," occurs in "various departments of life," and "covers a whole world of different things." In the western world, for example, Weber finds a unique rationalism not only in the capitalist economic system, but also in the domains of science, music, architecture, higher education, government administration, and law. Not only does the process of rationalization move simultaneously on "several tracks" and in different and sometimes conflicting directions, but it also engenders a wide range of consequences, both desirable and undesirable depending on one's perspective. The theme of rationalization is central to Weber's diagnosis of the modern condition.[4]

The meaning of rationalization varies according to the form it takes and the social sphere in which it is found, so no single definition will suffice. At the risk of simplification, however, it might serve as a useful starting point to think of the process of rationalization as involving some kind of *systematic ordering.* Social action, for example, is rationalized to the extent it is *systematically ordered* by conscious deliberation, planning, and calculation. Belief systems or worldviews are rationalized to the extent they are *systematically ordered* by a process of intellectual refinement, rendering them more consistent and comprehensive. Social practices and institutional processes, including everything from meditation rituals to job training programs to the operation of government agencies, are rationalized to the extent they are *systematically ordered* by the implementation of explicit rules and standardized procedures. We see a similar *systematic ordering* and a corresponding pattern of uniformity throughout the modern rationalized or, what George Ritzer calls "McDonaldized," service economy—in fast food restaurants, shopping malls, movie theaters, and motels, and in the provision of education, health care, and entertainment. Wherever we might look, in fact—in the workplace, the classroom, the prison, the hospital, the military—the imprint of rationalization is visible in the presence of orderly and predictable routines. The process of rationalization, touching virtually every area of social life, is a systematizing and organizing force.[5]

The difference between the present and the past, however, is not so much the greater orderliness of the modern world as it is the nature of that orderliness. While the social order of traditional society rests on an "organically prescribed cycle of natural life" bolstered by habit and custom, the social order of modern society reflects the increasing power of human beings to control the social and natural forces of the world. The modern social order is achieved rather than ascribed. It is a distinctly *rational* order—a product of deliberate calculation, willful planning, scientific management, the exploitation of expert knowledge, and the application of advanced technologies.[6]

In the rest of this chapter, I discuss Weber's theory of modernity, focusing on how the process of rationalization plays out in different arenas of social life and how it illuminates the transition from the traditional world to the modern world. I begin at the simplest level by discussing Weber's analysis of the rationalization of social action. Following this, I explore in turn the development of modern capitalism and the rationalization of economic life, the rise of rational-legal authority and the rationalization of domination, the growth of bureaucratic administration and "bureaucratic rationalization," and the development of modern science and the resulting disenchantment of the world.[7]

THE RATIONALIZATION OF SOCIAL ACTION

Sociology, Weber states, is "a science concerning itself with the interpretive understanding of social action and thereby with a causal explanation of its course and consequences." Social action is present wherever individuals attach a "subjective meaning" to their behavior—a motive, purpose, or intention. He identifies four types of social action, each constructed as a pure or ideal type. In reality, he acknowledges, any particular instance of behavior typically consists of some combination of these pure types.[8]

Affectual action is determined by emotions or "feeling states," reflexive reactions to stimuli as, for example, when we impulsively take a swing at someone in a bout of anger, not really in control of ourselves or even altogether aware of what we are doing.

Traditional action is determined by "ingrained habituation." Along with other customary and unpremeditated daily behaviors, this might include, for example, the ritual greetings we unthinkingly give our colleagues when we arrive at work each morning.

Value-rational action is "determined by a conscious belief in the value for its own sake of some ethical, aesthetic, religious, or other form of behavior." Such action, carried out regardless of consequences, is governed by a commitment to some higher duty or moral ideal as, for example, when a person, even at the risk of his or her own life, complies with the principle of non-violence. In contrast to the automatic and unreflective observance of tradition, value-rational action presupposes a process of conscious deliberation through which individuals, in devotion to a religious creed, political cause, or philosophical doctrine, conduct their lives according to certain self-chosen ultimate values.

Instrumentally rational action is determined by means-ends calculations. Action is rational in this sense, Weber states, "when the end, the means, and the secondary results are all rationally taken into account and weighed." A high school graduate acts in an instrumentally rational manner when she looks to the future and contemplates her options, when she considers tuition expenses and job prospects and comes to the conclusion that going to college is more sensible than immediately entering the labor market, and when she chooses the most affordable college suited to her interests and selects a major appropriate to her career goals. She is a rational actor, deliberately plotting a course of action, taking into account existing conditions and available resources, assessing costs and benefits, gauging likely consequences, and measuring the advantages and disadvantages of the alternatives at hand—all for the purpose of figuring out what objectives are worth pursuing and how best to pursue them.

Affectual action and traditional action, Weber explains, because they are more or less unconscious and unthinking, are on the borderline between truly meaningful action and merely reactive behavior. Rational action, however, because it embodies a definite thoughtfulness, is unequivocally meaningful. But instrumentally rational action and value-rational action are meaningful in significantly different ways. The thoughtfulness characteristic of instrumentally rational action takes the form of *calculation*—the conscious and deliberate appraisal of competing lines of conduct evaluated according to their probable costs, consequences, and likelihood of success. We see this type of rationality at work when people make investment decisions or choose a neighborhood to live in. By contrast, the thoughtfulness characteristic of value-rational action takes the form of *conviction*—the conscious and deliberate adoption of certain values or ideals. The value-rational actor is oriented unconditionally toward the fulfillment of what he or she perceives to be a binding duty, cause, or demand. We see this type of rationality at work in the case of artists committed to their craft, soldiers going off to war out of patriotism, or idealistic followers of a rigorous philosophy of life. But precisely because such principled action is carried out for its own sake—and damn the consequences—it is irrational from the viewpoint of instrumentally rational action.[9]

Weber's conception of the rationalization of action rests on this typology. Behavior is rationalized to the extent it ceases to be merely emotional or habitual and is instead subject to the controlling influence of conscious thought. More precisely, the rationalization of action involves the displacement of unreflective emotional behavior (affectual action) and the "unthinking acceptance of ancient customs" (traditional action) in favor of the "deliberate adaptation to situations in terms of self-interest" (instrumentally rational action) and the "deliberate formulation of ultimate values" (value-rational action). Weber, of course, does not anticipate the disappearance of affectual or traditional action, but he is proposing an empirical generalization that illuminates one aspect of the ongoing process of rationalization in the modern western world. What we see with this process at the level of individual behavior is a shift from impulse to intention, from instinct to premeditation, from reflex to reflection, from the force of habit to the exercise of reason.[10]

Weber's analysis of rationalization attributes special significance to the increasing prevalence in the modern world of self-interested market behavior, the prototype of instrumentally rational action. With "its clarity of self-consciousness and freedom from subjective scruples," this type of action, he says, "is the polar antithesis of every sort of unthinking acquiescence in customary ways." Instrumentally rational action in the form of self-interested economic behavior, what Marx calls "egoistic calculation," not only displaces affectual and traditional action, Weber suggests; it also suppresses value-rational action, the "devotion to norms consciously accepted as absolute values." In the era of modern capitalism, he argues, the construct of the rational actor enshrined in economic theory, an actor conceived as adapting to market conditions according to cost-benefit calculations, has become the way of the world, implicating "the destiny of ever-wider layers of humanity. And it will hold more and more broadly, as far as our horizons allow us to see." What we are left with then is not just the rationalization of action, but a *skewed* rationalization of action, with instrumentally rational action crowding out value-rational action. The rational behavior of the individual in the modern world is, Weber argues, increasingly characterized by *calculation* rather than *conviction*, by the self-interested adaptation to circumstances rather than the principled commitment to ideals. [11]

MODERN RATIONAL CAPITALISM

Capitalism occupies center stage for Weber just as it does for Marx. For Weber, however, capitalism is not the defining feature of modern society but rather one embodiment of a more encompassing phenomenon: western rationalism. The modern world is a capitalist world, but more fundamentally it is the product of a multifarious and far-reaching process of rationalization. Though extending well beyond the economic domain, this process penetrates the innermost structure and functioning of western capitalism. When Weber turns his attention to the origins, dynamics, and implications of the modern economic order, his primary object of analysis is not *capitalism* per se, but *rational* capitalism.

By referring to capitalism as "rational," Weber does not mean to imply "moral approval." His usage is intended to be descriptive, not evaluative. Modern capitalism, he maintains, is "formally" rational, but not necessarily "substantively" rational. To say that capitalism, or any other social phenomenon, is rational in a substantive sense is to judge it as commendable, consistent with certain ethical notions. Formal rationality, by contrast, is a value-neutral designation. Modern capitalism is rational in this formal sense—this is Weber's key point—to the extent that business operations are conducted according to systematic planning based on economic calculation and monetary accounting. This rational planning comes into play when business owners determine what goods to produce, in what quantity, how to produce them, for what markets, and so on. Capitalist enterprises, as profit-seeking organizations, are formally rational insofar as their managing decisions are consistently guided by the impersonal and quantitative assessment of costs and revenues. The expression "nothing personal, it's just business" alludes to this type of formal rationality, while at the same time alerting us to the potential divergence between formal rationality and substantive rationality, between what is rational from a bottom-line accounting perspective and what is rational from an ethical perspective. [12]

Capitalism: Modern and Pre-Modern

Capitalism, understood as the pursuit of profit, is neither a uniquely modern nor a uniquely western phenomenon, according to Weber, but what he calls "rational capitalism" is *both* uniquely modern *and* uniquely western. He underlines the distinctiveness of modern rational capitalism by contrasting it with the many other "species" of capitalist profit making that have existed around the world for "thousands of years." He cites, among other types, "politically-oriented capitalism," "adventure capitalism," "pariah-capitalism," and "robber capitalism." What he has in mind here are early forms of capitalism where profit is made by speculating in foreign trade ventures; or by taking advantage of opportunities opened up by colonial expansion; or by lending money; or by financing wars, bribing politicians, and otherwise exploiting fortuitous political developments. These forms of capitalism, Weber observes, have an "irrational and speculative character," with profit derived less from ongoing market operations than from opportunistic investments and the forcible acquisition of "booty." [13]

Modern rational capitalism is quite different, though not easily captured by a simple definition. Weber insists on one point at the outset, however, namely that modern rational capitalism cannot be equated with the "acquisitive drive," or the "unlimited greed for gain," or the "pursuit of selfish interests by the making of money." A ruthless orientation toward accumulation, he observes, is present in human history nearly everywhere and at all times. In fact, he suggests, modern capitalism, tempered by the businesslike pursuit of profit, is if anything characterized by a more restrained acquisitive impulse than the *"compulsive,* irrational, unbridled" lust for riches commonly found prior to and outside the modern capitalist world. [14]

Modern capitalism, according to Weber, is an economic system where the provision of human needs is satisfied through the continuous operation of privately owned and profit-minded business firms. These capitalist enterprises are distinguished by their reliance on a legally free labor force, their resolute orientation toward market opportunities, and a mode of operation governed by monetary calculation. Modern capitalism has a more durable presence than its predecessors. Since the 1800s an increasingly large share of all economic activity has come to be organized according to the principle of profit making. The daily needs of people in the modern era, far more than in the past, are supplied on a purely capitalist basis. The modern capitalist world, also far more than in the past, is dominated by more or less permanent business firms that, instead of intermittently pursuing "speculative opportunities for profit," are continuously "attuned to a regular market." What distinguishes the modern economic system accordingly, Weber asserts, is the rational pursuit of profit, "and forever *renewed* profit," by means of "rigorous calculation, directed with foresight and caution toward" long-run economic success. For Weber, in sum, the chief mode of economic activity in the western world since the middle of the nineteenth century is not political, speculative, or adventure capitalism, but something qualitatively different: "sober bourgeois capitalism." [15]

Modern Rational Capitalism: Preconditions and Characteristics

On several occasions, Weber identifies what he variously refers to as the "causes," "presuppositions," or "distinguishing characteristics" of western capitalism. I present below a summary of this list of factors. This is intended to further clarify Weber's conception of the nature and origins of modern capitalism and his view of how it differs from earlier types of capitalist profit making. This should also help us better understand what Weber means when he describes capitalism as rational. [16]

Private Ownership. Modern capitalism presupposes private ownership of the means of production with entrepreneurs firmly in charge. Ownership gives capitalists or their representatives the authority to manage the production process, direct the labor force, and make investment decisions—all guided by monetary calculations and oriented toward the goal of profit maximization. The formal rationality of the capitalist enterprise is dependent on managers being able to carry out the business of the firm based solely on considerations of profitability.[17]

Free Labor. The rationality of modern capitalism also presupposes a labor force that is legally free but compelled by "the whip of hunger" to offer its services on the labor market. Free labor—where workers can be hired, deployed, and fired at will—is an important precondition of capitalist rationality for two reasons. First, where workers sell their labor on the market for a wage, employers can reliably estimate the costs of production in advance. Second, free labor, along with private control over the means of production, facilitates workplace discipline. As a condition for receiving a wage, laborers voluntarily submit to the authority of the capitalist, who is then able to direct and monitor their work behavior, thus permitting greater control over the labor process and a "higher level of economic rationality." The ability of the capitalist business firm to achieve "exact calculation," Weber emphasizes, is dependent on the capitalist organization of free labor.[18]

Free Market. The process of capitalist rationalization presupposes a free market. The efficient operation of the capitalist business enterprise and the reliable determination of expected profits are possible only with the elimination of all market restrictions and other "irrational limitations on trading." This requires that market transactions be purely impersonal, free from the influence of any sentimental, religious, or ethical infringements. The "watchword" of the free market, Weber says, is "without regard for persons." The "market community," he explains, is the preeminent sphere of rational self-interested action.[19]

Capital Accounting. A rational capitalist enterprise, Weber states, is one that determines the merit of investment opportunities by means of modern bookkeeping methods. By comparing income with expenses, by measuring revenues against costs, capital accounting provides a uniquely rational method for evaluating the efficacy of economic ventures, both retrospectively and prospectively, and for directing capitalist business firms toward profitable market opportunities. Monetary calculation, carried out through the use of double-entry bookkeeping, is "formally the most rational means of orienting economic activity."[20]

Technology and Mechanization. Modern capitalism presupposes rational technology and the mechanization of production and distribution. Technology enhances efficiency, but more importantly for Weber, because it permits accurate estimates of output, it facilitates rational accounting and precise calculation.[21]

Calculable Legal and Administrative System. Modern capitalism presupposes "calculable law" and a dependable legal and political environment. The rationality of the capitalist business enterprise requires a durable and trustworthy legal and political system whose functioning is predictable. For this reason, Weber argues, the development of the modern bureaucratic state, "adjudicating and administering according to rationally established law and regulation," goes hand in hand with the development of modern capitalist industry.[22]

Commercialization. Modern capitalism presupposes the "commercialization" of economic life. By "commercialization," Weber means "the appearance of paper representing shares in enterprise" and "rights to income." Typified by the emergence of the stock company, this development, he argues, "has taken place only in the modern western world."[23]

Separation of Household and Business. Finally, modern capitalism also presupposes, as a requisite for rational bookkeeping, the "separation of business from the household." This entails both a "spatial separation" between residence and work and, more importantly, a "legal separation" between the personal wealth of the business owner, his or her private assets, and the corporate wealth of the business enterprise, the capital invested in or available to the firm.[24]

Appearing only in the modern western world, this constellation of conditions, Weber argues, enables capitalist business enterprises to achieve "a maximum of formal rationality." This quality—its rational organization and calculability—is precisely what makes capitalism such a formidable economic system. The unique rationality characteristic of modern capitalism, where economic activity is guided by monetary calculations oriented to the goal of profit making, is manifest from top to bottom: in the systematic organization of the production process, the management of the workplace, the specialized division of labor, the application of science and technology, the "military discipline" of the factory, the decision-making processes of the firm, the operation of the market, and the predictable functioning of external legal and political institutions.[25]

In a brief summary of his theory of the origins of modern capitalism, Weber says that "in the last resort the factor which produced capitalism is the rational permanent enterprise, rational accounting, rational technology and rational law." But, he adds, these institutional conditions alone are not sufficient. Other factors are also necessary, most importantly a "rational spirit, the rationalization of the conduct of life in general, and a rationalistic economic ethic." Thus the formal rationality of capitalism has yet another presupposition: it requires the presence of a new type of person, the "carriers" or "bearers" of a "rational ethic" and a new and specifically methodical way of life. Weber takes up this side of the story in *The Protestant Ethic*.[26]

THE PROTESTANT ETHIC AND THE SPIRIT OF CAPITALISM

The *Protestant Ethic* was originally published as a two-part article in 1905, and then republished in a revised edition in 1920. This book touches on a number of themes central to Weber's work as a whole: the transition from traditional to modern society, the origins of modern capitalism, the unique qualities of western rationalism, the role of ideas in history, the influence of religious ethics on economic conduct, the characteristics and fate of the modern individual, and the prospects for individual freedom in the modern rationalized world.[27]

Weber's premise is that modern capitalism, at least in the early "heroic" stage of its development, is characterized by a particular culture or "spirit." To explain the origins of this spirit is his primary objective. The central argument of the *Protestant Ethic*, sometimes referred to as the "Weber thesis," is that the spirit of capitalism, as well as the type of person embodying this spirit, can be traced back to certain religious influences originating from the Reformation. He thus posits a congruence or affinity between two worldviews: Protestantism on the one hand and the culture of modern capitalism on the other. These two otherwise divergent belief systems—one altogether religious in nature, the other thoroughly secular—share a common conception of the value of a sustained and disciplined work life. Weber's ultimate purpose, as he modestly puts it, is to demonstrate that the modern vocational culture, with its affirmation of the ideal of diligent labor in a specialized calling, is "in some way *religiously* based."[28]

The Spirit of Capitalism

Weber derives a "provisional description" of the spirit of capitalism from the writings of Benjamin Franklin. Among other everyday virtues, Franklin preaches industry, prudence, frugality, honesty, and punctuality. He advises his readers to save money, maintain creditworthiness, keep an "exact account" of income and expenses, and avoid idleness and waste. He furthermore admonishes individuals to accumulate wealth and earn "more and more money," while at the same time warning against frivolous spending and the "spontaneous enjoyment of life." Franklin's wise old sayings, Weber states, illustrate the spirit of capitalism "in almost classical purity." Moreover, he stresses, criticizing Marx's historical materialism, this spirit is no mere reflection of economic circumstances. Indeed, when Franklin set forth his moral precepts, the modern capitalist economic system was still only on the horizon. The *spirit* of capitalism appeared prior to the *system* of capitalism (in its modern form), and can conceivably be counted therefore among the causal factors contributing to the development of that capitalist economic system.[29]

What Weber finds most interesting is that Franklin's philosophy has the quality of an ethos. It is not a manual for achieving economic success, nor does it imply the glorification of self-interest or greed. It is rather an ethic "for the conduct of life." This ethic introduces something new into the culture: a morally imbued attitude toward work and profit making. Where the spirit of capitalism prevails, the lives of individuals revolve around and are made meaningful by the faithful and methodical fulfillment of occupational or professional responsibilities. Capitalists feel a devotion to their businesses, and workers feel a commitment to their jobs. Labor, traditionally thought of as a necessary evil, is transformed into "an absolute end in itself." The spirit of capitalism thus sanctions an ascetic or disciplined way of life, one systematically and purposefully organized around the performance of vocational duties. This cultural ethos, so unique in its qualities and profound in its implications, is what Weber sets out to explain.[30]

Weber emphasizes the peculiarity of the spirit of capitalism, its radical divergence from the traditional norm. "A man does not 'by nature' wish to earn more and more money," he says, "but simply to live as he is accustomed to live and to earn as much as necessary for that purpose." This mind-set, which he calls "traditionalism," is evident among pre-capitalist laborers who are content with maintaining a customary style of life rather than constantly striving to increase their earnings. Economic traditionalism is also evident among pre-capitalist employers who, rather than being driven to accumulate, take a more relaxed approach to business, looking only to preserve a given rate of profit and a comfortable level of economic activity.[31]

With the rise of the culture of modern capitalism, economic traditionalism with its leisurely attitude toward work and business comes to be regarded as morally objectionable. A new ideal—economic rationalism—is born, upending the "natural" order of things. Moneymaking, considered throughout most of human history as a mere means for the satisfaction of material needs, becomes a moral duty, the very purpose of life. This circumstance, "where a man exists for the sake of his business, instead of the reverse," is a profound alteration of the human experience. With its compulsive work ethic, unceasing pursuit of profit, and self-denying abstention from enjoyment, this manner of economic conduct, Weber observes, is anything but ordinary. To the "pre-capitalist man," it is "incomprehensible and mysterious," contrary in fact "to the ethical feelings of whole epochs." The restless acquisitiveness of the modern individual and the idea of work for its own sake are also utterly "senseless to any purely worldly view of life" and completely unintelligible from the "view-point of personal happiness." From just about any common-sense standpoint, the economic rationalism of the modern capitalist culture is deeply irrational.[32]

How did this peculiar spirit originate? How did it manage to overcome the "stubborn resistance" of economic traditionalism and create a new type of "economic man"? To answer these questions, to account for the rise of "our specifically worldly modern culture," Weber turns to another revolutionary development, the religious upheaval inaugurated by the Reformation. The spirit of capitalism, he argues, "was born" from "the spirit of Christian asceticism," that is, from the Protestant ethic.[33]

Ascetic Protestantism

With the Reformation of the sixteenth century, Protestantism broke from Catholicism, creating a division within Christianity. The reform movement, prompted by the writings of Martin Luther, put forward a new—"infinitely burdensome and earnestly enforced"—set of commandments for living a devout life. The faithful, it was now taught, can best serve god not by retreating into a monastery or withdrawing into the church, but by attentively carrying out the mundane obligations imposed upon them by their place in the world. Luther's concept of the "calling" (a "task set by God") embodied this new principle: "the valuation of the fulfillment of duty in worldly affairs as the highest form which the moral activity of the individual could assume." The Protestant Reformation thus had the effect of investing everyday life, the domain of work in particular, with great religious and moral significance. According to Weber, however, Luther gave this ethic an essentially "traditionalist interpretation." Rather than urging economic acquisition and advancement, he proposed only that individuals abide by the demands of the occupations in which, by divine providence, they have been placed. Effectively reinforcing traditionalism and restraining economic rationalism, Luther counseled individuals to adapt to but not surpass their god-given "station in life."[34]

The revolutionary implications of the Reformation, Weber argues, and its contribution to the development of economic rationalism, occur only with the rise of ascetic Protestantism, particularly in the form of Calvinism. The central dogma of Calvinism is the doctrine of predestination. According to this doctrine, the most pressing issue in the lives of believers—whether they are among the saved or the damned—is predetermined at the moment of creation by an omnipotent and inscrutable god. In contrast to their Catholic counterparts, able to wash away their sins in the confessional, faithful Calvinists can do nothing—no prayers, sacraments, supplications, or offerings of any kind—to influence their fate. Religious authorities are likewise incapable of helping believers attain a state of grace. God's plan is altogether impervious to human intervention. Individuals are on their own, doomed to uncertainty. Admitting no "magical means to salvation," Protestantism contributes to what Weber refers to as the "disenchantment" of the world, a topic I discuss more fully below.[35]

The fatalism associated with the doctrine of predestination was psychologically intolerable, leaving believers with "a feeling of unprecedented inner loneliness." To help assuage anxiety, local pastors began instructing the faithful that they had an "absolute duty" to consider themselves among the chosen and that the best way to ward off doubt and exhibit the "certainty of grace" was through "intense worldly activity," meaning specifically hard work. This advice, which had the practical effect of substituting active striving for fatalistic acceptance, was predicated on a conception of the individual as an instrument of god, the "tool of the divine will." For Calvinism, we are not put on earth to idle away our hours or have a good time or even achieve salvation. Our sole reason for existence, rather, is to honor the greater glory of god through the methodical and disciplined undertaking of our worldly endeavors. If, however, individuals prove themselves successful in serving god—if for example they run a profitable business—it would only be reasonable to interpret this productivity as a sign of grace. Though not a logical derivation from the Calvinist creed, this line of thinking, where economic achievement is taken to be a sign of personal worthiness, was how the doctrine of predestination played out in the everyday lives of the Protestant faithful.[36]

By calling for unrelenting self-discipline, Calvinism gave a powerful psychological inducement to a rational way of life. As servants of god in the everyday world, believers were instructed to maintain constant vigilance, exercise rigorous self-control, suppress their natural urges, restrain their impulses and emotions, and lead an always alert, wakeful, and "intelligent life." The faithful could stave off fears of damnation only by submitting their lives to "deliberate regulation" and "a systematic rational ordering." What god required was not simply occasional good works—neither deathbed contributions nor last-minute confessions—"but a life of good works combined into a unified system." This was a demanding religion, subjecting the totality of an individual's life—and not just the life of the religious "virtuoso" but the entire laity—to an unceasing regimen of self-regulation. The strict asceticism preached by Calvin is not unique to Protestantism, of course. Monks, for example, practice an equally rational, systematic, and orderly way of life. But while their type of asceticism is monastic or "other-worldly," a discipline requiring adherents to withdraw from worldly affairs, the asceticism of the Protestant religion is "inner-worldly." It takes the rational and methodical conduct of life out of the monastery and into the everyday realm of economic activity, transforming the world in the process.[37]

When the Protestant faithful enter the mundane world, they are obliged to work strenuously, avoid leisurely pursuits and unnecessary pleasures, and make constructive use of the limited time at their disposal. The Protestant ethic calls upon believers to devote themselves to an occupation, work hard, and take advantage of (god-given) opportunities. More to the point, however, what it demands is "restless, continuous, systematic work"—"not labour in itself but rational labour in a calling." The natural result of this virtuous performance of vocational demands is the accumulation of wealth. This is highly commendable, perhaps even a sign of salvation, but the use of such wealth for the enjoyment of life is morally unacceptable. Idleness, relaxation, contemplation, and recreation, because they detract from the fulfillment of vocational duties, are also sinful. Such superfluous leisure activities are an impious waste of time—time better spent *working* to glorify god. For Protestantism, while time is not money as it was for Benjamin Franklin, it is, Weber suggests, the spiritual equivalent.[38]

With this we arrive at the key conclusion of Weber's argument. Toward the end to the *Protestant Ethic*, he asks us to ponder the relationship between ascetic Protestantism and the spirit of capitalism.

> One only has to re-read the passage from Franklin, quoted at the beginning of
> this essay, in order to see that the essential elements of the attitude which was
> there called the spirit of capitalism are the same as what we have just shown to
> be the content of Puritan worldly asceticism, only without the religious basis,
> which by Franklin's time had died away.

The spirit of capitalism, as interpreted by Weber, is a secular outgrowth of
the Protestant ethic.[39]

From Ascetic Protestantism to Modern Capitalism

Weber's primary objective in the *Protestant Ethic* is to demonstrate a connection between one idea system, ascetic Protestantism, and another idea
system, the spirit of capitalism. But in the course of his analysis, he touches
on a larger issue: the influence of religious ideas on the formation of the
modern capitalist economic system itself. In the final chapter of the *Protestant Ethic*, Weber explicitly pursues this topic, identifying several pathways
through which Protestant asceticism, with its concept of the calling, contributed to "the development of a capitalist way of life."[40]

Protestantism favored the rise of capitalism by endowing profit making
with an "amazingly good" conscience. It not only applauded economic acquisition, previously inhibited by "traditionalistic ethics"; it transformed the
accumulation of wealth into an ethical imperative "willed by God." Instead
of being merely tolerated, moneymaking became venerated, indeed a sign of
moral worth. The combination of this "release of acquisitive activity" from
the constraints of tradition and the condemnation of luxury fueled the expansion of capitalism by giving a powerful stimulus to savings and the "productive investment of capital."[41]

The Protestant ethic legitimated profit making, but it also provided ideological support to capitalism by justifying inequality, poverty, and low
wages. To the "bourgeois business man," it gave the "comforting assurance"
that "the unequal distribution of the goods of this world was a special dispen-
sation of Divine Providence." It likewise legalized the exploitation of labor,
advancing the convenient idea that "faithful labour, even at low wages," is
"highly pleasing to God." Protestantism sanctioned both the wealth of the
rich and the poverty of the poor. By endowing mundane business pursuits
with the quality of a moral mission, moreover, Puritanism made an ethical
hero out of the "sober, middle-class, self-made man." Meanwhile, it provided
that same bourgeois businessman with a reliable labor force, a population of

"sober, conscientious, and unusually industrious workmen, who clung to their work as to a life purpose willed by God."[42]

Along with the role it played in legitimating the class system of modern capitalism, ascetic Protestantism, Weber argues, promoted the development of the capitalist way of life in two other respects as well. First, with its emphasis on the value of specialized work and the importance of a "fixed calling," it "provided ethical justification of the modern specialized division of labour." Second, the ascetic condemnation of decorative ostentation, re-garding clothing, for example, and its call for "sober utility" contributed to the "powerful tendency toward uniformity of life," thus aiding "the capitalist interest in the standardization of production."[43]

The Protestant Reformation, by giving birth to a peculiar economic ethos and a new type of person with a particularly practical and resolute set of attitudes and dispositions, contributed to the breakthrough into the modern world. It promoted "the development of a rational bourgeois economic life," and it produced the "modern economic man," more specifically, "the man of vocation." When "asceticism was carried out of monastic cells into everyday life," Weber says, "it did its part in building the tremendous cosmos of the modern economic order." But this outcome did not occur by design. The Protestant faithful were preoccupied by one thing only: the "salvation of the soul." Through their religiously motivated conduct, however, they uninten-tionally called forth the modern capitalist economic system. This result, We-ber emphasizes, was entirely "unforeseen" and "unwished-for." Calvinism paved the way for the rise of modern capitalism, but this was an unanticipat-ed consequence of a purely religiously inspired ethic of conduct.[44]

The Rise of the Capitalist System

Weber refers to the *Protestant Ethic* as a modest "contribution to the under-standing of the manner in which ideas," in this case religious ideas, "become effective forces in history." By demonstrating the influence of ascetic Protes-tantism on the formation of the vocational culture of modern capitalism, he challenges what he takes to be the economic determinism of Marx's histori-cal materialism. Though acknowledging the value of Marx's materialist per-spective when construed as a hypothesis, Weber insists that the course of history is determined not only by economic forces but by ideal or cultural forces as well—by life-shaping belief systems. He not only emphasizes the cultural roots of the modern economic order, but draws attention to the unique cultural characteristics of modern capitalism as well. Indeed, for Weber, the presence of the spirit of capitalism is precisely what distinguishes modern capitalism from other forms of capitalism and from other non-capitalist economic systems.[45]

But once the modern capitalist system is up and running, Weber acknowledges, it no longer requires the spiritual ethos that got it off the ground. Ascetic Protestantism contributes to the rise of western capitalism, but once the capitalist economic system is "in the saddle," he says, now sounding a lot like Marx, it takes on a life of its own, becoming a "tremendous cosmos" to which everyone, employers and employees alike, must submit. A mature capitalist system, Weber recognizes, no longer requires the "support of any religious forces" or the spiritual conformity of the individual. It assumes rather the form of an objective, machine-like system, "an unalterable order of things" to which individuals are compelled to adjust. The process of capitalist rationalization, once it reaches a certain threshold, forces everyone to "follow suit" or "go out of business." While the "Puritan wanted to work in a calling," under the circumstances of present-day capitalism "we are forced to do so."[46]

THE RATIONALIZATION OF LEGITIMATE AUTHORITY

The problem of social order, a central theme in Durkheim's writings, is an important topic in Weber's sociology as well. But while Durkheim attributes social stability to moral integration—shared values in the pre-modern world and bonds of interdependency in the modern world—for Weber it derives primarily from configurations of "domination" or "authority"; in other words, relations of power. Typically, however—with slavery being a notable exception—the exercise of power produces an enduring social order only if it manages to "justify itself," only if it is able to secure a "certain minimum of consent," at least on the part of the most "socially important" segments of the governed. This idea underlies Weber's concept of "legitimate authority." When he speaks of legitimacy, however, he is not making a value judgment or asserting that a particular relationship of power or structure of domination is in some normative sense *just*. Weber treats legitimacy from a strictly empirical standpoint. Legitimate authority obtains when the power to command is deemed valid, that is, when persons subject to authority voluntarily offer their obedience.[47]

Weber identifies three possible bases of legitimacy and, correspondingly, three types of legitimate authority, with each of these taking a variety of forms. The legitimacy of *traditional authority* derives from the sanctity of custom ("Obey me because this is what our people have always done."); the legitimacy of *charismatic authority* rests on the extraordinary qualities of the leader ("Obey me because I can transform your life."); and the legitimacy of *rational-legal authority* follows from the observance of formally established rules and procedures ("Obey me because I am your lawfully appointed superior."). These are ideal types, meant only to serve as a conceptual starting point for empirical investigation. Real-world systems of legitimate authority are more complicated, typically taking a mixed form. [48]

Traditional Authority

Originating from the rule of the father figure or master over his household, traditional authority is the form of power exercised by the patriarch, the lord, the prince, or the king. This type of authority is grounded in the venerability of the "eternal yesterday," the "sanctity of everyday routines," the sacred quality of "age-old rules and powers," the validity of that "which has always been." The authority of traditional rulers stems from their occupancy of customarily sanctioned positions of power. While traditional leaders encounter no legal restraints on their authority, they do not possess unlimited discretion. They too are "bound by tradition." They risk their legitimacy, and may even provoke a "traditionalist revolt," if their commands fail to respect the time-honored ways of the past. [49]

In systems of traditional authority the person in command, usually assuming power through inheritance, occupies the status of "lord" or "master." Those in a subordinate position occupy the status of "subjects." And the administrative staff—typically consisting of "personal retainers" recruited from loyal family members and friends—occupies the status of "servants." Predisposed toward keeping things the way they are, traditional authority is an inherently conservative force, rooted in and reinforcing "traditional attitudes." It is also "irrational," meaning in this context not governed by established rules, fixed procedures, or legal precedents. Within the limits set by sacred traditions, leaders are free to command according to their own personal inclinations, introducing an element of arbitrariness and unpredictability into the exercise of power. [50]

Charismatic Authority

Charismatic authority, a term Weber uses once again in a purely "value-free sense," derives from the extraordinary qualities of the exceptional individual. Examples include the religious prophet, the military hero, the great orator, or more specifically a Gandhi or a Martin Luther King Jr. The power to command possessed by charismatic figures does not come from their occupancy of official positions, whether attained through inheritance or election. They are obeyed not because of "tradition or statute," but because their followers believe in them. The authority of charismatic leaders, their ability to inspire people to abandon their normal lives and take up a historic cause, rests entirely on their own personal "gifts" or deeds: the force of their example, the potency of their message, the righteousness of their mission. But just as traditional authorities maintain their legitimacy only if they adhere to sacred traditions, so too is the validity of charismatic authority contingent on leaders' continued success in demonstrating their heroism, proving themselves through victories, and obtaining benefits for their followers.[51]

In the case of charismatic authority, the person in command occupies the status of "leader." Those in a subordinate position occupy the status of "disciples" or "followers." And the administrative staff consists of a "charismatic aristocracy composed of a select group of adherents." Like traditional authority, charismatic leadership is irrational, and uniquely so. It is not only "foreign to all rules," but because it is inherently unstructured and short-lived, antagonistic to normal routine, charismatic authority is also the "direct antithesis" of all "everyday forms of domination," whether traditional or rational-legal. In addition, while traditional authority is a conservative force, rooted in the past and committed to the way things are, charismatic authority is a revolutionary force, an enemy of the status quo. Charismatic figures typically appear during times of hardship, crisis, and contention. They enter into the fray, rally converts, and demand change, whether in the internal values and beliefs of followers or in the external structure of the existing social order.[52]

In contrast to the two other types of legitimate domination, charismatic authority, because it originates from the qualities of persons and their accomplishments, is intrinsically unstable and transitory. Leaders may lose their gifts and the confidence of their followers. They may become victims of their own success, as their authority becomes institutionalized, embedded in the everyday practices of a governing organization. Or they may die, raising the issue of succession—how to replace a remarkable leader and how to keep the

charisma alive. The typical pattern, Weber argues, is for charismatic authority to undergo a process of "routinization," gradually shedding its extraordinary qualities and giving way to either traditional authority or rational-legal
authority. The fate of charisma, which appears only as a temporary interrup-
tion of more enduring forms of domination, is "to recede before the powers
of tradition or of rational association."[53]

Rational-Legal Authority

Rational-legal authority, typically associated with bureaucratic organization,
is the specifically modern form of legitimate domination. This type of authority rests on "legality," on a "system of consciously made *rational
rules*"—the rule of law rather than persons. The commands issued by legal
power holders are justified in the name of impersonal rules enacted according
to "formally correct procedure" rather than "personal authority." The right to
exercise power is bestowed on individuals as temporary incumbents of an
office, not on persons in themselves; it is sanctioned by legal statutes, not
hallowed traditions; and obedience is owed to "the legally established impersonal order," not to the individual lord or master. And just as traditional
leaders are expected to abide by the sanctified ways of the past, so too are
legal authorities, no less than ordinary citizens, obliged to comply with the
law and follow prescribed procedures.[54]

   In systems where rational-legal authority predominates, persons in command, either elected or appointed, are "servants of the state"; they occupy the
status of "superiors." Those in a subordinate position occupy the status of
"citizens," or "members" when speaking of organizations (e.g., political parties or trade unions). And the administrative personnel, consisting of salaried
and trained professionals, occupy the status of "officials." Among the most
significant features of rational-legal authority is an administrative staff organized in the form of a bureaucratic body with no particular personal loyalty
to ruling authorities. These bureaucratic officials are recruited on the basis of
technical qualifications, they operate within a fixed area of specialization,
and they are expected to fulfill their duties in an impartial and impersonal
manner. Along with the rule of law, the presence of bureaucratic administration, discussed more fully below, is the primary source of the distinctive
rationality characteristic of legal authority.[55]

Legitimate Authority, Modernity, and Rationalization

The three types of legitimate authority, Weber insists, cannot "be placed into a simple evolutionary line," nor is this typology meant to be the foundation of any philosophy of history. Nevertheless, Weber does acknowledge two historically significant patterns, both relevant to his diagnosis of the modern condition. First, just as traditional authority is the preeminent form of domination throughout most of pre-modern history, so too is rational-legal authority a uniquely modern phenomenon. Thus, alongside the rationalization of action discussed above, we also observe in the modern western world a corresponding rationalization of legitimate authority. This development represents a profound reordering of the structure of social power. It signifies a transition from allegiance to sacred traditions to allegiance to abstract norms, from the rule of persons to the rule of laws, and from power relationships of a more personal nature to power relationships of a more impersonal nature.[56]

Second, unlike traditional and rational-legal authority, charismatic authority is not specific to any particular social context; it "has emerged in all places and in all historical epochs." Weber admits, however, that the rational-legal order characteristic of modern society is less conducive to an "eruption of charisma" than is the traditional social order. The rational, military-like discipline embedded in the "capitalist factory" and the "bureaucratic state machine," along with other modern institutions, creates a rule-bound orderliness that "more and more restricts the importance of charisma." "Only extraordinary conditions," he observes, "can bring about the triumph of charisma over the organization." While Weber envisions the waning of charisma in an increasingly rationalized world, as we will see in later chapters, he still holds out the possibility of a modern-day though perhaps attenuated version of charismatic leadership.[57]

BUREAUCRATIC RATIONALIZATION

Bureaucracy, "the purest type of exercise of legal authority," is the preeminent mode of administration and organization in the modern western world. The advance of bureaucracy, like the advance of capitalism, is a rationalizing and revolutionary force, remaking the world while in the process destroying traditional forms of authority and traditional ways of life. The process of modernization, for Weber, is a process of bureaucratization. Modern society is fundamentally and inevitably a bureaucratic society. This is apparent in nearly every domain of human association, including the army, religious institutions, charitable organizations, interest groups, hospitals, and universities. Even more important is the undeniable presence of bureaucratic administration in the economic and political spheres, in the organization and operation of the two central institutions of modern western society: the state and the capitalist business enterprise. Neither government nor industry could conceivably conduct their affairs without the services of a full-time bureaucratic body made up of technically trained personnel. The development of both the modern state and "modern high capitalism" is essentially a story of increasing bureaucratization. The state, in particular, Weber emphasizes, "is absolutely dependent upon a bureaucratic basis." The growth of "bureaucratic officialdom," he observes, has been the "unambiguous yardstick for the modernization of the state."[58]

Weber's concept of bureaucracy is an ideal type, an abstraction constructed to underline the rational properties of bureaucratic administration and highlight the contrast between bureaucratic rule and traditional rule. Actually existing bureaucratic institutions depart from this ideal type to a greater or lesser extent. But even if bureaucratic organizations are never altogether bureaucratic, the fact remains, according to Weber: "the future belongs to bureaucratization." Along with the factory, he states, bureaucracy is the "modern form of organization" that most determines "the character of the present age and of the foreseeable future." In what follows, I provide an overview of Weber's ideal-type representation of bureaucratic administration. My objective is to clarify his thinking about bureaucracy and, more specifically, draw attention to the bases, nature, and consequences of the particular rationality characteristic of bureaucratic organization.[59]

Formalism. Bureaucracy exhibits a high level of formalism insofar as official business is conducted on the basis of written rules, administrative regulations, and fixed procedures. These designate what is to be done, by whom, and how. They specify the duties and responsibilities of the administrative staff, their obligations and powers, their areas of jurisdiction, and the distribution of authority and command. The rational formalism of bureaucracy requires that administrative actions be handled in a uniform fashion—by the book—not on an individual, case-by-case basis and not according to the personal predilections of bureaucratic officials.[60]

Impersonality. The formalism of bureaucracy is evident also in its impersonality. Bureaucratic officials, in adherence to their vocational demands, perform their functions in a purely objective and matter-of-fact manner, in accordance with "calculable rules" and "without regard to personal consider-ations." Indeed, Weber argues, the more fully developed the bureaucracy, "the more it is 'dehumanized,' the more completely it succeeds in eliminat-ing from official business love, hatred, and all purely personal, irrational, and emotional elements which escape calculation." The impersonality of the mar-ket economy has its counterpart in the impersonality of bureaucratic adminis-tration.[61]

Predictability. Formalism and impersonality ensure that organizational behavior under bureaucratic auspices is optimally predictable. Bureaucracy, Weber states, permits a "high degree of calculability of results," both for those heading the organization and "for those acting in relation to it." This calculability is particularly important in the relationship between the modern bureaucratic state and the capitalist business enterprise. The efficient opera-tion of the capitalist economic system requires a state bureaucracy capable of conducting its administrative affairs with speed and precision. The capitalist market economy depends on the existence of a stable and predictable govern-ing system, and this is precisely what bureaucratic administration offers.[62]

Knowledge. The rationality of bureaucracy and its superiority as a method of administration derive also from its reliance on a staff consisting of knowl-edgeable professionals and technical specialists. The prominence of this type of person, a product of training and education, is unique to the modern world. The process of bureaucratization gives rise to a social order characterized by "the ever-increasing importance of experts and specialized knowledge" and by an "absolute and complete dependence" on a "specially trained organiza-tion of officials." This development alters the structure of social power. Bureaucratic administration, Weber states, "means fundamentally domina-tion through knowledge." As society is bureaucratized, the technical special-ists employed in bureaucratic offices come to comprise a new "privileged stratum," one distinguished by their educational qualifications. The power possessed by bureaucratic officeholders stems from their training, their expe-rience, their access to "*official information*," and their familiarity with the rules of the bureaucratic game. They not only have the requisite knowledge, but as bureaucratic insiders they also know the ropes and they know how to get things done. This circumstance means that the "political 'master,'" the person standing at the head of the bureaucracy, "always finds himself, vis-à-vis the trained official, in the position of a dilettante facing the expert."[63]

Efficiency. Bureaucratic organization is characterized by an office hierar-chy consisting of well-defined channels of authority and lines of supervision and by the presence of a trained staff of career officials with specialized areas of competence. In a fully developed bureaucracy, the process of administration, carried out on the basis of expert knowledge and impersonal rules, is notable for its continuity, stability, reliability, and consistency. By virtue of these features, Weber argues, bureaucracy—"this human machine"—is technically superior to any other form of organization. It is the most efficient and "most rational known means of exercising authority over human beings." The "bureaucratic apparatus," he explains, is to other forms of organization what the machine is to "non-mechanical modes of production." Due especially to this fact—its sheer technical efficiency—bureaucratization is an inexorable force, perhaps even the "final destiny of the modern world."[64]

Indispensability. Bureaucracy, the purest embodiment of formal rationality, is an indispensable feature of modern society. It is a uniquely efficient mechanism for administering the collective affairs of society. Bureaucracy's unrivaled capacity for "organized action" is the source of its technical superiority, power, and permanency. The very existence of modern society depends on bureaucratic organization. Short of sacrificing the achievements of modernity, there is no other way of running the state or the economy. Bureaucracy, Weber argues, is "escape proof" and "practically indestructible."[65]

Weber's analysis of bureaucracy adds one more ingredient to his conception of western rationalism and his theory of modernity. Alongside the rationalization of capitalism, the rationalization of social action, and the rationalization of legitimate authority, we can now include the rationalization of organization and administration. The bureaucratization of the world, and the process of rationalization more generally, is reflected in a pattern of *increase* in numerous dimensions of social existence: the regulation and organization of social activities according to formal rules and written procedures, the impersonality and dehumanization of social relations, the predictability and calculability of social life, the specialization of functions, the role of training and education, the reliance on professionals and officials, the importance of knowledge and expertise, and the overall level of efficiency in the management of human beings and social processes. These developmental tendencies, rooted in the process of bureaucratic rationalization, are among the most important markers of the transition from traditional society to modern society.

SCIENCE, DISENCHANTMENT, AND THE CRISIS OF MEANING

Modern science is both an outcome and an engine of western rationalism. As the go-to institution for empirical knowledge and technical expertise, science joins forces with capitalism and bureaucracy to fashion an orderly and calculable world. But while it increases humanity's technical mastery over reality, Weber argues, science also strips the world of meaning. This is its unique contribution to the process of rationalization. Science enhances our ability to understand and control the social and natural environments, but at the same time it renders the world meaningless. [66]

As in the case of his analysis of capitalism and bureaucracy, Weber is primarily interested in the cultural significance of science—what the rise of science means for the life of the individual and the "fate of our times." He pursues this objective by delineating the boundaries of science and by mapping (and patrolling) the borderlines between science and religion, science and ethics, and science and politics. In the process he distinguishes those issues science can and cannot legitimately address and the purposes it can and cannot legitimately serve. [67]

The Circumstances of Science in the Modern World

The philosophers of the French Enlightenment regarded science as an instrument of progress, a vehicle of social and moral betterment. The growth of empirical knowledge and the application of reason, they believed, by delivering people from the bondage of ignorance, superstition, and poverty, would usher in a new era of human freedom and well-being. Weber rejects this "naïve optimism." He also criticizes the conventional German view of academic intellectuals as spiritual leaders, cultural guardians, and modern-day wise men. Opposing the lofty image of the scholar held by many of his colleagues, Weber locates the practice of science in the mundane world of occupations. Science, he maintains, is a "vocation," a profession like any other with its own prosaic duties and responsibilities. It is not "the gift of grace of seers and prophets dispensing sacred values and revelations." Though he is among the most ardent defenders of science, Weber, always deflating one balloon or another, is determined to lower expectations about what science can achieve, what questions it can answer, and what it can promise for the future. To gain a deeper understanding of Weber's conception of what is, after all, his own chosen vocation, in what follows I discuss his view of the circumstances, characteristics, and meaning of science in the modern rationalized world.[68]

First, for Weber, like Durkheim, the era of the dilettante, the "cultivated man," has given way to the era of the expert, the "'specialist' type of man." Nowhere is this more apparent than in the academic world. Science, Weber says, has "entered a phase of specialization previously unknown." Genuine intellectual achievement is nowadays possible only through "strict specialization" and a workmanlike though passionate commitment to a delimited field of inquiry. This circumstance is the inevitable condition of any further intellectual progress. It requires a willingness on the part of would-be scholars to renounce the "Faustian universality of man" and devote themselves solely to their professional responsibilities and the specific research tasks at hand. In the modern world, science is a job reserved for full-time specialists.[69]

Second, all scientific work, Weber observes, "is chained to the course of progress," destined to be "antiquated in ten, twenty, fifty years." Unlike a work of art, a Beethoven symphony or a Shakespeare play, which may continue to edify and inspire for centuries, the accomplishments of an empirical scientist will inevitably be surpassed. Individuals with a calling for science must resign themselves to this fact. They must accept the reality that their work will eventually cease to have value and will be consigned to the dustbin of history. No scientific achievement can ever be truly definitive, and no scientist can ever expect to accomplish anything lasting.[70]

Third, the meaningfulness of science is questionable also because the value of scholarship cannot be proven by scientific methods. There are no objective criteria for determining what is worth knowing. Nor are the questions science poses and the problems it addresses dictated by the nature of reality itself. What becomes an object of empirical investigation, what is selected for study from the "absolute infinitude" of reality, depends on what is deemed culturally significant; it is contingent on the "evaluative ideas" and cognitive interests of scholars themselves. Though it can claim objective validity for its findings, science rests on an inherently subjective presupposition, an irrational leap of faith that the striving for empirical knowledge is worth the effort.[71]

Fourth, no matter how advanced it may be, science can never reveal the world as it truly is in all of its "infinite multiplicity." "All knowledge of cultural reality," Weber asserts, "is always knowledge from *particular points of view*." The study of social life requires the *selection* of a phenomenon of interest, a "one-sided" conceptualization that carves out a particular object of inquiry. Weber's focus on the rationality of modern capitalism illustrates this point. He does not presume to set forth an all-encompassing theory, but rather to shed light on the modern economic order from a selective and inherently partial vantage point. This underscores yet another limitation of science. It can produce factual knowledge, but it can never give us a complete picture of reality or an exhaustive account of why things are the way they are.[72]

Fifth, the different "points of departure" one might take in approaching the social world are limitless—at least as long as the intellectual domain does not become so stagnant as to preclude our "setting new questions to the eternally inexhaustible flow of life." The socio-historical sciences, because there are always new ways of looking at the world and "new ways of formulating problems," are "eternally youthful." Science is not only inherently perspectival; it is also inevitably incomplete, fated never to come to an end.[73]

The Disenchantment of the World

The rise to supremacy of empirical science marks a shift from a pre-modern view of the world as enchanted to a modern view of the world as disenchanted. The first conceives the world as consisting of a multitude of magical, spiritual, and supernatural powers, both good and evil. These paranormal forces intervene in the world for their own obscure purposes and—through prayers, potions, incantations, rituals, and the like—are also potentially susceptible to human manipulation. The enchanted world is a meaningful world, filled with purpose, significance, and mystery. Science construes the world differently, perceiving it simply as an object of knowledge, nothing more than a "causal mechanism." In the passage from the pre-modern to the modern era, the "world's processes become disenchanted," Weber observes; they "lose their magical significance, and henceforth simply 'are' and 'happen' but no longer signify anything." The disenchantment of the world means "there are no mysterious incalculable forces that come into play, but rather that one can, in principle, master all things by calculation." For Weber, it is important to recognize, disenchantment or, more literally, demagification is not necessarily something to be regretted, nor certainly does he look forward to some re-enchanted future.[74]

As science develops, as it takes on an increasingly analytic, empirical, and mathematical cast, it more and more comes into conflict with conceptions of the world as "God-ordained" or as somehow constituting a "*mean-*

ingful and ethically oriented cosmos." The view of the world as operating according to the principle of cause and effect and the view of the world as inherently meaningful, as exhibiting some grand purpose or design, stand in "irreconcilable opposition." The process of intellectualization and disenchantment relegates religion to the realm of the subjective and the irrational and, by transforming the world into a neutral object of empirical science, it divests it of any cosmic significance. But while science dethrones religion, it cannot perform the same function the latter once served: it cannot give meaning to the world or to people's lives. Nor can scientists legitimately adopt the role of secular prophets or priests. "The fate of an epoch which has eaten of the tree of knowledge is that it must know that we cannot learn the *meaning* of the world from the results of its analysis, be it ever so perfect." In the modern era, as a consequence, individuals in search of meaning are thrown back on their own resources. This is the existential predicament of the modern individual: those who aspire to a meaningful life must somehow create it themselves.[75]

Empirical Judgments and Value Judgments

Weber's seemingly bleak view of the role of science rests on his understanding of the logical distinction between empirical judgments, statements about what "is," and evaluative judgments, statements about what "ought to be." Empirical or factual propositions fall within the domain of science and can claim universal validity. Evaluative or normative propositions fall within the domain of ethics or politics and are matters of individual conscience and personal conviction. Where empirical issues are at stake, conflicts of opinion can in principle be settled through scientific investigation. But science cannot resolve evaluative issues, it cannot prove the relative validity of competing ideals, and it cannot distinguish between what is desirable from what is undesirable. Economists, for example, are able to calculate the rate of unemployment, document its causes and consequences, and assess the costs and benefits of alternative policy responses. But in the final analysis they cannot tell us what, if anything, we should do about the problem. This is a value judgment. It depends on our ethical feelings and political beliefs, our sense of what is fair, and our vision of the kind of society we wish to live in. Because these are evaluative issues rather than factual issues, the scientific expert is no more suited to propose a course of action than is the ordinary citizen. "It can never be the task of an empirical science," Weber declares, "to provide

Chapter 4

binding norms and ideals from which directives for immediate practical activity can be derived."[76]

For Weber the "ought" cannot be derived from the "is," values cannot be deduced from facts, and political or ethical decisions cannot be inferred from the results of empirical analysis. Science can tell us what is true and false, but not what is right and wrong or what is just and unjust. "A choice among ultimate commitments," Weber says, "cannot be made with the tools of science." Refusing to shy away from the unhappy implications of his own argument, Weber, citing Tolstoy, acknowledges that science is "meaningless." "It gives no answers to our question, the only question important for us: 'What shall we do and how shall we live?'" Science cannot give us guidance on those matters that matter most. This responsibility falls to "the acting, willing person."[77]

In calling for the separation of factual judgments and evaluative judgments, Weber's primary interest is not the issue of scholarly objectivity. His concern is less to protect the practice of science from the biasing effect of values than it is to shield the realm of values from the dispiriting influence of science. The problem he worries about, in other words, is not the politicization of science but the scientization of politics. In espousing "value freedom," Weber's hope is to preserve a space for individual autonomy, to ensure that ethical standpoints, political commitments, and philosophies of life—precisely the realm of value-rational choice where people are able to define and give meaning to their existence—are not reduced to technical issues or handed over to experts. Weber offers this clarification of his position:

> The reason why I take every opportunity . . . to attack in such extremely emphatic terms the jumbling of what ought to be with what exists is not that I underestimate the question of what ought to be. On the contrary, it is because I cannot bear it if problems of world-shaking importance—in a certain sense the most exalted problems that can move a human heart—are here changed into a technical-economic problem of production and made the subject of a scholarly discussion. We know of no *scientifically* demonstrable ideals.

He argues similarly in another context, "One does not wish to see the ultimate and highest personal decisions which a person must make regarding his life confounded with specialized training."[78]

Cultural Differentiation and Value Pluralism

The process of intellectualization and disenchantment undermines the unifying authority of religion and its power to endow the world with certitude and meaning. But while science displaces religion, it cannot function as a substitute. Science cannot give direction to people's lives or help them make sense of their existence. Nor can science alleviate the "experience of the irrationality of the world," explain why bad things happen to good people, or promise compensation or solace for "undeserved suffering," "unpunished injustice," and senseless death.[79]

The rise of science and the marginalization of religion leave a world bereft of meaning. The resulting vacuum is filled by a multitude of competing worldviews. The monotheism of the past gives way to the "absolute polytheism" of the present. The culture of the modern era, as a result, becomes increasingly differentiated and fragmented, with conflict arising not only "between 'class interests' but between general views on life and the universe as well." With a unitary culture no longer possible, the modern world is an irrevocably divided world, as "irreconcilably antagonistic" political ideologies, ethical doctrines, and attitudes toward life enter into constant conflict with one another. In this context, the individual cannot help but "feel himself subject to the struggle between multiple sets of values." He is forced "to choose which of these gods he will and should serve, or when he should serve the one and when the other." But "at all times," Weber states, "he will find himself engaged in a fight against one or another of the gods of this world."[80]

At the same time, intensifying this conflict and amplifying the process of cultural differentiation, the transition to modern society gives rise to several distinct and autonomous "value spheres" or "life orders." Alongside the religious sphere, Weber singles out the economic, the political, the aesthetic, the erotic, and the intellectual (science). These spheres represent more or less institutionalized ways of life, different avenues through which individuals might respond to or escape from the conditions of the modern world. Each is bound to its own norms, driven by its own imperatives, and subject to its own "immanent laws." These value spheres, furthermore, as he illustrates in his essays on politics and science as vocations, impose rules and place demands on the individuals who choose to enter them. Calling attention to the difficulty of submitting to more than one "god" at a time, Weber also underlines the tension that exists among these spheres, their "mutual strangeness." This is particularly evident, as we have already seen, in the relationship between science and religion and between science and politics. But consider also the conflict between the religious ethic of universal "brotherliness" and the violence inherent to the sphere of politics. Or consider the mixture of incomprehension and disdain with which the practically minded businessperson looks upon pointy-headed intellectuals and freethinking artists; or the reverse, the disrepute with which intellectuals and artists view the profane and corrupting world of commerce. [81]

For Weber, the antagonism among competing worldviews and among incommensurable value spheres is irresolvable. Modern culture, inevitably, is a domain of value pluralism and never-ending conflict. The "ultimate possible attitudes toward life are irreconcilable," he says, and "hence their struggle can never be brought to a final conclusion." Science can neither arbitrate nor resolve this conflict, nor can it relieve individuals of the responsibility to decide which among the "warring gods" they will serve. In the face of value pluralism, the only recourse left for the individual is to take a stand, to make an ultimately "irrational" choice, to find and obey "the demon who holds the fibers of his very life." As a result of the disenchantment of the world, individuals are left without any fixed meanings or moral absolutes, but what they gain in return is a certain freedom. They are, depending on one's perspective, either compelled or liberated to make their own decisions about which ultimate values they will follow. [82]

The Value of Science

Though he is relentless in exposing the limitations of science in the modern world, Weber does believe there is much it can offer. In the first place, science contributes to the development of cognitive skills, intellectual tools, and "methods of thought." It also enhances our ability to control and master the external world, the natural world as well as the social world, and it assists us in resolving technical questions and achieving practical purposes. The expertise science provides is indispensable if we wish to travel to other planets, eliminate hunger, or combat global warming. Whether any of these things are worth doing, of course, is not a question science can answer. How we should allocate our resources, prioritize our goals, and choose among competing policy objectives are political matters, inherently evaluative issues. But once we have chosen a goal, science can tell us how best to accomplish it. [83]

Science can play another and far more fundamental role. Both in the classroom and in the larger public arena, it can be put to work in the service of moral and political education. It cannot *authorize* judgments of value, of course, but by means of its empirical, logical, and analytic tools, science can *inform* those judgments. It can help individuals evaluate their options, think through their views of the world, achieve a better understanding of what they truly believe, and assess the logical coherence and empirical implications of their political positions and moral beliefs. Despite his insistence on the absolute disjunction between the realm of facts and the realm of values, Weber argues that science, in the form of "technical criticism," can nevertheless play a constructive role in ethical and political decision making. Within the limits imposed by the current state of knowledge, science can provoke reflection and rethinking by raising certain kinds of issues about the values or ends to which individuals may subscribe. For example: (1) It can assess the feasibility of a particular end, for example, direct democracy, by ascertaining whether the means necessary to achieve it are available or whether its realization is possible given existing circumstances. (2) If an aim is feasible, scientific investigation can estimate the costs required to achieve it and can raise the question of whether the end truly justifies the means. (3) It can also determine empirically the negative as well as positive repercussions of pursuing a particular end and once again ask whether the realization of that end is worth all the "subsidiary consequences." (4) It can also serve the interest of clarity by identifying the often hidden trade-offs and ethical implications entailed by adhering to certain principles, and it can bring to light through logical analysis those values that, implicitly, one either accepts or rejects. (5) The same kind of analytic operation can elucidate an individual's tacit hierarchy of ideals and principles, helping a person to see which of their potentially competing values they rank more highly, for example, social justice or individual liberty. Ultimately, however, Weber cautions, technical criticism, while performing an invaluable clarifying function, cannot generate any definitive moral or political decisions, and it cannot "save the individual the difficulty of making a choice."[84]

As a strictly empirical and analytic enterprise, science is thus not without value, even where moral and political questions are at issue. By making explicit what otherwise remains implicit, science, Weber observes, is in a position to help individuals become more fully conscious of their own "ultimate standards of value." It is also capable of informing individuals about the meaning of their choices and actions, for example by revealing what the pursuit or attainment of a desired end will cost "in terms of the predictable loss of other values" or the sacrifice of other ends. Science can perform

another important educational service as well—Weber in fact refers to this as
the "primary task of a useful teacher"—it can confront individuals with "inconvenient facts," facts that challenge their political identities, and it can
force individuals to see "the realities of life in all their starkness." Through
the application of this kind of "technical criticism," the scientist as educator
promotes "self-clarification and a sense of responsibility." The fulfillment of
this duty, Weber states—now drawing attention to the *value* of science—
might even be considered a genuine "moral achievement."[85]

MODERNITY AND RATIONALIZATION

As the pre-modern traditional world gives way to the modern rationalized
world, things change. Science supersedes religion as the source of authoritative knowledge, the credentialed specialist prevails over the cultured dilettante, the bureaucratic official replaces the village elder, technical expertise
supplants ancient wisdom, precise calculation displaces rule-of-thumb guess-
work, and the predictability of explicit rules and formal procedures triumphs
over the caprice of personal judgment. What was once haphazard and casual
becomes codified and routinized. Individual behavior takes an increasingly
instrumental turn, guided by cost-benefit estimates rather than customary
norms. With the expansion of bureaucracy and the market, furthermore, social relations that were once personal and affective, imbued with sentiment
and feelings of moral obligation, become increasingly impersonal and detached, pervaded by a spirit of "rational matter-of-factness." In even the most
private spheres, including marital relations and child rearing, social practices
once governed by long-standing traditions are nowadays regulated by legal
precepts, the findings of scientific research, and the scrutiny of trained professionals. In the larger public arena too, with the rationalization of economic
and political institutions, the everyday lives of individuals—so different from
their traditional counterparts—are increasingly dominated by the "inani-
mate" machinery of the capitalist factory and the "animate" machinery of the
bureaucratic organization. What we see with the process of rationalization, in
sum, as Rogers Brubaker explains, is "the depersonalization of social relationships, the refinement of techniques of calculation, the enhancement of the
social importance of specialized knowledge, and the extension of technically
rational control over both natural and social processes."[86]

While Weber uses the various permutations of the term "rational" in a
purely neutral, descriptive sense, he nevertheless implies three normatively

tinged conclusions about the process of rationalization. First, it is not altogether a bad thing. Rationalization enhances efficiency, control, and predictability, and it endows individuals with the capacity to live a self-conscious and meaningful life. Second, it is not altogether a good thing. Rationalization intensifies the constraining qualities of modern society and the regimentation of social life, posing a threat to the freedom of the individual. Third, for good and bad, it is an inescapable thing. Whether we like it or not, rationalization is the inevitable condition of modern existence, the "fate of our times." The issue for Weber, therefore, as we will see more fully in later chapters, is not how we might collectively revolutionize the modern rationalized and bureaucratized world, but how we might as individuals find a way within this world to preserve some measure of autonomy and meaning.[87]

Part II

Themes

Chapter Five

The Modern Condition

This chapter and the three other thematic chapters to follow focus on four topics central to Marx, Durkheim, and Weber's theories of modern society: the perils of the modern condition (chapter 5), the fate of the individual (chapter 6), the prospects for democracy (chapter 7), and the question of socialism (chapter 8). With these four thematic chapters, building on the preceding overview chapters, we will attain a more comprehensive picture of Marx, Durkheim, and Weber—as sociologists, as theorists of modernity, and as politically engaged public intellectuals. I also identify and explore key intellectual and political differences among the three in these four chapters, thus giving readers an opportunity to wrestle with the conflicting ideas of preeminent sociological theorists concerning modern society's present and future.

Marx, Durkheim, and Weber witnessed revolutionary changes in the cultural, political, and economic landscape of the western world. In opposition to the backward-looking traditionalists of their day, they welcomed the rise of modern industrial civilization. At the same time, however, they spent much of their lives documenting and interrogating the contradictions and irrationalities of the modern era. Indeed, among their most enduring contributions to the sociological tradition are their penetrating examinations of modern society's pathologies. The objective of this chapter is to explain the thinking of Marx, Durkheim, and Weber on the problems of modern life and compare their diagnoses of the modern condition.

The present chapter sets the stage for the three other thematic chapters. Marx, Durkheim, and Weber differ in what they perceive as the chief ail-

ments of modern society, in how they interpret those ailments, in the remedies they propose, and in what they envision for the future. These differences, in turn, underlie their contrasting perspectives on the predicament of
the modern individual (chapter 6)—in what they regard as the chief threats to
a worthy individualism and in what they believe is required to promote
individual freedom, dignity, and self-realization. Their contrasting analyses
of the pathologies of modern life also go a long way toward explaining the
divergence among the three in their views of democracy (chapter 7) and in
their assessments of socialism (chapter 8). And just as we cannot fully understand their arguments on the issues of individualism, democracy, and socialism apart from their diagnoses of the modern condition, so too we cannot
fully understand Marx, Durkheim, and Weber's diagnoses of the modern
condition without working through their arguments on the issues of individualism, democracy, and socialism. These four thematic chapters, in sum, combine to give us a reasonably thorough overview of Marx, Durkheim, and
Weber's theories of modernity, and they provide us with an account of how
and why these three classical sociologists arrived at such different views of
the modern world.

KARL MARX: THE FATE OF THE WORKING CLASS

Marx was a "man of science," his longtime collaborator Friedrich Engels
said at his graveside, but more than anything else he was a "revolutionist."
His life's mission was to promote the "overthrow of capitalist society" and
the "liberation of the modern proletariat." Motivated by this revolutionary
mission, Marx's diagnosis of the modern condition—carried out from the
standpoint of the working class—takes the form of a critique of capitalism.
He approaches the modern world through an eye-opening examination of
how the dynamics of the capitalist economy affect the lives of workers,
especially their lives *as workers*, toiling from day to day within the harsh
industrial workplace. In his writings on capitalism's origins, inner workings,
and developmental tendencies, the central question Marx pursues is this:
What does the capitalist mode of production mean for the "fate of the working class"? By adopting this class perspective, he is able to unveil certain
"inconvenient facts" (to use Max Weber's expression) and raise issues typically neglected in the conventional thinking about the free enterprise system.
What he discovers, ultimately, is an economic order that is not only crisis
prone, but also fundamentally irrational and inhumane. The normal function-

ing of the capitalist system, Marx maintains, as I explain below, is premised on the exploitation, immiseration, and alienation of the working class.[1]

The objective of Marx's critical diagnosis is to separate reality from illusion, unearth the "scientific truth" concealed by "the delusive appearance of things," and shatter the ideological mystifications justifying capitalism's existence. Instead of a harmonious relationship between the classes, Marx perceives an inherent antagonism of interests, with the capitalist class and the working class standing in opposition to each other as "oppressor and oppressed." Instead of an economic utopia where market forces ensure individual freedom, Marx uncovers a system of forced labor, with propertyless workers compelled to sell their labor power to the wealthy owners of the means of production. Instead of a society enabling individuals to develop freely and fully their potential as human beings, Marx finds an exploitive social order, with one class living off the unpaid labor of another. Instead of an economy designed to satisfy the needs of the population, Marx reveals a system where the sole object of production is the maximization of profit. And instead of accepting the assumption that capitalism is "an eternal natural necessity," the final destiny of humanity, Marx envisions a better society on the horizon, a post-capitalist society where class domination and wage slavery have been eradicated.[2]

The Developmental Tendencies of Capitalism

While both Durkheim and Weber show great interest in the passage from pre-modern to modern society, neither examines in much detail how the modern economic system evolves over time. For Marx, however, this issue is central to his diagnosis of the modern condition. We cannot properly understand the problems and prospects of present-day society, he believes, without taking into account the characteristic of capitalism as "an organism constantly engaged in a process of change."[3]

Propelled onward by its "unlimited mania for wealth," capitalism, Marx emphasizes, is a uniquely revolutionary and self-transformative mode of production. The "essential locomotive force" of the system—the proximate cause of its tendency toward ceaseless expansion—is the competition among capitalists and between capital and labor. In response to the "coercive laws of competition," each capitalist must be more ruthless than the next or be driven out of business. The capitalist class is thus continuously compelled to modernize the instruments of production, speed up the work process, and lower the costs of labor. The result of capitalism's competitive dynamic for the system as a whole is a progressive increase in the application of machinery, the division of labor, the scale of production, and the concentration and centralization of capital. For workers, however, the inexorable escalation of capitalism's productive power only heightens their exploitation and dependence. "Accumulation of wealth at one pole," Marx says, "is at the same time accumulation of misery, the torment of labour, slavery, ignorance, brutalization and moral degradation at the opposite pole."[4]

In the following pages I explore Marx's analysis of the dynamics of capitalism more fully, first by discussing the process of "valorization," the motivating force of the capitalist mode of production, and second by summarizing his historical account of the transition from manufacture (making by hand) to modern industry (making by machine). Against this backdrop, I then turn to the heart of Marx's diagnosis of the modern condition: how the development of capitalism affects the lives of workers.[5]

The Process of Valorization

Labor—a process in which humans appropriate and transform nature through work—is a necessary condition of human existence. Regardless of the type of society in which people live, they need to find some way to produce the necessities of life. With the rise of the capitalist mode of production, where profit making is the "absolute law," the labor process attains a new form and a new reason for existence. It becomes an instrument of what Marx calls "valorization," the process through which capitalists—"vampire-like"—extract surplus value by devouring the "labour-power of the worker." The history of the modern economy, from this standpoint, is a tale of how capitalists, in their determination to maximize the production of surplus value, are compelled to introduce increasingly efficient methods for the extraction of unpaid labor from the working class. Marx thus presents a picture of capitalism in which its "civilizing" side, the growth of society's productive forces, is inseparable from its dominant characteristic as an exploitative economic system, one in which the creation of wealth comes at the expense of the humanity of the worker.[6]

From Manufacture to Modern Industry

Capitalist production first appears when owners of capital take over the handicraft trades, bringing formerly independent artisans under the same roof and transforming them into wage laborers. Instead of working on their own, tailors or carpenters, for example, are gathered together within a single work-place and made subject to the "directing authority" of their newfound em-ployer. This transformation in the social relations of production, with the labor power of the workforce placed under the "despotic" command of the capitalist, is, according to Marx, the starting point of capitalism. The ensuing reorganization of the labor process augments the creation of surplus value, but it does not initially entail any significant alteration in the methods of production. The technical conditions of labor, including the tools and skills employed in the production process, remain the same. What changes is the social status of workers. As wage-dependent laborers, they now find them-selves in a "coercive relation," assembled together as propertyless employ-ees, subordinated to "the powerful will of a being outside them" and forced to labor according to "a plan drawn up by the capitalist."[7]

The period of manufacture proper, lasting in England from the middle of the sixteenth century to the last part of the eighteenth century, begins with a profound economic innovation—the introduction of the detailed division of labor within the workplace. In their effort to increase productivity and strengthen their control over the workforce, capitalists gradually begin divid-ing up the labor process. The skilled watchmaker, for example, is displaced by numerous specialized workers, each manufacturing a separate component part—the casing, the hands, the mainspring, the glass. The finished commod-ity, previously the "individual product of an independent craftsman," be-comes the collective product of a combination of "one-sidedly specialized workers." This detailed division of labor is the defining characteristic of the manufacturing period. As this new system of production takes hold, the labor process is fundamentally restructured. Workers, who previously exercised a variety of different skills, are increasingly confined to one exclusive sphere of activity, repeating the same movements over and over again with "the regularity of a machine." And while this benefits the capitalist by increasing productivity, it does so "by crippling the individual worker."[8]

The introduction of the division of labor in the era of capitalist manufac-ture furthers the objective of valorization by means of a more efficient organ-ization of the production process. The rise of modern industry, embodying the "principle of machine production," carries the exploitation of labor even further. During this period, the age of the Industrial Revolution, advances in science and technology are employed to automate the process of production. The emergence of the "machine system" transforms the labor process into an "industrial form of perpetual motion." Machines replace tools as the primary instruments of production. For workers, the "lifelong speciality of handling the same tool now becomes the lifelong speciality of serving the same machine." As manufacture gives way to modern industry, furthermore, a new mechanism of labor control is put into place. The "formal subsumption of labor under capital" is replaced by the "real subsumption of labor under capital." While the manufacturing worker is subordinated to the personal authority of the capitalist, the industrial worker, "regulated on all sides by the movement of the machinery," is subordinated to the objective power of the mechanized labor process itself. Formerly the worker made use of tools, but in the automated factory the machine makes use of the worker. And with the wage laborer now functioning as a mere "appendage of the machine," work is thoroughly deprived of its "individual character" and "all charm for the workman."[9]

The Immiseration of the Working Class

As explained in chapter 2, the concept of exploitation, because it unlocks the secret of profit making, is the centerpiece of Marx's analysis of the capitalist mode of production. The lifeblood of capitalism, he contends, is the unpaid labor siphoned from the working class. But beyond showing that workers are forced to perform surplus labor for the benefit of the capitalist, he also documents in graphic and indignant detail many other adverse effects of capitalist production on the well-being of the proletariat. Alongside his theory of exploitation, Marx proposes a theory of immiseration.

The concept of immiseration is typically understood as implying a tendency, as capitalism matures, for workers' wages to decline, whether in absolute terms or relative to the capitalist class. In either case, the result is increasing class polarization, with a widening divide separating wealthy capitalists on the one side from impoverished workers on the other. In a pamphlet published in 1864, Marx, taking note of this tendency, cites the contradictory "fact that the misery of the working masses has not diminished from 1848 to 1864, and yet this period is unrivalled for the development of its industry and the growth of its commerce." And even when wage levels do rise above the norm, he remarks, the "enjoyments of the worker" still tend to fall "in comparison with the increased enjoyments of the capitalist." As workers' living standard in the United States and the rest of the advanced capitalist world improved during the post–World War II era, many observers concluded that Marx's thesis had been proven wrong. Since the 1970s, however, with widespread wage stagnation and the dramatic surge in economic inequality, the idea of immiseration has acquired a new life. [10]

As Joseph Fracchia argues, however, it is mistaken to interpret Marx as equating immiseration with "wage impoverishment." He draws attention to the "corporeal" dimension of Marx's critique. The development of capitalist industry causes suffering on the part of workers not only because they are poorly paid, but also, and more importantly, because they are poorly treated. The damage resulting from the exploitation of labor is felt not only in the pocketbook of workers, but in their bodies and minds as well. Marx condemns capitalism not just because workers are divested of their labor time, but also because the relentless production of surplus value inflicts physical and psychological harm. [11]

Profit making for the capitalist "is an end in itself" and workers a "mere means of production," and once they are no longer useful in the process of valorization, they are "thrown onto the street." In the capitalist system, where workers are used up and then discarded, the accumulation of wealth is "brought about in contradiction to and at the expense of the individual human being." The power of capital, Marx declares, is "enriched through the impoverishment of the worker." And as capitalism develops, he states, drawing attention to an issue that clearly goes beyond "wage immiseration," the "situation of the worker, *be his payment high or low*, must grow worse." This concept of immiseration is meant to capture the reality that while workers' earnings may sometimes go up, the relentless dynamics of capitalist production take an increasing toll on their humanity. [12]

The unrestrained growth of modern industry, Marx observes, alluding to the corporeal dimension of immiseration, requires "ceaseless human sacrifices" from the working class. In the "mitigated jails" of the factory, he declares, citing Charles Fourier, workers are robbed of the very necessities of life, including light and air. Limited to a narrowly specialized function in the detailed division of labor, the worker is mutilated, turned "into a fragment of himself," a "crippled monstrosity." The introduction of machinery only makes matters worse, "confiscating every atom" of the worker's freedom, "both in bodily and intellectual activity." Forced to work long hours, furthermore, workers are also deprived of "time for education, for intellectual development, for the fulfillment of social functions, for social intercourse, for the free play of the vital forces of his body and mind, even the rest time of Sunday." And as the scale of production increases, continually reproducing the capital–labor relationship, the "perpetual dependence" of the working class is "constantly renewed," forcing them to return day after day to the capitalist workplace. For Marx, in sum, capitalism is characterized by a "dialectical inversion" where "all means for the development of production" become instruments of domination and exploitation and where "the whole lifetime of the worker and his family" is turned into "labour-time at capital's disposal for its own valorization." In the capitalist economic system, Marx argues, the human individual is sacrificed at the altar of profit maximization. [13]

The Alienation of Labor

Workers are exploited, Marx claims, insofar as their unpaid labor is appropriated by the capitalist in the form of profit. Workers are immiserated insofar as the system of capitalist production causes them physical and mental harm. And insofar as they are condemned to live a less than truly human life, workers are also alienated. These three concepts are among the central ingredients of Marx's critique of the capitalist mode of production, each opening a somewhat different window on the inner workings of the capitalist system and the oppressive circumstances of the working class.

Marx's theory of alienation, set forth most explicitly in his early writings of 1844, elucidates the pathologies of capitalist society from the vantage point of a philosophical conception of human nature, human capacities, and human needs. We can distinguish four distinct, though interrelated, aspects of the phenomenon of alienation. Each of these illustrates the detrimental effects of capitalism on the lives of the working class. [14]

First, workers under capitalism are alienated from the products of their labor. The wealth they create is not theirs to possess, consume, or enjoy. The objects they produce are the property of the capitalist, and workers have no say over what becomes of them. They put their lives into their work, but the goods they make, including the productive power of capital itself, now confront them "as *something alien*, as a *power independent* of the producer." This facet of alienated labor attests to the perversely inverted world of capitalist society: "It is true that labor produces for the rich wonderful things—but for the worker it produces privation. It produces palaces—but for the worker, hovels. It produces beauty—but for the worker, deformity." [15]

Second, workers under capitalism are alienated from their productive activity, from work itself. Labor is compulsory, not voluntary, a means of subsistence, not an end in itself, and a source of hardship, not a channel for self-realization. Rather than being a *"free manifestation of life,"* work is a "*forced* activity," a "*torment*" imposed on workers by the need to earn a living. Rather than contributing to the cultivation of the physical and mental energies of the individual, work under capitalism mortifies both the body and the mind. The alienation of the worker from his or her own productive activity means that real life begins only at the point work ceases. As a result, Marx says, the worker "only feels himself freely active in his animal functions"—"eating, drinking, procreating, etc." And in his labor, this uniquely human function, "he no longer feels himself to be anything but an animal."[16]

Third, workers under capitalism are alienated from their essential nature, their "species-being." The distinguishing quality of human beings, according to Marx, is the capacity for free and self-actualizing labor. He describes this "exclusively human characteristic" in a famous passage from *Capital*:

> A spider conducts operations which resemble those of the weaver, and a bee would put many a human architects to shame by the construction of its honeycomb cells. But what distinguishes the worst architect from the best of bees is that the architect builds the cell in his mind before he constructs it in wax.

This human essence—the ability of individuals to conceive a purpose and realize it through their laboring activity—is corrupted under capitalism where work serves an external need and is performed under the dictatorial control of the capitalist. Because wage laborers as sentient beings are treated as mere instruments of production, no better than non-human animals, work under capitalism is contrary to human nature, quite literally dehumanizing.[17]

Fourth, individuals under capitalism are alienated from their fellow human beings. Capitalism transforms all social relationships into competitive economic relationships, resulting in the "*estrangement of man from man*." Rather than each of us being the condition for the self-realization of the other, as in a "true community," we each regard the other as a means or obstacle to the achievement of our own egoistic interests. In the dog-eat-dog world of capitalist society, people are brought together only through "the selfishness, the gain and the private interests of each." Every individual "looks only to his own advantage. . . . Each pays heed to himself only, and no one worries about the other."[18]

Workers in capitalist society, Marx argues, are not only exploited and immiserated; they are alienated as well. They are deprived of the fruits of their labor, unable to take pleasure or affirm themselves in the objects they produce. They are forced to relinquish control over their own laboring activity, with their work lives subservient to and under the command of the "alien will" of the capitalist. Because their work is involuntary, a mere means to an end, they are precluded from expressing their individuality through labor. And finally, as capitalist norms of behavior cause people to become increasingly egoistic and asocial, they experience an *"estranged* form of social intercourse," contrary to any genuine *"human community."*[19]

Alienation is a condition of society, Marx contends, not a state of mind or an inescapable concomitant of human existence. It is not a psychological malady that can be cured through drugs or therapy; it is not an ontological fact that must be endured; and it is not a problem that can be remedied within the framework of capitalism. The alienation of labor, for Marx, originates from the inner workings of the capitalist system of production and cannot be overcome except through the abolition of that system.

The Irrationality of Capitalism

For the defenders of the free market economy, capitalism is an eminently rational way of organizing the production and distribution of goods. It promotes the efficient allocation of resources, fosters economic growth, provides opportunities for ambitious individuals to get rich, and offers consumers a vast array of products to choose from. Marx presents a far more critical view of capitalism, partly because he employs a different yardstick in his evaluation of the system. First, instead of assessing capitalism from the standpoint of the capitalist, mainly concerned about making a profit, or the consumer, mainly concerned about the price of goods and services, Marx asks what the operation of the system means for the well-being of the direct producers, for workers themselves. Second, instead of focusing exclusively on the market, the locus of individual freedom in mainstream economic theory, Marx draws back the curtain on the largely invisible world of work. He asks what the labor process, configured as a process of valorization, means for the millions of people who spend the bulk of their waking hours trapped within the confines of the capitalist workplace. And third, instead of taking a snapshot picture, Marx draws attention to the contradictory dynamics of the capitalist economic system, to its crisis-prone, injurious, and ultimately self-destructive pattern of development. Marx sees capitalism differently in sum because he looks at it from the viewpoint of the working class, from inside the "hidden abode of production," and as a "historically transient stage of development."[20]

EMILE DURKHEIM: THE MALAISE OF MODERN SOCIETY

The modern world, Durkheim says, suffers from a "condition of profound unrest," an "alarming moral destitution," a "wave of sadness and discouragement," a "state of mental confusion," a "moral mediocrity." Among the most visible symptoms are these: unrestrained egoistic individualism, an abnormally high and rising rate of suicide, industrial crises and commercial breakdowns, exploitive labor contracts and unjust economic relations, class conflict and political turmoil, and the disorganization and demoralization of the entirety of economic life. Durkheim's central project is to diagnose the nature of this uniquely modern illness. What are its underlying causes, what does it imply about the modern condition, and how might the malaise of modern society be alleviated?[21]

Durkheim's assessment of the modern era sets him apart from both the "reactionary school" to his right, calling for the restoration of the old regime, and from the socialist movement to his left, agitating for a "complete remolding of the social order." In opposition to both its traditionalist and socialist critics, Durkheim offers a defense of modern society. The state of crisis in which the European societies of his day find themselves, he insists, does not discredit modernity itself, which after all is still only in its infancy. The illness afflicting the modern era rather is temporary and remedial, due to certain abnormal circumstances. We need to take a longer view, he advises, looking beyond the present and admittedly pathological state of society to consider its future potential, what it is destined to become. Indeed, far from being doomed to dissolution, the modern world, Durkheim suggests, contains within itself the seeds of its own perfection.[22]

A State of Transition

For Marx, as we have seen, the pathologies of modern society—the exploitation, immiseration, and alienation of the working class, along with the crisis-prone pattern of economic growth—are inherent features of the capitalist mode of production, and as capitalism matures its contradictions are bound only to worsen. For Durkheim, in contrast, the current state of crisis is not due to any intrinsic characteristics of modernity, nor is it an inevitable outgrowth of the system of private ownership. It is, instead, an aberrant product of a tumultuous passage from the pre-modern period to the modern period. This transition is an ongoing source of instability, he argues, because it is at once profound, rapid, uneven, incomplete, and contradictory. *Profound* insofar as it altered the fundamental structure of people's lives, giving rise to an entirely new social type, a "mainly industrial" society. *Rapid* insofar as the passage from the old world to the new world occurred at an extraordinary velocity, too quickly to be anything other than disruptive. *Uneven* insofar as the speed of economic change outpaced the development of corresponding cultural adaptations, leaving the new economic system without an appropriate moral framework. *Incomplete* insofar as archaic sentiments and practices from the past, including the institution of inheritance, continue to linger on into the present, hindering modern society's maturation. *Contradictory* insofar as the new industrial economy in its currently unregulated state excites egoistic motives and extravagant aspirations, freeing desires and appetites from all authoritative restraints. In sum, Durkheim concludes, modern society is in a state of crisis because the "new life that all of a sudden has arisen has not been able to organise itself thoroughly."[23]

The malaise of the modern era is a transitional problem. The old world is not yet altogether dead, and the new world is not yet fully born. European societies persevere as unstable mixtures of two antagonistic social systems—one in the process of decline, the other in the process of emergence. The institutions of the pre-modern world have become anachronistic, but not enough time has passed for new institutions to take their place. The resulting state of upheaval, Durkheim emphasizes, constitutes a crisis of integration and solidarity—in short, a *moral* crisis. Though originating from a sweeping economic transformation, the problem does not stem from any failings of modern industry, but is due instead to the absence of a moral order sufficient to regulate the emerging economic order.[24]

The Crisis of Modern Society

Durkheim's diagnosis of the modern condition pinpoints three key problems: egoism, "the anomic division of labor" (more simply, anomie), and "the forced division of labor" (more simply, injustice). These three—egoism, anomie, and injustice—are the chief pathologies of modern society. In the following subsections, I discuss each of these in turn. I then examine Durkheim's conception of the "corporative system," one aspect of his thinking about how modern society might be reformed to more closely approximate its ideal or normal state.[25]

Egoism: The Absence of Group Life

The rise of modern society, by opening up new economic vistas, liberates the individual from the sometimes stifling influence of family ties, ascribed groups, and communal associations. While this transformation overcomes one abnormal state, where the individual is excessively absorbed into the collective, it threatens to cause another: egoism. As Durkheim explains in *Suicide*, egoism exists where society is insufficiently present in the life of the individual. In this egoistic state, people are isolated in their own personal worlds, unencumbered by social ties, and detached from the influence of collective forces. Caught up entirely in their own individual lives, they pursue personal inclinations rather than societal goals, they are guided by self-interest rather than collective codes of conduct, and their own egoistic calculations take precedence over higher social ideals. This "excessive individuation," Durkheim observes, is a common problem in the modern era where the ethos of individual freedom is exceptionally strong and a stable group life appropriate to an industrial society has yet to form.[26]

This "state of affairs," Durkheim says, where a "fierce individualism" is the norm and the "spirit of association" is weak—referring specifically to the France of his day—"constitutes a serious crisis." No lasting social and political order is possible if individuals serve only their own personal ends, if they are not joined together by collective aims and ideals. Where individuals lack this commitment to a common project, where they succumb to the pathology of egoism, society is reduced to "a pile of sand that the least jolt or the slightest puff will suffice to scatter." A society is "devoid of moral character," no real society at all, if it consists only of an aggregate of solitary and self-interested individuals each looking out for number one. In response to this pathology, Durkheim calls for the subordination of "individual and selfish ends" to "ends that are truly social and consequently moral." To stem the tide of egoism, what is needed, he proposes, is a unifying "faith in a common ideal."[27]

Anomie: The Absence of Moral Regulation

Durkheim singles out three notable features of the process of economic modernization: the expansion of the market, the rise of large-scale industry, and the growth of workplace specialization. These developments, occurring with little planning or regulation, cause widespread economic turmoil and social disorder. First, as the market for goods and services extends beyond the local community, becoming national and even global, the balance between supply and demand is disrupted. Manufacturers are unable to gauge accurately the needs of consumers, sometimes producing too much and sometimes too little. This market anarchy underlies the ruinous ups and downs of the business cycle, destructive competition, business bankruptcies, and the recurrence of "industrial or commercial crises."[28]

Second, in the small workshops of the pre-industrial era, Durkheim says, employers and employees worked alongside each other as equals, sharing a common life. The rise of large-scale manufacturing fundamentally alters this more or less intimate and cooperative relationship. Employers, now industrialists, and employees, now wage laborers, reside in separate worlds, occupy unequal class positions, and encounter one another in a "state of permanent hostility." With this hardening of the class system, strikes, boycotts, and even violent conflict become common features of the industrial landscape.[29]

Third, the development of large-scale industry is accompanied by increasing workplace specialization. Tied to the new factory regimen, workers become isolated in their tasks, disconnected from co-workers, and confined to a monotonous routine with little sense of purpose. Recalling Marx's theory of alienation, Durkheim describes the industrial worker as a "lifeless cog" set in motion by an "external force," impelled "always in the same direction and in the same fashion." "Plainly," he observes, this is nothing less than a "debasement of human nature."[30]

Durkheim's concerns about the modern economic system—economic crises, antagonistic class relations, the dehumanization of labor—are strikingly similar to those raised by Marx. For Durkheim, however, while the current functioning of market forces, big industry, and factory workplaces is pathological, these economic institutions themselves are not to blame. The real culprit, he asserts, is the anomic state of industrial relations—that is, the absence of legal and moral regulation. The problem is not the modern economic system per se, but a *disorganized* modern economic system. So how and why did the currently chaotic condition of economic life come about?[31]

Durkheim pursues this question by first briefly surveying what he considers the normal course of modernization. With the advance of the division of labor, he observes, it is natural for occupational or professional associations to proliferate. People typically come together and form relationships around their shared economic pursuits and work experiences, creating an enduring group life. As these group structures multiply and stabilize, they each develop their own system of "professional ethics," moral rules specific to the varied occupational spheres. These serve two functions vital to the preservation of social stability: they regulate occupational practices, engendering an orderly professional world, and they provide a moral life for individual members. Durkheim mentions several professions where moral codes and regulative institutions are already in place, including the army, law, medicine, government, and education.[32]

In the world of industry, however, because it materialized so suddenly, no such moral organization, no system of professional ethics, has yet emerged. The entire domain of economic life thus exists "in a state of legal and moral anomie." Business activities are carried out in a moral vacuum, with no clear-cut precepts distinguishing between "the permissible and the prohibited, between what is just and what is unjust." There are, for example, no authoritative rules of conduct regulating market transactions, setting prices and wages, moderating competition among rival business firms, or specifying the respective rights and duties of employers and employees. In denouncing this economic anarchy, Durkheim, notably, takes a stand against the classical economists for whom all rules and regulations are considered a tyrannical infringement of the natural workings of the free market. From a laissez-faire standpoint, industrial anomie is a desirable condition, the ideal state of economic life. For Durkheim, it is a recipe for disaster. "Economic functions," he says, cannot operate "harmoniously nor be maintained in a state of equilibrium unless subjected to moral forces which surpass, contain, and regulate them."[33]

The problem of anomie is a particularly serious threat, Durkheim emphasizes, because of the preeminence of economic activity in the lives of modern individuals. Pre-modern people pass the bulk of their time in the close embrace of families, churches, and communities. The advent of modernity, however, causes a shift in society's center of gravity. The economic realm becomes the principal locus of social existence, with people spending "their lives almost entirely in an industrial and commercial environment." This combination of an increasingly industrial society and the persistently "amoral character of economic life" is inevitably a "source of moral deterioration." In the anomic state of the modern world, where economic pursuits predominate, the "greater part" of people's lives, Durkheim warns, is "divorced from any moral influence."[34]

Injustice: The Absence of Economic Equality

The disorganized and demoralized state of modern society causes egoism and anomie with all their attendant problems. It also causes injustice, yet another source of discontent and instability. For Durkheim, injustice in economic relations is a pathological phenomenon, inconsistent with modern moral principles and public sentiments which demand that individuals be treated equally and fairly.[35]

A just social order exists only when there is "absolute equality in the external conditions" under which individuals develop their abilities, compete for jobs, and stipulate to a contract. Justice, according to Durkheim, requires both *equality of opportunity*, so that individuals are free to cultivate their capabilities to their fullest, and *equality of exchange*, so that individuals are remunerated fairly for their economic contributions. Because of the persistence of "sharp class differences" and the institution of inheritance, the division of labor in modern industrial society currently fulfills neither of these conditions.[36]

A normal and just division of labor takes the form of a meritocracy, with individuals allocated to positions in the occupational system according to their aptitudes. In a just society there is a "harmony between individual natures and social functions," a close fit between the abilities and skills of individuals on the one hand and the roles and positions they occupy on the other. Everyone has a job suited to their talents, everyone rises to their level of competence, and everyone is rewarded according to their performance. A just social order, Durkheim asserts, is one in which the distribution of "social inequalities" corresponds to the distribution of "natural inequalities."[37]

This happy outcome is possible only if the competition for employment is "spontaneous," meaning unconstrained, equally open to all eligible candidates. Justice requires that the process through which individuals are matched to jobs be merit based, leaving no one either unduly advantaged or unduly disadvantaged. Where this condition is not realized, where equality of opportunity is lacking, we have what Durkheim calls a "forced" division of labor, the opposite of a just division of labor. In this pathological state—the current state of modern society—free and equal access to opportunities is undermined by barriers of caste and class; by inequalities deriving from "the accident of birth" and "family status"; by lingering prejudices and favoritism; by outdated customs, conventions, and laws that restrict admittance to certain occupations; and, perhaps most importantly, by the hereditary transmission of wealth, which confers benefits unrelated to "personal value." This forced division of labor is a violation of the principle of justice, it renders existing inequalities illegitimate, and it yields dissatisfaction and disintegration rather than solidarity and social order.[38]

For justice to prevail, it is not enough that individuals enter the market as equals; they must also bargain in the market as equals. This takes us to the second form of economic injustice: unfair contracts. A contract is formed when two parties consent to the terms of an agreement. But this amounts to a *just* contract, Durkheim insists, only if consent is truly free. If one party acquiesces to an agreement "under duress," if he or she lacks options or is otherwise in a weak position, then the outcome is not a morally valid contract but a "case of extortion." A just contract exists only where the parties negotiate from a position of equality, where the one faces no more pressure to settle than the other. According to Durkheim, therefore, to be counted as truly just, a contract must fulfill two conditions: first, contracting parties must negotiate under equal circumstances, with the "weapons" of each side matched "as nearly as possible"; and second, the terms of the contract must be objectively equitable, with the services exchanged being "equivalent in social value." A just contract requires equality from start to finish, from the commencement of the bargaining process to the completion of the final exchange.[39]

Economic injustice, with unfair labor contracts being the prime example, is—as with inequality of opportunity—due primarily to inequitable class divisions. Because of class differences in resources and power, employers and employees confront one another under greatly unequal bargaining positions, enabling the first to exploit the second. According to Durkheim, "if one class in society is obliged, in order to live, to secure the acceptance by others of its services, whilst another class can do without them, because of the resources already at its disposal," then "the latter group can lord it over the former." Durkheim draws a radical conclusion from this: "there can be no rich and poor by birth without their being unjust contracts." This reasoning leads him to single out the institution of inheritance for special criticism, describing it as an "archaic survival" that has "no part in our present-day ethics." The "inherited fortune," he says, because it "loads the scale and upsets the balance," undermines fairness in economic relations and contradicts the modern spirit of egalitarianism. For Durkheim, in sum, as long as "sharp class differences exist in society," and as long as these differences are kept sharp by the inheritance of wealth, then "the system operates in conditions which do not allow of justice."[40]

This pathological system cannot endure, Durkheim claims. The destabilizing social and economic abnormalities of the present are destined to wither away as modern society matures. The driving force of this progressive evolutionary process is the powerful "thirst for justice" embodied in the aspirations and passions of the modern individual. With its reverence for egalitarian principles and the rights of the individual, modern society, Durkheim says, is on a "mission for justice." This mission is bound to be successful, he suggests, because injustice is "not founded in the nature of things," not based on reason, and not consistent with modern moral notions. Inequality and injustice are repugnant to the "public consciousness." The heightened "moral sensitivity" of the modern individual is aroused when undeserved suffering is inflicted, when the strong take advantage of the weak, and when some claim "the lion's share" and others receive less than their due. Through the pressure exerted by this egalitarian cultural imperative, Durkheim suggests, the basic institutions and practices of society will gradually be reshaped and realigned to ensure the realization of social justice.[41]

Corporate Organizations

Durkheim's diagnosis of the modern condition exemplifies his conception of sociology as serving practical as well as theoretical purposes. He intends not only to explain the pathologies of the modern world, but also to "put ourselves in a position where we can better resolve them." His research thus leads him to propose certain recommendations for reorganizing society. The key to alleviating the malaise of the modern era, Durkheim concludes, is to discover a collective force capable of regulating the burgeoning sphere of economic activity and introducing a new moral order appropriate to an industrial society. The family, because the scope of its influence is too limited and because it occupies a progressively smaller place in modern people's lives, is not up to the task of providing an encompassing moral environment. Traditional religious institutions are not sufficient either. In the modern "freethinking" milieu, they cannot possibly regain the authority they once had in the past. The state, because its powers are certain to expand as society progresses, is a more likely contender for the job. And though Durkheim foresees it playing an essential role, he does not believe the state is equipped to solve the problems of economic anarchy and moral anomie. First, it is too distant from the workings of the economic system to monitor and regulate business practices, employer-employee relations, and other day-to-day economic activities. Second, the state is also too far removed from people's everyday lives, and its connections with them too irregular, for it to exert a "sufficiently effective and continuous" moral influence. As far as the provision of economic and moral regulation is concerned, the state, Durkheim believes, is a blunt instrument, a "clumsy machine."[42]

Rejecting alternative solutions to the crisis of modern society, Durkheim pins his hopes on the formation of occupational associations, what he typically calls "professional groupings" or "corporate bodies." Already more or less present in some non-industrial spheres, for example, medicine and law, these intermediate organizations, as he conceives them, would be situated between the state and the individual, filling the vacuum created by the destruction of the guilds during the era of the French Revolution. Occupational groups, for Durkheim, hold out the promise of creating an authoritative collective presence in addition to the state, and one much more closely tied to the everyday lives of individuals. He envisions these groupings as public institutions, bringing together people working in the same industries. Unlike labor unions or business associations which function as private interest groups, these occupational organizations would include both employers and employees, forging closer ties between two often antagonistic camps. To accord with the expansion of the market and the growing reach of the economy, these would be organized nationally, but with regional centers as well to accommodate the varied circumstances and needs of different localities. In addition, while remaining separate and autonomous, occupational groups, to prevent them from falling victim to "professional selfishness" or "corporate egotism," would also be subject to the "general supervision" of the state.[43]

The corporate organization, Durkheim maintains, because of its capacity to exercise a moral influence, is uniquely suited to remedy the pathologies of the modern era—egoism, anomie, and injustice. It has "everything necessary to give a framework to the life of the individual, to remove him from his state of moral isolation; and, given the present inadequacy of other groups, it alone can fill this essential role." First, professional organizations, as envisioned by Durkheim, would reinvigorate group life, enliven the currently impoverished "spirit of association," and thereby rein in the rule of self-interest. They would serve as an antidote to egoism by creating within the economic world a multiplicity of "*moral milieux*" and by fostering "ideas and needs other than individual ideas and needs"—ideas pertaining to duty, obligation, and fairness. Second, occupational groups, by regulating business activities, industrial relations, and market forces, would also alleviate the anomic state of modern economic life and help prevent economic crises. In addition, by including employers and employees in the same organizations, by placing these often warring parties in regular contact with each other, and by specifying their respective rights and duties, occupational groups would help relieve industrial society of its "sad class conflict." Third, corporate organizations would help combat injustice by protecting the weak against the strong, reminding people of their "mutual duties" and "the general interest," and enforcing the "law of distributive justice." In sum, "what we particularly see in the professional grouping," Durkheim says, "is a moral force capable of curbing individual egoism, nurturing among workers a more invigorated feeling of their common solidarity, and preventing the law of the strongest from being applied too brutally in industrial and commercial relationships."[44]

Occupational groups, or something akin to these, have a long history, Durkheim states. Their endurance over time implies they are neither archaic institutions having little relevance to modern times nor the arbitrary constructions of utopian theorists. Indeed, Durkheim argues, the historical ubiquity of occupational groups suggests they serve a vital social function and "correspond to deep and lasting needs." Given the predominantly industrial and occupational nature of modern life, these would seem to be even more clearly necessary in the current era. The occupational group, Durkheim suggests, is a "normal" feature of modern industrial society. To say then that he proposes or recommends the establishment of occupational organizations is not quite accurate. He is not setting forth an abstract ideal or "inventing a new system," at least not to his own way of thinking, as much as he is projecting into the future from the facts of the past and the present. His preferred solution to the crisis of the modern era, reflecting a certain "evolutionary optimism," is found within the logic of modernity itself. In calling for the establishment of occupational associations, he is rallying the forces of his society to a winning cause, one already in motion and perhaps even destined for success.[45]

MAX WEBER: THE IRON CAGE

If Marx is a the theorist of revolutionary aspirations and Durkheim a theorist of liberal hopes, then Weber is a theorist of disillusionment. Neither revolution nor evolution, he argues, will bring about a future of peace, happiness, and equality. For Weber, there is no prospect of achieving human emancipation or social harmony. Moreover, he claims, the truly fundamental problems afflicting modern society are neither abnormal nor temporary, nor are they rooted in the historically contingent dynamics of the capitalist mode of production. They derive instead from the very nature of modern social life. What is history for Marx and Durkheim is destiny for Weber, the "fate of our times."[46]

Marx's critique of the industrial society of his era calls attention to the crisis-prone nature of the capitalist economic system and the exploitation, immiseration, and alienation of the working class. Durkheim highlights the problems of egoism, anomie, and injustice, attributing these to the absence of an appropriate moral framework. Weber's perspective is grounded in his analysis of the rationalization, bureaucratization, and disenchantment of the world. He warns about individuals being imprisoned in an "iron cage" arising from the uniquely modern machinery of rational capitalism and bureaucratic administration. He worries about the loss of meaning, the routinization and petrification of everyday life, and the erosion of individual liberty and autonomy. He also underscores the impersonal and ethically indifferent quality of contemporary social institutions, including the capitalist system itself. For Weber, however, in contrast to Marx and Durkheim, there is no resolution to the dilemmas of the modern age. We can, though, respond to the demands of the present in more or less sensible ways. And within the constraints imposed by the conditions of modernity, Weber argues, as I explain more fully in the next chapter, it is possible for the individual (or at least *some* individuals) to live a meaningful life and find a measure of personal freedom.

The Iron Cage

On several occasions Weber uses the expression "iron cage" or some equivalent to characterize a particular feature of modern society or to warn of a possible future. Though often cited in the secondary literature as the centerpiece of his diagnosis of the modern condition, the precise meaning of this metaphor and what it is intended to imply are not perfectly clear, and its usage also varies from one context to another. To further muddy the waters, the primary referent of this concept appears to shift from capitalism in Weber's earlier writings to bureaucracy in his later writings. In addition, as Peter Baehr, among others, has observed, the term "iron cage" is not the best rendering of the German phrase (*stahlhartes Gehäuse*), which might be more accurately though less vividly translated as "shell as hard as steel."[47]

Weber employs the concept of the iron cage to evoke the coercive circumstances of life in the modern rationalized world. Though only occasionally using the specific term, he frequently discusses how individuals are constrained by the dominant institutions of modern society—forced to comply with the dictates of formally rational procedures, the imperatives of the market economy, the demands of the industrial workplace, and the regimentation of the bureaucratic order. People in the modern age, he suggests, are by no means altogether free to shape the conditions of their own lives or exercise their capacity for autonomous action. To cite just a few examples, individuals today, Weber states, are bound "with irresistible force" to the "technical and economic conditions of machine production," obliged to accommodate to an industrial system they did not will. They are subject to a regime of "rational discipline," particularly in their role as employees, expected to carry out orders without question, like soldiers in the military. They inhabit a social world inevitably circumscribed by "structures of dominancy" and "the inequality of the outward circumstances of life," with a permanent divide separating a "positively privileged" minority from a "negatively privileged" mass. And just as the working class is deprived of means of production and relegated to a subservient position in society, so too is nearly everyone else— including university professors, civil servants, technical personnel, and administrative employees—condemned to a state of dependency by virtue of their not having command over the instruments, equipment, and resources necessary to earn a living.[48]

Capitalism: The Most Fateful Force in Our Modern Life

Weber borrows the term "masterless slavery" to characterize the functioning of the modern economy. Capitalism, he says, echoing Marx, embodies a uniquely impersonal form of domination, a "special kind of coercive situation," one resulting from the "purely economic 'laws' of the market." The merciless operation of the capitalist system cannot be ascribed to the depredations of any "concrete master" or the villainy of any particular individual. Consider for example the state of the working class. While it is true, Weber acknowledges, that employees often receive only a subsistence wage, are subject to an inhumane workplace discipline, and are perpetually vulnerable to unemployment, this unhappy circumstance is not due to the moral blindness of the capitalist, but to the requirements of the system itself—to "the need for competitive survival and the conditions of the labor, money and commodity markets." The behavior of actors in the modern economy—employers and employees, as well as bankers, shareholders, and mortgage holders, all of whom are locked in the competitive struggle for existence—is determined not by personal motivations for which they might be held ethically accountable, but by "impersonal forces." And for those who refuse to abide by these forces, the result is "extinction." The capitalist who fails to make a profit will be driven out of business, and the worker who is unwilling to adjust to the status of wage laborer will starve. For Weber, as Wolfgang Mommsen points out, underlining the similarity to Marx, the modern capitalist system is an "irresistible social force" which compels everyone to "quasi-voluntarily" submit to its demands "regardless of whether they like them or not."[49]

When Weber introduces the iron cage metaphor in the *Protestant Ethic*, it is meant in just this way—to signal the coercive nature of modern, mature capitalism. While in an earlier era, the Puritans fulfilled their occupational duties as autonomous agents acting out of the "highest spiritual and cultural values," the individual today, with the capitalist system firmly "in the saddle," experiences the modern economic order not as a "locus of freedom" but as a "compulsive apparatus."

> The capitalist economy of the present-day is an immense cosmos into which the individual is born, and which presents itself to him, at least as an individual, as an unalterable order of things in which he must live. It forces the individual, in so far as he is involved in the system of market relationships, to conform to capitalist rules of action. The manufacturer who in the long run acts counter to these norms, will just as inevitably be eliminated from the economic scene as the worker who cannot or will not adapt himself to them will be thrown into the streets without a job.

Under the "domination of capitalism," Weber says, "any sober observer would have to say that all *economic* indicators point in the direction of growing 'unfreedom.'" As capitalism matures, as economic life is more and more circumscribed by the impersonal demands of the market, the individual is increasingly held captive in an iron cage of economic necessity.[50]

If the concept of the iron cage is meant to signify a loss of freedom, then for the modern industrial working class this is no mere nightmarish possibility but a palpable reality. The freedom of the free wage labor, for Weber no less than for Marx, is largely illusory. In principle workers have the right to accept or refuse a labor contract. But lacking access to their own means of production, they are in fact at the mercy of employers, who, by virtue of their stronger market position, are typically able to "set the terms, to offer the job 'take it or leave it.'" Constrained by the "threat of joblessness" and the prospect of an "empty pocketbook" and a "hungry family," workers have little choice but to accede to the dictates of the property-owning class. And once they hire themselves out to an employer, they are denied even the "slightest freedom" in determining the conditions of their work. Upon entering the capitalist workplace, they are subject to a rationalized "military discipline," tied to the rhythms fixed by a process of "scientific management," and placed in the service of the machinery of the modern factory which thoroughly dominates "their everyday working life." Work under capitalism is thus deprived of its "worldly attractiveness" and characterized by a "joyless lack of meaning." In the capitalist economic system, Weber concludes, workers are inevitably subordinated to the authority of the capitalist class and its representatives. This, he says, is the "fate of the entire working class." For Weber, in contrast to Marx, there is no alternative. The subjugation of the working class, he insists, is an inevitable condition of modern industry, whether organized on a capitalist basis or a socialist basis.[51]

Bureaucracy: A Structure of Domination

When Weber employs the metaphor of the iron cage in reference to capitalism, he is portraying what he sees as the existing reality of an economic system where market imperatives and workplace discipline restrict the freedom of the individual. But when he uses this concept in reference to bureaucracy, he is issuing a warning about the future as much as he is describing a current state of affairs. The specter of a bureaucratic "shell of bondage" is a worrisome possibility for Weber, something "which men will *perhaps* be forced to inhabit some day," not an inescapable destiny. How far the process of bureaucratization progresses is an "open question," he observes, thus holding out hope that the movement toward bureaucratic domination might still be held in check.[52]

Bureaucracy, Weber argues, is the supreme instrument for the organization and mobilization of collective action, but it is also a "structure of domination." It is a uniquely efficient system for managing the affairs of society, but it is also a potent "means of exercising authority over human beings," both those employed within the bureaucratic machinery and those subject to it. Bureaucracy thus exhibits a dual quality: it is technically indispensable *and* dangerously powerful. Because it is such a formidable system of domination and prone to spread like a virus, bureaucracy, Weber believes, is hazardous to both the autonomy of the individual and the dynamism of society.[53]

Increasing bureaucratization jeopardizes the freedom of the individual, but it is not entirely clear whose freedom is at stake, what this imperiled freedom entails, how it is put at risk by bureaucratic administration, or what other negative consequences result from "the irresistible advance of bureaucratization." In some passages, Weber's critique addresses the plight of individuals employed within bureaucratic organizations, caught up in the soul-sapping shallowness of the bureaucratic rat race. The professional bureaucrat, he says, "is chained to his activity," reduced to "a small cog in a ceaselessly moving mechanism which prescribes to him an essentially fixed route of march." With more disdain than empathy, he elsewhere describes bureaucratic officials as "little cogs, little men clinging to little jobs and striving towards bigger ones." Harnessed to the bureaucratic order, these "little men," incapable of independent action, are trapped in an apparatus they cannot "squirm out of." But they also share a common interest in the perpetuation of that apparatus—the cause of their impotence but also the source of their social status—and in "the persistence of its rationally organized domination." As more or less willing participants in their own servitude, bureaucratic office workers, Weber suggests, are no less alienated than the industrial proletariat.[54]

But while he sometimes describes bureaucratic functionaries as "little cogs," at other times he envisions them forming a privileged social stratum. As members of a professionally trained elite, bureaucratic officials possess a "tremendous influence," Weber asserts, referring specifically to the occupants of the state bureaucracy. They not only enjoy a "distinctly elevated *social esteem* vis-à-vis the governed," but the dominant position they derive from their unrivaled expertise within the system of administration also puts at risk the freedom of those subject to their authority. This circumstance is all the more troubling, Weber states, because the power exercised by bureaucratic officeholders—by virtue of their technical proficiency, experience as career administrators, and access to "official secrets"—is "practically indestructible."[55]

The rise of bureaucracy and the ascendancy of the bureaucratic official, according to Weber, have deeper cultural ramifications as well, creating not only a pervasive and omnipotent system of authority, but a unique type of human being, a modern "bureaucratic self." This new breed of men and women, marked by a rule-bound bureaucratic mentality, are the carriers of a submissive ethic of "adaptation." Trained in the observance of procedure and predisposed toward a regulated way of life, the modern bureaucratic self, he says, needs "'order' and nothing but order." Weber fears a future where the world is populated by "no men but these." This problem is particularly salient in his own country because the bureaucratic ethos aggravates what in his view is already the great weakness of the German nation—its inclination toward security, docility, and obedience.[56]

Bureaucracy makes "little cogs" of ordinary people, but for Weber the growing power of bureaucratic officialdom is even more harmful for another reason. As it penetrates the spheres of government and business, bureaucracy suppresses innovative political and economic leadership. The advance of bureaucracy infringes on the struggle for political power and the give-and-take of market competition—two dynamic, counter-bureaucratic arenas which Weber regards as invaluable testing grounds for the training and selection of leaders. The more the "spirit of bureaucracy" and the "civil-service mentality" prevail, the less space there is for the cultivation of visionary politicians and risk-taking entrepreneurs. Only these social types, Weber contends, possess the ambition, the sense of responsibility, and the capacity for independent action required of genuine leaders. By contrast, the bureaucratic official, accustomed to working "according to rules and instruction," is singularly unequipped to fulfill the role of the "directing mind" or the "moving spirit." The qualities of a competent leader, Weber insists, diverge sharply from those of a competent bureaucrat.[57]

By inhibiting the development of effective leadership and promoting the value of order above all else, the process of bureaucratization contributes to political and economic stagnation. As David Beetham explains, bureaucracy for Weber threatens individual freedom, but more to the point, reflecting the rather elitist tone of his diagnosis, it narrows "the scope for exceptional individuals to exercise a socially creative role in both economy and state." Such individuals are an energizing force. Only they are capable of setting forth new goals and aspirations, new values and ideals. The ceding of power to the bureaucrat at the expense of the politician and the entrepreneur tightens the bars of the iron cage—stifling private enterprise, hardening the already "rigid casing" of capitalism, and leaving the nation-state without vitality and direction. The encroachment of bureaucracy constrains the decision-making authority of economic and political leaders, limiting the potential for rejuvenating social change and the periodic disruption of "rational rule." The tendency toward stagnation in modern society can be combated, according to Weber, only if the leaders of government and industry—the counterweights to bureaucratic power—have the leeway to intervene in an otherwise routinized world and interject an element of charisma into an increasingly ossified bureaucratic structure.[58]

Bureaucracy for Weber is a realm of order whose advance threatens to erode the realm of freedom. If left unchecked, the expansion of bureaucracy is certain to exacerbate the coercive and enervating qualities of modern social life, strengthening the present-day "iron cage" or "shell of bondage." How can we moderate this tendency? Weber wonders. How can we resist the "supreme mastery of the bureaucratic way of life," and how can we "possibly save any remnants of 'individualistic' freedom" in the modern rationalized world? I explore Weber's response to these questions more fully in the following chapters. [59]

Formal and Substantive Rationality

Weber's diagnosis of the modern condition, besides exposing the coercive features of rational capitalism and bureaucratic organization, also draws attention to the ethical indifference of modernity's defining institutions. Distinguishing between two conflicting forms of rationality—formal and substantive—Weber discloses an apparent paradox: the irrationality of the modern rationalized world.

Formal and substantive rationality are similar insofar as both contribute to making social action more orderly, consistent, and coherent, but they do so in different and often contradictory ways. The first promotes orderliness by submitting social practices to a *technical* criterion, for example, profitability (in the case of economic activity) or procedural legality (in the case of law and bureaucratic administration). Where formal rationality prevails, social life is organized through the application of established protocols, set procedures, and fixed rules, making the workings of society more calculable and predictable. The second promotes orderliness by submitting social practices to a *value* criterion, an ultimate end of one kind or another. Where substantive rationality prevails, social life is organized by reshaping the workings of society so they are more in harmony with some ethical or political ideal, for example, fairness or equality. [60]

These two forms of rationality, Weber believes, are typically at odds with each other. For example, the greater the formal rationality of an economic system, the more it is governed by money prices and market calculations, and the less it serves substantive normative goals. The greater the substantive rationality of an economic system, the more it is designed to fulfill ethical aims and the less it is able to achieve the productivity of a market economy. From the viewpoint of formal rationality, what matters most is long-term profitability. From the viewpoint of substantive rationality, what matters

most is whether the organization of economic activity and the ends it serves
are consistent with ethical principles.[61]

Weber employs this distinction to explore the moral ambiguity of the
modern condition. The formally rational quality of modern-day social institutions, he argues, engenders numerous substantive irrationalities, as the following examples illustrate.

The Capitalist Business Enterprise. The formal rationality of the capitalist
economy, made possible by the technique of capital accounting, depends on
economic activity being based exclusively on money prices. Business operations, focused on the monetary bottom line and free of any ethical infringements, are guided solely by market opportunities. This exemplifies the antagonism between formal rationality, oriented toward the calculable goal of
continuous profitability, and substantive rationality, oriented toward specific
ultimate ends. "The more the world of the modern capitalist economy follows its own immanent laws," Weber asserts, reflecting on this conflict of
principles, "the less accessible it is to any imaginable relationship with a
religious ethic of brotherliness." More generally, what we observe is an
irresolvable tension between the rational, profit-minded functioning of the
capitalist economic system and commonly held normative, religious, and
political values.[62]

The Free Market. The same antagonism between formal and substantive
rationality is evident in the operation of the free market, the "most impersonal" sphere of action "into which humans can enter with one another." In the
market arena, Weber states, the norm of business "matter-of-factness" predominates. There is no room for moral considerations, for "obligations of
brotherliness." People are treated not as ends in themselves, but as means in
an exchange relationship or as combatants in the struggle for existence. The
"economically rationalized" and impersonal world of commercial transactions precludes "any caritative [or charitable] regulation of relations." The
formally rational free market is substantively irrational, Weber says, "an
abomination to every system of fraternal ethics."[63]

The Industrial Workplace. The formal rationality of modern capitalism
also demands that workers, at the cost of their very humanity, submit to the
harsh discipline of the industrial workplace. For Weber, as we have already
seen, the rationality of capitalism requires a rigidly organized labor process
where workers are compelled to obey the commands of the capitalist. This
state of affairs, he recognizes, is an insult to common notions of human
decency. "The fact that the maximum of *formal* rationality in capital account-

ing is possible only where the workers are subjected to domination by entrepreneurs is," Weber asserts, "a further specific element of the *substantive* irrationality in the modern economic order."[64]

Bureaucratic Administration. Bureaucratic administration achieves the highest degree of formal rationality where officials conduct their business "according to purely objective considerations" and "without regard for persons." A rational bureaucratic organization functions with the efficiency and impersonality of a machine, with people processed according to *"calculable rules,"* regardless of their personal needs or individual circumstances. "Bureaucracy develops the more perfectly, the more it is 'dehumanized,'" Weber says, "the more completely it succeeds in eliminating from official business love, hatred, and all purely personal, irrational, and emotional elements which escape calculation." This formally rational quality of bureaucratic administration—the cause of its often being disparaged as heartless—is precisely what makes it substantively irrational.[65]

The Modern Legal System. According to Weber, the formal rationality of the modern legal system, where rulings are derived from abstract legal concepts and procedural logic, enables the system to operate in a highly predictable manner, "like a technically rational machine." This legal formalism, however, with law kept separate from ethics, is incompatible with the "ideals of substantive justice." Indeed, Weber declares, the conflict between these two principles is "insoluble." What is just from a purely legal standpoint— corporate tax avoidance strategies, to take a modern example—is not necessarily just from an ethical point of view.[66]

As the process of rationalization plays out in the capitalist business enterprise, the free market, the industrial factory, the bureaucratic organization, the legal system, and other institutional realms, social relationships become increasingly divorced from ethical considerations. The rationalized world is one in which people, who from a moral outlook might be conceived as unique individuals deserving kindness, sympathy, and respect, are treated instead in an impersonal, objective, and matter-of-fact manner—as cases in a courtroom, clients in a bureaucracy, competitors in a market, or employees in a workplace.

Formal rationality is a systematizing and regulative force, making the world more calculable, orderly, and predictable, but at the same time it is an ethically irrational force, undermining the motivating power of value-laden religious beliefs, moral ideals, and political principles. The presence of this contradiction is, for Weber, the price we pay for living in a modern society.

In offering this diagnosis of the modern condition, therefore, Weber's intention, in contrast to Marx and Durkheim, is not to provoke social change or set forth an agenda for social reform but rather to alert us to certain "uncomfortable facts" and compel us to see "the realities of life in all their starkness."[67]

MARX, DURKHEIM, AND WEBER
ON THE MODERN CONDITION

What are the defining characteristics of the modern era? What new economic, political, cultural, and social forces are at play? What are the chief ailments of the modern world, what are their causes, and how might they be remedied? What is the trajectory of modern society, where are we headed, and on what grounds might we be either optimistic or pessimistic about the future? These are among the key questions raised by Marx, Durkheim, and Weber. But as we have seen in this chapter, and as we will see further in the chapters to follow, they differ in their analyses of the modern condition and in their beliefs about what we can and should do to make the world a better place. These differences give us the opportunity to compare three provocative yet conflicting perspectives on the problems and possibilities of modern life. Setting Marx, Durkheim, and Weber against one another in this manner also provides us with an abundance of ideas and insights that we can draw upon to deepen our own thinking about the modern world and reexamine our own intellectual assumptions and political identities.

The Diagnosis of Modernity

Marx's diagnosis of the modern condition calls attention to the exploitation, immiseration, and alienation of the working class. These problems derive from the inner logic of capitalism and the inherently antagonistic relationship between the capitalist class and the working class. Durkheim's diagnosis underlines the pathologies of egoism, anomie, and injustice. These problems arise from the absence of a regulative framework appropriate to the industrial era. Weber's diagnosis singles out the process of rationalization, the threat of bureaucratic domination, and the impersonality and ethical indifference of modern social institutions. These problems originate from realities of modern life that are largely inescapable.

Marx adopts a distinct vantage point in his diagnosis of the modern condition. First, more so than either Durkheim or Weber, he conceives the modern society of his day as foremost a capitalist society, and he puts forward a theory of modernity that takes the form of a theory of capitalism. For Marx, there is virtually no quality of modern life that can be adequately comprehended in isolation from the workings of the capitalist economic system. Second, his perspective is unique also for its focus on the "fate of the working class." He urges us to consider an often neglected phenomenon—how the functioning of the capitalist mode of production specifically affects the lives of workers, the millions of people who perform society's labor. Third, his analysis of the dynamics of capitalism and the circumstances of the working class is notable as well for the light it sheds on the "hidden abode of production." Marx's thinking about the modern condition stands out for directing our attention to the innermost recesses of the capitalist system and the daily experiences of wage laborers inside the capitalist workplace. Fourth, his view of modern society differs also because he perceives capitalism not as the endpoint of human history, but as a passing stage in the process of social evolution. Marx foresees the future development of a higher form of modern society, a modern socialist society.

Durkheim conceives the modern society of his day as an industrial society. The defining characteristic of this society is the division of labor. People in the modern world, unlike their pre-modern counterparts, occupy specialized roles and perform specialized tasks. Despite his perception of its essentially industrial nature, however, what most distinguishes the modern era for Durkheim is not the presence of a new mode of production or increasing technological innovation or growth in the productivity of labor. The advent of modernity gives rise to a new economic order to be sure, but it is not the narrowly economic dimension of this order that attracts Durkheim's attention. What most interests him, rather, is the quality of the social relationships and social bonds that characterize a modern industrial society. With the expansion of the specialized division of labor, people more and more relate to one another through exchanges and contracts, they become dependent on one another, they forge a multitude of cooperative ties, and they come to see that they are part of something larger than themselves. As individuals join together in this new way, they are compelled to develop a set of moral rules to regulate their interactions—to define what is right and wrong, lawful and unlawful, just and unjust. Typically regarded only in its economic aspect, the real significance of the division of labor, according to Durkheim, is that it gives rise to a new moral and legal order and a new set of collective beliefs and sentiments. While Marx analyzes modern industry with the aim of disclosing the dynamics of the capitalist economic system, Durkheim's purpose, by contrast, is to reveal the foundations of a new and uniquely modern moral framework.

Durkheim acknowledges, however, that the establishment of such a framework takes time. At the present, he observes, the old world has not yet completely died out, and the new world has not yet been fully born. Modern society is an *industrial* society, but it is still an *immature* industrial society. More specifically, he argues, while the industrial economy has experienced explosive growth, the development of a suitable system of moral rules lags behind, leaving modern economic life in a state of moral anarchy. For Durkheim, this moral impoverishment is modern society's central problem, not the private ownership of the means of production. The crisis of modernity, he argues, is ultimately *moral* rather than *economic* in nature. It is not due to the contradictions of an aging capitalism, but to the moral disorganization of a still youthful industrial society. Nor is this pathological state an inherent outgrowth of modern industry. It is rather a temporary and abnormal by-product of a difficult period of transition. Durkheim is confident that with the passage of time and the implementation of modernizing reforms, including particularly the creation of corporate organizations, the malaise of modern society will be resolved, and without the need for violent revolution. [68]

For Weber the modern society of his day is characterized by the prevalence of formal rationality. Social practices and arrangements are formally rational to the extent that they operate according to standardized rules, written regulations, and established protocols. Formal rationality is a systematizing and organizing force; it contributes to making modern life more orderly, calculable, and predictable. We see this kind of rationality on display in the operation of the modern state and the private business enterprise, in the factory and the market, in the military and the legal system, in science and education, and nearly everywhere else we might look. For Weber, in contrast to both Marx and Durkheim, what most distinguishes the modern western world is the ubiquity of this peculiar rationality.

Although he shares with Marx an understanding of the coercive dynamics of the capitalist mode of production, Weber's diagnosis of the modern condition attributes greater importance to the bureaucratic nature of modern society than to its capitalist nature, and he attributes greater importance also to the danger of bureaucratic domination than he does to the danger of class domination. Bureaucracy, according to Weber, is the epitome of formal rationality. Evident especially in government and industry, bureaucratic administration is also a pervasive phenomenon. We might even say that for Weber modern society is essentially a bureaucratic society. In any case, this is certainly the characteristic of the modern world that draws his attention. Because of its technical efficiency, Weber asserts, bureaucracy is indispensable to the functioning of modern social institutions, but it is also a worrying system of power. The expansion of bureaucracy, he argues, imperils the freedom of the individual, limits the scope for effective and creative leadership, gives birth to a timidly bureaucratic self, fashions an increasingly orderly and regimented world, and exacerbates the tendency toward social and cultural stagnation.

The process of rationalization according to Weber not only shapes the functioning of modern social institutions; it also engenders social relationships of a uniquely modern form. In the modern rationalized world, he observes, people's relations with one another take on an increasing impersonal and matter-of-fact quality, as in the case of market transactions and legal processes. Such relations are not only bereft of emotion, but they are also free of ethical considerations. The affairs of the modern business enterprise and the modern bureaucratic organization, for example, are not governed by ethical norms or moral principles. They are instead carried out according to monetary calculations, standardized procedures, or legal precepts. Social relations in the modern rationalized world, Weber finds, are characterized by impersonality and ethical indifference.

The contrast on this issue between Weber and Durkheim is striking. While Weber sees the rise of modern society as resulting in the *de-moralization* of human relationships, Durkheim envisions a process of *re-moralization*. The division of labor, he argues, establishes ties between people that are bound to produce empathic feelings of interdependence, an increase in sympathy and compassion, and a growing recognition that every individual is deserving of dignity and respect. For Weber, on the other hand, the predominant tendency in modern society is toward the depersonalization and dehumanization of interpersonal relationships. Modern individuals relate to one another according to rules and regulations, as in bureaucratic organizations and the legal system, or in a purely calculative and instrumental manner, as in the workplace and the market. While Durkheim anticipates a future in which collective moral principles and ideals play a larger and larger role in modern life, Weber denies that a unifying moral framework is conceivable in the modern disenchanted and pluralistic world. Moral ideals might survive the process of rationalization, he acknowledges, but they can exist only in the form of antagonistic individual value commitments.

In his writings on the pathologies of the modern era, "Marx proposes a therapy," Karl Löwith observes, as does Durkheim, I would add. Weber, however, "has only a 'diagnosis' to offer." As a judgment of Weber, this is not altogether true, but Löwith certainly has a point. Weber does not propose any grand solutions to the problems of humanity. He presents himself instead as a gloomy realist, warning against the refusal "to see uncomfortable facts and the realities of life in all their starkness." Many of the most disturbing features of the modern era, including those cited by Marx and Durkheim, are, according to Weber, simply unavoidable. Inequality, domination, injustice, coercion, alienation, conflict—these "realities of life" can only be endured; they cannot be overcome. They are among the ineradicable conditions of human existence. Though Weber seems naturally inclined toward the view that things are likely to get worse, he nevertheless holds out the promise that things might instead get better. Change is possible, he recognizes, but any conceivable change is possible only within rather narrow limits. This somber vision of human history places him in opposition to Marx and Durkheim, both of whom foresee a much brighter future on the horizon.[69]

Progress and Social Change

Marx, Durkheim, and Weber differ in how they view both the present and the future. They differ also in how they imagine the present giving way to the future, with each assuming a different developmental logic and each perceiving a different pattern of social change. For Marx, the process of economic development plays the pivotal role in shaping the course of history. He highlights in particular the tendency, greatly accelerated with the rise of capitalism, for the forces of production to accumulate over time. The result is a more or less continuous growth in human productive power. This wealth-producing potential in turn, by making it possible for individuals to be liberated from the oppression of alienated labor, creates the economic underpinnings for a future socialist society. Marx's theory of history thus implies a concept of progress.

The same is true for Durkheim. But while Marx gives primacy to economic forces, Durkheim gives primacy to cultural forces. Just as the advent of modernity for Marx unleashes society's productive power, so too for Durkheim does it unleash certain irresistible collective sentiments and ideals. Modern society, he argues, is impelled forward by a collective need for justice and a collective belief in the sanctity of the individual. Firmly rooted in the conditions of modern life, these powerful moral impulses, he suggests, push society in the direction of a more rational and humane social order. Both Marx and Durkheim are optimistic about the course of social change. They both see dynamics at work in modern society—economic dynamics for Marx and cultural dynamics for Durkheim—that portend a better future.

The same cannot be said for Weber. As Jeffrey Alexander observes, Weber "did not see hopeful and progressive signs in the empirical development of Western society either in the short or in the long run." Indeed, Weber rejects the "ideology of progress" altogether, partly because he denies that there is any scientific or objective metric according to which one can assess whether things are getting better or worse. In any case, Weber suggests, the evolution of modern society, understood as a process of rationalization, does not unequivocally imply human progress, *however* this might be defined. It does not bring us moral certainty, or peace, or justice, or happiness; nor does it free us from the uncomfortable realities of modern life. The modern world for Weber is a new world certainly, qualitatively different from the pre-modern world. But it cannot be conceived as a stage in the inevitable advancement of humankind. One can identify achievements associated with modernity, particularly in the areas of science and technology, but whether these necessarily translate into an improvement in the well-being of society or in the circumstances of the individual is questionable.[70]

The End of History?

Marx, Durkheim, and Weber agree that the rise of the modern industrial economy constitutes a fundamental break from the pre-modern past. For Marx, this transition represents the triumph of capitalist exploitation over feudal exploitation; for Durkheim, organic solidarity over mechanical solidarity; and for Weber, economic rationalism and rational authority over economic traditionalism and traditional authority. On one key point, however, Marx's analysis of the transition from the past to the present differs from that of Durkheim and Weber. Despite his recognition of capitalism's profoundly unique and revolutionary nature, Marx perceives more continuity in the passage from the pre-modern world to the modern world than does either Durkheim or Weber. Like slavery and feudalism before it, Marx notes, capitalism too is an exploitative class society. It is an economic system, similar to preceding modes of production, in which a dominant class appropriates the surplus or unpaid labor of a subordinate class. In "its limited bourgeois form" and with its antagonistic class relations, the modern epoch, Marx argues, is still part of the "prehistory of human society." The victory of capitalism, he suggests, is not so much the beginning of a new era as it is the final stage of an old era.[71]

In contrast to Marx, both Durkheim and Weber leave the impression that the modern world as they perceive it—whether capitalist or socialist—will remain essentially the same into the foreseeable future. Neither views the society of their day as set in stone, of course, but neither do they anticipate anything fundamentally different. For Durkheim, modern society is still in its infancy, neither completely formed nor fully separated from the past. The world of the future, he believes, will take the form of a more mature and "normal" extension of the world that currently exists. He does not imagine a radical departure, but rather a working out and refinement of ideals and institutions already inscribed within the present. For Durkheim, in agreement with Marx, the society of the future will be a qualitatively *better* society. It will not be a qualitatively *different* society, however, unlike Marx's socialism, but rather an improved version of what is already in place.

Weber's conception of modernity allows for less wiggle room than is true for either Marx or Durkheim. With the appearance of the modern world, Weber argues, certain inexorable forces are set in motion—rationalization, bureaucratization, industrialization, and disenchantment. These forces establish the parameters of any possible future. In agreement with Durkheim, accordingly, Weber does not anticipate a world that will be qualitatively *different* from the present. But in contrast to both Durkheim and Marx, he also does not anticipate a world that will be qualitatively *better* than the present. Indeed, to the extent that his fears of an iron cage are realized, the future might even be worse. The question for Weber is not how we might create a more perfect society, but how we might contain the threat of bureaucratic domination and respond intelligently to the harsh realities of modern life. His diagnosis of the modern condition, as Stephen Kahlberg reminds us, leaves room for alternative paths of societal development. But any future, Weber suggests, throwing cold water on utopian dreams, will certainly be a recognizable variation on what currently exists.[72]

Weber envisions neither a qualitatively different society in the future nor a qualitatively better society. Durkheim envisions a qualitatively better society, but not one that is qualitatively different. Marx envisions a qualitatively different society, and one that is also qualitatively better—a "higher form of society in which the full and free development of every individual forms the ruling principle." Though he attributes profound significance to the passage from feudalism to capitalism, Marx foresees another stage of historical development, a transition still to come from a modern capitalist society to a modern socialist society. For Marx, in contrast to Durkheim and Weber, the story of modernity has yet another chapter.[73]

Chapter Six

The Fate of the Individual

The individual and individualism—as philosophical constructs, normative ideals, and objects of empirical inquiry—have been among the most enduring interests of sociology and social theory. When first introduced into the public discourse in nineteenth-century Europe, the term "individualism" evoked two different sets of ideas. On the one hand, it signified a *political* creed exalting the "Rights of Man" and the sovereignty of the individual. On the other hand, it signified an *economic* creed extolling free market economics and the unfettered pursuit of self-interest. Both conceptions were modern in origin, the first growing out of the Enlightenment and the French Revolution, and the second accompanying the rise of laissez-faire capitalism. Whether political or economic, the phenomenon of individualism initially aroused fears of anarchy and dissolution, with conservative defenders of the old regime first sounding the warning bell. But over the course of the nineteenth century, individualism acquired a more positive connotation. It still had its dark side in the form of unrestrained egoism, but when understood as referring to the sanctity of the person, individualism ultimately attained membership—along with freedom and equality, liberty and democracy, reason and autonomy—in the pantheon of modernity's cherished ideals. [1]

Here lies the paradox. While modern culture consecrated the principles of freedom, autonomy, and individualism, modern institutions threatened to undermine those ideals at their very inception. What modernity gave with one hand, it took away with the other. How can individual rights and liberties thrive in the shadow of the modern bureaucratic state? How can individuals develop fully their human qualities when confined to a tiny niche in the specialized division of labor? How is human dignity possible in a world populated by self-interested competitors, each perpetually at war with the other? What remains of equality and autonomy when people are trapped in the impersonal market economy and the despotic capitalist workplace?

Marx, Durkheim, and Weber each attribute great value to personal freedom and individual dignity. And while well aware of the perilous circumstances of the individual, they each believe that modern society contains within itself the means through which an authentic and worthy form of individualism might yet be realized. For Marx, the logic of capitalism demands the exploitation, immiseration, and alienation of the working class. But the dynamics of capitalist development also prepare the way for a socialist future in which "the full and free development of every individual forms the ruling principle." For Durkheim, the rapid emergence of the modern industrial economy gives rise to egoism, anomie, and injustice. But within the womb of modern society a new moral order is being born, with the individual destined to become the sacred object of a secular "religion of humanity." For Weber, the process of rationalization threatens to leave the individual imprisoned in the iron cage of the "modern economic order." But that same process endows individuals with a capacity for self-empowerment and the inner resources necessary for constructing a meaningful life.[2]

KARL MARX: FREE INDIVIDUALITY

Capitalism is often presumed to be the only economic system consistent with the values of individualism and freedom. By comparison, communism (or socialism) is thought to be a vastly inferior alternative. Marx offers a diametrically opposed opinion. Capitalism, he claims, frustrates the full development of human individuality and the full flourishing of human freedom. These ideals, he insists, can be truly realized only in a communist society. In the United States, certainly, this assessment is likely to be greeted by eye-rolling skepticism if not worse. But it is precisely because his perspective is so contrary to today's conventional wisdom that Marx is still interesting, and worth taking seriously. He challenges us to reflect on our usage of the terms "individualism" and "freedom," consider what social conditions are necessary to fulfill these ideals, think critically about how well capitalism serves the higher needs of the individual, and ponder what a communist future might mean for the quality of human life.

Capitalism, Communism, and Individuality

Ian Forbes describes Marx as a "theorist of individuality." The object of Marx's interest, however, is not the individual in the abstract conceived apart from history, but "real living individuals" situated within historically specific conditions of production. As material beings living in a material world, humans satisfy their subsistence needs by utilizing their collective labor to appropriate the fruits of nature, everything from food to fuel. A requisite of social existence, this labor process, Marx argues, is the primary medium through which humans develop their individuality and fashion a way of life. As they enter into the struggle with nature, individuals exercise and refine their species' powers and capacities, in the process creating new qualities, new abilities, and new forms of association. What individuals are and how they relate to one another, Marx says, coincide "with *what* they produce and with *how* they produce."[3]

On the basis of this materialist perspective, Marx examines the formation and expression of individuality in different historical periods and under different modes of production. More specifically, he posits a three-stage process of development, with each stage corresponding to a particular economic epoch: (1) pre-capitalist society, (2) capitalist society, and (3) communist society. With the passage from one epoch to the next, individuals become increasingly autonomous and more fully capable of self-directed agency. His conception of the individual parallels his conception of the forces of production: over the long course of history, both are progressively liberated from constraining social conditions.[4]

The Individual in Pre-Modern, Pre-Capitalist Society

Individuals in the pre-capitalist world, Marx states, are bound by "relations of personal dependence." Absorbed in the group, they belong "to a greater whole"—the family, the clan, or the simple self-sufficient community. Neither free nor equal, pre-modern people are imprisoned within a fixed and seemingly natural social order, with their rights, duties, and obligations originating from their place within the hierarchy of traditional social relations. Submerged within their inherited roles, their personal identities are inseparable from their predetermined social identities. They exist not so much as differentiated individuals but as occupants of socially defined positions, for example, landlord and serf. And while they relate to one another personally, they do so, as Carol Gould explains, not as individuals per se, but "in accordance with their status, role, and function within the community." In this pre-modern stage of human development, for Marx as for Durkheim, the individual as a person in his or her own right barely exists. [5]

The Individual in Capitalist Society

The capitalist revolution inaugurates a world-changing transformation, undermining the communal existence of the pre-modern era. It eradicates the "motley feudal ties that bound man to his 'natural' superiors" and sweeps away "all traditional, confined, complacent, encrusted satisfactions of present needs." The spread of the market economy releases the individual from the parochialism of "old ways of life" and stimulates constant change in methods of production and patterns of consumption. New human capacities and needs arise, setting the stage for the "cultivation of all the qualities of the social human being." Capitalism, for Marx, is a "civilizing influence," not only because it accelerates the growth of productive forces, but also because it rescues the individual from archaic relations of "personal dependence" and creates the material conditions for the appearance of an "all-sided" and "rich individuality." [6]

In the transition from pre-capitalist to capitalist society, the circumstance of the individual undergoes a corresponding change, from "personal dependence" to "personal independence." But within the framework of capitalism, this newfound individuality is both greatly limited and partially illusory. Despite the abolition of feudal bonds, relations of domination persist, but in a disguised form. The personal independence of the individual, manifest especially in the freedom to engage in market transactions, is "founded on *objective* dependence." While in the pre-capitalist stage the dependence of the individual "appears as a personal restriction" of one individual by another—the serf by the lord, for example—in the capitalist stage this dependence takes the form of "an objective restriction of the individual" by abstract socioeconomic forces. Marx's usage of the term "*objective* dependence" is meant to capture the unique nature of modern forms of power—their impersonal, autonomous, and even invisible quality. To put it simply, while individuals in the pre-capitalist period are subordinated to their social superiors, individuals in the era of capitalism are subordinated to the system itself whose presence they experience as an objective reality, an "external necessity." As independent participants in relations of exchange, beholden to no one, individuals *imagine* themselves to be freer than ever, but they are in fact less free, Marx says, "because they are to a greater extent governed by material forces . . . over which they, as separate individuals, have no control."[7]

The Individual in Communist Society

The evolution of the individual is limited by "relations of personal dependence" in the pre-capitalist stage, with individuality sacrificed to community, and by "personal independence founded on *objective* dependence" in the capitalist stage, with community sacrificed to a stunted, egoistic individuality. In the third stage, the communist stage, relations of class domination give way to a "real community" of freely associating individuals, a synthesis of individuality and community. The defining characteristic of this culminating stage, Marx says, is "free individuality."[8]

Just as capitalism represents an advance over pre-capitalist society, so too, Marx argues, does communism represent an advance over capitalist society. Communism makes possible what capitalism precludes: the opportunity for every individual to achieve their potential and develop their human capacities to their fullest. Most people under capitalism, forced to sell their labor power to earn a living, enjoy a limited freedom at best. Though no longer subject to the authority of the feudal lord, they nevertheless remain subservient to a system of production they encounter as an alien power "existing outside them as their fate." With communism, Marx maintains, the situation is reversed. The system of production is subordinated to the "power of the united individuals," to their collective will, "manageable by them as their common wealth." While capitalism compels the individual to serve the goal of production, under communism by contrast, production, now under "communal control," is organized to serve the needs of the individual. With this transformation in the social relations of production, according to Marx, the era of human servitude, the "prehistory of human society," comes to an end.[9]

Capitalism, Communism, and Freedom

Marx's perspective on individuality rests on his concept of freedom. What he means by freedom will become clearer as we go on, but for a start it is fair to say that for Marx freedom implies self-determination, "the positive power" of individuals to assert their "true individuality." The freedom of the individual in this sense, in contrast to a nowadays fashionable view, requires much more than simply limiting the scope of government. "Real freedom," Marx argues, exists only where individuals have control over their own labor, where as workers they have the right to choose their own goals and realize their own aims. By this criterion, he suggests, the capitalist mode of production is anything but a *free* economy. [10]

Marx distinguishes between capitalism on the one hand and slavery and serfdom on the other. All three are class societies, each with a dominant class living off the unpaid labor of a subordinate class. But the status of the "direct producers" in these three modes of production differs. While the slave belongs to the slave owner and the serf belongs to the land, the wage laborer is a free person. For Marx, however, a closer look reveals that the free worker has more in common with the slave and the serf than the defenders of capitalism would care to admit. He sometimes even refers to the "slavery" or "enslavement" or "servitude" of the supposedly free worker. What makes capitalism different, however, is that wage laborers *appear* to be free. Unlike slaves or serfs, they are not coerced to perform unpaid labor by custom, law, or any other "direct extra-economic force." They are *legally* free, but they are constrained by their "*objective* dependence," by their economic standing as a propertyless mass. The working class is forced to labor not by the dictates of any particular authority, hence the illusion of freedom, but by the "silent compulsion of economic relations." [11]

In the following pages I explain Marx's thinking about the conflict between capitalism and freedom more fully, focusing in turn on (1) the limited freedom of the free market, (2) the absence of freedom in the capitalist workplace, (3) the confiscation of workers' free time, and (4) workers' lack of opportunity to develop their human potential.

The Illusory Freedom of the Market

In the market, the sphere of exchange, "free persons" gather as independent individuals, "equal before the law," obeying nothing other than their own "free will." When the commodity labor power is in play, capitalists appear in the market as buyers, looking to hire, and workers appear as sellers, looking for a job. They each need the other, a perfectly free and reciprocal relationship. Mutual self-interest, so it seems, is the "only force bringing them together." [12]

The illusion that capitalists and workers meet in the market under conditions of "equality and freedom" is sustained only by viewing them as abstract individuals, ignoring their class circumstances. In reality, Marx asserts, workers, needing to earn a living and possessing only their bodies and minds, have little choice but to sell their labor power to the capitalist owners of the means of production. Unlike slaves or serfs, he observes, workers are "formally" free. They are not compelled to sell themselves to any capitalist in particular, and are periodically at liberty to change "masters," but they cannot survive for long without selling themselves to one capitalist or another.[13]

Some workers, Marx admits, will find a way to escape the system or even join the ranks of the bourgeoisie, but for the working class as a whole, freedom from wage labor is not an option. What makes work compulsory in the capitalist system is that individuals who choose not to work will starve. The wage laborer, unlike the slave, is not "held in chains," but he is tied to "his owner by invisible threads," "compelled to sell himself of his own free will." Workers are imprisoned by the system itself, which produces and reproduces their "perpetual dependence," ensuring their ongoing subservience to the capitalist class. For Marx, in sum, because workers are forced to sell their labor power to capitalists, they experience only the semblance of freedom, not the real thing.[14]

The Despotism of the Workplace

While in the marketplace the two classes meet as buyers and sellers of labor power, in the workplace they confront one another formally as capitalists and workers. Here even the semblance of freedom vanishes. Once workers cross the threshold into the factory, they are unequivocally subject to the rule of the capitalist class. When workers agree to a labor contract, they effectively relinquish their freedom, ceding control over their labor power to their employer, who thereby gains "command over the use of workers' bodies and their persons." Within the workplace, wage laborers are subject to capitalist authority, tethered to the predetermined routine of the labor process, relegated to a "one-sided vocation" within the detailed division of labor, and subsumed under the mechanized system of machine production. Workers receive a wage in return for the alienation of their labor. But to earn this "mess of pottage," as Marx calls it, they pay a heavy price. Their essential life activity, their capacity for labor, is reduced to a mere instrument of production.[15]

The Appropriation of Time

Disposable time is an essential element of freedom for Marx and a precondition for individual self-realization. Free time, he says, including both "idle time" and "time for higher activity," is a prerequisite for human development. It is "real wealth," the leeway to act "according to one's inclinations" and the opportunity "for enjoyment, for leisure." Indicative of their impoverishment, however, workers in capitalist society suffer from a shortage of free time. "Apart from the mere physical interruptions by sleep, meals, and so forth," their lives serve only one purpose: to feed capitalism's voracious appetite for surplus value. Bound to the wage-labor system and deprived of free time, the worker, Marx declares, is "less than a beast of burden."[16]

Besides extracting unpaid labor from the working class, capitalists also usurp workers' time. In capitalist society, Marx says, "free time is produced for one class by the conversion of the whole lifetime of the masses into labour-time." In short, the labor expended by workers begets the leisure enjoyed by capitalists. The "free development" of the capitalist class, Marx states, "is based on the *overwork*, the *surplus labour* time," of the working class, which is left with no time for its own "free development." When capitalists exploit workers, therefore, they not only appropriate their labor power; they also appropriate the time workers might otherwise use freely to cultivate their human faculties.[17]

Capitalism is deeply inhumane, according to Marx, but as he stresses, it is also a historically progressive system, preparing the way for a better society in the future. The issue surrounding the use and distribution of time brings the contradictory nature of capitalism into full view. When capitalists seek to boost productivity by introducing more and more efficient machinery, their aim is not to shorten the workday but to increase profitability by economizing on labor and cheapening the costs of production. This dynamic results in the growth of society's productive power and a reduction in the human energy required in the labor process, in the total number of labor hours it takes to make a car, for example. In this manner, capitalism, "despite itself," is an emancipatory force. By exploiting advances in science and technology, it creates the possibility for reducing labor time "for the whole society to a diminishing minimum, and thus to free everyone's time for their own development." Within the framework of capitalism, however, this opportunity is squandered, as gains from increasing productivity are instead pocketed by the capitalist in the form of profit. But in a socialist society, Marx argues, where machinery is freed to serve the needs of the individual, the development of the forces of production will "rebound" to the benefit of the working class in the form of free time.[18]

Under capitalism, time is money; it is a "dominating, alien force." Under communism, time is freedom; it is a "'space' for the development of human capacities." The emancipation of the individual, as conceived by Marx, is a matter of unleashing society's productive power for the purpose of extending free time as far as possible. In a well-known passage, Marx draws the connection between free time and "free individuality." Freedom, he states,

> can consist only in this, that socialized man, the associated producers, govern the human metabolism with nature in a rational way, bringing it under their collective control instead of being dominated by it as a blind power; accomplishing it with the least expenditure of energy and in conditions most worthy and appropriate for their human nature. The true realm of freedom, the development of human powers as an end in itself, begins beyond it, though it can only flourish with this realm of necessity as its basis. The reduction of the working-day is the basic prerequisite.

The productive potential created by capitalism can in a future society be rationally utilized to reduce the "realm of necessity," the period of time people must devote to producing their means of subsistence, and increase the "realm of freedom," the free time people have at their disposal to develop their human nature.[19]

The distinction between the realm of freedom and the realm of necessity, as James Klagge observes, is a distinction between productive activity that is an end in itself and productive activity that is a means to an end. Marx recognizes that in no society can necessary labor be entirely eliminated, but it need not be forced or alienating. Productive activity, even when necessary, is free to the extent that (1) it is subject to the rational and democratic control of the "associated producers"; (2) it is voluntary, the expression of free choice, not imposed on the individual by an external force; (3) it is agreeable, carried out under conditions "worthy" of and "appropriate" to human nature; (4) it is organized so that no worker is confined to "one exclusive sphere of activity," thus preventing the one-sided crippling of the individual; and (5) it is a communal activity where work is fairly divided among able-bodied persons, ensuring that "one section of society" does not benefit at the expense of another.[20]

Real human freedom, in this vision, requires reducing the realm of necessity to a minimum, thus enabling individuals to spend the bulk of their time engaged in pursuits of their own choosing. Real human freedom also requires restructuring the realm of necessity, thus liberating individuals from exploitation, immiseration, and alienation even in the performance of necessary labor. The abolition of capitalism, for Marx, is an essential precondition for achieving this real freedom.

Freedom, Self-Realization, and Human Flourishing

Marx criticizes the capitalist system not primarily because it is wasteful or because it widens the gap between the rich and the poor, but because it restricts individual self-development and human freedom. The problem with capitalism, he suggests, is not that it is *too* individualistic, but that it is not individualistic *enough*. It allows for a limited individualism only, a selfish and paltry form of individualism. With the rise of capitalism, the individual is *set loose*, released from the constraints of the feudal order, but not *set free*. The predicament in capitalist society is that individuals have little real control over their own lives. They are personally independent but utterly powerless, effectively enslaved by an economic system where profit making is the prime directive. What capitalism elicits is a form of individualism distorted by the absence of freedom.

The concept of "self-realization" or "free individuality" is the underpinning of Marx's condemnation of capitalism and his commitment to socialism. A good society for Marx is one that promotes the all-around cultivation of human qualities, the full realization of the individual's capacities and needs, and the "absolute working out of his creative potentialities." The primary avenue for individuals to pursue their self-realization, according to Marx, is labor broadly speaking, including work in the narrow sense but also activities ranging from gardening to cooking, from playing a musical instrument to writing a book. Free labor in this sense is not merely "fun" and "amusement," Marx insists, but "damned serious, the most intense exertion." In fact, he suggests, work is most liberating when it is demanding, when it requires the "overcoming of obstacles."[21]

Though he attributes great importance to individual freedom and individual self-realization, Marx does not perceive any necessary opposition between "free individuality" and "true community." A social or communal life, he believes, is essential for individuals to flourish. We affirm ourselves through our work by satisfying the needs of others and by winning their recognition for our accomplishments. The human animal, furthermore, as a "social being," is capable of individuation, "personal freedom," and the cultivation of "his gifts" only in a communal context. In the "real community" of the future, he declares, "individuals obtain their freedom in and through their association." While in capitalist society the individual achievement of one person comes at the expense of another, in the communist society pictured by Marx, the "free development of each is the condition for the free development of all."[22]

EMILE DURKHEIM: MORAL INDIVIDUALISM

Durkheim is famous for proclaiming the priority of society over the individual. The job of sociology, as he conceives it, is precisely to establish the superiority of society and cultivate a "collective spirit." Among the most important practical services sociology can perform, he asserts, is to promote respect for society, to "make the individual understand what society is, how it completes him, and how little he really is when reduced to his own forces alone." The educational system too has a role to play in combating excessive individualism and nurturing a social consciousness. The chief imperative for schools, he argues, is to make children aware of society's transcendent reality and instill in them an "inclination toward collective life" and a "spirit of association."[23]

Given his seeming deification of society, one might think that Durkheim is an anti-liberal antagonist of individualism. This is far from true. While he rails against individualism of a certain type, he is also a fervent defender of the rights and dignity of the individual and the principles of free thought, free inquiry, and free discussion. He even singles out as an essential purpose of the modern educational system "to make of the individual an autonomous personality." Though he regards some of its forms as unworthy and harmful, he is anything but an unconditional enemy of individualism.[24]

For Durkheim, there is no contradiction in affirming both the divinity of society and the sacredness of the individual, in part because "individualism itself is a social product," a gift from society. Under normal conditions, the individual and society are not in conflict with one another, and in the modern era, he contends, social solidarity and individual autonomy are mutually reinforcing. One does not have to choose between valuing society and valuing the individual. Far from being an adversary, society is the cradle of individualism and the protector of the individual. The presence of a healthy society is a requirement for the flourishing of individuality. Only "on the condition that he is involved in society," Durkheim maintains, echoing Marx, can the individual "fully realize his own nature."[25]

The Road to Individualism

There are two consciousnesses within the individual, Durkheim declares, a collective consciousness, the set of beliefs and values we share with other members of society, and an individual consciousness, our personal thoughts and feelings. In the early stages of human evolution, where "the individual personality is lost in the depths of the social mass," the collective consciousness predominates, resulting in everyone being like everyone else, leaving little room for diversity. In the pre-modern world, Durkheim says, "society is all, the individual nothing."[26]

But "little by little," as the history of humanity unfolds, "things change." The individual comes to occupy an increasingly prominent place in society. This process of individuation is fueled by the expansion of the division of labor. Roles and occupations become more and more specialized, with each person gravitating toward his or her own particular "sphere of action." People's life conditions become more varied, the power of the collective consciousness diminishes, and the "individual personality grows stronger." In today's world, rather than being steered in an exclusively "collective direction," everyone is "oriented to a different point on the horizon," each seeking their own place within the occupational system. As the power of the group mind decreases, undermining the "old conformism of former times," the individual consciousness attains a measure of independence.[27]

The historical narrative Durkheim constructs—"the road to individualism"—is not one in which individuals emancipate themselves from society, but one in which the evolution of society induces the liberation of the individual. Indeed, he argues, in the pre-modern world, individuality is not suppressed; it simply does not exist. Individualism is not a natural or primordial phenomenon. It is the "fruit of historical development," the product of society itself. Individuals come into their own not in *opposition* to societal demands, but in *response* to societal demands. First, individuals as distinct personalities with diverse aptitudes and aspirations are necessary to fill the varied occupational slots in the division of labor. Second, individuals as autonomous agents capable of reflective thinking are also necessary because in today's society, a premium is placed on reasoning. As traditional beliefs are "swept away," Durkheim explains, people are reliant on their own independent thought processes to navigate their way in the world. Individualism is essential to the existence of modern society because of the need for people able to perform specialized functions and to think for themselves.[28]

As the pre-modern era gives way to the modern era, the moral rules governing people's conduct undergo a corresponding change. In traditional society, the moral duty of the person is to "resemble everyone else," to conform to the "collective type." In modern society, the moral duty of the person is to specialize, to equip oneself *"to fulfill usefully a specific function."* In both cases, however, the rules of conduct that people follow serve social needs and foster social cohesion. The individualism of the modern era is no less a moral obligation than is the conformism of the traditional era. The emancipation of the individual, Durkheim insists, "does not imply a weakening but a transformation of the social bonds. The individual does not tear himself away from society but is joined to it in a new manner."[29]

Individualism as Pathology

Individualism is a requirement for the functioning of modern society. But in the Europe of his day, Durkheim acknowledges, individualism—like the division of labor itself—exists in an abnormal form. Instead of engendering social harmony, it is a disintegrative force. Because of the still incomplete transition from the pre-modern world to the modern world, the inhabitants of today's industrial society live an impoverished collective existence. The rapid pace of social change has left people lacking the two central elements of a moral life: "the spirit of discipline," the absence of which causes anomie, and "attachment to social groups," the absence of which causes egoism. The spirit of discipline is necessary to regulate individuals' desires, limit their otherwise unquenchable aspirations, and orient them toward realizable goals. By ensuring that people pursue achievable ends, moral discipline enables individuals to live happy and balanced lives. The attachment to social groups is necessary to inhibit individuals' egoistic inclinations and orient them toward the "richer reality" of collective interests. By ensuring that people devote themselves to shared ideals, group attachments enable individuals to live meaningful and moral lives. In the distressed state of modern society, however, individuals neither are subject to adequate moral regulation nor possess an adequate group life. Deprived of moral discipline, they are at the mercy of voracious appetites and infinite ambitions, perpetually dissatisfied and frustrated. Deprived of social bonds, they are guided only by considerations of self-interest, inwardly directed, isolated, and socially disengaged. The dilemma for Durkheim is how to remedy the predicament of the individual and resolve the larger crisis of modern society without abandoning the

achievements of modernity or sacrificing the benefits of individuality. He
takes up this issue in the context of the Dreyfus affair of the late 1890s. [30]

Moral Individualism

In 1894, Alfred Dreyfus, a Jewish captain in the French army, was falsely
convicted of treason and served five years of a lifetime sentence before being
exonerated. The politically charged controversy surrounding this case, besides bringing the issue of anti-Semitism to the surface, split the nation. It
pitted the right against the left, the protagonists of a religious authoritarian-
ism against the supporters of a democratic Third Republic, and the military
and the church against liberal-minded intellectuals and academics. In 1898,
in the midst of this divisive conflict, Durkheim, an outspoken supporter of
Dreyfus, published an essay entitled "Individualism and the Intellectuals." In
this defense of modernity, Durkheim offers a powerful response to the anti-
liberal, anti-intellectual, and anti-individualistic standpoint of the partisans of
the old regime. [31]

For traditionalist critics, the egoistic individualism unleashed by the rise
of modern society is an altogether destructive force. On this particular point
Durkheim agrees. The unbridled pursuit of self-interest, with people given
unlimited license to act on their personal desires, is an undeniable threat to
social stability. A "communal life is impossible," he emphasizes, "without
the existence of interests superior to those of the individual." But the solution
is not to renounce modern society, rescind the rights of the individual, or
reestablish the oppressive traditions of the past. "It is a matter of completing,
extending, and organizing individualism," he argues, "not restraining and
combating it." If individualism of one kind is the disease, an individualism of
another kind is the cure. Durkheim envisions the possibility of a new and
distinctly modern social order where the insatiable desires of individuals are
contained and their egoistic urges curbed, but where at the same time the
ideal of individualism is strengthened. His argument hinges on the distinction between moral individualism and egoistic individualism. [32]

Moral Individualism and Egoistic Individualism

In their rush to condemn egoistic individualism, the opponents of modernity,
Durkheim argues, fail to perceive the presence of "another sort of individualism." This is moral individualism, the very antithesis of egoistic (or utilitar-

ian) individualism. The contrast between these two opposing types, described below, is the centerpiece of Durkheim's analysis.[33]

First, egoistic individualism and moral individualism differ in their intellectual and socio-historical origins. The former, celebrated in the writings of orthodox economists, is an outgrowth of a "crass commercialism" and the spread of the market economy. The latter, moral individualism, with its conception of the individual as a being "preeminently worthy of respect," has its roots in the French Revolution, the Declaration of the Rights of Man, and the philosophies of Kant and Rousseau.[34]

Second, for egoistic individualism, the individual in question is the "tangible, empirical" person. For moral individualism, the individual "offered for collective love and respect" is not this or that person but "mankind in general, idealized humanity." Egoistic individualism glorifies the private interests of the particular self, while moral individualism reveres "humanity in the abstract." The first gives priority to the value of personal liberty, the freedom of individuals to act on their own wishes. The second gives priority to the value of human dignity, respect for persons as ends in themselves.[35]

Third, egoistic and moral individualism grow out of different, though equally natural, psychological impulses: desire or egotism on the one hand and sympathy or altruism on the other. Desire is a "centripetal" force. A handmaiden of the self, it looks out for the needs of the individual only. Sympathy is a "centrifugal" force. Directed toward an ideal outside the self, it reaches toward supra-individual ends. Unlike its self-interested opposite, moral individualism embodies a sensitivity "for all that is human, a broader pity for all sufferings, for all human miseries." The motivations underlying egoistic individualism are essentially selfish, while those associated with moral individualism, Durkheim explains, extend our self-regard to concern for others. In the modern world, he proclaims, precisely because each of us is an individual ourselves, "we take sentiments protecting human dignity personally to heart."[36]

Fourth, with egoistic individualism, the actions of the individual are oriented toward the achievement of purely *personal* or amoral objectives. We strive to satisfy our passions, fulfill our needs, and realize our private ambitions. With moral individualism, the actions of the individual are oriented toward the achievement of *impersonal* or moral objectives. We aspire to create a more perfect society and advance the cause of justice. While egoistic individualism "flatters our instincts" and furthers our personal interests, moral individualism "fixes before us an ideal." It offers up a set of shared values, beliefs, and practices that—in sharp contrast to any notion of self-interest—forces "the individual to rise above himself."[37]

Finally, while egoistic individualism is bound up with the development of the modern industrial economy, moral individualism, with scholars and artists among its most vocal champions, emerges in alliance with the growth of reason and science. This sort of individualism, Durkheim says, "implies a certain intellectualism." It "has as its primary dogma the autonomy of reason and as its primary rite the doctrine of free inquiry." It values reflection, freedom of thought, and intellectual independence. The defense of intellectualism is inseparable from the defense of individualism.[38]

For Durkheim, moral individualism arises from the essential conditions of existence of the modern world, and as modern society matures, it is destined to become more and more firmly established. With the advance of civilization, the individual, "originally nothing at all," becomes a sacred object of respect, and individualism becomes a unifying moral ideal, the "rallying-point" of humanity. "Everything indicates," he declares, "that we are becoming more alive to what touches on the human personality."[39]

Moral Individualism as the Religion of Humanity

In the passage from the pre-modern era to the modern era, an essentially religious worldview is replaced by an essentially secular worldview. But if religion is "nothing other than a body of collective beliefs and practices endowed with a certain authority," if it is separated from the idea of a supernatural being, then a religion of a new kind is present even in modern society. The influence of traditional religious beliefs has waned, Durkheim observes, but in their place the individual has become the object of a uniquely modern secular religion. Like its predecessors, this "religion of humanity" has a common faith, a conception of the sacred, and a collection of moral commandments. In this new religion, "man has become a god for men." We no longer pray to the old gods, whose time has now passed, but we do nowadays "worship the dignity of the human person." We perceive the individual as invested with a "sacrosanct character," and we thus regard any harm or injustice inflicted on human beings as "sacrilegious." This new concept of the individual as a "sacred thing par excellence," Durkheim states, is perhaps the "fundamental axiom" of our modern morality. Moral individualism—the "cult of the individual"—takes center stage as the religion of the modern era, "a religion in which man is at once the worshiper and the God."[40]

Because it places before us something we can all believe in, moral individualism is not only the antithesis of egoistic individualism, according to Durkheim, it is also the solution to the social disintegration that egoism causes. The individual pursuit of self-interest pulls us apart, but the ideal of a shared humanity brings us together. "Far from detaching individuals from society and every goal beyond themselves," moral individualism, unlike egoistic individualism, joins "them in a single thought and makes them servants of a single task." The religious quality of moral individualism is manifest in precisely this capacity to forge a "communion of minds and wills" united around a sacred principle and a collective aspiration. This individualistic ethic, Durkheim argues, is in fact "the only system of beliefs which can ensure the moral unity of the country." So while the critics of modernity attack individualism because of its putatively anarchic consequences, Durkheim supports individualism (of a different sort) precisely because it is a source of social solidarity, indeed, "the only tie which binds us all to each other." In defending the "rights of the individual" therefore, he proclaims, one is also defending "the vital interests of society."[41]

Moral Individualism, Moral Education, and Collective Rituals

The ideal of human dignity derives from collective sentiments that are inherent to the modern condition. Moral individualism is an ascendant ethic. But, Durkheim recognizes, it is not yet fully or securely embodied in society's practices and institutions, and it cannot yet claim universal support. He cites, for example, "the extreme ease with which we have accepted an authoritarian regime several times in the course of this century—regimes which in reality rest on principles that are a long way from individualism." To fight "old habits," he emphasizes, it is not enough to enunciate a new doctrine. Society itself must be restructured to make "an individualistic moral code" truly "feasible and durable." As I explain below, the new religion of humanity, Durkheim argues, needs to be nurtured in the minds of each succeeding generation, and it needs to be continuously enlivened in the public consciousness. To achieve the first he proposes a system of moral education, and to achieve the second he calls for periodic collective rituals.[42]

Moral Education. The modern world, Durkheim observes, is in a period of profound transformation, and this in turn demands an equally profound transformation of the educational system. Despite the industrial nature of modern society, what is most needed today is not vocational education but moral and civic education, not the perfection of technical skills but the reshaping of people's ideas, beliefs, and feelings. "It is not a matter of training workers for the factory or clerks for the warehouse," he states, "but citizens for society." This requires, above all else, "moral instruction." The foremost objective of such citizenship education is "to sever minds from selfish views and material interests, to replace a vanishing religious piety by a kind of social piety." In the modern world accordingly, Durkheim explains, the teacher displaces the priest as the "interpreter of the great moral ideas" of the day.[43]

The primary aim of the educational system in the present era, according to Durkheim, is to create the kind of person required by the conditions of modern life. This necessitates two complementary tasks. The first responsibility of the educator is to disseminate the ideals associated with moral individualism—to encourage among students a respect for reason and science, nurture the "sense of the dignity of man," and foster a "greater thirst for justice." The second responsibility of the educator is to transform students into autonomous beings, to ensure they possess a critical mind and a capacity for moral reasoning. The mission of the teacher is not to indoctrinate but to explain, not to instill an unreflective "parrot-like morality" but to promote an "enlightened allegiance" to modern values and ideals. The goal of moral education is to produce intelligent assent not unthinking acquiescence; to motivate individuals to observe moral rules; and to ensure that they do so "consciously and knowing why." For Durkheim, in sum, moral education serves a twofold purpose: to spread the gospel of moral individualism and at the same time contribute to the formation of an autonomous, reflective, and rational individual—in other words, precisely an individual of the sort that is deserving of dignity and respect.[44]

Collective Rituals. It is not enough to educate citizens in the ideals of moral individualism, Durkheim argues. It is also necessary, through "moments of collective ferment," to keep those ideals alive in the hearts and minds of the populace. Public gatherings are essential for stirring people's passions and emotions, breathing life into society's sacred principles, and renewing the common faith in the individual as an "exalted object of moral respect." By inciting enthusiasm and exhilaration, collective rituals temporarily increase the intensity of social existence; they generate a collective energy or vitality, what Durkheim calls "effervescence." Under normal conditions, people are preoccupied by their own private affairs; they retreat into themselves. This weakens the power of social ideals and threatens "moral stagnation." But through ceremonies, parades, celebrations, and other public assemblies—periodic breaks from the ordinary and the routine—individuals, "pressing close to one another," are transported to a higher plane. Reminded of "social things," they reexperience the enrichment of being part of something larger than themselves. Public rites, according to Durkheim, play a key role in reaffirming the "moral identity" of the group, recharging society's commitment to the ethic of individualism and reinforcing the belief in the ideal of humanity.[45]

Moral individualism for Durkheim is a uniquely modern phenomenon, at once an ethical ideal, a collective aspiration, and a cultural imperative. It is embodied in modern society's common consciousness, sentiments, and feelings. No less than industrialization itself, it is a modernizing force, remaking the world. Durkheim envisions a future state where the regulative power of this individualistic ethic helps keep people's otherwise unlimited desires in check; where the presence of this social ideal orients individuals to common ends outside themselves, thus restraining their egoistic instincts; and where the collective need for justice and the belief in the dignity of the individual prohibit the strong from exploiting the weak and the rich from taking advantage of the poor.

MAX WEBER: THE ETHIC OF PERSONALITY

The fate of the individual in the modern era was among Weber's central preoccupations. This concern led him to ask some fundamental questions, both sociological and existential. How can individuals respond in a dignified and responsible manner to the stark realities of modern life? What leeway do they have within the confines of the iron cage to exercise their uniquely human capacity for autonomous agency? What opportunities exist for people to create meaningful lives for themselves in an age of moral uncertainty? In addressing these issues, Weber presents a scholarly diagnosis of the modern condition. But at the same time he sets forth an ethic for the conduct of life, a morally charged statement of how the individual in the modern rationalized world might salvage a measure of freedom and forge an independent "personality."

Unlike the *philosophes* of the Enlightenment, and in contrast to Marx and Durkheim as well, Weber is skeptical about the idea of progress. He certainly does not believe that the course of history is leaning toward the liberation of the individual. Nor does he anticipate that through some radical social transformation humanity will be delivered into a state of peace and happiness.

Though he is not a doomsayer, he does not foresee a particularly bright future either. He is even sometimes said to have a "tragic vision of history." This is not to say, however, that Weber preaches resignation. Just the opposite, in fact. He calls upon individuals to face up to the uncomfortable realities of everyday existence and embrace the world—but on their own terms, guided by their own self-consciously chosen values and principles. Even within the iron cage of modern industrial society, Weber claims, individuals have the resources to carve out a free and meaningful life.[46]

Weber's Concept of Freedom

It is generally agreed that the problem of freedom is a central theme in Weber's work. But his usage of the term is sometimes vague, and its meaning varies from one context to another. Donald Levine clarifies matters by distinguishing between two concepts of freedom in Weber's writings: "situational freedom" and "subjective freedom." The lack of situational freedom refers to an objective state of affairs, a circumstance in which there are material constraints on the alternatives available to individuals and the opportunities they have for acting on their ideals and interests. According to Weber, as we saw in the previous chapter, the two major threats to the situational freedom of the individual just happen to be the two institutional pillars of modern society: capitalism and bureaucracy. The first imperils the freedom of the individual by compelling economic actors to abide by "capitalistic rules of action." The second limits the space for "individually differentiated conduct" by imposing a uniform orderliness on the world. These two fateful forces profoundly shape the options available to us and the lives we lead.[47]

While the concept of situational freedom draws attention to the constraints on the choices people make, the concept of subjective freedom has to do with the quality of those choices. The contrast here is between *being* free, in the sense that alternative lines of action are available to us, and *acting* free, in the sense that our life decisions are reflective rather than reactive, intentional rather than impulsive. We are free in the subjective sense to the extent our actions are *rational*, and they are rational to the extent they cease to be merely emotional or habitual and originate instead from the agency of thoughtful deliberation. As Weber states,

> We associate the highest measure of an empirical "feeling of freedom" with those actions which we are conscious of performing rationally—i.e., *in the*

absence of physical and psychic "coercion," emotional "affects" and "accidental" disturbances of the clarity of judgment, in which we pursue a clearly perceived end by "means" which are the most adequate in accordance with the extent of our knowledge.

While situational freedom varies according to the presence of structural obstacles, subjective freedom varies according to the rational mindfulness of the acting individual. I addressed the problem of situational freedom in Weber's writings in the previous chapter and will continue to explore this theme in the next two chapters. In the following pages, I focus primarily on the issue of subjective freedom.[48]

The Routinization of Everyday Life

Weber calls attention to the coercive conditions of a mature capitalist society and the ever-present threat of bureaucratic domination. Individual freedom, however, is endangered by another, more subtle source as well: the "enslavement to the lifeless routine of everyday existence." Rather than living alert and purposeful lives, individuals instead—in a "state of inarticulate half-consciousness"—may simply give in to the mundane requirements of the daily grind. Narrowing their horizons and focusing on immediate and practical objectives, these "fully-adjusted men of a bureaucratic age" passively adapt to the commonplace exigencies of the everyday world. They go through the motions, fulfilling their daily duties, but they lack any strongly held values or personal convictions to give their lives direction and meaning.[49]

Weber sometimes uses the expression "practical rationalism" to describe this way of being in the world. Individuals exhibit this type of rationalism when they orient themselves toward immediate goals in a pragmatic and utilitarian manner, methodically setting out to attain ends through "an increasingly precise calculation of adequate means." A practical rationalism of this sort is evident in the mind-set that "sees and judges the world consciously in terms of the worldly interests of the individual ego" and, from this standpoint, seeks an expedient accommodation to existing circumstances. Instead of being motivated by deeply felt commitments of a religious or political nature, for example, a practical rational life entails a narrowly self-interested and un-heroic adaptation to things as they are. According to Stephen Kalberg, Weber feared that the "looming onset" of this way of life

"would eventually call forth a stagnant society populated by highly conform-
ing persons lacking high ideals, individualism, and a 'devotion to a cause.'"[50]

Practical rationalism originates from worldly pressures that tempt individuals onto the path of least resistance, inducing them to live orderly and
ordinary lives. Underlining the issue of subjective freedom, Weber claims
that this practical rationalism results also from a failure of individual will.
People get so caught up in the "shallowness" of their "routinized daily existence," he states, that they "do not become aware, and above all do not wish
to become aware" of their potential for autonomous action.

> The fruit of the tree of knowledge, which is distasteful to the complacent but
> which is, nonetheless, inescapable, consists in the insight that every single
> important activity and ultimately life as a whole, if it is not to be permitted to
> run on as an event in nature but is instead to be consciously guided, is a series
> of ultimate decisions through which the soul—as in Plato—chooses its own
> fate, i.e., the meaning of its activity and existence.

For Weber, the modern world is characterized by a plurality of "irreconcilably antagonistic values." Science cannot tell us which of these competing
values we should serve; it cannot tell us how we should live our lives. This
responsibility falls on the shoulders of the "acting willing person." But by
allowing themselves to become habituated to their daily routine, individuals
evade this responsibility. They effectively relinquish the freedom to find
their own causes and choose their own destiny, thus denying themselves the
possibility of living a genuinely meaningful life.[51]

The routinization of modern life and the triumph of an "ethic of 'adaptation'" are indicative of another development: the suppression of value-rational action in favor of instrumentally rational action. These two types of social
action correspond to conflicting "forms of life conduct." The first involves
the "deliberate formulation of ultimate values," and the second involves the
"deliberate adaptation to situations in terms of self-interest." When individuals orient their lives in an instrumentally rational manner, they follow the
dictates of immediate self-interest rather than striving to realize ultimate
values, they adjust to prevailing circumstances rather than seeking to
transcend them, and they accommodate to the world as it is rather than
struggling against it. The tendency in modern society is for instrumentally
rational action to crowd out value-rational action. This development, Weber
suggests, represents the victory of acquiescence over innovation, the ordinary
over the extraordinary. It implies the "waning of charisma" and the "dimin-

ishing importance of individual action." By this, he means action that is subjectively free, motivated by self-chosen value commitments. Instrumental rationality, of course—with its matching of means and ends and weighing of costs and benefits—is an essential element of social action, not something we can do without. But Weber worries about a future in which value-rational action and personal conviction recede into the background, with individuals conducting their lives based exclusively on calculations of advantage.[52]

The Concept of Personality

In reflecting on how individuals might live a dignified and meaningful existence in modern society, Weber, following in the footsteps of Immanuel Kant, arrives at the concept of "personality" (or personhood) as a moral ideal. To the extent the individual achieves personality, his or her life ceases to be an "event in nature," like a leaf floating down a stream, and becomes instead a unified "whole placed methodically under a transcendental goal." The life of a personality, rather than being a mere "series of occurrences," is organized around self-selected values that give it coherence and purpose. These might include personal virtues, like honesty or loyalty, or political causes such as democracy, equality, or nationalism. Regardless of the guiding values one chooses, to possess personality is to be a fully conscious individual, to have a fully integrated identity and to live a fully rational life, one that is subject to willful and rigorous self-discipline. The ethic of personality affirms a way of being in the world that is the antithesis of both an unthinking routinized existence and a practical rational life of adaptation. In what follows, to further clarify Weber's moral vision, I discuss four qualities associated with the idea of personality: (1) the deliberate choice of an ultimate value, (2) the systematic organization of life conduct, (3) vocational specialization, and (4) subjective freedom.[53]

A Commitment to Ultimate Values

The achievement of personality requires a "deliberate formulation of ultimate values." These values make up the "innermost elements" of personality. Like an anchor, they secure the individual's identity, functioning as an "autonomous counterweight" to external pressures. The stabilizing force of these values helps individuals maintain a certain distance from the world, ensuring they do not passively surrender to the circumstances of everyday life. Empowered by strong value commitments, the personality—like the charismatic figure—stands apart from the world and, as Harvey Goldman explains, has "leverage over the world" through the tension that is created "between the believer and the world."[54]

To aspire to personality, individuals, through a value-rational act of self-determination, must make a "decisive choice." They need to decide which of the "warring gods" they will serve and which they will oppose. They need to make clear to themselves what they are for and what they are against. Weber implies that this is perhaps less a choice than a discovery. Since there are no scientifically objective grounds for favoring one value over another, all we can do is search within our own conscience and find and obey "the demon who holds the fibers" of our very existence. Through this process of self-reflection, we reveal to ourselves those values, beliefs, and principles we regard most highly. In so doing, we disclose who we are and where we stand. The hallmark of personality is thus the ideal of the individual who, in "constant thought" and with "constant motives," is dedicated to a purpose or committed to a cause. The "dignity of the 'personality,'" Weber says, "lies in the fact that for it there exist values about which it organizes its life." These values, which supply us with moral imperatives and binding norms for behavior, are what give life "meaning and significance."[55]

A Systematic Ordering of Life Conduct

For individuals to approach the ideal of personality, it is not enough that they make a choice among rival values. They also need to live up to the values they choose. Their actions, their entire life conduct, must consistently reflect their beliefs. The concept of personality, Weber says, "entails a constant and intrinsic relation to certain ultimate 'values' and 'meanings' of life." True personalities—whether their ultimate allegiance is to work or family, to the principle of non-violence or the ideal of feminism—live demanding and methodical lives of devotion. To stay on the path one has chosen requires a vigilant regimen through which the purposeful will of the individual, by repressing the instinctive urges of the self, brings a rational order to one's life. "Whatever the value or object or law one adopts," Harvey Goldman explains, "personality lies in subjecting the self to it and taming desire, feelings, inclination, vanity, and the natural self." For Weber, it is precisely this ceaseless effort to adhere to one's ideals that invests life with integrity, transforming it into something more than a mere string of events.[56]

Vocational Specialization

In the modern industrial era, according to Weber, the vocational sphere is the primary arena in which individuals can aspire to personality. Just as their Protestant ancestors sought salvation through methodical and systematic labor in a calling, so too is vocational specialization the main route for modern individuals to forge a dignified self and prove their worth. A specialized vocation presents individuals with a "definite field" in which they can exert themselves and accomplish something valuable. [57]

The fulfillment of the obligations of one's "professional activity" is an ethical imperative, Weber suggests, a point he underlines in his famous essays on the vocations of politics and science. "Every professional task has its own 'inherent norms' and should be fulfilled accordingly," he states. This demands "self-restraint," the disciplined subordination of one's self to the duties of the job. "In the execution of his professional responsibilities," he continues, "a man should confine himself to it alone and should exclude whatever is not strictly proper to it—particularly his own loves and hates." To be a personality, Weber declares, requires "the whole-hearted devotion" to occupational demands. The paradox, as Harvey Goldman notes, is that for Weber the "elevation of the self" to personhood requires the subordination of the self to vocational duties. Individuals achieve personality only by becoming *servants* to their values, causes, or professional obligations. Self-abnegation is a pre-requisite for self-realization. [58]

Subjective Freedom

The actions of individuals are free, according to Weber, the less they have the character of an "event in nature" and the more they are distinctly human, and they are distinctly human the more they derive from rational judgment—that is, purposive and thoughtful deliberation. Freedom is embodied in actions guided by the autonomous will of the individual. By contrast, freedom is lacking where actions are unthinking responses to external or internal stimuli or are influenced by moods, affects, and other irrational psychological factors. The difference here, as Rogers Brubaker states, is between *human actions* that are "rational, free and meaningful" and *natural events* that are "non-rational, unfree and devoid of meaning." [59]

As Stephen Turner observes, Weber proposes an "ascetic notion of freedom." He locates individual freedom in the "inner quality" of self-control, in the will to reason and choose. Individuals are free when they are unimpeded by impulse or habit and when they self-consciously select their courses of action by reference to their ultimate values and the availability of means necessary to achieve their ends. To accomplish one's purposes "within the world but against it"—this, Karl Löwith explains, "is the positive meaning of the 'freedom of movement' with which Weber was concerned." Freedom in this sense has to do with the ability of individuals, within the limits imposed by situational constraints, to act on their own values and determine their own destinies. The freedom of the individual, fully realized in the ideal of personality, is dependent foremost on self-clarity, self-mastery, and rational judgment. This is the essence of Weber's concept of subjective freedom.[60]

Personality, Individual Freedom, and the Iron Cage

Unless we are prepared to relinquish the benefits of modernity—not even a remotely realistic option in Weber's judgment—we cannot do away with large-scale industry or bureaucratic organization. There is no escape from the essential conditions of modern society, no way out of the iron cage. However, it is possible, he believes, to protect at least some space for individuality through policies that might moderate a maturing capitalism's tendency toward stagnation, restrain the march of bureaucratization, and preserve democratic institutions and civil liberties. Beyond these measures, though, not much else can be done to increase the situational freedom of the individual. The course of history is not set in stone, but one thing is certain: there is no future in which the mass of humanity will be liberated from the coercive conditions of the modern rationalized world.

Nevertheless, Weber insists, individuals do have it within their power to lead free and meaningful lives. Even if there is little latitude for altering the objective circumstances of modern society, how people conduct themselves within those circumstances matters. While they may have limited situational freedom, if individuals possess the necessary inner strength and self-discipline, they can endow their lives with a meaningful purpose. This is where the ethic of personality and subjective freedom come into play. People have no choice but to accommodate to the conditions of modern life, but they do not have to accommodate thoughtlessly or submissively. They can engage the world on their own terms. They can self-consciously organize their lives around ultimate values, devote themselves to a chosen vocation, and commit themselves to fulfilling the "demands of the day." Being trapped within the iron cage does not prevent us from leading attentive, purposeful, and ethical lives. This is Weber's message.[61]

Weber's ethic of personality proposes a response to the modern condition that is individual and existential rather than structural and political, a response that calls for self-transformation rather than societal transformation. Indeed, he contends, there are no viable collective solutions to the predicament of the individual, no prospect for advancing the cause of human freedom through large-scale social change. The only recourse is for individuals themselves to take responsibility for their life outcomes. They are not entirely on their own, however. The formation of personality is a matter of self-examination, but in this process individuals may benefit from a particularly important kind of social support—education, moral education specifically.

First, as we saw in chapter 4, Weber argues that teachers can perform a valuable moral service. They can compel students to recognize the necessity of moral choice, enable them to gain clarity about their own ultimate values, and provide instruction on how to reason logically about ethical matters. A competent teacher can encourage a student to give "*an account of the ultimate meaning of his own conduct*," thus helping that student to develop an independent personality. [62]

Second, Weber also suggests that voluntary organizations can play an important educational and socializing role, shaping the inner life and personality of the individual. He attributes particular significance to "associations of every kind based on *selective* choice of members." Unlike "churches," for example, where membership essentially derives from birth, in selective associations—what Weber calls "sects"—individuals gain admission only by exhibiting high moral standards. They must *earn* membership, and to maintain good standing within the group, with each person keeping a close eye on the other, they must also continuously demonstrate their moral qualifications. These sect-like associations ensure the good character of their members by constantly monitoring behavior and testing moral worth. Both through their exclusivity and their intense supervision, selective associations mold the ethical qualities of members and call upon them to adopt a rationally disciplined organization of life conduct. As with the formal education students receive in the classroom, the informal education acquired from participation in voluntary organizations may also contribute to the moral development of individuals, pushing them to live up to higher ideals. [63]

By adhering to the ethic of personality, the individual can achieve a degree of subjective freedom and create a meaningful life. This is, of course, a purely personal response to the problems posed by the modern condition. It is also a solution possible only for the exceptionally resolute person. The ethic of personality, because of the extraordinary demands it puts on the individual, is what Weber calls a "heroic" ethic as opposed to an "average" ethic. He appears to believe that most people do not have the inner resources necessary to exercise the arduous self-discipline and unceasing devotion required to live a truly purposeful life. The ethic of personality, as Rogers Brubaker observes, implies a "radical bifurcation of humanity": the "mass of men are condemned to the meaninglessness of a merely natural existence; only the ethical virtuosi are privileged to lead a truly human existence." Weber's pessimist analysis of the modern condition leaves him with a solution to the predicament of the individual that is, on the one hand, a purely individual solution and, on the other hand, one available only to the most strong-willed segment of the population. [64]

THE INDIVIDUAL, INDIVIDUALISM, AND MODERNITY

Marx, Durkheim, and Weber demonstrate a shared "moral problematic"—an abiding concern for the freedom and dignity of the individual. They agree also that the *real* state of the individual falls well short of the *ideal* state. The current circumstances of modern society, they find, hinder the ability of individuals to live truly human lives. Their interpretations of this problem reveal significant points of disagreement, however. These in turn are indicative of deeper differences among the three in their conceptions of modern society, their basic sociological assumptions, and their personal political convictions. [65]

Common Ground

There is considerable common ground in the thinking of Marx, Durkheim, and Weber on the individual and individualism. I touch on other commonalities below, but for now I briefly discuss three broad areas of agreement. First, they each repudiate what Steven Lukes calls the idea of the "abstract individual." According to this image, humans are equipped with a fixed human nature, an invariant set of characteristics that exists independently of history and society. While not necessarily denying that human beings are characterized by certain essential qualities, Marx, Durkheim, and Weber attribute far more importance to how individuals are constituted by sociohistorical forces. Marx, for example, describes the individual as an "historical result," "something evolving in the course of history." Durkheim says almost exactly the same thing. It is only through "historical analysis," he writes, that we can "discover what makes up man, since it is only in the course of history that he is formed." Weber argues similarly. The most fundamental character traits of individuals, he claims, are shaped by the "life orders" or institutional environments in which they are located. The kinds of people that come to prevail at any point, according to Weber, are determined by the cultural and organizational characteristics of society.[66]

Second, while all three see the rise of the modern era as creating a profoundly new economic order, they see it as creating a new kind of person as well, a modern individual. Marx calls attention to the "new-fangled" industrial workers of the present day, insisting that they "are as much the invention of modern time as machinery itself." For Durkheim, too, the individual as a being with an autonomous personality exists only in the era of modern industry—thanks primarily to the development of the division of labor. Weber also perceives the emergence of a new "type of *human being*" in the western world, a vocational person, peculiarly devoted to a life of disciplined service in an occupational calling. For all three, in short, modern individuals are something of a unique species of humanity, fundamentally different from their pre-modern counterparts.[67]

Third, Marx, Durkheim, and Weber are in agreement also in rejecting the equation of individualism with the unfettered pursuit of self-interest. Indeed, the vision of individuality they each defend is explicitly conceived in opposition to the egoistic individualism lauded by the mainstream economists of their day. For Marx, the individual of the present era, acting only on "naked self-interest," is a deformed product of a capitalist system that transforms all personal relations into monetary relations. He puts forward instead an ideal in which "free individuality" is achieved not at the expense of others, but only through mutual association in a "real community." Durkheim too denounces egoistic individualism, attributing this "sickness" to the "crass commercialism" of the modern age "which reduces society to nothing more than a vast apparatus of production and exchange." He calls for a moral individualism, an ideal predicated on a representation of the human person as a sacred being inherently deserving of dignity and respect. Weber also worries that modern individuals, lacking firm convictions, are increasingly inclined toward the mere self-interested adaptation to circumstances. As an alternative to this shallow and uninspiring way of life, he proposes an ethic of personality. Individuals, he believes, can achieve a truly meaningful and virtuous existence only by living in devotion to certain self-chosen values or causes.

Despite their differences, Marx, Durkheim, and Weber are united in their refusal to regard the example of the self-interested actor as the embodiment of the ideal of individualism.[68]

Modern Society and Individual Freedom

Marx, Durkheim, and Weber each presuppose what might be called a two-dimensional view of freedom. They each imply that freedom has both an outer dimension and an inner dimension—that it pertains to both action and thought. Individual freedom is dependent on both the characteristics of one's social environment and the qualities of one's state of consciousness. For convenience's sake, I call the first "objective freedom" and the second "subjective freedom." We can say that people are objectively free to the extent their life trajectories are not unduly restricted by external constraints, and they are subjectively free to the extent they possess the autonomy necessary for rational reflection and self-direction. Individuals lack freedom if their choices are unreasonably limited by social forces beyond their control or if their thought processes are impaired by ideological blinders, traditional prejudices, or irrational psychological influences. Marx, Durkheim, and Weber each rely on some dualistic idea of freedom conceived along these lines, and they each suggest that the attainment of human freedom requires both the reform of society and the reform of consciousness.

Objective Freedom and the Reform of Society

People are objectively free, as Steven Lukes explains, if they are masters of their own fate—able to determine their own "life course," realize their "human potentialities," and exercise their "capacity for self-development." This requires that individuals have *real* alternatives to choose from and *real* opportunities to pursue their plans and act on their preferences. Marx, Durkheim, and Weber, as we have seen in this and the previous chapter, each single out certain features of modern society that limit the objective freedom of the individual. The lives of people in the modern era, they agree, are constrained by institutional forces, coercive pressures, and barriers to the formation and expression of human individuality.[69]

For Marx, the capitalist mode of production is the foremost obstruction to individual freedom in the modern world. Only by abolishing capitalism and creating a socialist society can the promise of human freedom and true individuality be realized. By its very nature, he insists, capitalism offers workers neither real alternatives to the exploitative system of wage labor nor real opportunities to affirm their individuality. Due to their economic dependence within the capitalist system, workers, as individuals, are denied the uniquely human capacity for self-determination. Capitalism, Marx concludes, is the enemy of freedom.[70]

In *Suicide*, Durkheim introduces the concept of "fatalistic suicide." This type of suicide arises in circumstances where the lives of individuals are "excessively regulated and pitilessly confined." In a brief footnote he denies that such circumstances can be found in the modern era. Elsewhere in his writings, however, and often, he acknowledges that blocked opportunities, undue constraints, and other oppressive conditions are continuing problems in modern society. This concern is evident, for example, in his objection to restrictions on free speech and free inquiry, his dismay over the monotony and purposelessness of factory labor, and his worries about the persistence of economic inequities. For Durkheim, objective freedom is imperiled when individual rights are violated, when opportunities are wrongly limited, when labor is not fairly compensated, and when external obstacles hamper "the free unfolding of the social force each individual contains within himself." In Durkheim's writings, social and economic injustice is the main impediment to objective freedom.[71]

For Weber, in agreement with Marx, the coercive imperatives of the capitalist economic system restrict the freedom of the individual. But the phenomenon of bureaucratization, he suggests, is an even more serious threat, portending the formation of an indestructible "shell of bondage." The formally rational system of bureaucratic administration, with its vast apparatus of rules, regulations, and procedures, fashions a regimented social order that leaves little room for the free play of individual initiative. Weber worries that the suffocating effects of a bureaucratically imposed orderliness jeopardize the autonomy of the individual. Given the "irresistible advance of bureaucratization," he asks, how is it possible to "save *any remnants* of 'individualistic' freedom in any sense"? This, in Weber's view, as Wolfgang Mommsen states, is "the most pressing problem of our time."[72]

If we want freedom according to Marx, we need to abolish capitalism and create a classless society where each and every individual has the opportunity to develop his or her creative powers. If we want freedom according to Durkheim, we need to establish just economic relations, meaning, specifically, equal opportunity and fair contracts. Marx and Durkheim, at least on the surface, are not dramatically far apart in what they deem desirable. They are alike also in their optimistic belief that individuals will be far freer in the future than they are in the present. They disagree, however, about whether the overthrow of capitalism is necessary for the achievement of individual freedom, with Marx saying yes and Durkheim saying no. While Durkheim suggests that economic injustice is bound to give way naturally and peacefully to the cultural imperative of moral individualism, Marx insists that a free society can be achieved only through political agitation and, ultimately, socialist revolution. On the issue of objective freedom, Weber offers a more pessimistic picture. He believes that the advance of bureaucracy might be restrained, thus preserving some room for individuality. But he rejects the possibility of a future in which individuals will achieve anything approximating complete liberation from the oppressive and constraining realities of modern industrial society.

Subjective Freedom and the Reform of Consciousness

Marx, Durkheim, and Weber each claim that individuals in some sense have been psychologically debilitated by pathological social conditions and, if they are to live free and meaningful lives, they need to undergo what we might call a reform of consciousness. Freedom requires that individuals have alternatives and opportunities, but it also requires that their thought processes are unburdened by external social forces and internal barriers to rationality and autonomy. To attain subjective freedom, individuals, in effect, need to get their heads right, and this requires some process of political or moral education.

   For Marx, the working class—exploited, immiserated, and alienated—is a product of the capitalist mode of production, and it "looks upon the requirements of that mode of production as self-evident natural laws." Given the unrelenting hardships they endure and their inclination to accept the capitalist system as a given, how can Marx possibly imagine workers becoming subjectively free or acquiring a true consciousness of their class circumstances? He answers this question by pointing to the educational value and liberating experience of political activism. As people endeavor collectively to make their lives better, they change themselves in the process, extricating themselves from the psychological and ideological baggage of the capitalist system. In their struggles to achieve objective freedom, individuals achieve subjective freedom as well. In "revolutionary activity," Marx says, "the changing of oneself coincides with the changing of circumstances." Elsewhere he declares that a revolution is necessary "not only because the *ruling* class cannot be overthrown in any other way, but also because the class *overthrowing* it can only in a revolution succeed in ridding itself of all the muck of ages and become fitted to found society anew."[73]

While Marx maintains that subjective freedom is won in the course of political struggle, Durkheim and Weber, offering remarkably similar arguments, emphasize the necessity for moral restraint. More specifically, they each identify three conditions for the attainment of subjective freedom: (1) the taming of the natural self, (2) the rational control of one's life conduct, and (3) the adherence to moral rules. First, for both Durkheim and Weber, freedom is possible only where individuals are able to master their primordial desires and emotional urges, rein in their egoistic inclinations, and liberate themselves from the influence of taken-for-granted habits and customs. Second, Durkheim and Weber also suggest that for individuals to neutralize the irrational impulses of their natural selves, they need to conduct their lives in a rigorously systematic and rationally disciplined manner. Third, a disciplined life, in turn, requires the presence of a guiding moral code. Individuals are truly free only when they devote themselves to higher ideals or ultimate values, only when they commit themselves to something that transcends their own immediate self-interest. The concept of subjective freedom in the writings of Durkheim and Weber thus revolves around three central ideas: self-mastery, rational discipline, and moral action.

Durkheim and Weber agree that a moral code is the anchor of a free, meaningful, and autonomous life. It enables us to emancipate ourselves from slavery to our natural instincts, and it equips us with a rational basis for monitoring, regulating, and orienting our life conduct. They differ however in their interpretation of this moral code. According to Durkheim, the moral values that guide the behavior of the individual are social in origin, acquired through a process of socialization. According to Weber, on the other hand, the moral values that bring coherence to the life of an individual are self-selected, acquired through a process of reflection. Durkheim's theory of moral action, underlining the importance of group attachments and shared ideals, is weighted toward a concept of *social* control. Weber's theory of moral action, with its emphasis on the rational will of the autonomous personality, is weighted toward a concept of *self*-control.

This relates to another difference between the two. In modern society, Durkheim argues, moral individualism is destined to become a system of beliefs that claims universal allegiance. By following the moral rules embodied in this new religion of humanity, furthermore—that is, by treating others with sympathy, respect, and dignity—we simultaneously assert our individuality and affirm our common humanity. There is, accordingly, no conflict between the freedom of the individual—which indeed is only realized by acting in conformity with social ideals—and the solidarity of society. But while Durkheim envisions the advent of modernity giving rise to a unifying moral code, Weber foresees the proliferation of warring gods. Though agreeing that individuals can attain freedom only through the observance of moral rules, Weber claims that this is bound to result in an interminable struggle among irreconcilable values and conflicting ideals. In contrast to Durkheim, Weber perceives a tension between individual freedom and social order. The triumph of a worthy individualism, he believes, is less likely to bring us all together, as both Marx and Durkheim anticipate, than it is to drive us all apart.

Individualism, Freedom, and Self-Realization

Marx, Durkheim, and Weber each regard individual self-realization as a paramount normative ideal. Beyond this, furthermore, they each also identify labor or work as a primary medium through which individuals might express their individuality and forge a meaningful existence. For Marx, the concept of self-realization underlies both his critique of capitalism and his vision of socialism. Individuals realize themselves through truly free labor, he argues—that is, by engaging in activities that are self-directed, that are free from external control, and that afford sufficient opportunities for individuals to exercise their creative powers and develop their human potential.

For Durkheim, the moral duty of modern individuals is to equip themselves to perform differentiated occupational functions. In carrying out this duty, moreover—in dedicating themselves to a "definite task"—individuals also affirm their individuality. While Marx cites the crippling effects of the division of labor, Durkheim regards occupational specialization as both a moral obligation and a primary way for individuals to live socially useful and fulfilling lives. He acknowledges that economic reforms are necessary to ensure a normal and just division of labor. We need to "smooth the functioning of the social machine," he says, so that all individuals are able to develop "their abilities without hindrance." In contrast to Marx, however, for whom the defect lies in the very nature of the capitalist labor process, for Durkheim market imperfections—mainly unequal opportunities and unjust labor contracts—are the chief impediments to individual self-realization. [74]

Weber also emphasizes the occupational arena as a sphere of individual self-realization. Unlike Marx and Durkheim, however, he does not anticipate the need for or possibility of any substantial structural reforms. The ability of individuals to achieve self-fulfillment and aspire to "personality" through work is less dependent on the organization of the production process (Marx) or the distribution of jobs and wages (Durkheim) than it is on the willingness of individuals to commit themselves fully to the particular demands of a chosen occupation. Freedom, for Weber, is experienced in the self-aware and responsible performance of vocational duties. This, in turn, demands self-restraint, devotion to the tasks at hand, and strict adherence to the "internal norms" associated with one's profession. For work to be a meaningful activity, what counts most, according to Weber, are the inner qualities of the individual, not the external qualities of the occupational environment.[75]

Marx, Durkheim, and Weber agree that individuals need freedom and autonomy to achieve their full potential and that labor or work is a particularly suitable avenue for self-realization. They disagree, however, about what might be done to improve the prospects for individuals to live truly human lives. Consider first the contrast between Marx and Weber. For Marx the predicament of the individual in modern society is a structural problem, rooted in the system of capitalism. He proposes a political solution, namely proletarian revolution. For Weber, the predicament of the individual is essentially an existential problem, rooted in the very nature of modern existence. He proposes a largely individual solution, namely the ethic of personality. Bryan Turner pithily captures the differences between the two: "Whereas Weber's existential solution was individualistic, inward, and despairing, Marx's solution was collectivist, external, and hopeful." What about Durkheim? Like Marx, Durkheim proposes a structural interpretation of the problem. He attributes the unhealthy state of the individual to the youthfulness of modern society. Unlike Marx, however, he vehemently opposes any disruptive political solution. He argues instead that the problems of the present will work themselves out naturally as modern society matures. Like Marx, and unlike Weber, however, Durkheim is optimistic that change will come and that the lives of individuals—all of them, not just some of them—will improve significantly over time. In contrast to the more pessimistic Weber, both Marx and Durkheim envision a future in which freedom and individuality will flourish.[76]

Chapter Seven

The State and Democracy

Beginning in the late eighteenth century, with the French Revolution leading the way, the rise of democratic movements and the appearance of democratic institutions—phenomena that were integral to the process of modernization—presented a profound challenge to the traditional political order. Throughout the 1800s, pro-democracy forces in Western Europe, often pursuing a larger social justice agenda, demanded popular sovereignty, political equality, universal suffrage, civil liberties, and human rights. In its most radical form, the call for democracy enunciated a revolutionary idea: "that 'the people,' down to its lowest ranks, were entitled to govern themselves." Over the course of the nineteenth century and since, as the concept of democracy gained respectability, the precise referent of the term became increasingly contentious. In his survey of the field, David Held thus identifies numerous competing "models of democracy," and he raises what has become an unavoidable theoretical and practical question: "What should democracy mean today?" This question figures prominently in the political writings of Marx, Durkheim, and Weber. [1]

The passage from traditional to modern society, as we saw in the previous chapter, brought to the forefront the issue of individualism and, as we will see in this chapter, it placed the issue of democracy center stage as well. The affinity between modernity and democracy was not lost on the classical sociologists. Marx, Durkheim, and Weber were each deeply committed to the idea as well, though their conceptions of democracy, and their very usage of the term, could hardly have been more different. This partly stems from their conflicting political convictions and allegiances. But the divergence in their thoughts about democracy followed also from their contrasting diagnoses of the modern condition and their contrasting views of the fate of the individual. I mention this to underscore the connection between these three themes— modernity, individualism, and democracy; to emphasize the continuity between this chapter and the previous two thematic chapters; and to offer a reminder that while this chapter is focused on the issue of democracy, it is intended also to shed further light on the differences among Marx, Durkheim, and Weber in their theories of modern society, their interpretations of the pathologies of modern life, and their visions of the future.

KARL MARX: TRUE DEMOCRACY

Marx does not fit the popular image of a Marxist. As the most famous of all self-proclaimed communists, we might expect him to desire a society where the aspirations of the individual are subordinated to the needs of the collective. But as we saw in the previous chapter, he attributes the highest value to individual freedom and autonomy. We might also expect him to prefer a political system where ultimate power is invested in an imperious state bureaucracy. But as we will see in this chapter, he is instead an impassioned advocate of unrestricted political participation. He calls for a genuine democracy where public affairs are managed by the public itself, not by bureaucratic officials or professional politicians. Marx is not a communist because he hates freedom and democracy. His communism, in fact, is an extension of his uncompromising commitment to the ideals of human freedom and popular self-government—ideals that are, he believes, permitted only a limited and distorted existence within the framework of capitalist society.

Marx's Early Political Writings

In the period from 1842 to 1844, Marx addresses three broad topics: the division between civil society and the state, the relationship between economic forces and political forces, and the contradiction between the various particular interests in society and the general interest. Though well worth reading in their own right, we can perceive in these early writings the rudiments of Marx's later theory of the state, the inception of his concept of democracy, and the development of a radical vision of human emancipation.

Marx's Critique of Hegel's Political Theory

In his 1843 critique of Hegel's political philosophy, Marx examines a problem unique to modern times: the separation of the economic and the political, the split between the private sphere of civil society and the public sphere of the state. During the eighteenth century, commerce and industry were gradually liberated from political regulation. Economic activity acquired an independent existence, manifest in the growth of a laissez-faire market economy. The result, Marx explains, was the creation of two "heterogeneous" arenas: civil society, a system of private rights (including property rights) where individuals are given license to pursue their selfish interests, and the state, a system of public duties where communal-minded citizens are expected to promote the general interest. Individuals in the modern era live a "heavenly" existence within the abstract community of the state and an "earthly" existence within the Hobbesian world of civil society where each is at war with the other.[2]

How is a harmonious society possible on this contradictory basis? For Hegel, the duality of modern life is resolved within the state itself through the mediating role of three institutions: first, the monarch, the very "personality of the state," whose inherited position purportedly ensures his independence and impartiality; second, the bureaucracy, a "universal class" entrusted with the task of tending to the communal interest; and third, a legislative system where representatives from the crown, the bureaucracy, and the various economic groupings (or "estates") within civil society gather together to work out the general good. The modern state in Hegel's vision is endowed with a transcendent, spiritual quality. It stands above and apart from the mundane materialism of egoistic pursuits. It plays the role of neutral arbiter, reconciling the conflicts endemic to civil society. And as the embodiment of universality and reason, it functions to secure the common interest and bring unity to the life of the nation.[3]

Though crediting him for recognizing the contradiction between civil society and the state, Marx argues that Hegel's speculative method leads him to substitute a theoretical phantasm for the world itself. Hegel mistakes the ideal for the real, just as we sometimes portray our own political system through the filter of a fanciful image of American democracy. In reality, Marx argues, the clash of egoistic concerns and the conflict among private interests permeate every nook and cranny of the state, undermining its claim to serve as an impartial moderator in the worldly struggle for existence.[4]

Political Emancipation and Human Emancipation

In wrestling with the relationship between the state and society, Marx also takes up the problem of human freedom. In an 1843 article, "On the Jewish Question," a contribution to an ongoing debate about Jewish civil rights, he distinguishes between "political emancipation" and "human emancipation." Political or legal emancipation entails the extension of citizenship rights to all persons regardless of religion, economic status, or other restrictive qualifications. This is a "big step forward," Marx acknowledges, but the granting of political rights leaves intact the inequalities and injustices of civil society. The monopolization of private property, for example, continues to exert a detrimental effect on the lives of the poor even if property ownership is no longer a requirement for political participation. Political equality in itself does little to mitigate the pernicious influence of self-interested behavior, unrestrained competition, and economic deprivation in the larger society "*outside* the sphere of the state." The politically emancipated individual lives a bifurcated existence: "equal in the heaven of the political world yet unequal in the earthly existence of society." Furthermore, by sealing off the sphere of private interests from government interference, establishing a preserve for the free play of egoistic pursuits, political emancipation has the effect of reinforcing the "materialism of civil society." For Marx, in sum, political freedom falls short of true human freedom. The state can be a "free state," he says, one in which in which every adult is accorded citizenship status, "without man being a *free man*." The attainment of real freedom, which requires something more than political reform, is precisely the goal of human emancipation.[5]

In an article published the following year reporting on a revolt by impoverished weavers in Silesia, Marx distinguishes between "political revolution" and "social revolution," paralleling his earlier contrast between political emancipation and human emancipation. The typical interpretation of poverty and other social maladies, he observes, if not simply blamed on the victims themselves, is to attribute these to some failing of government—defective administration, for example, or the misguided policies of this or that political party. This tendency to think exclusively "*within* the framework of politics," ignoring the underlying socioeconomic conditions, fails to grasp the essence of the problem. For Marx, the true cause of social ills is not bad government, but the very existence of the state itself as an institution separate from people's ordinary lives and its rootedness in and dependence on a factional civil society. A political revolution is needed to overthrow the existing government leadership, he admits. But the crucial imperative, beyond this first step, is a social revolution, a "protest against a dehumanized life," a transformation of the social order as a whole. In this article we see Marx once again taking a radical stance, drawing attention to the inherent inability of the state to solve social problems and the limitations of a purely political perspective. Real human emancipation, he insists once again, is possible only by revolutionizing the economic structure of society.[6]

Marx's concepts of "human emancipation" and "social revolution," though presented rather abstractly, do point to the need for social change that goes beyond conventional political measures. But by the time he completed his article on the Silesian weavers, Marx was already moving in a new direction. From this point on, he situates his theory of the modern state and his concept of social revolution in the larger context of a theory of the capitalist mode of production. And while previously his primary concern was the division between civil society and the state and the contradiction between particular interests and the general interest, Marx now adopts a class perspective, underlining the antagonistic relationship between the capitalist class and the working class.

Marx's Theory of the Capitalist State

Marx's later political writings bear the mark of the materialist conception of history. Turning Hegel right side up, he maintains that it is not the state that shapes economic life, but economic life that shapes the state. Following a line of thinking implicit in his critique of Hegel, Marx argues that the state is not an "independent entity" existing separately from the economic workings of society. Just the opposite. The specific form taken by the state, the ends it pursues, and the policies it enacts are dependent on society's "economic base," on the social relations of production.[7]

Marx's theory of the capitalist state is not as systematically developed as his theory of the capitalist economy. His writings on the state are incomplete and scattered. They are also inconsistent, partly indicative of changes in his thinking, but also reflecting the variation in political circumstances from one country to another and from one time period to the next. We can thus find in Marx's writings at least two different theories: the ruling class theory of the state and the parasite theory of the state. In the first, featured prominently in the *Communist Manifesto*, he describes the state as the instrument of the capitalist class. In the second, found most notably in the *Eighteenth Brumaire*, he portrays the state as a "parasitic body," operating relatively inde-

pendently from class interests. In neither case, however, is the state a protector of the common good or an ally of the working class.[8]

The Ruling Class Theory of the State. According to Marx's ruling class
theory, the state in capitalist society is the political form in which the capitalist class asserts its "common interests" and pursues its "internal and external
purposes." The function of the state, according to this theory, is to promote
the interests of the bourgeoisie. Far from being a neutral institution looking
out for the well-being of society as a whole, the primary role of the state is to
serve the needs of the economically dominant class and ensure the continued
existence of the capitalist system. The "executive of the modern State," Marx
famously declares, is "a committee for managing the common affairs of the
whole bourgeoisie." Making a point central to his theory of power, he emphasizes however that the capitalist class is a politically ruling class because
it is an economically dominant class, not the reverse. The capitalist monopolization of private property does not "arise from the political rule of the
bourgeoisie," he explains, but rather "the political rule of the bourgeois class
arises from these modern relations of production." The ultimate power of the
capitalist class derives from its ownership of the means of production, not its
occupancy of government. The state is an organ of class rule, a political
weapon in the conflict between the bourgeoisie and the proletariat. In this
capacity it protects the system of private property and facilitates profit making. But the root source of capitalist class power—evident in its controlling
position within the system of production—is the ownership of capital itself.[9]

The Parasite Theory of the State. "Political power," Marx maintains, is
"the organized power of one class for oppressing another." But under exceptional circumstances, when the capitalist class is weak or divided, for example, or when "history is caught in the flux of becoming," as Hal Draper puts
it, the state may take a more autonomous form. This is precisely what happened in the aftermath of the French Revolution of 1848, when Louis Napoleon Bonaparte, in December 1851, seized power in a coup d'état. Bonaparte's triumph resulted in the victory of the "*executive power over the
legislative power,*" replacing the "despotism of a class" with the "despotism
of an individual." In the person of Bonaparte, with the support of the army,
the government "made itself an independent power." Marx describes this
ascendant executive authority with its vast "state machinery" and "enormous
bureaucratic and military organization" as an "appalling parasitic body."
Bonaparte's regime, the Second French Empire, which remained in power
until 1870, is significant because it attests to the possibility of the state

attaining a relative autonomy from the immediate influence of class forces. But it also reveals Marx as a critic of the state not only when it is directly under the thumb of the capitalist class, but also when it asserts its own supremacy and becomes, as he observes elsewhere, a "parasite feeding upon, and clogging the free movement of, society." Whether in the form of a class state, serving the interests of the bourgeoisie, or a parasite state, serving the interests of state officials themselves, the modern state for Marx is the enemy of human freedom and the antithesis of true democracy. [10]

True Democracy

Marx introduces the concept of "true democracy" in his critique of Hegel's defense of constitutional monarchy. The foundation of a true democracy, he states, is "unrestricted suffrage," the "greatest possible universalization of voting," and the "most fully possible universal participation in legislative power." The aim is to convert "the state from an organ superimposed upon society into one completely subordinate to it." By opening the doors of government to all the people, true democracy abolishes the political domain as the private province of a governing elite and reabsorbs public affairs into the "real life of the people," making citizenship an essential part of the individual's everyday world. Only on this basis can the individual be said to live a truly free and human life. True democracy, Marx says, is "*human existence*," the realization of human emancipation. [11]

Marx's commitment to democracy is the thread connecting his early writings, before he declares his allegiance to communism, to his later writings. But Marx is not just another proponent of democracy. He is, as Hal Draper observes, a "democratic extremist," urging "*the complete democratization of society*." The form of political life he envisions departs substantially from what normally passes for democracy. His conception of popular self-government, as I explain below, is based on several premises central to his political thought. [12]

Against Elitism. At the very outset of his political career, in several articles defending the free press, Marx attacks the arrogant attitude of government censors who deem the public dangerously immature while presupposing their own superior capacity for political judgment. The practice of censorship rests on an "unlimited trust" in government officials and an "unlimited distrust" in private persons. Marx derides this elitist view, regarding it as no more than a convenient excuse to impose restrictions on democratic institutions. He rejects the assumption that state functionaries or other supposedly enlightened elites possess some exceptional power to discern the common good or know better than ordinary citizens how to run the affairs of society. Marx's commitment to democracy is based on this anti-elitist faith in the intelligence of the public. [13]

Against Bureaucracy. For Hegel, bureaucratic administration, carried out by a cadre of independent and disinterested civil servants, is the essence of the rational state. Indeed, Marx admits, this is bureaucracy's self-image. It claims the state as its own "private property," it assumes the mantle of a "universal class," and it passes off its particular interests as the general interest. The "closed society" of bureaucracy conceives itself as the expression of the common good and the incarnation of "universal intelligence." But for Marx these qualities can only reside in the public as a whole. Universality is an attribute exclusive to a class composed of "every citizen." Bureaucracy is a danger, he argues, because it inevitably takes on a life of its own, elevating itself above society and in opposition to the people it allegedly serves. As the rule of a remote and privileged elite, the bureaucratic state is a violation of the democratic principle. [14]

Against the Professionalization of Politics. Consistent with his anti-elitist convictions, he not only denounces rule by bureaucrats; he also opposes rule by politicians. For Marx, a true democracy, as Richard Hunt explains, is a "democracy without professionals," a genuinely participatory democracy where political matters, instead of being the exclusive responsibility of a small minority class, are handled by ordinary citizens. Marx proposes a "government of the people by the people," where the affairs of the public are decided directly by the public itself. Besides restoring to individuals the role of citizen, this de-professionalization of political life has the added advantage of ensuring that the interests of the rulers do not differ from the interests of the ruled. For Marx, the existence of an elite class of professional politicians, as in the case of bureaucratic rule, is contrary to the democratic ideal. [15]

The Abolition of the State. A true democracy requires not only dismantling the political as a discreet sphere of life but also abolishing the state in anything like its current form. Once the era of class domination comes to an end, Marx declares, "there will be no more political power properly so-called," "no state in the present political sense." In a classless society, the state will cease to exist. But what precisely does this mean? Marx anticipates the state disappearing in the following respects: (1) as an instrument of capitalist class rule; (2) as a self-serving "parasitic body" feeding off the public; (3) as the exclusive province or "private property" of bureaucratic officials and professional politicians; and (4) as a superior and "special organism," "the master instead of the servant of society." But to say "the public power will lose its political character" in a self-governing system does not imply that all public powers or state functions will necessarily disappear, for example, the administration of production, health services, and education. What Marx does suggest, however, is that all remaining public responsibilities, the "legitimate functions" of the state, would be constituted differently. As he makes clear in his discussion of the Paris Commune, "public functions" would continue to exist, but they would be performed by ordinary citizens, as *"real workmen's functions."* The post-capitalist state, a truly democratic state, no longer severed from society, differs from the capitalist state both in the interests it serves and in the machinery and methods of its operation.[16]

The Dictatorship of the Proletariat. Marx also foresees the state being abolished in another sense: as a coercive instrument. But, as I explain more fully in the next chapter, this can occur only after the working class seizes political power and uses the authority of the state to overcome the resistance of the capitalist class and abolish the system of private property. For Marx, the state as an instrument of force is necessary to effect the transition from capitalism to communism and to create a *"classless society."* Only then will the state as a coercive apparatus cease to exist. During this transitional period, Marx declares, the state takes the form of a "dictatorship of the proletariat." But unlike the undemocratic dictatorship of the bourgeoisie it replaces, the rule of the proletariat takes the form of a *democratic* dictatorship— democratic because it is a workers' government, a political body that comes into existence through a popular revolution, and democratic also because it represents the interests of the vast majority of society.[17]

The Paris Commune

In 1871, toward the end of the Franco-Prussian War, the Parisian masses overthrew the city's government and "took into their own hands the direction of public affairs," establishing the so-called Paris Commune. As a workers' government, the Commune, lasting only two and a half months before being brutally suppressed, did not go very far toward establishing a socialist system. Marx nevertheless refers to it as a "glorious harbinger of a new society." The Commune, he says, is "the political form at last discovered under which to work out the economic emancipation of labour" and uproot "the economical foundations upon which rests the existence of classes, and therefore of class rule." Marx's analysis of the Commune offers a rare glimpse into his vision of the post-revolutionary future, and it also serves as a practical illustration of two key ideas: true democracy and the dictatorship of the proletariat.[18]

The working class, Marx insists, cannot "lay hold of the ready-made state machinery and wield it for its own purposes." The state as it presently exists is part of the problem and is incapable of being used to liberate the proletariat. "The political instrument of their enslavement," he explains, "cannot serve as the political instrument of their emancipation." To create a true workers' government, it is insufficient therefore simply to replace the current personnel of the state with representatives from the working class. The state is an oppressive institution not primarily because of the class membership of its officials, but because of its very structure as an independent and bureaucratic body, a "parasitic excrescence." Only by dismantling the state in its current form and creating new institutions of democratic self-rule can the working class emancipate itself. This is precisely what Marx credits Parisian workers with doing. He thus describes the Commune not simply as a working-class revolt, but as "a Revolution against the *State* itself," a revolution against the "horrid machinery of Class-domination."[19]

We can examine this political revolution from two angles: first, by identifying the characteristics of the existing state the Commune overturned, and second, by identifying the political measures the Commune implemented. Regarding the first, the main aim of Parisian workers was to disassemble the centralized power of the state and its pervasive bureaucratic apparatus. Among other reforms, the Commune abolished the standing army, replacing it with a people's militia; it stripped the police force of its autonomous standing; it separated the affairs of the church from the affairs of the state, thus eradicating "parson-power" and sending priests "back to the recesses of private life"; it abolished the "sham independence" of the judiciary by selecting judges and magistrates through open elections; and it fused the executive and legislative powers, ending the subordination of the latter to the former. Through these and other means, the Commune destroyed a remote and hierarchical state bureaucracy in which "public functions" were monopolized by the "Central Government."[20]

Regarding its more positive program, the essential purpose of the communards was to create a truly participatory democracy, a "real self-government," with the "people acting for itself by itself." "Instead of deciding once in three or six years which member of the ruling class was to misrepresent the people," the Commune fully applied the principle of universal suffrage. This entailed several innovations all with the purpose of de-professionalizing politics, maximizing public participation, and ensuring the accountability of government officials: (1) all government positions, including administrative positions, were made elective; and all officeholders were (2) subject to recall at any time; (3) bound to the mandate of their constituencies, serving more as delegates than representatives; and (4) paid only workers' wages. By ridding the system of politicians and enhancing the power of the vote, politics, Marx proclaims, was turned over to the people themselves. The achievement of the Commune was to establish a political system where "plain working men for the first time"—and without the inducement of an outsized paycheck— "dared to infringe upon the governmental privilege of their 'natural superiors' and, under circumstances of unexampled difficulty, performed their work modestly, conscientiously, and efficiently." The Commune, as Marx saw it, created a real people's democracy, with ordinary citizens carrying out the functions of government and with the state itself no longer existing as an independent entity separate from and superior to society.[21]

Democracy Equals Communism

Marx radicalizes the concept of democracy. True democracy requires not simply the democratization of politics, but the democratization of economic life as well. A system where people are presumably equal and free in the political sphere, but subject to exploitation and domination in the economic sphere, is a meager and illusory democracy. The struggle for complete democratization, however, is bound to find itself in opposition to the system of private ownership and the rule of the capitalist class. A genuine commitment to democracy thus necessarily entails a corresponding commitment to socialism. Marx defines "*consistent democracy in socialist terms, and consistent socialism in democratic terms.*" He was, according to Hal Draper, "the first socialist figure to come to an acceptance of the socialist idea *through* the battle for the consistent extension of democratic control from below. . . . He was the first to fuse the struggle for consistent political democracy with the struggle for a socialist transformation." Communism, as envisioned by Marx, is the realization of true democracy, meaning not just a democracy that universalizes citizenship rights, but a democracy that also liberates people from class servitude and offers opportunities for the full flourishing of every individual. For Marx, true democracy equals communism equals human emancipation.[22]

EMILE DURKHEIM: THE FUTURE BELONGS TO DEMOCRACY

Durkheim's political writings, which focus primarily on the modern state and democratic government, have two noteworthy peculiarities. First, they ignore many of the ordinary features of political life. Though touching on electoral arrangements, Durkheim says little or nothing about power, political parties, interest groups, social movements, or the legislative process. He generally downplays the more contentious and disruptive side of politics. Second, though he typically refuses to grant scientific validity to theories concerned with what ought to be rather than what is, Durkheim's own political writings are far more normative than empirical. In discussing the state and democracy, he expresses himself more like a philosopher than a sociologist. Instead of examining the actual functioning of the state and the real world of democratic politics, he presents us with a political ideal, a conception of the state and democracy as we might wish them to be, not as they really are. In his defense, it might be said that Durkheim's objective is to discover the ideal in the real, to show what modern society has the potential to become—and this is an empirical project of sorts. His intention is not to describe precisely how things stand at the moment, but to uncover through observation the formative moral and political principles of the modern era and to reveal the outlines of a future political order immanent in the facts of the present. [23]

The Role of the State in Modern Society

Social theorists have conflicting ideas about what the primary functions of the state are or should be. Among the leading contenders are these: defend the interests of the dominant class, serve the needs of the public, preserve social order, mediate conflicting political preferences, maximize economic growth, safeguard the operation of the free market, and advance the nation's political and military standing. Like many other political theorists, Durkheim too defines the state by its functions, but his conception of these is unconventional. He envisions the modern state playing three key roles: (1) it is the "brain" of society, (2) the "liberator of the individual," and (3) the "organ of justice."

The State as the Brain of Society

As societies become increasingly complex, the state emerges as a separate institution playing its own special role. Durkheim reserves the term "state" to refer to the group of officials—"agents of the sovereign authority"—who have the job of *thinking* about public affairs. The state in this conception is distinct from administrative agencies that carry out decisions and execute orders. For Durkheim, the state proper, standing at the apex of the larger sphere of government, is essentially a deliberative body, the "brain" of society, the "very organ of social thought." It thinks for a political purpose, formulating ideas and aims that serve to "frame decisions" and "guide collective conduct."[24]

Durkheim is not very specific in explaining what the state thinks about in its capacity as society's brain. Presumably, among other things, it thinks about how to regulate the functioning of society, solve social problems, and improve society's ability to realize its collective ends and ideals. Ordinary citizens ponder the very same questions. What distinguishes the state, therefore, is not *what* it thinks about but the *quality* of its thought. In contrast to lay individuals, absorbed in their own occupational specialties, state officials, precisely because political matters are their chief business, apply a deeper intelligence to the issues of the day. The state, as the institutional locus of expert knowledge and authoritative reasoning, contributes to the well-being of society by introducing "an element of reflective thought into social life."[25]

Durkheim's theory of the state thus rests on the distinction between two "different forms of collective psychic life." First, there is the broader collective consciousness, the amorphous and muddled mentality of the larger public. Rooted in custom and habit, this consciousness consists of vague and obscure beliefs and opinions, sentiments that have not been exposed to rigorous examination. Second, there is the "government consciousness," the more fully articulated and coherent sensibility of the state. This consciousness originates from concerted reflection on the part of government officials. It takes shape as ideas are exchanged and scrutinized in the context of assemblies, councils, hearings, and debates. Through these and other deliberative forums the state rationalizes society's psychic life, bringing the social consciousness to a heightened level of intelligibility and awareness.[26]

The responsibility of the state as the brain of society is to assimilate, clarify, and evaluate the typically ill-formed and murky ideas of the larger public and employ its collective intelligence to forge a sharper, clearer, and more knowledgeable vision of where society is and where it is going. As in conventional political theory, the state functions as a mediator of sorts, but a mediator of divergent ideas, not competing interests. Its purpose, moreover, is not to find some middle ground, but to submit popular beliefs to an informed and critical appraisal. The state in this manner acts as an independent "organ of reflection," giving direction and cohesiveness to society and helping it attain a more refined sense of itself.[27]

The State as the Liberator of the Individual

Individuals in pre-modern societies, submerged in the collective life and subject to an all-encompassing religious authority, barely exist as distinct personalities. But over the course of history, with the development of the division of labor, the individual gradually emerges from the undifferentiated mass and becomes an "autonomous centre of activity." At the same time, Durkheim observes, the role of the state inevitably expands—its functions multiply, its aims proliferate, and it intervenes in more and more areas of social life. The process of modernization thus gives rise to a seeming paradox: the simultaneous increase in the freedom of the individual and the power of the state.[28]

For Durkheim, however, and in contrast to an influential viewpoint in conventional political theory, there is nothing at all contradictory about this combination of "individualism" and "Statism." Indeed, he asserts, far from being a despotic institution, the modern state is the "liberator of the individual." Under normal conditions, the "more active the State becomes, the more the individual increases his liberty." Durkheim suggests three specific ways in which a strong state furthers individual freedom: (1) by legislating the rights of the individual, (2) by protecting individuals from the potential tyranny of group life, and (3) by promoting the dignity of the individual as a moral and practical ideal.[29]

First, the view of the state as the enemy of the individual depends on the false assumption, one common to the discipline of economics, that individuals come into the world as self-subsistent actors invested with natural rights. This premise makes it plausible to imagine that the growth of the state necessarily infringes on the presumably inherent liberties of the individual. For Durkheim, however, individual rights, for example, the right to vote and the right of free speech, are not inborn or given in nature. They have to be won, maintained, and exercised. This is where the state enters the picture. Only through the agency of the state are individual rights implemented, inscribed in law, and enforced in practice. It is the state, he says, "that creates and organizes and makes a reality of these rights." Individuals, Durkheim declares, are not naturally free; they are made free by the state.[30]

Second, the state plays a liberating role also by preventing individuals from being oppressed by parochial group affiliations and local attachments. Secondary groups, intermediate between the state and the individual—including the family, the church, the community, and professional associations—can jeopardize individual autonomy by greedily demanding the loyalty and subservience of their members. Only through the counterbalancing power of a higher authority—namely, the state—can the centripetal force of these "partial societies" be restrained. Thus Durkheim credits the state with rescuing the child from "patriarchal domination," freeing the citizen from archaic "feudal groups," and liberating "the craftsman and his master from guild tyranny." The threat of despotism, he even goes so far as to suggest, is more likely to arise from within society itself than from the state. For individuals to be free, therefore, the state needs to be strong. By shielding the individual from "specific local groups that tend to engulf him," the state, Durkheim concludes, "redeems the individual from society."[31]

Third, in contrast to laissez-faire advocates and small-government proponents, Durkheim anticipates the state playing a large and decidedly interventionist role. Rather than this endangering liberty, however, he believes that only on the basis of a strong state can the sanctity of the individual be assured. As the voice of moral authority and the guardian of society's collective ideals, the state is the one institution capable of effectively promulgating the principle of human dignity and establishing an "individualistic moral code." Beyond this, an active state is also necessary to transform the ideal of moral individualism into a practical reality. Only through the initiative of a powerful state can society be organized to reduce individual hardships, sustain peaceful and cooperative relations, and create a social milieu where the individual "may realize himself more fully" and "develop his faculties in freedom." For Durkheim, in sum, a strong and effectual state is necessary to secure the liberty and autonomy of the individual.[32]

The State as the Organ of Social Justice

In less advanced societies, according to Durkheim, the state, oriented outward, pursues primarily militaristic objectives, for example, territorial expansion and the conquest of rival nations. In more advanced societies, however, the state is directed inward, "toward the interior affairs of society," with moral purposes taking center stage. One of the state's fundamental moral duties, as we have seen, is to protect the dignity of the individual, and this in turn requires that individuals be treated equally and fairly. The state is thus compelled to assume another moral duty: to "bring about the reign of greater justice."[33]

Durkheim attributes to the state a higher "moral activity." Its purpose is to set society's "house in order" by infusing an element of justice into the sphere of economic relations—seeing to it that individuals are treated as they deserve, "freed from an unjust and humiliating tutelage," and permitted to realize their individuality. Societies in the modern world, where a strongly felt "need for justice" prevails, are in a favorable position. They "can have their pride, not in being the greatest or the wealthiest, but in being the most just." For Durkheim, the proper objective of the modern state is neither military prowess nor material wealth, but "the goal of realizing among its own people the general interests of humanity—that is to say, committing itself to an access of justice, to a higher morality."[34]

For Durkheim, the greatest threat to justice originates from class divisions, buttressed by the inheritance of wealth, and the persistence of other inequalities unrelated to merit. "Sharp class differences," deriving from circumstances of birth, are inconsistent with modern individualistic and egalitarian principles. A state of affairs where some are rich and others poor, where one person is placed at the mercy of another, undermines equality of opportunity, fair contracts, and equal exchanges. It enables the powerful to exploit the powerless and denies to disadvantaged individuals the dignity and respect they deserve. Though he is not specific in how it might address this complex of problems, the state, Durkheim declares, "is the necessary instrument through which equality, and consequently justice, is attained." Its task is to ameliorate "individual suffering," moderate the power of capital over labor, prevent the accumulation of "monstrous" inequalities of wealth, and structure society so as to create a "closer correspondence between the merit of its citizens and their conditions of life." As the "organ of justice," the primary responsibility of the state is to introduce a "greater equity into our social relationships."[35]

The State and Democracy

Durkheim warns against two popular misconceptions. First, like Weber, he rejects the commonplace assumption that democracy means self-government. Except in the most primitive societies, he asserts, anything approaching a direct democracy, where the entire population participates equally in the conduct of government, is inconceivable. In the modern era, no matter how developed the democracy, the state is destined to operate as an authoritative governing entity separate from the rest of society. The division between a minority group of governing officials and a majority group of ordinary citizens is a necessary and inevitable condition of modern society.[36]

Second, Durkheim also denies that democracy obtains only where government policies consistently reflect the will of the people. For government to operate effectively, the state must not only be separate from the larger society, he argues, but it must also possess a significant degree of autonomy. Even in a democracy, the state is called upon to carry out the singular function of thinking about political matters. Its duty as the brain of society is not to channel the preferences of the public, but to act as an independent organ of intelligence. Rather than simply expressing and summing up "the unreflective thought of the mass of the people," Durkheim says, the role of the democratic state is "to superimpose on this unreflective thought a more considered thought, which therefore cannot be other than different." While in a democracy the views of the public *inform* the decision of the state, they do not *determine* those decisions. The job of democratic government is not to echo the will of the people, but to marshal its superior intelligence to discover what is best for the people.[37]

So then, what is democracy if not a system where government is perfectly representative of the public? For Durkheim, as I explain below, democracy exists in modern societies to the extent there is (1) open government, (2) back-and-forth communication between state officials and the larger public, (3) a critical and reflective spirit in the political life of the nation, and (4) a sufficiency of "secondary groups" located between the individual and the state.[38]

Democracy as Open Government

One test for the presence of democracy, Durkheim believes, is whether the thinking and deliberating functions of government are carried out behind closed doors or take place "in the full light of day." While in a despotic system government is the private province of distant and insular elites, in a democratic system the activities of the state are conducted in the public sphere. Democracy does not mean self-government, but it does mean open government. This in turn necessitates the existence of public forums and assemblies of various kinds, permitting the deliberations of state officials to be "heard by all" and giving ordinary citizens the opportunity "to follow the workings of government." Where the state operates in the open, lay individuals are able to pose to themselves and others the same questions contemplated by government officials. In a democracy, therefore, the boundary between the "government consciousness" and the broader collective consciousness is permeable, meaning the larger public is able to share in the higher intelligence embodied in the brain of society.[39]

Democracy as Two-Way Communication

Democracy does not eradicate the distinction between governors and governed, Durkheim insists, but it does require "regular and organized" communication between these two bodies. Each must remain in close contact with the other, creating an ongoing circuit of mutual awareness. This requires institutional arrangements—political hearings and periodic elections, for example—that enable the state to communicate its thinking to the public and the public to communicate its sentiments to the state. For Durkheim, this "two-way" communication is the "gist of democracy." Two conditions are required for this back-and-forth communication to work properly. First, government officials, without sacrificing their autonomy, must be responsive to the needs of the public. Second, the public must be adequately educated in the duties of citizenship and in the "essential principles" of "democratic morality." Thus Durkheim calls upon the school system to teach respect for reason and science and inspire students to subordinate their "selfish views and material interests" to the higher ideals of modern society. A thriving democracy, whose lifeblood is public deliberation, needs both good institutions and good citizens.[40]

Democracy as Reflective Government

Democracy, Durkheim says, is "the political system by which the society can achieve a consciousness of itself in its purest form." This results from a twofold process. First, the reach of the state increases as more and more areas of social life fall under the purview of government intervention, including education, health, business, and the administration of justice. Second, the power of the state as an organ of social thought expands as an ever-growing domain of society is subject to sustained public deliberation. In a democracy, Durkheim claims, no tradition or institution is exempt from being judged before the court of reason. Everything is "open to question." A society is less democratic where it remains "tied to the past," where common customs, sentiments, and beliefs evade public scrutiny. Because it institutionalizes reflection, shining the light of critical thought on all social conventions, democracy is the enemy of routine and the ally of progress. A democratic society regards no social arrangements or practices as sacrosanct. This makes it easier to adapt to new circumstances and carry out "the almost continuous changes that present-day" conditions demand. For Durkheim, the more "deliberation and reflection and a critical spirit play a considerable part in the course of public affairs, the more democratic the nation."[41]

Democracy and Corporate Organizations

The defining characteristics of democracy are open government, two-way communication, and a spirit of reflection. But a democratic polity also requires an appropriately organized society. For Durkheim, this means an abundance of "secondary groups," public institutions located between the individual and the central government, separate from but still subject to the "general supervision" of the state. Where there is an absence of intermediate organizations, precisely the problem he finds in the France of his day, individuals are reduced to a formless and unstable mass, and the state is left as the only durable collective force. This pathological circumstance, Durkheim argues, is the chief cause of the "political malaise" afflicting modern societies. In the industrial world of the modern era, where individuals spend the bulk of their time engaged in economic pursuits, the corporate or professional association, uniting people of the same occupation, is the most suitable type of secondary group to fill the void. As we saw in an earlier chapter, Durkheim imagines these corporate organizations playing a key role in invigorating the moral life of the nation, and he foresees them playing a vital political role as well.[42]

Just as the state functions to deter secondary groups from absorbing the individual, so too, Durkheim maintains, do secondary groups function to deter the state from becoming despotic. If "not limited by some collective power that restrains it," the state, he warns, will "develop out of all proportion and in turn become a threat to individual liberties." A proper balance between secondary groups and the state, each curbing the other, is essential for both the well-being of democracy and the freedom of the individual. When this balance is upset, tyranny is the result, with the individual either subject to the absolute authority of the state or to the coercive pressures of group attachments. By serving as a counterweight to the central government, occupational organizations are a necessary institutional component of a healthy democracy.[43]

Secondary groups are politically significant for Durkheim primarily because they protect the individual from the potentially oppressive power of the state. But they serve other important political functions as well. First, as an institutional intermediary between the state and the public, secondary groups facilitate the two-way communication necessary for democratic deliberation. Second, well-developed occupational associations, by mediating and moderating the political participation of the populace, insulate the government from excessive and direct pressure by citizens, thus allowing the state to maintain its needed autonomy. Third, because people's lives are closely intertwined with their occupation groups, these are well positioned to function as agents of political socialization. The communal environment occupational associations provide gives them sufficient presence and moral authority to inhibit egoistic drives, form socially minded citizens, and instill the higher principles of a democratic morality. Finally, Durkheim also expects corporate organizations, because they more accurately reflect "the diversity of social interests," to supplant geographical regions as the "true electoral unit" and the basis of political representation in modern democratic societies.[44]

The Future Belongs to Democracy

Only in a democracy does the state achieve its fullest expression as the brain of society, the liberator of the individual, and the organ of justice. For Durkheim, democracy is the culmination of the modern political ideal. It is the government form "societies are assuming to an increasing degree." What accounts for this pattern? Why is Durkheim so convinced that democracy is destined to prevail in the modern world? He gives two arguments, one emphasizing its practical superiority, the other its cultural ascendancy.[45]

One reason democracy is the dominant political system in the modern world, according to Durkheim, is that it fulfills a pressing societal need. Under the governance of pre-modern regimes, society's affairs are carried out according to habit, tradition, and "blind routine." But given the complexity of the modern world and the ever-present necessity to introduce changes and enact reforms, society can no longer function effectively without the heightened capacity for reflection, deliberation, and innovation that democratic government makes possible. In the simpler period of the past, "things go on happening in the same way." But survival in the modern era depends on the state being able to make constant adjustments, respond thoughtfully to the flux of circumstances, and plan for the future with intelligence and foresight. Democracy is the government of choice in the modern world, Durkheim claims, because of its superior capability as society's brain.[46]

Democracy is also the form of government most culturally suited to the modern world, most in line with "our inmost moral concepts," and most attuned to "our present-day notion of the individual." As a distinctly modern rallying cry, democracy is one part of a larger collection of other increasingly influential social ideals, including individualism, egalitarianism, and justice. Together these add up to a powerful moral force, an aspiration deeply rooted in the sentiments, beliefs, and values of the modern collective consciousness. Democracy is the wave of the future because it responds to an insistent popular demand. Everywhere, Durkheim exclaims, democracy "is carrying the day," with nations "swept along on a broad democratic current that would be absurd to seek to resist."[47]

A democratic government is a practical necessity in complex industrial societies and the only political form consistent with modern cultural values. For these two reasons, Durkheim argues, the future belongs to democracy. This prognosis reflects his generally optimistic view of the course of social evolution. Obstacles to progress remain, of course, including the continued opposition of anti-liberal defenders of the old regime. Nevertheless, despite his recognition of all the work yet to be done, Durkheim, as a proponent of individualism and democracy, and in sharp contrast to Max Weber, felt himself to be swimming with the tide.[48]

MAX WEBER: LEADERSHIP DEMOCRACY

In his political writings—and in much of the rest of his work as well—Weber adopts the role of "political educator." He presents himself in this capacity as a hardheaded "exposer of nonsense," saying "things people do not like to hear," telling it like it is. He urges us to acknowledge "uncomfortable facts" and see "the realities of life in all their starkness." As a determined anti-utopian, his objective is to burst our illusions about the world and infuse our political judgment with an element of tough-minded realism.[49]

Weber's analysis of the modern condition reveals what he believes are certain inevitabilities—value conflict and bureaucratic organization, for example. These inevitabilities define the parameters of any conceivable future. Declaring that we cannot evade the "laws of this earthly world," Weber admonishes us to abandon romantic dreams about what the future might hold. His mission in exposing the "facts of social life" in this manner is "the education of judgment about practical social problems." This, he insists, is the duty of scholars like himself. The immediate goal is to help cultivate among citizens (referring specifically to the German nation and the German bourgeoisie in particular) a more mature and responsible political outlook. In this undertaking, as Peter Breiner observes, Weber is a theorist of political "prudence." His intention is to sharpen our ability to distinguish between what is feasible and what is not and to determine which political goals are worth pursuing, which are too costly, and which are simply unattainable.[50]

Weber's writings on the state and democracy incorporate a mix of empirical claims and evaluative judgments, scholarly analysis combined with partisan exhortation. He sets out to educate but also to persuade. He asks his audience to see things as they are, but he also wants to enlist allies to his causes. On the one hand, from a scholarly perspective, he examines the objective possibilities and likely consequences of different political programs or ideals. Can we have democracy, peace, and socialism? What form might these take, how might they be achieved, at what price? On the other hand, as he freely admits, he also assesses political programs from a normative perspective, from the vantage point of his own political principles, including foremost the "power-interests" of the German nation. Weber wants us to see the world as it is, but he also wants us to see it as he sees it—that is, with sympathetic consideration for values and ends that are, from his political standpoint, not just feasible but also desirable.[51]

In the next section I briefly discuss Weber's theory of the state and his conception of political action. Following this, in a longer section, I examine his thinking on the topic of democracy. My primary aim here is to explain why Weber rejects "direct" or participatory democracy in favor of "leadership democracy," how he envisions a leadership democracy functioning, and what he perceives to be the advantages of this type of political system in the modern rationalized world.

The State and Politics

Political theorists sometimes refer to the state as the servant of the people, or the instrument of the common good, or the mediator of conflicting interests. Weber views it in less rosy terms. The state, he declares, is a "relation of men dominating men," an institution through which rulers wield power over the ruled. Its basic function is to secure the "orderly domination" of a territory and its population. Beyond this broad purpose, however, Weber defines the state not by the ends it serves, which are innumerable, but by the means at its disposal. Here again, he does not try to paint a pleasing picture. The state stands out from other institutions, he says, because it "claims *the monopoly of the legitimate use of physical force* within a given territory." It "alone is accorded 'legitimate' power over life, death, and liberty." Coercion and violence are not the sole means employed by the state, of course, nor are such means exclusive to the state, but only the state has the *lawful right* to use such means. According to Weber, the legitimate use or threat of force, whether applied to external or internal enemies, "is a means specific to the state."[52]

Weber describes the state as a neutral tool, "a purely technical instrument," whose coercive power can be employed in the service of any conceivable aim. Politics, accordingly, is the struggle among competing individuals and groups to gain influence within the state for the purpose of furthering their causes, promoting their worldviews, and advancing their material and ideological interests. Power struggles—with some striving to impose their will against the resistance of others—are an inherent feature of political life. Politics, Weber states, "means conflict." The political field is a battleground of clashing goals and irreconcilable values. This is particularly true in the modern disenchanted world where the unifying power of traditional religious beliefs has given way to a proliferation of "warring gods" and a never-ending antagonism among contending interests, ideologies, and doctrines. Anyone contemplating a career in the "tough business" of politics, Weber cautions, must "recognize the fundamental reality of an ineluctable eternal war on earth of men against men." Dashing all utopian hopes, he argues that there is no imaginable future in which people might achieve some state of lasting social harmony, or realize the "dream of peace and human happiness," or escape the necessity of conflict, or free themselves from relations of domination.[53]

Power, violence, struggle, domination, conflict—these are the keywords of Weber's political theory. Individuals entering the world of politics, in service to its "diabolical powers," are bound to get their hands dirty. Political action inevitably raises "ethical paradoxes." Only a "political infant," Weber says, can fail to see that "it is *not* true that good can follow only from good and evil only from evil." The distasteful political reality is this: the use of "morally dubious" means, for example, violence, is often necessary for the attainment of desirable ends. This circumstance—what he refers to as the "ethical irrationality of the world"—guarantees that political actors will find themselves in morally compromising situations. A political life is not suited to those who wish to remain pure of heart. On the other side, however, the vocation of politics, Weber suggests, does have the appeal of being a unique realm of freedom and self-expression. It is an arena in which individuals can define themselves by taking up causes of their own choosing. Politics offers an opportunity for people to act on their ideals and create a meaningful life for themselves in defiance of the "lifeless routine of everyday existence."[54]

Democracy

Weber today is typically thought of as a "liberal." This judgment is based on his defense of individualism, his belief in personal freedom, and his commitment to democracy. Like any reputable liberal, he acknowledges the invaluable "achievements of the age of the Rights of Man." He worries about the threat of "growing unfreedom" in the modern rationalized world. And he is a "resolute follower of democratic institutions," outspoken in his support for popularly elected leaders, parliamentary government, unrestricted suffrage, political parties, and universal citizenship rights.[55]

Despite these credentials, however, Weber is generally regarded as something of a *qualified* liberal. He is, as Sven Eliaeson puts it, a liberal "of a sort" advocating a democracy "of a sort." In contrast to many of his British and European counterparts, Weber's liberalism—more elitist than egalitarian—is not motivated by any moral imperative to create a more equal society, eradicate poverty, or alleviate the misery of the working class. Nor is he an advocate of economic redistribution or a proponent of the welfare state. And while he defends democratic institutions, he does not see any "necessary connection between democracy and freedom and/or equality," and he attributes far more importance to the need for strong political leadership than to the value of popular political participation. As David Beetham states, Weber is a "liberal without liberal values."[56]

Direct and Participatory Democracy

Direct and participatory forms of democracy are intended to maximize the involvement of the public in the political process. This conception of democracy, the embodiment of the traditional democratic ideal, rests on the belief that all citizens are capable of undertaking public affairs. The functioning of a popular democracy of this sort requires either regular public meetings or frequent elections, along with some procedure for rotating political offices and duties so that everyone has the opportunity to serve. Where officeholders are present, they are held strictly accountable to the electorate; they function only as agents of the people, obliged to comply with the wishes of the public;

and their discretionary authority—their "power to command"—is reduced to a minimum. In a direct or participatory democracy, the people are simultaneously the rulers and the ruled.[57]

Weber acknowledges that this kind of democracy is feasible in small and homogenous political communities. In the mass society of today, however, the population is far too large for every citizen to be actively involved in the governing process. For many other reasons as well, he argues, a participatory democracy *of even a limited form* is not a realistic option in the modern era.[58]

First, increasing "economic differentiation" corrupts the principle of political equality by affording unequal opportunities for political involvement. Most people, immersed in the economic struggle for existence, have little time for political activism. This includes the least advantaged, those "forced to work for a living," as well as industrialists absorbed in their day-to-day business pursuits. This circumstance results in government positions falling into the hands of rentiers, landowners, and other members of the more or less idle rich. Only they have the time and resources necessary to devote themselves full time to politics. The imperatives of modern economic life make it impossible to fulfill the arduous demands of a participatory democracy.[59]

Second, the growing complexity of administrative tasks requires that government positions be filled by personnel with specialized expertise. A system where the people themselves run the day-to-day affairs of government is technically impossible, or at least prohibitively inefficient. The modern state, Weber declares, cannot function in the absence of a "specially trained *organization* of officials." Any effort to create a direct democracy at the expense of parliamentary institutions, furthermore, would only diminish the countervailing influence of professional politicians, thus exacerbating the tendency toward "uncontrolled bureaucratic domination." What "democracy" can mean, he concludes, is radically altered with the advent of bureaucratic administration. And under modern conditions, Weber insists, democracy *cannot* mean a system in which the people themselves play an active governing role.[60]

Third, institutional devices designed to give the public a more direct political voice—including referenda, the right of recall, and the imperative mandate (the requirement that representatives adhere to the preferences of their constituents)—are inconsistent with the need for timely decision making. Referenda and other such procedures convey only periodic and insufficiently detailed information about the will of the people. Elected officials cannot know precisely what the public wants in any particular circumstance, and under the rules of a direct democracy they lack the leeway to make independent decisions. This hinders their ability to respond quickly to unexpected developments and undertake the necessary political work of negotiation, compromise, and "horse-trading." A direct democracy, Weber suggests, is a recipe for political paralysis.[61]

Fourth, electoral contests and legislative battles in the modern political world are necessarily carried out under the auspices of mass political parties. Their presence establishes an intermediate level of organization in the political sphere, and where such organization exists, "the law of the small number" prevails. Inevitably, a select few—with the benefit of experience, expertise, and the "maneuverability" possessed only by small groups—"assume the active direction of party affairs." Rank-and-file members serve merely as followers, carrying out a political program formulated from above. The larger electorate plays an even smaller role, appearing on the political stage only as occasional "objects of solicitation" by the contending parties. For Weber, mass political parties deepen the division between those citizens who are "politically active" and those who are "politically passive," further compromising the democratic ideal of political equality.[62]

Fifth, Weber's assessment of the political capabilities of ordinary people, the propertyless working class in particular, also leads him to reject more participatory forms of democracy. The "masses," he says, reflecting his rather elitist viewpoint, think "only in short-run terms," they are particularly vulnerable to "purely emotional and irrational" influences, and they are inclined toward a "reckless and unreserved political idealism." Caught up in the daily struggle for survival, they are "susceptible to all emotional motives in politics, to passions and momentary impressions of a sensational kind." Only the coolheaded and responsible leadership of professional politicians, Weber argues, can prevent a disorganized "democracy of the streets," mitigate the predominance of "emotional elements" in politics, and achieve "the orderly *leadership* of the masses." In Weber's view, meaningful popular political participation is not feasible, and given the irrationality of the masses, it is not desirable either.[63]

Weber's critique of direct and participatory democracy draws attention to what he assumes are certain unavoidable features of the modern political landscape: the persistent inequality in political influence between the "positively privileged" classes and the "negatively privileged" classes; the inviolable divide separating elites and masses, rulers and ruled, leaders and followers; the inescapable bureaucratization of government administration; the irrationality and political immaturity of the masses; and the limited opportunities for ordinary citizens to participate directly in the operations of government. The domination of a power-holding minority over a relatively powerless and largely passive majority, Weber argues, is an inherent feature of modern political life. And while he welcomes the presence of democratic institutions—voting rights, free elections, representative institutions, and political parties—he denies that these will ever confer power on the people or lessen the domination of the many by the few. According to Weber, any "thought . . . of removing the rule of men over men through even the most sophisticated forms of 'democracy' is 'utopian.'"[64]

Leadership Democracy

Despite his critique of the classical ideal, Weber maintains that democracy is still a viable possibility; but it will not take the form of a participatory democracy, and it will not "mean an increasingly active share of the subjects in government." In the present era, only a limited form of democracy is possible and—turning a necessity into a virtue—the type of democracy Weber thinks feasible, "leadership democracy," is also the type he deems most desirable.[65]

Weber's point of departure in his writings on democracy is not the relationship between elites and masses, as is typically the case, but the relationship between two different categories of elites: political elites and bureaucratic elites. The choice, he argues, is not between elite rule and popular self-government, but between rule by professional politicians and rule by civil servants. Democratic institutions are preferable to Weber not because they guard against the threat of elite domination (this is inevitable), but because they guard against the threat of bureaucratic domination. No modern democracy can empower the masses vis-à-vis the elites, but under the right circumstances it can empower politicians vis-à-vis bureaucrats.

The type of democracy Weber advocates is not intended to enhance the power of ordinary citizens. Indeed, in any modern democratic system, he argues, the masses are destined to play a supporting role only. The purpose of leadership democracy, rather, is to create opportunities for the rise of forceful and independent political leaders, politicians capable of counteracting the bureaucratization of political life and advancing the interests of the German nation. Weber favors democratic institutions not because they have any intrinsic value, but because they are more likely to ensure that politicians rather than bureaucrats control the reins of national power. He thus justifies democracy primarily on instrumental grounds. It is "a technique, a means to an end." "Constitutional arrangements," he argues, are of secondary importance; what matters far more is whether "politicians . . . are the ones who rule."[66]

Parliamentary Democracy

In a series of articles originally published in 1917, Weber describes the German parliament in the post-Bismarck era as "completely powerless." The weakened condition of parliament impedes its ability to contain the expansionary tendency of the state bureaucracy. The result is the bureaucratization of politics, with leadership positions taken over by bureaucratic officials rather than genuine politicians. The problem with this, Weber argues, is that only experienced politicians—practiced in the struggle for power and possessed of a strong political will—have the qualities necessary to serve as the "directing mind" of government. The trained officials who make up the ranks of the civil service, by contrast, are accustomed to obeying instructions and following procedures. While skilled in the performance of administrative duties, their bureaucratic mentality makes them ill equipped to occupy governing positions. Policy making, Weber proclaims, "is not the business of the professional civil servant." And where "'administrative' officials" usurp the job of "'political' officials," incompetent leadership inevitably results. This is precisely the predicament Weber finds in the Germany of his day.[67]

In response to this leadership problem, Weber calls for institutional reforms to upgrade the parliamentary system. With the British model in mind, he advocates a "working" parliament—not just a "speech-making" body, but an institution possessing a "positive share in government." He wants a parliament that would have the authority to oversee the bureaucratic apparatus, serve as a "recruiting ground" for the highest political offices, and offer meaningful career opportunities for "men with political ambition and the will to power and responsibility."[68]

Weber envisions a working parliament performing several important functions. First, it would serve as a "proving-ground for political leaders." It would enable aspiring politicians to gain experience in the "difficult art" of political struggle, get training in how to recruit allies and build a following, and learn the "craft of demagoguery." Only by increasing its powers and responsibilities, Weber argues, can parliament perform the vital role of cultivating leadership qualities and furnishing politicians the opportunity to test their abilities and demonstrate their fitness for rule.[69]

Second, because of the powerlessness of parliament, Weber laments, ambitious and talented people, through a process of "negative selection," are diverted away from politics and into the more promising field of business. But if a career in parliament allowed members to exert real influence and placed them on a pathway to national leadership, then individuals with a taste for power could make their mark in the world of politics instead. A strengthened parliament would thus attract a more gifted class of potential political leaders.[70]

Third, a working parliament is necessary to restrain the power of state officialdom and ensure that bureaucrats limit themselves to purely administrative roles. Politicians, Weber says, "must be the countervailing force against bureaucratic domination." He thus proposes expanding the prerogatives of parliament to enable it to exercise supervisory authority over the state bureaucracy—what is today sometimes called legislative oversight. This includes especially the "right of inquiry"—the right to question bureaucratic officials, request official information, inspect documents, scrutinize records, and otherwise "force administrative chiefs to account for their actions." Beyond enhancing the power of politicians over bureaucrats, the added advantage of such open investigations, Weber emphasizes, is that they would help inform the public about the operations of government.[71]

Fourth, according to David Beetham, Weber desired a strong working parliament not only because it would promote effective political leadership, but also because it would function to sustain democratic values and preserve individual liberties. Unlike bureaucratic rule, which operates behind the scenes, a parliamentary democracy, with contending politicians engaged in open political struggles, guarantees at least a minimal degree of elite accountability. Political leaders and party officials are "exposed to public scrutiny through the criticism of opponents and competitors." This allows the electorate an opportunity to evaluate the qualities of political figures and gives the public a say in the process through which politicians are selected for top leadership positions.[72]

A well-functioning parliament increases the transparency of government, offers a modicum of elite accountability, and helps ensure the preservation of individual liberties. For Weber, however, the primary purpose of a working parliament is to establish a political counterforce to the state bureaucracy and provide politicians with an avenue for developing their political leadership qualities and gaining experience in the competitive struggle for power. After 1918, according to Wolfgang Mommsen, Weber's support for parliamentary democracy increasingly took a backseat to his call for plebiscitary democracy. Disillusioned by a business-as-usual parliamentary system, he came to believe that great leadership and effective political rule could only come in the form of a charismatic politician with a mass following. In the last few years of his life, Weber became a strong proponent of "plebiscitary leadership democracy."[73]

Plebiscitary Democracy

In a plebiscitary democracy, political leaders attain office through direct elections, as in the case of the U.S. president. They are chosen by the people themselves rather than being selected through parliamentary procedures. Weber favors precisely such a system. It is essential, he asserts, referring to the Germany of his day, "to create a *head of state* resting *unquestionably on the will of the whole people*, without the intervention of intermediaries." This form of democracy is a "variant of charismatic authority," with politicians coming to power primarily on the basis of their personal qualities rather than their political programs. Would-be leaders prove themselves through their demagogic skills and their ability to attract a devoted following. While they derive their formal legitimacy from the "will of the governed," Weber states, plebiscitary leaders, in typical charismatic fashion, rule by virtue of the "trust and faith of the masses."[74]

In contrast to popular democracy, in a plebiscitary system, Weber recognizes, power flows from the top down, not from the bottom up. Leaders do not respond to public opinion; they shape it. And the people do not govern; they are governed. The plebiscitary ruler is an "elected leader" not an "elected official." The "official," Weber explains, "acts according to the expressed or surmised will of the voters." But the "leader," backed by the confidence of the electorate, acts "according to his own discretion." This is the essence of leadership democracy. The primary objective of such a system is not to empower the public, but to permit the rise of strong and independent charismatic figures capable of governing the nation. As reported by his wife, Marianne, when asked to explain his idea of democracy, Weber gave this response: "In a democracy the people choose a leader whom they trust. Then the chosen man says, 'Now shut your mouths and obey me. The people and the parties are no longer free to interfere in the leader's business.' . . . Later the people can sit in judgment. If the leader has made mistakes—to the gallows with him!" A "popularly elected president," Weber states elsewhere, means the "subordination to leaders one has chosen for oneself."[75]

Political leaders selected through direct elections, Weber suggests, have the advantage of being able to invoke a mandate. With the backing of the people, they are authorized to lead as independent agents, free to act on their own initiative, empowered to assert a visionary political agenda. Popular support gives politicians the latitude to set forth new ideas and inject a creative and dynamic element into an otherwise stagnant and ossified political environment. This is what Weber finds uniquely attractive about plebiscitary leadership: it is a distinctly counter-bureaucratic force. The innovative energy of a charismatic leader, he believes, is a much-needed corrective to routinized bureaucratic administration and the uninspired wheeling and dealing of normal parliamentary politics.

Particularly in light of the subsequent rise of German fascism, Weber's defense of plebiscitary leadership democracy raises obvious concerns. Most importantly, it is not clear how his desire for strong leadership can be reconciled with his commitment to liberal democracy or how the abuse of power can be avoided in a system explicitly intended to augment the autonomy of political leaders. As Steven Pfaff argues, Weber's vision of plebiscitary democracy skirts "the division between democracy and dictatorship, between a liberal and authoritarian order." Wolfgang Mommsen makes a similar point, observing that Weber's concept of charismatic leadership applies to both "good" demagogues and "bad" demagogues. What is there to ensure that a leadership democracy produces "charismatic leadership" rather than "charismatic domination"? Weber did not confront these issues in sufficient depth. Perhaps his negative view of the masses led him to be excessively preoccupied with the issue of strong leadership. Or perhaps any concerns he might have had about authoritarian leadership were outweighed by his fear of bureaucratic despotism. In any case, Weber did not adequately come to terms with the dangers inherent in the idea of plebiscitary democracy.[76]

Weber, as we have seen, does not advocate democracy because it possesses some inherent value or fulfills some moral imperative. Nor does he justify democracy by reference to a principled belief in popular sovereignty, a deep commitment to egalitarian ideals, or a strong sense of social justice. "The peculiarity of Weber's position," David Beetham states, is that he favors democracy because he believes it promotes the rise of powerful political leaders. The leitmotif of his vision of democracy is leadership, not citizenship. Ultimately, Weber's worries about bureaucratic domination, his skepticism about the political capabilities of the masses, his pessimism regarding the prospects for anything resembling a participatory democracy, and his preoccupation with the problem of effective leadership lead him to propose a vision of democracy that is, as Beetham explains, "anything but democratic."[77]

MARX, DURKHEIM, AND WEBER
ON THE STATE AND DEMOCRACY

The writings of Marx, Durkheim, and Weber on the state and democracy include a combination of empirical analysis and prescriptive theory. From a social science standpoint, they each examine the realities of political life in the modern era; and from a normative standpoint, they each also affirm a certain ideal system of government. In this concluding segment, I focus primarily on the normative side of Marx, Durkheim, and Weber's political writings. In the first section below I briefly compare their conceptions of the state, and in the longer second section I explore their contrasting visions of democracy.

The State in Marx, Durkheim, and Weber

Marx's perspective on the state is altogether hostile. He describes it as either an oppressive parasitic body draining the resources of the public or an instrument of the dominant class. In a socialist society, he anticipates, the state as an autonomous institution and coercive force will gradually wither away to be replaced by a true democracy. Both Durkheim and Weber have a more positive view of the state. But there are some striking differences between the two. They agree that the state, when functioning properly, is the directing authority in society—the "prime mover," as Durkheim puts it—and an essential source of dynamism and change. But they ascribe the innovative power of the state to two very dissimilar agencies. For Durkheim, the transformative potential of the state derives from the specialized capacity of government officials to reason about the affairs of society. For Weber, this potential depends on the presence of political leaders who, by virtue of their charismatic qualities, can mobilize the power necessary to pursue a visionary agenda. The primary resource of the state in its role as an instrument of change is, for Durkheim, rational deliberation and, for Weber, forceful leadership. Underlying this difference is the contrast between a theory of the state as a body possessing a superior faculty for thinking versus a theory of the state as a body possessing a monopoly on the legitimate use of force.[78]

Both Durkheim and Weber advocate an active state, but they differ in the ends they see it serving. The fundamental duty of the state for Durkheim is to protect the dignity of the individual, and for Weber to serve "the interests of national *power*." Durkheim envisions state intervention as a *moral* force, oriented in a primarily "internal" or "inward" direction, toward the goal of promoting equality and fairness. Calling upon the state to elevate the moral standing of society, he emphasizes the primacy of domestic policy. In marked contrast, Weber envisions state intervention as a *political* force, oriented in a primarily "external" or "outward" direction, toward the goal of enhancing "Germany's position in world politics." Declaring that the job of the state is to promote the "economic and political *power* interests" of the nation, he emphasizes the "primacy of foreign policy." This contrast between Durkheim's moral idealism and Weber's realpolitik could hardly be greater.[79]

Though they differ in their conceptions of the role of the state, for both Durkheim and Weber the services it performs are indispensable to the well-being of society. Marx takes a far more critical view. He questions the implication in Durkheim and Weber that the modern state is a sufficiently autonomous and impartial institution to serve in a beneficent or independent governing capacity. The state, Marx observes, is inhibited from playing a guiding role in society because it is simply another playground for the pursuit of egoistic interests. In addition, he emphasizes, the constraints imposed by the capitalist economic system and the interests of a politically powerful capitalist class severely limit what the state can accomplish. Within the framework of capitalism, he suggests, the state's vulnerability to the influence of economic forces precludes it from functioning in the manner in which Durkheim and Weber wish it to function. In any case, Marx points out, far from being a part of the solution to the ills of modern society, the very existence of the state is an integral part of the problem. As an institution standing above and apart from the lives of ordinary people—assuming the role of "master" of society—the state is an obstacle to democratic government and individual freedom.[80]

The Idea of Democracy in Marx, Durkheim, and Weber

Marx, Durkheim, and Weber differ in how they picture democracy, the purposes they see it serving, and why they find it desirable. In each case, however, their preference for and conception of democracy are intimately connected to their diagnoses of the modern condition. All three regard democratic government as an essential condition for alleviating the pathologies of modern society.

Marx calls for a participatory or "true" democracy, with the responsibilities of government managed by ordinary citizens. The struggle for democracy and the struggle for socialism, he believes, are two sides of the same coin. The objective of both is to put an end to class domination and turn power over to the people. Durkheim advocates a deliberative or communicative democracy, with governing officials engaged in a continuous process of public reasoning. For Durkheim, democracy means open government and responsive leadership, but it also entails a form of life where social conventions are subject to the scrutiny of society's collective intelligence. Weber favors a leadership or plebiscitary democracy in the expectation that popularly elected and charismatic leaders might be able to hold off the advance of bureaucracy, inject an element of dynamism into the culture, and protect the interests of the German nation. He values democracy because it is a potentially counter-bureaucratic force and an antidote to stagnation and routinization.

Neither Marx nor Durkheim regards democracy as a political system narrowly conceived. It is rather a type of society or a way of life, and an end in itself. Both conceive democracy as the embodiment of freedom and equality and, accordingly, both endow it with a certain moral standing. For Weber, on the other hand, democracy is not a type of society; it is simply a form of government, a method for the selection of leaders. Nor does it have any particular affinity with freedom and equality or otherwise possess any intrinsic moral worth. Weber's commitment to democratic institutions, though certainly genuine, nevertheless takes a more instrumental form. "For me," he says, "'democracy' has never been an end in itself. My only interest has been and remains the possibility of implanting a realistic national policy of a strong, externally oriented Germany."[81]

Elites and Masses

Marx, Durkheim, and Weber differ in the place each assigns to the mass of citizens in modern democracy. In contrast to Marx, both Durkheim and Weber deny the feasibility of popular self-government. In the modern world, the state necessarily exists as a specialized institution, differentiated from the rest of society, and this autonomy is a prerequisite for the proper performance of its functions. Politics too, they propose, is a specialized occupation, a profession suited only to those with the appropriate experience, training, and skills. Both thus envision an enduring division between a minority group of governing officials and the majority of lay individuals. For Weber, this division separates politically active elites from a politically passive mass, and for Durkheim, it separates a superior "government consciousness" from a less well-formed public consciousness.

While both Weber and Durkheim see government as the specialized activity of professionals, they differ in their view of the relationship between elites and masses. In Weber's conception of democracy, the role played by ordinary citizens is relatively minor and purely formal, with most people entering the political arena only in their capacity as voters. In Durkheim's theory, however, citizens play a more central and ongoing role. The very essence of democracy, he argues, is the regular back-and-forth communication between governing officials and the larger population. This continuous two-way interaction is necessary to ensure the responsiveness of the state to the concerns of the people and to enlighten the thinking of the public. For Weber, by contrast, the communication between elites and masses proceeds in a mostly one-way direction, from the top down; and it typically takes the form of emotional appeals on the part of leaders striving to win a following rather than rational discourse intended to educate a populace. Durkheim, by contrast, conceives democracy as necessarily "involved in the transformation of the population into an ever more rational and critical public." For Durkheim, as Jeffrey Prager says, the "democratic state" is democratic not because it takes a democratic *form*, but because it endeavors to produce a "democratic public."[82]

In contrast to Durkheim and Weber, Marx is committed to the ideal of popular self-government. He advocates a democracy where ordinary citizens, rather than being consigned to the sidelines, occupy the political playing field itself. A genuine democracy, he argues, one truly committed to the ideal of popular sovereignty, necessarily takes the form of a "government of the people by the people." Marx thus departs from Durkheim and Weber on several issues. First, he is adamantly opposed to the professionalization of politics. The active participation of citizens in the governing of their society, he argues, is an essential condition of individual freedom and self-realization. Second, as a determined enemy of elite rule, Marx rejects the assumption that ordinary citizens lack the mental temperament or intellectual ability necessary to carry out the functions of government and make judgments about the common good. Third, he also rejects any political system where the state exists as a superior body standing apart from the rest of society. Finally, while agreeing with Durkheim on the educational value of democratic

government, Marx suggests that public enlightenment comes not from communication between elites and masses but only through people's direct participation in political life.[83]

The Prospects for Democracy

Marx, Durkheim, and Weber differ in their analyses of the characteristics and
trajectory of modern society and, following from this, they differ also in their
assessment of the prospects for democracy. Marx is optimistic not only that
democracy will prevail in the future, but that it will take a radically participatory form. This hopefulness follows from a theory of how the development of
capitalism gives rise to an increasingly revolutionary workers' movement,
one whose interests naturally incline it toward the complete democratization
of society. For Durkheim, too, democracy is the wave of the future. But
while Marx gives priority to economic and political forces, Durkheim emphasizes cultural and moral forces. Democracy, he argues, is an imperative
rooted in powerful collective beliefs and sentiments, impelled by a growing
and indelible popular demand for a more just and equal society. While Marx
believes that democracy must be won through political agitation, for Durkheim it is riding the wave of an irresistible and peaceful cultural dynamic,
one destined to carry the day. In evaluating the prospects for democracy,
Durkheim thus attributes far more weight to the role of ideas in history than
does Marx—and far more than Weber as well. The power of the democratic
ideal, according to Weber, is no match for the obstacles to democracy inherent in the modern condition. While Durkheim finds within the logic of modernity an inducement to democracy, Weber finds a hindrance. The domination of the many by the few, he argues, is an inevitable outcome of the
necessity of bureaucratic organization, the need for professional personnel
and technical experts, the durability of economic and political inequality, and
the hierarchical structure of industrial production. These irrevocable conditions of modern life, Weber claims, mean that any genuinely participatory or
deliberative democracy is simply inconceivable.[84]

For both Marx and Durkheim, the future belongs to democracy; for Weber, it belongs to bureaucracy. Durkheim does not directly address the topic,
but the differences between Marx and Weber on bureaucracy partly explain
why the former is optimistic about the prospects for democracy and the latter
pessimistic. For Weber, the professionally trained occupants of the bureaucratic apparatus play an indispensable role in the management of society's
affairs. Power naturally flows in their direction, hence the ever-present threat

of bureaucratic domination. The authority and influence that bureaucratic personnel possess by virtue of their technical expertise and insider knowledge pose an insuperable obstacle to any kind of popular democracy. Bureaucratic domination can be contained, Weber argues, but only "from above," only by a determined political elite, and thus only at the expense of popular self-government.[85]

For Marx, however, the oppressive machinery of bureaucratic organization is less a technical necessity than an instrument of class rule. He finds bureaucracy objectionable, furthermore, not because it thwarts effective leadership but because it is contrary to democratic principles. The real obstacle to democracy, Marx argues, is not bureaucratic domination per se, but class domination. The overthrow of capitalism and the creation of a classless society, he believes, will pave the way for the realization of the democratic ideal, and this, in turn, will diminish the pernicious effects of bureaucracy by subjecting it to a "democratic control from below." Weber, however, in opposition to Marx, rejects the feasibility of mass participation, and he thus denies the possibility that bureaucracy can be contained by the democratic empowerment of ordinary citizens. The advent of socialism, for Weber, accordingly, will result in a more *bureaucratic* society, not a more *democratic* society. This contrast—Marx's optimism about the prospects for democracy and Weber's pessimism—is among the most fundamental differences between the two. It goes to the heart of their opposing political views and, as we will see in the next chapter, it underlies their conflicting thoughts about socialism as well.[86]

Both Marx and Durkheim might be accused of overestimating the strength of the popular demand for democracy and of having unrealistic expectations for a democratic future. Or, stated otherwise, they might be criticized for underestimating the obstacles to democratic reform and the strength of the anti-democratic opposition. Weber on the other hand is vulnerable to the charge of overestimating the impediments to democracy and downplaying the influence and democratic promise of mass social movements and popular resistance to elite rule. If Marx exaggerates the revolutionary potential of the working class and Durkheim exaggerates the democratic potential of modern cultural values, Weber pays too little attention to the forces in society pressing for democratization. By turning a blind eye to the political struggles of ordinary citizens and the pressures for democracy from below, Weber underestimates the possibilities for participatory politics and leaves an unduly pessimistic picture of the prospects for democracy. As

Mark Warren observes, while Weber presents a thoughtful critique of direct democracy, he too quickly rules out "less demanding forms of participatory democracy."[87]

Both Marx and Durkheim envision the triumph of democracy, and both also anticipate that the achievement of democracy will mean a qualitatively better society. Weber's outlook is much less hopeful. There is no escaping the unpleasant realities of the present, he insists, and no getting around the limits these impose on the possibilities for the future. The democratization of society can only go so far, he argues, and certainly not far enough to fulfill any dreams of a qualitatively better society. From Weber's standpoint, therefore, Marx and Durkheim are faulted for expecting the impossible. It is worth noting, however, as Weber himself admits, that "the possible is often reached only by striving to attain the impossible that lies beyond it."[88]

Chapter Eight

Socialism and Capitalism

The same great transformation that gave rise to modern capitalism also gave rise to its antithesis, the theory and practice of socialism. Socialist ideas appeared in the nineteenth century in response to the massive dislocations accompanying the triumph of capitalism. As warring ideologies, antagonistic political forces, and competing systems of economic organization, socialism and capitalism have waged an ongoing though lopsided battle since the very beginnings of industrialization. Given its current global dominance, we might be tempted to declare capitalism the winner. But even in the United States, where the word "socialism" is commonly used as a slur, a 2011 poll from the Pew Research Center found that a surprisingly large percentage of the public (31 percent) had a "positive reaction" to the term. And among younger people (18–29), "socialism" elicited a more positive response (49 percent) than did "capitalism" (46 percent). These findings are difficult to interpret, of course. We do not know precisely what definitions individuals attribute to the two concepts or what specifically they mean to say when giving either a positive or negative response. Nevertheless, it would seem that the debate that started in the nineteenth century has not yet been settled. A close look at the contrasting views of Marx, Durkheim, and Weber can illuminate this controversy while also helping us sort through our own thoughts on the question of socialism versus capitalism. [1]

The passage from traditional society to modern capitalist society not only brought the issues of individualism and democracy to the forefront, but it did the same for the issue of socialism. Though important in its own right, the topic of socialism is significant also—crucially so, in fact—for comprehend-

241

ing Marx, Durkheim, and Weber's diagnoses of the modern condition and for understanding the differences among the three in their basic worldviews, their sociological assumptions, their political commitments, and their visions of what is possible and desirable in the future. We cannot fully understand these three theorists without recognizing the centrality of the "social question" in their work (what can be done to improve the circumstances of the working class?) and without coming to grips with their writings on socialism specifically. What Marx, Durkheim, and Weber each has to say about socialism and socialism versus capitalism is uniquely revealing, perhaps shedding more light on their respective theoretical orientations and political standpoints than just about any other issue. This is the last of the thematic chapters, and it can be justifiably regarded as a culminating chapter as well.

KARL MARX: THE SELF-EMANCIPATION OF THE WORKING CLASS

The term "socialist," whether in reference to a person, a doctrine, a movement, or a political party, does not have a definitive meaning. To pin the label "socialist" on someone or something is not particularly informative, probably revealing more about the labeler than the labeled. It is not sufficient therefore to call Marx a socialist or a communist and leave it at that. Socialism preceded Marx's birth, it appeared in various forms during his lifetime, and it has lived on in even greater diversity since his death. Marx was a socialist, but not all socialists or socialisms are Marxist, and Marx himself was critical of many contemporaneous socialist ideas and programs. Given socialism's varied manifestations and the uncertain usage of the term, we should resist any temptation to infer the substance of Marx's socialism from the theory and practice of socialism generally, whether in the past or the present, or from the image of socialism promulgated by either its sympathizers or its detractors.[2]

How did Marx become a socialist, and what sort of socialist did he become? What led him to join the socialist cause, what was his political standpoint within the socialist movement, and how did he see a socialist society differing from a capitalist society? To shed some light on these issues, I begin by tracing the development of Marx's thinking up until around 1846, by which time he had become a recognizably *Marxist* socialist. I then discuss his theory of revolution and his perspective on the politics of the working class and the strategies and goals of the socialist movement. Following this, I briefly take one final look at a topic alluded to in earlier chapters—Marx's vision of the socialist future.

Marx's Road to Socialism

Marx first confronted economic questions in two articles published in 1842 and 1843 in the *Rheinische Zeitung*, a weekly newspaper he edited for about six months until its suppression by the German government. According to Engels, Marx later singled out these writings as being pivotal in leading him "from pure politics to economic relationships and so to socialism." In the 1842 article, he protests a legislative proposal on behalf of property owners to impose criminal penalties on the gathering of wood on private forestland. His analysis reveals three noteworthy features of the political landscape: the corrupting influence of powerful economic groups on the functioning of the state, legislative policy that sacrifices the needs of the poor to the interests of the rich, and the elevation of the property rights of wealthy landowners over the customary rights of dispossessed peasants. In the 1843 article, another early foray into socioeconomic issues, Marx addresses the impoverishment of Moselle winegrowers and questions the ability of the government bureaucracy to respond adequately to their economic plight. These two pieces reveal a young Marx in the early stage of becoming a Marxist. He investigates concrete social problems, takes notice of the sharp economic divisions in society, challenges the sanctity of private property, exposes the subversion of government by privileged interests, and demonstrates a "passionate identification with the poor and oppressed."[3]

With the government shutdown of the *Rheinische Zeitung* in 1843, the twenty-five-year-old Marx spent the next several months writing a critique of Hegel's political philosophy and reading books in political theory and history. According to Richard Hunt, Marx's "moral commitment" to communism took shape during this period, motivated by his radical democratic outlook and his critical view of the state. Though still not explicitly referring to himself as a communist, Marx's devotion to the ideal of popular democracy pushed him to call for a classless society and the abolition of private property. In demanding a "true democracy," Marx effectively, if not yet explicitly, announced his allegiance to the communist cause. But at this early point, he viewed communism primarily as a means for resolving the political, rather than the economic, contradictions of modern society.[4]

The relationship between economic forces and political institutions emerges as a central theme in the writings of the young Marx. His early efforts at clarification converge on five key points. First, he underlines what he perceives to be the untenable division between civil society, the private sphere of everyday life, and the state, the public sphere, responsible for upholding the general interest. Second, he draws attention to the pathological condition of civil society, an arena marred by the presence of private property, egoistic pursuits, and class antagonisms. Third, in recognition of the powerful influence of socioeconomic forces, he asserts the primacy of civil society, the economic sphere, over the state, the political sphere. Fourth, by denying the supremacy of the state, treating it as dependent on civil society, he casts doubt on the capacity of government to act as an independent agent in service to the common good. Fifth, following from this, he comes to the conclusion that the state, hemmed in by the forces of civil society, is incapable of overcoming economic injustice, poverty, and other pressing social problems. Political reforms by themselves, he concludes—for example, changing the leadership of government or expanding civil rights—are insufficient to eliminate the ailments of civil society or resolve the pathologies of modern life. What is needed is a transformation of the very economic structure of society itself, including specifically the class-based system of private property.[5]

But who will carry out the revolution necessary to achieve this transformation? In an article published in early 1844, Marx takes another step toward his mature socialist position—he identifies the proletariat as the historical agent of social change. The proletariat is the "heart" of human emancipation, he declares, because it is a class "which has *radical chains*," "which has a universal character because its sufferings are universal," and "which does not claim a *particular redress* because the wrong which is done to it is not a *particular wrong* but *wrong in general*." As the complete negation of existing society, the proletariat, Marx argues, is uniquely situated to serve as the vehicle of revolutionary change. At this point in Marx's thinking, however, the proletariat enters the picture less as an empirical reality than an intellectual construct, a "purely speculative deduction."[6]

Shortly after discovering the proletariat in theory, Marx moved to Paris, and there he found a flesh-and-blood proletariat gathered in the streets, salons, and socialist sects of the "new capital of the new world." By all accounts his yearlong stay in Paris was a formative experience, bringing him into contact with a vibrant workers' movement and a variety of socialist thinkers and organizations. At the same time, partly through the influence of Engels, Marx's attention was drawn to the Chartist movement, the struggle of English workers to win citizenship rights and civil liberties. A revolt by Silesian weavers in June 1844 added to his ongoing political education. He was particularly impressed by the class consciousness of these German workers and by the "striking, sharp, unrestrained and powerful manner" in which they, even more so than their French and English counterparts, proclaimed their opposition "to the society of private property." Influenced by these examples, Marx came to see the proletariat from a less paternalistic viewpoint, not simply as a poverty-stricken mass, but as a potentially revolutionary working class.[7]

Marx took another step down the road to socialism while in Paris: he began to study political economy, including the writings of Adam Smith. The first by-product of this encounter was a collection of notebooks which have come to be known as *The Economic and Philosophic Manuscripts of 1844*. In this work we see a significant advance in Marx's thinking. First, his primary concern shifts from politics to economics, from the critique of the state to the critique of capitalism. Second, while previously equating the proletariat with the poor and the dispossessed, from here on, adopting a more precise and modern usage, he employs the term "working class" to refer primarily to the population of industrial wage laborers. Third, he places class conflict at the heart of his description of the capitalist system, declaring in the opening sentence of the *Manuscripts* that wages "are determined through the antagonistic struggle between capitalist and worker." Fourth, he introduces a theory of alienation that highlights the capital–labor relationship in the workplace, thus according center stage to the process of production rather than the market. Finally, in the Paris *Manuscripts*, Marx for the first time explicitly identifies himself as a communist.[8]

In 1845 and 1846, in collaboration with his partner Engels, Marx wrote a lengthy manuscript setting forth the materialist conception of history. Marking a decisive break with the tradition of German idealist philosophy, this work, *The German Ideology*, is generally regarded as the point of arrival on Marx's path to socialism. This was also the period, not coincidentally, in which he first ventured into the world of politics, forming the Communist Correspondence Committee in 1846, an association intended to establish lines of communication among European socialists, and joining the Communist League in 1847, the organization under whose auspices he and Engels wrote the *Communist Manifesto*. In the *German Ideology* and in the "Theses on Feuerbach," written in 1845, Marx insists on a point crucial to his view of socialism—that changing the world is a *practical* matter, something to be accomplished through politics not philosophy, through revolution not criticism. Communism, Marx says, is not a fixed ideal awaiting realization, "a *state of affairs* which is to be established." It is, rather, an observable tendency growing within the womb of capitalism, a "real movement" destined to abolish "the present state of things." This insight is central to his thinking about the liberation of the working class.[9]

Marx's Conception of Socialism and the Socialist Movement

Over a two- or three-year stretch in the early 1840s, Marx came to believe that human emancipation was possible only through a working-class revolution that would abolish the system of private property, end the regime of class domination, and overthrow the capitalist mode of production. Marx had become a socialist, more specifically a *Marxist* socialist. What most set him apart from other socialists was his perspective on the socialist movement and the political struggles of the working class. In the following pages, organized into several short segments, I discuss Marx's conception of communism as a "highly practical movement, pursuing practical aims, by practical means."[10]

Capitalism as a Precondition of Socialism

Marx condemns capitalism because of its inhumanity, but he embraces socialism because of its possibility. A qualitatively better society is feasible, he believes, for two reasons. First, as he states repeatedly, there is nothing preordained, eternal, or natural about the capitalist economic system. It is just another temporary way station in the history of humanity, a "transient stage of development," no less destined to be superseded than any preceding mode of production. In denouncing capitalism, he is not merely lamenting the awful state of the world; he is also anticipating the prospect of a more desirable future. For Marx, in contrast to those for whom "there is no alternative"—a viewpoint popular enough in today's era to have its own acronym, TINA—capitalism does not represent the end of human history.[11]

Second, socialism is a real possibility and not just the "quixotic" fantasy of utopian dreamers, Marx argues, because capitalism itself, by spurring the growth of modern industry, establishes the objective conditions necessary for a socialist society. Capitalism is not just a historically transitory system; it is a historically progressive system as well. Its "historical mission" is "to expand the productivity of human labour," thus creating the stored-up economic potential necessary for the emancipation of the working class. Within the framework of capitalism, Marx foresees a new and better world being born—a world in which the burden of unpleasant labor is reduced and every individual afforded the time and opportunity to pursue his or her own self-realization. Capitalism, Marx adds, prepares the way for socialism not only by increasing society's productive capacity, but also by calling into existence its own "grave-diggers," a revolutionary working class. It is a progressive force in history not only because it sows the *economic* seeds of a new society, but also because it sows the *political* seeds of its own destruction. For Marx, the capitalist system produces the social conditions that "enable and compel the workers to lift this historical curse."[12]

An Uncompromising View of Socialism

Marx's socialism is uncompromising, distinguished both by the radicalism of its opposition to capitalist society and by the radicalism of its vision of socialist society. The goal of the workers' movement is not to make capitalism more bearable, but to overthrow the system in its entirety. There is no room for conciliation in a society where the "man of labour" is subservient to "the monopoliser of the means of production." Marx preaches revolution, not reform. Instead of piecemeal palliatives, which serve only to perpetuate "the continued existence of bourgeois society," he calls for the "*complete emancipation*" of the working class, a goal achievable only by overturning the "very system of wages labour and capital rule." The proper objective, he states, is not the "alteration of private property" but "its annihilation, not the smoothing over of class antagonisms but the abolition of classes, not the improvement of existing society but the foundation of a new one."[13]

Nevertheless, Marx does recognize the value of trade union struggles to win immediate reforms, emphasizing in particular efforts to attain universal suffrage, shorten the working day, increase wages, and improve working conditions. But these "guerilla fights," he cautions, combat the *effects* of the system only. They address the symptoms, not the disease. The appropriate "motto" for the socialist movement, he pronounces, is not "a fair day's wage," but the "abolition of the wages system." Just as better food, clothing, and treatment do not alter the status of the slave, so too a bigger paycheck does not put an end to the exploitation of labor or restore to workers "their human status and dignity." Workers suffer from low wages and long hours, but the deeper problem, Marx insists, is that as dependent wage laborers, they are denied the freedom to control their own productive activity.[14]

The Self-Emancipation of the Working Class

Marx emphatically rejects the elitist view that workers are "too uneducated to emancipate themselves" and that their well-being and advancement can only be secured through the beneficent guidance of enlightened superiors. Intellectuals like himself, he acknowledges, can serve a useful supporting function. They can demystify social conditions and bring clarity to the political struggles of the working class. But they cannot effectively contribute to the socialist cause if they assume the role of "schoolmaster," or prescribe ready-made recipes for action, or fabricate detailed blueprints of the future, or demand that workers bow down before their theoretical principles. Any such doctrinaire programs, Marx argues, are less than useless. They "serve only to distract from the present struggle."[15]

In what is perhaps the central plank in his conception of socialism, Marx proclaims that the "emancipation of the working classes must be conquered by the working classes themselves." They cannot count on anyone else to liberate them from the servitude of wage labor. He urges workers to form their own independent political parties and organizations. Only through their own protracted struggles can workers hope to emancipate themselves and construct an alternative to capitalist society. Marx envisions a social movement unprecedented in its scale and import. "All previous historical movements were movements of minorities, or in the interests of minorities," he observes. But the "proletarian movement is the self-conscious, independent movement of the immense majority, in the interests of the immense majority." A socialist revolution, according to Marx, must be a working-class movement—carried out under the leadership of the working class, undertaken to promote the interests of the working class, and with the objective of building a society where the working class itself governs its own collective affairs.[16]

Class Struggle and Socialist Revolution

Marx's socialism is uncompromising not only in its antagonism toward capitalism and its vision of the future, but also in its insistence on the necessity of class struggle as the means for overthrowing the rule of the bourgeoisie. The working class, he emphasizes, cannot emancipate itself through conciliation and compromise, through rational appeals to the dominant class, or through "empty phrases about 'justice.'" He thus declares his refusal to cooperate with people who regard political agitation as too distasteful and who "spurn all *revolutionary* action." Repelled by the coarse world of politics, these "apostles of political indifferentism" want to "deny to the working class any real means of struggle." Marx finds this same aversion to political engagement in the writings of the utopian socialists. They naively hope to "attain their ends by peaceful means," by the persuasive power of their designs for the future or the shining example of their small-scale experiments in communal living.[17]

In sharp contrast to this "political indifferentism," Marx takes a radical standpoint. Instead of pleas for help, tempered dialogue, or "the play of the imagination on the future structure of society," he advocates revolutionary activity. The emancipation of the working class, he claims, is attainable only through class struggle, the "great lever of modern social revolution." A workers' revolution is necessary because the capitalist class cannot be expected to give up their political power and economic privileges without a fight. "Material force," Marx says, "can only be overthrown by material force." In the few countries where democratic institutions are in place, citing England and the United States, this revolution, Marx acknowledges, might take a peaceful form, through the ballot box. But even in most European nations at the time, democracy was either non-existent or underdeveloped, leaving workers with no means for advancing their interests except for non-institutionalized and likely violent political confrontation.[18]

Proletarian Revolution and the Conquest of Political Power

The bourgeois revolution transferred ruling power in society from the feudal lords to the capitalist owners of industry. Capitalists accomplished this revolution by gradually introducing a new mode of production in the interstices of the feudal system and then over time leveraging their growing economic power to secure their political dominance. This option is not available to the proletariat, partly because on the economic front "capital is the stronger side." The dependent status of workers as wage laborers precludes them from building an alternative economic order within the framework of capitalism. Because the "only social power of the workmen is their number," they are compelled to follow a different revolutionary path: to first attain political supremacy and then use their power as a majority force to sweep away the system of private property.[19]

The *economic* emancipation of the working class, Marx argues, can be achieved only through a *political* movement, only by the working class forming itself into a political party and seizing control of the state. Marx thus proposes a two-stage model of revolution, beginning with the "conquest of political power." The "first step in the revolution," he states, is to "raise the proletariat to the position of ruling class, to win the battle of democracy." Once the proletariat has attained political power, the next step is to begin the process of abolishing the system of private property, meaning the private ownership of the means of production, the basis of the capitalist economy. In this second stage the working class deploys its newly won political power to initiate the lengthy process of reorganizing the economic foundation of society. This objective cannot be achieved except through the forcible intervention of government by means of "despotic inroads on the rights of property, and on the conditions of bourgeois production." "Between capitalist and communist society lies the period of the revolutionary transformation of the one into the other," Marx explains. "Corresponding to this is also a political transition period in which the state can be nothing but *the revolutionary dictatorship of the proletariat*." During this period of transition, the state becomes the means through which the working-class majority carries out the abolition of the capitalist mode of production.[20]

Marx's Vision of a Socialist Society

Marx offers a *vision* of a socialist society but not a detailed *blueprint*. He refused to write recipes "for the cook-shops of the future," but he does set forth some general principles and ideals, mainly extrapolated from the negative example of capitalism. Despite his resistance to speculation, however, in at least one important sense, Marx *was* a utopian theorist: he believed that a better society was possible.[21]

Marx was a radical, though as Richard Hunt argues, more so in the ends he sought than in the means he advocated. He anticipated a qualitative break from the capitalist society of the present to the communist society of the future. The advent of communism represents a new stage of history, bringing within reach possibilities for human emancipation frustrated by the irrationality of the capitalist mode of production. In what follows, I briefly identify some of the central elements of Marx's radical vision of the communist future. (1) Under communism the means of production are placed under common ownership, thus freeing society's "wealth producing powers from the infamous shackles of monopoly" and subordinating them "to the joint control of the producers." (2) By abolishing private property, communism puts an end to the system of class exploitation where one group of people is compelled to do all the work while another reaps all the rewards. (3) A communist society, by uncoupling the sphere of work from the imperative of profit making, overcomes the alienation of labor, enabling workers to assume control over their own productive activity. (4) By eliminating the capitalist division of labor where "each man has a particular sphere of activity, which is forced upon him and from which he cannot escape," communism makes possible "the all-round development of the individual." (5) By subordinating the system of production to the needs of the individual and by reducing the sphere of necessary labor, communism maximizes the potential for human flourishing by affording people the free time necessary to realize their true individuality. (6) Communism abolishes the antagonism between the individual and society, creating a genuine community, where the full development of each individual is the condition for the full development of all individuals. (7) Under communism the polity takes the form of a radical participatory democracy, with the state no longer existing as a separate institution standing apart from and above the individual. [22]

Communism for Marx is a point of departure, not a point of arrival. It signals the end of the "prehistory of human society," but it is only the beginning of a truly human history where the individual is the master of his or her own destiny. The arrival of communism does not complete the project of human self-development, Marx suggests; it initiates that project. [23]

EMILE DURKHEIM: A CRY OF GRIEF

Durkheim gave every indication of being a socialist. He wrote and lectured extensively on the topic of socialism, he was close to several prominent figures in the French socialist movement, and many of his students and colleagues were committed to the socialist cause. One might also suspect socialist leanings from his enduring commitment to equality and democracy, his lifelong preoccupation with the "social question," and his vehement opposition to the doctrine of laissez-faire. He might also be assumed to have socialist sympathies from what he regarded as the chief pathologies of modern society: economic injustice, the imbalance of power between employers and employees, the exploitation of workers, unbridled egoistic individualism, and the anarchy of the market. The same conclusion might be inferred by considering some of the reform measures he favored: the abolition of inheritance, fair labor contracts, and economic regulation. Finally, to cite one last piece of evidence, in a 1915 letter pondering the future of France, Durkheim even went so far as to declare that "our salvation lies in socialism." [24]

But still, as Steven Lukes observes, Durkheim was only a "socialist of sorts." Though supportive of egalitarianism and drawn toward certain socialist ideals, he was never a political activist or a participant in the socialist movement, and he was adamant in his opposition to any program calling for revolutionary class struggle or the complete overturning of the industrial order. His judgment of socialist theory, including Marx's *Capital*, was largely negative, dismissing it as lacking in scientific validity. He emphasized the distinctly industrial nature of modern society, but unlike Marx, he never undertook a systematic analysis of the inner workings of the developing capitalist economy, refraining even from using the term "capitalism," and he showed "little interest in the economics of socialism." Though he was certainly influenced by socialist thinkers, Saint-Simon among others, Durkheim's particular brand of socialism was a departure from the mainstream of the European socialist movement, including especially Marxian socialism.[25]

Socialism and Sociology

Durkheim saw in socialism an imperfect sociology. Though often claiming the mantle of science, socialism, he argues, is essentially a practical doctrine. It is concerned "less with what is or was than what ought to be." Rather than presenting an empirically rigorous account of the modern world, it proposes instead an "artificial and unreal" plan for an imaginary future. And because it traffics mainly in ideals rather than realities, he asserts, socialism cannot help us understand or find solutions to the crisis of modernity. Downplaying the empirical contributions of socialist theory, Durkheim portrays it as little more than a utopian vision of the future. This critique, not incidentally, as Dick Pels observes, has the effect of elevating by comparison the standing of sociology, legitimating the latter as the one true science of society.[26]

Though socialism is of "minor interest" as a scientific doctrine, Durkheim concludes, it has performed the valuable service of energizing reflection about the modern condition, posing new problems, and stimulating scientific research. Socialism in this respect has spurred the advancement of sociology. In addition, he emphasizes, socialism is of the "highest importance" if considered as a social fact in its own right—and like sociology itself a product of and response to the advent of modernity. While it may not be a genuine "work of science," therefore, socialism is a worthy "object of science." However dubious its empirical claims and misguided its political ambitions, socialism, Durkheim states, has the provocative quality of bearing witness to the ills of modern society. Recalling Marx's view of religion as "the sigh of the oppressed," Durkheim describes socialism as "a cry of grief, sometimes of anger." While it falls short as a science, socialism is a potent symptom of the malaise of the modern period.[27]

Beyond this, socialism is significant also as an expression of a powerful current of opinion working itself out within the "soul of society." This "socialism from below," rising up from the "half-conscious" needs, desires, and yearnings of the public, takes the form of a "confused drive," an amorphous desire for change, a diffuse aspiration for "a different moral, political and economic regime." In this popular manifestation, emerging from modernity's cultural depths, socialism is a reflection of moral sentiments uniquely characteristic of modern times—a demand for equality and fairness, an affirmation of the rights and dignity of the individual, a lament for human suffering. Inspired by a "thirst for a more perfect justice," this socialism from below, Durkheim suggests, enunciates the modern religion of humanity.[28]

The study of socialism as a social fact, he claims, much like the study of suicide, is valuable for its potential contribution to understanding the pathologies of modern society and discovering how these might be resolved. Durkheim thus sets out to submit the phenomenon of socialism to the scrutiny of science; extract from the varied socialist doctrines their rational core, separating the scientific wheat from the ideological chaff; and excavate socialist ideas for the purpose of illuminating the crisis of the modern era.[29]

Durkheim's Definition of Socialism

The first step in undertaking a study of socialism, as with any other social fact, is to construct a definition of the phenomenon under investigation. Durkheim's approach, intended to avoid imposing any personal preconceptions, is to discover the true nature of socialism by identifying the core principles common to all socialist doctrines. The application of this criterion leads him to reject certain conventional views. He finds, for example, that some tenets typically ascribed to socialism are not peculiar to it, for example, support for egalitarianism, or are not central to all socialist theories, for example, allegiance to the cause of the working class.[30]

But all forms of socialism do have something in common. They all take economic conditions as their point of departure, they all protest the unruly state of the modern economy, and they all promote measures to regulate economic activity. Indeed, Durkheim credits socialism for pinpointing the central problem of the modern world—the disorganized state of economic life. Socialist theory, in particular, draws attention to how business firms, each pursuing its own narrow interests, "lack a common purpose," and how the entire sphere of economic activity more generally—"what goes on in factories, in mills, and in private stores"—proceeds outside the awareness and influence of the administrative authority of the state. Advocates of socialism, in Durkheim's view, are troubled by precisely the same problem he explores in the *Division of Labor*—"the state of legal and moral anomie in which economic life exists at the present time."[31]

This takes Durkheim to his definition of socialism. The distinctive "spirit of socialism," he says, is the demand for organization. This is a specifically modern spirit, "part and parcel of the very nature of higher societies," and already manifest in the army, education, and other arenas. To put it simply, he asserts, socialism "is essentially a movement to organize." It aspires to a system where economic functions are connected "to the directing and conscious centers of society," where economic activity is brought under society's conscious control.[32]

Durkheim contra Marx

Durkheim's strategy for defining socialism ostensibly functions as a neutral method intended only to render it an object of scientific examination. By a "curious feat of coincidence," however, in applying this procedure he divests socialism of nearly everything associated with the doctrine he finds objectionable. The features of socialism he judges to be inessential—not truly characteristic of the phenomenon—also happen to be precisely the same features of socialism he deems undesirable. He ultimately arrives at a conception of socialism that is very nearly the antithesis of Marxism. In the following pages, I take a closer look at Durkheim's vision of socialism— what he thinks it is and is not or, more accurately perhaps, what he thinks it should be and should not be.[33]

Socialism and the Working Class

In *The Communist Manifesto*, Marx reviews several different strands of socialist theory, including "critical-utopian socialism." "Socialists of this kind," he says, standing above the class struggle and appealing to "society at large," purport to represent the interests of "every member of society," regardless of class, the most advantaged as well as the least advantaged. This precisely defines Durkheim's socialism. Though workers too will be among its beneficiaries, socialism, properly understood, he argues, is neither a movement by the working class nor a movement for the working class. A true and efficacious socialism, he contends, cannot be "an exclusively class-based party"; it must be concerned with the common problems experienced by the entire population. As his nephew Marcel Mauss explained, Durkheim "desired change only for the benefit of the whole of society and not of one of its parts."[34]

Durkheim, of course, is fully aware of the difficult circumstances encountered by workers. But these, he believes, are symptoms of a more fundamental problem. "The malaise from which we are suffering is not rooted in any particular class," he insists. "It is general over the whole of society," afflicting "employers as well as workers." In opposition to Marxism, Durkheim is intent on ridding socialism of its "obsession" with the working-class question. Instead, he calls for a renewed and reinvigorated socialism, one determined to confront "the present malaise in all its dimensions" and promote the interests of society as a whole, not merely those of one segment of the population. Durkheim has no use for a socialism that pits the poor against the rich, employees against employers, as though "the only possible solution" to the illness of modern society consists of taking from one segment of society and giving to another. Indeed, he argues, to achieve a harmonious society, the desires of the poor need to be restrained no less than the ambitions of the rich. In sum, Durkheim says, socialism "goes beyond the workingman's problem" and "is far from being an exclusively workingman's affair." Even if not always recognized as such, the real aim of socialism, one destined to benefit the entirety of society, is to overcome the problem of economic anarchy by bringing economic activities under the control of the public consciousness.[35]

Socialism and Class Struggle

Durkheim disagrees with Marx about the interests socialism serves, but also about the means required to achieve it. For Marx, a socialist society can be created only through the sustained struggles of a revolutionary proletariat, only by workers mounting a political challenge to the system of capitalist production. Durkheim strongly objects to this view. "All his life," Mauss recalls, Durkheim "was reluctant to adhere to socialism" because of its sometimes "violent nature" and "its political and even politician like tone"; and he "was profoundly opposed to all wars of class or nation." Detesting violence and conflict, Durkheim rejects revolutionary socialism, judging it to be too "aggressive" and "hate-ridden," fueled only by "feelings of anger." He advocates instead a socialism motivated by "feelings of pity," and not just pity for the working class, but pity for the suffering experienced by society as a whole.[36]

Durkheim prefers a version of socialism not only denuded of its class perspective, but also committed to realizing its objectives without violence, conflict, or even politics. He denies that class struggle is necessary to accomplish socialism's mission, and he does not have much faith in "practical party politics" either. Political revolutions and parliamentary maneuverings, in his opinion, are "superficial, costly and more dramatic than serious." Indeed, for Durkheim, class conflict and political contention are among the chief pathologies of the modern era. Resorting to such dubious means can only aggravate the ills of modern society. Rejecting both proletarian agitation and political legislation, he instead pins his hopes for a socialist society on the educative power of reason and science and the efforts of writers and scholars to promote public enlightenment.[37]

Both Durkheim and Marx are optimistic about socialism's prospects. Their reasoning is similar too. Both are inclined to believe that modern society is naturally heading in the direction of a socialist future. But they disagree about how this will transpire. Marx foresees a revolutionary and likely violent transition from capitalism to socialism, while Durkheim envisions a process of gradual, evolutionary, and peaceful change. Socialism, he believes, is not something that must be forcibly brought into existence. It is already implied by the nature of things, an extension of the very logic of modernity, propelled by popular aspirations and the practical requirements of modern life.[38]

Socialism and Socialist Transformation

The classless society of the future, Marx argues, represents a profound break with the past, requiring the overthrow of the capitalist system. Durkheim resists this image of total revolution, this desire for "a complete remolding of the social order." He rejects the premise of a categorical "incompatibility between what ought to be and what is," arguing that the "ideal of tomorrow" is not entirely discontinuous from the "ideal of yesterday." He also rejects the implication that a more perfect society is possible only through the total eradication of the status quo.[39]

In Durkheim's assessment, modern industrial society is by no means irredeemable. Its pathologies are not so severe that it has to be thoroughly dismantled. And in any case, he claims, revolution—more a destructive than a creative force—is an ineffective instrument of social reform. "Great changes" do not occur overnight, he says; they need time, reflection, and "sustained effort." Durkheim in short favors reform over revolution, a gradual modification of existing conditions rather than a sudden and convulsive transformation. "It is not a matter of putting a completely new society in the place of the existing one," he says, "but of adapting the latter to the new social conditions." What is needed to achieve a desirable future is to develop and improve the industrial society of the present. "There can be no question of razing the social edifice to the ground in one day of revolution and then erecting another ab initio upon the ruins of the first." Durkheim, in sum, envisions continuity rather than rupture in the transition to socialism; and he envisions a socialist future arising through a protracted evolutionary process rather than through a massive social and political upheaval. [40]

Socialism and Capitalism

In contrast to Marx, Durkheim's commitment to socialism did not arise from a critique of capitalism, but from a concern about the more general malaise of modern society. His vision of the socialist future moreover is not anti-capitalist. For Durkheim, the objective of socialism is to organize economic functions by subordinating them to authoritative regulations, and this he believes is achievable within the framework of capitalism. Such regulations are necessary to assure equilibrium between supply and demand, restrain destructive competition, mitigate the power of capital over labor, and promote justice in economic relations. Laissez-faire capitalism is certainly unsustainable, he acknowledges, but he does not envision the reforms needed to create a good society as requiring an assault on the regime of private ownership. Contrary to revolutionary socialism, Durkheim believes that greater individual freedom and a "more distributive justice" can be introduced into society without abolishing "the entire system of property, production and exchange." There is no reason, he believes, "why the private enterprise system cannot be modified so as to make exchanges sufficiently equitable." [41]

For Durkheim, indeed, the "collectivist formula" will accomplish nothing. Even if the private property system were eradicated and the means of production delivered to collective control, he argues, "all the problems around us that we are debating today will still persist in their entirety." Simply transforming the system of ownership, he insists, will not obviate what remains the most pressing task: the creation of a "corpus of rules" specifying the rights and obligations of economic actors and regulating the operation of the various economic functions. Transferring the "machinery of labour" from one set of hands to another will not remedy the disorganization of economic life. This "state of anarchy," he declares, underlying his opposition to revolutionary socialism, "comes about not from this machinery being in these hands and not those, but because the activity deriving from it is not regulated."[42]

Here we see a key difference between Durkheim and Marx. For Durkheim, socialism means organization, and this is not incompatible with capitalism. For Marx, socialism means proletarian emancipation, and this demands the abolition of the capitalist system of production. For Durkheim, subject to proper regulation, the private enterprise system can be "socialized" and made to work in an orderly and just manner—for the benefit of society as a whole. For Marx, the capitalist system is inherently irrational, exploitive, and crisis prone—and it cannot be made otherwise. Both Durkheim and Marx look forward to a socialist future, but they disagree about how that might be achieved and what it would entail.

Socialism and Human Liberation

Durkheim's conception of human liberation is similar to that of Marx, with both upholding the ideal of individual self-fulfillment. For example, Durkheim speaks of the necessity of establishing an economic environment that allows for "the free unfolding of the social forces each individual contains within himself." Similarly, he ascribes to the state a duty to provide a social setting in which individuals can develop their "faculties in freedom" and realize themselves "more fully." Elsewhere, he talks about the importance of smoothing out "the functioning of the social machine" so that individuals are able to "reach all possible means of developing their abilities without hindrance." Both Durkheim and Marx recognize that individuals can flourish only if they are permitted the freedom and opportunity to realize their capabilities, and they both also insist that individuals can only be truly human as members of a community, as social beings.[43]

There is, however, Durkheim argues, a dangerous current in many socialist conceptions of human emancipation. Too often, he claims, referring specifically to Saint-Simon, socialism anticipates a future where production and consumption expand indefinitely and where individuals are completely liberated from all social constraints. Embracing this ideal, the socialist movement, he fears, threatens to throw fuel on the fire of one of the central pathologies of modern society: "the malady of infinite aspirations." Already, Durkheim observes, modern individuals suffer from unrestrained appetites, desires, and ambitions, incapable of ever being fulfilled. This yearning for more and more inevitably leaves people frustrated and unhappy. "Theories that celebrate the beneficence of unrestricted liberties," he states, whether in the form of anarchic socialism or laissez-faire capitalism, "are apologies for a diseased state." Indeed for Durkheim, what the modern individual most requires is not total liberation but moral discipline. Individuals can attain a healthy existence and a state of mental balance, he argues, only if their otherwise insatiable passions are contained by definite and achievable limits. "What is needed if social order is to reign," he says, in a passage with a notably authoritarian tone, "is that the mass of men be content with their lot" and "be convinced they have no right to more." This requires a "moral power," "an authority whose superiority they acknowledge and which tells them what is right." For Durkheim, individual liberty, properly understood, is not possible in the absence of moral rules. The image of the future advanced by socialists, he believes, because of its excessively materialistic concern with the problem of satisfying people's economic needs, overlooks the more fundamental issue, the problem of fulfilling people's moral needs. This last point takes us to the heart of Durkheim's critique of alternative socialist doctrines. [44]

Socialism and Moral Regulation

Socialism is a response to the social pathologies of an industrialized world. It is inclined to interpret these pathologies too narrowly, however, regarding them as economic problems or worker problems only. This, Durkheim contends, is the primary failing of socialism: it neglects the moral dimension of the crisis of modern society. Saint-Simon, for example, commits just this error in presuming that a stable society can be constructed "on a purely economic foundation." But for Durkheim, the troubles of the present are due ultimately to "the state of our morality," not "the state of our economy." What is most required to alleviate the ills of the modern world, accordingly, is a "moral restraint which can regulate economic life, and by this regulation control selfishness and thus gratify needs." Socialism is correct in demanding the organization of economic activity, but to overcome the malaise of modern society, "*organization*" must be joined with "*moralization*." In Durkheim's view, socialism's energies should be mobilized not only to pursue economic reconstruction, but to promote moral regeneration as well. [45]

Because of its materialist bias, socialism interprets social problems too much as issues of distribution, Durkheim argues, as bread-and-butter issues only. In his alternative conception, socialism "does not reduce itself to a question of wages, or—as they say—the stomach." It is impelled instead by an aspiration to rearrange "the industrial set-up" so that it is subject to the "control of the conscience." For Durkheim, a socialist society cannot be built from purely economic reforms. A stable, harmonious, and just social order requires that economic functions be "subjected to moral forces which surpass, contain, and regulate them." A transformation of the economic system, in the absence of moral enrichment, will accomplish little. New economic arrangements are crucial, Durkheim admits, including particularly the establishment of corporate organizations, but less for their own sake than to create the institutional conditions necessary to establish more effective moral regulation, to remake "the moral constitution of society." For Durkheim, economic reform is the servant of moral reform.[46]

MAX WEBER: THE DICTATORSHIP OF THE OFFICIAL

Weber describes the capitalist economy as a constraining system, an "unalterable order of things" to which everyone is compelled to submit—property owners and wage laborers alike. Capitalism is an ethically indifferent system as well. Its "rules of action," Weber states, require economic actors, if they wish to avoid "extinction," to behave in a purely self-interested, instrumental, and impersonal manner, at odds with both religious teachings and the humanistic values of the Enlightenment. He also denies that capitalism has any necessary "affinity with 'democracy' let alone with 'liberty' (in any sense of the word)," and he is dubious about the likelihood of these values enduring for long "under the domination of capitalism." More passages along these lines could be cited, but this should be sufficient to make the point: anyone looking for a ringing endorsement of the capitalist economic system will not find it in the writings of Max Weber.[47]

Given his critical view of the system, why does Weber prefer the capitalist market economy to the socialist planned economy? Why does he refuse to join the socialist cause? What line of reasoning motivates Weber to follow a political path so dissimilar from that taken by Marx? In the following pages, with a separate section devoted to each, I address in turn four questions: (1) Why does Weber think a socialist revolution is unlikely? (2) Why is he opposed to socialism and what problems does he foresee with a planned economy? (3) Why, even with all of its faults, does he defend capitalism, and what virtues does he attribute to a market economy? (4) How is Weber's assessment of the relative merits of capitalism and socialism related to his larger theory of modernity?[48]

Capitalist Development and Socialist Revolution

Marx believed that a socialist revolution was inevitable; Weber thinks it is improbable. Marx argued that the course of capitalist development would ultimately culminate in a working-class revolt and the formation of a socialist society. Writing more than a half century after the publication of *The Communist Manifesto*, Weber discerns a trajectory of social and economic change that does not fit the pattern predicated by Marx. The economic system has been and continues to be transformed in ways that Marx did not anticipate, and for any foreseeable future, Weber concludes, there is little prospect that capitalism will be superseded by socialism.

The Capitalist Class Structure

The Marxist perspective, as commonly interpreted, envisions an increasingly simplified and polarized class structure, with a growing and uniformly impoverished working class squaring off against a property-owning capitalist class. Weber identifies several contrary trends. He perceives an increasingly complex and differentiated class system—not just two classes, but a plurality of classes, each itself internally divided; and not a process of proletarianization, but the enlargement of the middle classes instead. He cites the growing population of white-collar clerks in the bureaucracies of the private sector and the emergence of a university-educated and professionally trained "specialist officialdom" within the bureaucracies of the public sector. The working class too, Weber observes, is undergoing a process of differentiation. Instead of a homogenous and unified proletariat, he finds evidence of a more heterogeneous working class, one divided by education, training, skill level, and occupational specialization.[49]

The ongoing transformation of the capitalist class structure, as Weber sees it, engenders new bases of affiliation, new lines of cleavage, and new forms of class struggle. Confounding Marxist expectations, however, it does not point toward any future confrontation between a handful of "capitalist magnates" and "millions upon millions of proletarians." Nor does it portend the creation of an increasingly large and powerful constituency for socialism. The interests of the new middle classes in particular, Weber emphasizes, do not correspond to those of the industrial proletariat and do not predispose white-collar workers or civil servants toward socialist revolution. "One cannot maintain at present," he states, "that there is a decline in the power and number of those with direct and indirect vested interests in the bourgeois order." All in all, Weber concludes, the development of the modern system of stratification is "far from being unequivocally proletarian."[50]

Class Consciousness and Class Action

Objective class location, Weber contends, does not necessarily translate into a corresponding subject identity or a corresponding readiness to organize for political action. He admits that people are normally inclined to act in conformity with their economic circumstances. But there is no guarantee this will happen. The relationship between class situation, on the one hand, and class consciousness, "class action," and class organization, on the other, is contingent. Workers, for example, do not always act on their economic interests alone. Even when they do, their interpretation of those interests and the direction in which they pursue them may vary greatly and may not necessarily lead them to adopt a radically anti-capitalist stance. In the typical case, in fact, he states, workers feel more antagonism toward their supervisors—their "immediate economic opponents"—than toward factory owners and shareholders. For Weber, in any case, it is anything but inevitable that the industrial working class will arrive at a unified proletarian consciousness, much less a revolutionary consciousness.[51]

Class Conflict and Socialist Revolution

Weber agrees with Marx that class conflict is a normal feature of modern capitalist society. But he rejects the Marxian view that the interests of capital and labor are entirely divergent, that class conflict is destined to intensify over time, that working-class struggles will inevitably take a revolutionary form, and that the advent of socialism will put an end to class antagonism and the domination of the few over the many.

While the interests of the capitalist class and the working class are by no means identical, Weber admits, they are not altogether opposed either. Capital and labor share some common ground, and they have common enemies as well. First, they both gain from a dynamic and growing economy, and for the "masses" in particular, Weber stresses, an efficient and productive economic system is necessary to make their existence at all tolerable. Both classes have a stake, he concludes, in the rationalization, modernization, and intensification of economic activity. On this "one essential issue," Weber states, the interests of workers and entrepreneurs "are identical." Second, both classes also stand to benefit from a policy of political and economic expansion abroad. To compete effectively in the global struggle for existence, he argues, and to increase the nation's "elbow-room in the world," Germany needs a strong export policy, and it needs to protect its access to overseas markets. A "decent life for the masses," he believes, depends on the "preservation and advancement of Germany's position as a great power." On this basis too—assuming workers can be led "to a better appreciation of nationalist politics"—Weber perceives a convergence of interests between capital and labor.[52]

Capitalists and workers are potential allies on another front as well. The interests of both "are diametrically opposed to the interests of all those strata in society" who—living from stipends, rents, and other types of unearned income—long for a "'leisurely' way of life" and hope to retain some sort of quasi-feudal existence. Because the working class and the capitalist class both gain from economic modernization, they are (or should be) united in their opposition to these backward-looking "forces of economic reaction." Weber thus implies that the immediate interests of the working class are not necessarily anti-capitalist, suggesting instead that their chief enemy is not so much the entrepreneurial class as it is the traditionalist champions of a preindustrial economic order.[53]

The relationship between capital and labor, Weber recognizes, does not cease to be antagonistic just because they have some shared interests. Indeed, he envisions no future in which workers will *not* be in conflict with capitalists. In opposition to Marxist predictions, however, Weber argues that the struggles of the working class do not invariably take the form of an attack on capitalism per se. Instead of trying to overthrow the system of private property, workers are more likely to engage in class actions intended to increase their share of the economic pie. "Trade unionism" adopts this approach, fighting for "high wages, shorter working hours, industrial protection and so on." The assumption underlying this strategy is that workers, if properly organized, can achieve significant gains *within* the capitalist system. Citing this more or less peaceful and reformist side of the working-class movement, Weber rejects the equation of class struggle and revolutionary politics.[54]

The Self-Destructive Nature of Capitalism

Weber is skeptical about the prospects for the formation of a revolutionary proletariat, and he also denies that the inherent contradictions of capitalism will result in the downfall of the system. Marxists are mistaken, he claims, in their assumption that the capitalist economy is unsustainable because of its vulnerability to recurring crises, and they are also incorrect in their belief that the logic of capitalism necessarily leads to the impoverishment of the proletariat. In Weber's view, the malfunctioning of the capitalist system is not so severe as to provoke either an economic collapse or a revolutionary outcry. The creation of business cartels and the regulation of credit by large banks have diminished tendencies toward over-production and over-speculation, thus mitigating the self-destructive effects of capitalist competition. Weber, indeed, turns Marx on his head, arguing that planned economies, with government bureaucrats filling in for industrial entrepreneurs, are more prone toward stagnation and ruin than market economies.[55]

Against Socialism

While for Marx socialism is both desirable and inevitable, for Weber it is neither. He admits that socialism is "theoretically conceivable," but even so, the reality of an actually existing socialist society, he believes, would be quite different from the ideal drawn up by its proponents. Weber argues, indeed, that the central promise of socialism—to put "an end to all rule by man over man"—is a utopian illusion, under no circumstances attainable. If anything, he claims, the substitution of a socialist planned economy for a capitalist market economy would result in an even more oppressive system of domination.[56]

Modern society is inevitably a bureaucratic society. Neither the modern state nor modern industry can be effectively managed in the absence of bureaucratic administration. The day-to-day functioning of government and business, Weber maintains, is thoroughly dependent on the expertise of professionally trained civil servants, on the one hand, and private sector white-collar office workers, on the other. By virtue of its unrivaled technical efficiency, bureaucracy is "escape-proof"; it is a "completely indispensable" feature of the modern era. But if left uncontrolled, the process of bureaucratization can jeopardize political and economic dynamism and can pose a serious threat to individual freedom. This is precisely the problem Weber anticipates with socialism. A planned economy, he predicts, would dangerously exacerbate the tendency toward bureaucratic domination that is already evident under capitalism.[57]

In a capitalist society, the bureaucracies of business and government exist side by side, "as separate entities." This has the advantage of enabling each to curb the power of the other. But under socialism, the "private and public bureaucracies . . . would be merged into a single hierarchy," a "single body with identical interests," no longer subject to any counterbalancing control. The bars of the iron cage will only tighten, Weber fears, "if the opposition between state bureaucracy and the bureaucracy of private capitalism is replaced by a system of bringing firms under 'communal control' by a unitary bureaucracy."[58]

This is Weber's main concern about socialism. By fusing economic and political authority, it would establish one system of power, with no countervailing force. If private ownership and the entrepreneurial class were eliminated, Weber warns, the "state bureaucracy would rule alone." State officials would be elevated to unchallenged leadership in a single bureaucratic structure. This convergence of business and government—already present under capitalism in the form of state intervention and private–public partnerships—would be fully accomplished under socialism. The ultimate result, Weber famously declares, would be "the dictatorship of the official, not that of the worker."[59]

Besides giving rise to an all-embracing state bureaucracy, a socialist society, because of the technical requirements of economic planning, would have two additional consequences. First, a planned economy would greatly expand the overall size and responsibilities of the bureaucratic apparatus. "Increasing public ownership in the economic sphere," Weber states, "unavoidably means increasing bureaucratization." Second, economic planning would also intensify the existing trend toward "the ever-increasing importance of experts and specialized knowledge." Socialism is advertised as a system intended to liberate the working class. In reality, Weber asserts, it would lead to the empowerment of bureaucratic officials and technical specialists, and it would result in the replacement of one structure of domination by another—capitalist domination by bureaucratic domination. Socialism's ostensible beneficiaries, the working class, would be worse off than ever. Instead of being under the thumb of the capitalist class, they would be subordinated to a state bureaucracy unconstrained by any competing power.[60]

For Capitalism

Weber was anything but a cheerleader for capitalism, but he vehemently defended the system against both its reactionary critics on the right and its socialist critics on the left. His position in these polemics, as Guenther Roth explains, was not so much pro-capitalist as it was "anti-anticapitalist."

Though he was less than an enthusiastic supporter of the system, he saw nothing better on the horizon. Beyond this, however, he did believe that a capitalist market economy had certain virtues that were lacking in a socialist planned economy.[61]

The system of modern capitalism, Weber emphasizes, exhibits a high degree of "formal rationality." This means that economic activities are guided by quantitative calculations, typically expressed in monetary terms. The behavior of capitalists, for example, is formally rational insofar as investment decisions are based on the numerical weighing of expected monetary costs and monetary returns. As Weber recognizes, however, the "formal rationality of monetary accounting" is indifferent to all "substantive" norms. For example, the system of rational capitalism, driven by the goal of profit maximization, does not yield a society where there is an equitable distribution of rewards or where everyone has the opportunity to engage in meaningful work. By these criteria—that is, from the standpoint of certain worthy ideals—modern capitalism is "irrational." However, Weber points out, capitalism does not look quite so bad "if the standard used is that of the provision of a certain minimum of subsistence for the maximum size of the population." Modern capitalism does not give us a just world, he confesses, but at some elementary level it does deliver the goods, it does have the virtue of providing for the basic economic needs of the population.[62]

Because of its formal rationality—because it maximizes the opportunity for rational calculation—capitalism has something else going for it as well, according to Weber. It is a uniquely efficient way of organizing the provision of goods and services. This advantage derives from its characteristic as a profit-oriented, competitive market system where the allocation of resources is based on monetary calculations of prices and profitability. Money, he says, "is the most 'perfect' means of economic calculation," the most "rational means of orienting economic activity"—for example, informing investment and consumption decisions. Purely from the standpoint of technical efficiency, therefore, capitalism, Weber argues, is superior to socialism.[63]

In agreement with Marx, Weber sees capitalism as a revolutionary system, always changing, expanding, and growing. This is what he seems to most admire about the capitalist economy—its unique dynamism, energy, and innovative power. He attributes these qualities to the risk-taking entrepreneur and the rough-and-tumble of market competition. The entrepreneur, for Weber, is the embodiment of a spirited individualism. Analogous to charismatic politicians in the political arena, the entrepreneurial class is a creative power and a counterbalancing force to the stifling effects of bureau-cratization. The system of market competition, with its "free fight for eco-nomic life," is another source of capitalism's vitality. Indeed, he regards the "'anarchy' of free enterprise"—a common target of socialist criticism—as an altogether desirable phenomenon, far preferable to the orderliness of bureau-cratic rule. The "moving spirit" of the entrepreneur and the give-and-take of market competition—these two capitalist institutions, he hopes, can help preserve some remnant of individual freedom in the modern bureaucratized world. This appears to be Weber's main reason for supporting capitalism over socialism.[64]

Weber's defense of capitalism consists partly of the lament that there is no better alternative. But, as we have seen, he also finds some positive virtues in the market economy. His preference for the capitalist system, how-ever, is also partly a matter of his own personal political and philosophical convictions. He values competition and struggle more than he values security and stability. He values efficiency and dynamism, which he associates with a market economy, more than he values the socialist ideals of equality and justice. He likewise prefers the economic rationality and productivity of capi-talism—necessary also for Germany to become a leading industrial power—more than he wishes to ameliorate the disempowerment and deprivation of the proletariat. He fears "the effects of socialist centralization and control" more than he fears "the effects of capitalist concentration of property." And he worries less about the destructive effects of market competition and profit seeking than he does about the regimentation of a bureaucratic order and the prospect of economic stagnation. Weber was "a serious critic of capitalism," as Fritz Ringer observes, but he was ultimately "much more radically critical of 'planned economies' than he was of 'market economies.'"[65]

Capitalism, Socialism, and Modernity

The socialist movement arose in response to the problems of an emerging industrial society, including especially the alienation and impoverishment of the working class. Many socialists, Marx included, attributed these problems to the unique characteristics of the capitalist mode of production. By over-throwing capitalism, accordingly, a socialist movement could thereby achieve the liberation of the proletariat and usher in a new era of human freedom.

Weber offers a more pessimistic appraisal. The hardships experienced by the working class, he argues—which socialists mistakenly blame on capital-

ism—derive instead from certain ineradicable features of modern economic
life. For Weber, socialism is a futile project, fueled by aspirations that cannot
possibly be fulfilled. A socialist revolution, he insists, will not alleviate the
subservience of the working class, and it may even make things worse. I
examine Weber's argument on this point by focusing on his discussion of
two key issues: the expropriation of workers from the means of production
and the subordination of workers within the system of modern industry.
Weber's analysis of these issues leads him to the conclusion that the alienation of labor, which Marx attributes to the logic of capitalism, is instead an
inevitable concomitant of modernity.

The Expropriation of Workers from the Means of Production

Workers under capitalism, Marx argues, are separated from the means of
production. They do not own land to grow crops or machinery to manufacture goods. All they possess is their capacity to labor, and this they are forced
to sell to one or another capitalist. As propertyless wage laborers, workers
are formally free, but they are anything but free in fact. Needing a job to earn
a living, they are dependent on capitalists within the labor market and subject
to their authority within the workplace.

Though largely in agreement with Marx's analysis, Weber argues that this
pattern of "expropriation" is occurring everywhere, not just in private industry, and it is happening to nearly everyone, not just the industrial proletariat.
Soldiers in the army, professors in the university, civil servants in the state,
technical and administrative personnel in the private sector—all these people
are "in precisely the same situation as any worker." As individuals, they are
deprived of the instruments, equipment, and resources necessary to carry out
their work; they function as cogs in a hierarchically organized bureaucratic
apparatus; they occupy a subordinate position within this apparatus, subject
to the authority of their superiors; and they are dependent on wage or salary
income. "Everywhere we find the same thing," Weber states: "the means of
operation within the factory, the state administration, the army and university
departments are concentrated by means of a bureaucratically structured human apparatus in the hands of the person who has command over this human
apparatus."[66]

This process of expropriation, Weber insists, does not result from the
workings of capitalism per se. It is rather a product of "*technical* factors" and
the requirements of efficiency. From a technical standpoint, Weber asserts,
the machinery of modern industry, the bureaucratic apparatus of the state, the

libraries of the university, and the instruments of modern warfare—all these means of operation, unlike the tools of the independent craftsman, exist on too large a scale to be under the control of each and every individual. The expropriation of workers, Weber states, is an inevitable by-product of the very "nature of present-day technology." In addition, he argues, the growth of a hierarchical system of bureaucratic administration and control, partly because of the opportunity it affords to manage and discipline the workforce, is due also to its greater efficiency. There is simply no other way of managing a modern economy. For these reasons, Weber submits, the pattern of expropriation is irreversible. It is an unavoidable characteristic of the modern economy, certain to outlive any socialist revolution.[67]

The Subjugation of the Working Class

Wherever the capitalist system prevails, Weber states, it is "the fate of the entire working class" to comply with the authority of the capitalist class. The creation of a socialist society, he suggests, will not alter this circumstance. In the modern industrial world, whether capitalist or socialist, whether the labor process is directed by private entrepreneurs or state bureaucrats, the population of workers is destined to occupy a subservient position in the system of production.[68]

For Marx, the alienation and exploitation experienced by the working class reflects the peculiarities of a historically transitory system of production devoted to the extraction of surplus value. For Weber, however, the "fate" of workers within the system of "large-scale industrial production"—chained to the machinery, subject to stringent factory discipline, and suffering the "extreme monotony" of specialized labor—is *independent* of whether that system is organized on a "capitalist" basis or a "socialist" basis. The subordination of the working class, he contends, is a technical necessity of modern industry, an essential requirement for the operation of a rational and efficient economy. Whether private property is abolished or not, "the steel frame of modern industrial work" will persist. The "fate of a worker who works in a mine does not change in the slightest," he states, "if the pit is a private or a state concern." Weber believes there is no possibility of transcending capitalism, at least insofar as this implies the creation of an altogether new society where workers are liberated from the affliction of alienated labor.[69]

Weber denies that a socialist system can reverse the expropriation of workers from the means of production or abolish the dehumanizing subjugation of the working class within the system of modern industry. A socialist revolution, he claims, will not bring about a more rational, humane, and democratic society, or improve the circumstances of the working class. Nor can socialism do anything about the growth of bureaucratic administration, or the increasing influence of technically trained specialists, or the requirements of machine production, or the persistence of class inequality, or the "rule by man over man." Socialism is powerless to change the unalterable conditions of modern life. Weber's portrayal of the modern world rules out the possibility of any radical transformation or any qualitatively better future. There is no realistic alternative to the way things are, he believes, and in the unlikely event that capitalism gives way to socialism, this will not result in any positive change in the conditions of humanity. Socialists, according to Weber, misread the present situation. They fail to see that the pathologies of modern society are not due to a replaceable capitalist system but originate instead from the inescapable conditions of modernity itself. [70]

MARX, DURKHEIM, AND WEBER ON SOCIALISM

Marx was dedicated to the socialist cause, Durkheim was a socialist of sorts, and Weber was a critic of socialism. Marx's socialism was radically anti-capitalist. Durkheim's socialism was not definitively anti-capitalist, but it was decidedly anti-Marxist. And Weber was a staunch opponent of socialism even while acknowledging capitalism's inherent irrationalities. Despite his support for socialism, Durkheim considered Marx an ideologue; despite his opposition to socialism, Weber held Marx in high regard; and despite their mutual rejection of Marxian socialism, neither Durkheim nor Weber mounted much of a defense of capitalism.

The Worker Question and the Pathologies of Capitalism

Marx, Durkheim, and Weber differ in their stance on socialism in part because they differ in their diagnoses of the modern condition. They do agree on one essential point, however: the situation of workers in the world of modern industry is deplorable. But they disagree about why this is the case, what it implies about capitalist society, and how this uniquely modern problem might be remedied.

Marx's analysis of the fate of the working class is rooted in his theory of capitalism. The capitalist free wage-labor system, he argues, is a forced labor system in disguise. Workers are *forced* into the labor market by economic necessity, and once on the job they are *forced* to do the bidding of profit-seeking employers. His critique is noteworthy especially for shedding light on the lives of workers within the hidden abode of production. Here, within the workplace, is where Marx uncovers the pathologies of the capitalist economic system: the exploitation, immiseration, and alienation of labor. Here is where he discloses the dehumanization of workers, treated only as disposable instruments for the production of surplus value. And here, within the workplace, is where he finds the moral imperative for the abolition of capitalism and a political force primed to fight for a socialist alternative.

Both Durkheim and Weber agree with Marx that the freedom enjoyed by the free wage-labor force is severely limited. Citing the forced division of labor and inequitable employment contracts, Durkheim denounces the injustice of a situation where job opportunities are unfairly restricted and where the advantages of class enable the wealthy to exploit the poor. "What can the unfortunate worker reduced to his own resources do against the rich and powerful employer?" he asks. Weber, similarly, referring to the "masterless slavery" of the modern proletariat, acknowledges that the weak position of workers in the labor market puts them at the mercy of capitalists and compels them to take just about any job that comes along. Durkheim and Weber also agree with Marx that workers encounter degrading conditions inside the capitalist workplace. For Durkheim, the monotonous routine of industrial labor, with the worker reduced to a "lifeless cog" set in motion by an "external force," is a "debasement of human nature." For Weber, too, the work life of the proletariat—structured by machine production, military-like organization, and the rationalized discipline of the factory system—is oppressive and unfulfilling. Durkheim and Weber thus confirm much of Marx's assessment of modern industry. But they differ from Marx, and from each other as well, in how they account for the predicament of the working class and what they propose to do about it.[71]

Durkheim admits that workers are extorted in the labor market and endure less than ideal conditions in the workplace, and he too finds this state of affairs to be unacceptable. He denies however that the mistreatment of the working class is an inevitable outcome of industrial capitalism and can be rectified only through the revolutionary overthrow of the private property system. The worker problem, Durkheim argues, in opposition to Marx, stems from the "state of our morality," not the "state of our economy." The anarchic system of laissez-faire capitalism is, without a doubt, inherently pathological. But through proper moral regulation, creating a more equitable and collaborative relationship between capital and labor, the system of private enterprise, he insists, can be made healthy and just. While for Marx the exploitation of the working class is a distinctly *economic* phenomenon, a necessary outgrowth of capitalism's ceaseless drive for profits, for Durkheim it is a *moral* phenomenon, a product of "legal and economic anomie." The proper course of action, therefore, is not the *destruction* of capitalism, but the *moralization* of capitalism. By this he means subjecting economic activity to binding moral rules, thereby mending the disorganized and unregulated state of economic life. Marx and Durkheim thus disagree on a fundamental question. Can the inhumane and unjust treatment of the working class be resolved within the framework of capitalism? Marx says no; Durkheim says yes. What unites the two, and what sets them apart from Weber, is that both are confident that change is possible, both believe that the working class can be freed from servitude, and both envision a more desirable future on the horizon.[72]

In contrast to Marx and Durkheim, Weber is far more pessimistic about the prospects for the working class. The dependent status of workers and their subjugation within the capitalist workplace are regrettable, he admits, but little can be done to alleviate this situation. He sees no realistic possibility of eliminating class inequalities, or transforming the hierarchical system of industrial labor, or liberating workers from the burden of alienated labor. These are among the inevitable conditions of modern economic life, and neither economic revolution nor moral reform can alter this circumstance. The unfortunate reality, according to Weber, is that the working class is destined to occupy a subordinate position within the modern system of production.

It does not follow, however, that nothing can be done to improve the situation of workers. Weber objects to social welfare policies, concerned that their paternalistic ethos might undermine workers' fighting spirit. But he does support trade union efforts and other measures intended to create a more level playing field in the competition between capital and labor. He holds out the possibility that workers, through their collective struggles *within* the system of capitalism, might be able to secure a more dignified existence and a greater share of society's rewards. But unlike both Marx and Durkheim, Weber does not foresee any fundamental change in the lives of workers, and he certainly does not anticipate a future of class harmony, economic equality, and social justice. The basic disagreement between Weber and Marx is whether it is feasible to radically alter the system of production and whether any such alteration would free workers from class domination and industrial labor's "joyless lack of meaning." Weber says no; Marx says yes. And similarly, on the question of whether a qualitatively better future is possible, while both Marx and Durkheim say yes, Weber says no.[73]

The concept of exploitation is the centerpiece of Marx's analysis of capitalism, but it plays a far less prominent role in the writings of Durkheim and Weber, and their usage of the term also differs significantly from that of Marx. When Durkheim and Weber raise the issue of exploitation, they typically mean inequitable exchanges in the labor market, with workers being unfairly remunerated for their labor services. The problem, they both suggest, is that employers are able to leverage their stronger bargaining position to underpay their employees and thus reap an excess reward. For Marx, however, the locus of exploitation is not the marketplace but the workplace. Capitalists exploit workers not in the sphere of exchange, but in the sphere of production, and they do this on a day-to-day basis by appropriating surplus value from workers' unpaid labor. Exploitation, for Marx, is not a contingent result of market imperfections. It is rather the key to understanding the secret of profit making and the innermost workings of the capitalist economy, and it is the key also to comprehending the "unavoidable antagonism" between these two classes and the dynamics of class conflict.[74]

Marx's theory of exploitation, along with his theory of alienation, gives his critique of capitalism its radical bite while at the same time informing his vision of the socialist movement. In contrast to the optimistic Durkheim, for Marx the dehumanization of labor can *only* be overcome through the abolition of capitalism, hence the *need* for a socialist revolution. In contrast to the pessimistic Weber, for Marx the abolition of capitalism creates the real possibility for *ending* the dehumanization of labor, hence the *value* of a socialist revolution. Ultimately, neither Durkheim nor Weber fully confronts Marx's critique of the ugly side of capitalism—the exploitation, immiseration, and alienation of labor. Durkheim skirts the issue by supposing that the adversities experienced by workers are destined to disappear through a natural course of evolutionary change, and Weber skirts the issue by supposing that such adversities are an inevitable feature of the modern condition.

Capitalism, Socialism, and Modernity

Marx came to socialism through a commitment to "true democracy," a radical critique of capitalism, and a passionate dedication to the emancipation of the proletariat. He perceived socialism as a *"real* movement" of workers engaged in a political struggle to emancipate themselves from the system of private property and the rule of the capitalist class. Durkheim, on the other hand, was drawn to socialism in search of a solution to the anarchic state of modern economic life. He vehemently rejected any notion of socialism that privileged the suffering of the working class or that called upon workers to launch a violent revolution. The primary objective of his reform-minded socialism was not to remedy the hardships experienced by the proletariat, but to alleviate the malaise common to society as a whole. Weber, though identifying himself as a class-conscious member of the bourgeoisie, was not unsympathetic to the plight of the working class. But a socialist revolution, he argued, would not free workers from their subordination within the system of industrial production or give rise to a more egalitarian society. In all likelihood, according to Weber, socialism would only worsen the oppression of the working class. [75]

In Marx's vision, a socialist revolution, by eradicating the system of class domination, would represent a radical break from the past, bringing an end to the "prehistory of human society." Durkheim and Weber, in contrast, perceive considerable continuity between the capitalist present and any socialist future. Socialism for both is the fulfillment of tendencies already present in modern industrial society—individualism and egalitarianism according to Durkheim and bureaucratization and rationalization according to Weber. For Durkheim, socialism would mean the perfection of what already exists, the ideal of an industrial society brought to fruition, the culmination of modernity's "mission for justice." For Weber, socialism would result in the consummation of a regimented bureaucratic order, the nightmare of the iron cage fully realized, and it would only further jeopardize the already imperiled freedom of the individual. [76]

Marx and Durkheim

Marx's diagnosis of the modern condition is premised on the distinction between two antithetical modes of production: capitalism and socialism. The achievement of the second requires the abolition of the first. Durkheim rejects this logic. Unlike Marx, he does not see socialism as an economic system at all, but as a "movement to organize." The objective of this movement is to place economic functions under the conscious control of society and invest them with an authoritative moral sensibility. What matters for Durkheim is not whether the means of production are privately or publicly owned, but whether economic activity is carried out in conformity with the moral ideals constitutive of a modern society. The enemy for Durkheim is not capitalism per se but economic anomie, and this is a problem that can afflict both market economies and planned economies. For Durkheim, in contrast to both Marx and Weber, the issue is not socialism versus capitalism. The socialism Durkheim favors, furthermore, is not conceived as an attack on or an alternative to capitalism, but as an effort to inject a moral element into the workings of the modern industrial economy.[77]

In sum, we can see four interrelated differences between Marx and Durkheim. First, for Marx the crisis of modernity originates from the capitalist economic system and the contradictions of a class society. For Durkheim, this crisis arises not from any inherent economic pathologies, but from a deeper problem: the unregulated and demoralized condition of modern economic life. Second, for Marx, the exploitation and alienation of the working class are normal and inevitable features of the modern capitalist economy, destined to worsen as capitalism expands. For Durkheim, the exploitation and alienation of the working class are abnormal and temporary conditions of the underdeveloped state of the industrial era, destined to be resolved as modern society matures. Third, the logic of Marx's argument leads him to the conclusion that the emancipation of the working class and the creation of a socialist society can only be attained through class struggle resulting in the abolition of the capitalist mode of production. The logic of Durkheim's argument, by contrast, leads him to the conclusion that socialism requires neither a violent revolution nor a fundamental transformation of the economic system. Fourth, for Marx, a socialist future, and any reforms within capitalism along the way, can only be achieved through the political mobilization of a class-conscious proletariat. Marx insists on the need for a political solution to the ills of the modern era. For Durkheim, political agitation and class conflict only aggravate society's problems. Socialism, he argues, can be achieved peacefully through moral education, public enlightenment, and the guiding light of social science research.

Marx and Weber

For Marx, the central feature of modern capitalist society (with the emphasis on "capitalist") is class domination. But since he believes that capitalism is destined to be superseded by socialism, Marx's analysis holds out the promise of a future classless society. For Weber, the central characteristic of modern capitalist society (with the emphasis on "modern") is bureaucratic domination. But since he believes that bureaucratic organization is an inescapable attribute of modernity, Weber's analysis precludes any future where

the rule of the few over the many ceases to exist. While for Marx the pathologies of modern society are rooted in the capitalist system of class exploitation, for Weber they are rooted in the process of bureaucratic rationalization.
By overthrowing the capitalist system, Marx argues, a socialist revolution
would solve the most pressing ills of modern society. Weber admits that a
socialist revolution might put an end to the system of private enterprise, but
because of the requirements of economic planning, it would only exacerbate
the tendency toward bureaucratic rule.[78]

Weber acknowledges the possibility of abolishing the private ownership
of the means of production and removing the capitalist as the managing force
in the economic system. He raises a good question, though. Who will be in
charge once the capitalist is out of the way? If entrepreneurs are no longer the
proximate decision makers, Weber contends, economic control will inevitably fall into the hands of professionally trained officials. The modern economy "cannot be managed in any other way." A socialist revolution will result
in the transfer of economic power from the capitalist class to government
bureaucrats, replacing one set of elites by another. Workers will continue to
occupy a subordinate position. The substitution of a planned economy for a
market economy, according to Weber, will not result in any improvement in
the conditions of labor within the workplace either. Because of the technical
requirements of modern industry and the need for efficiency, workers will
still be subject to a regimented and routinized production process. Any conceivable socialism, Weber assumes, will take the form of a centralized
planned economy—what is generally called "state socialism"—with specialized personnel running the show, both at the national level and the industry
level. This line of reasoning leads him to the conclusion that socialism will
result not in the "dictatorship of the proletariat" but in the "dictatorship of the
official." The socialist ideal of ending the "rule of man over man," Weber
declares, is illusory.[79]

Marx, of course, disagrees with this verdict. First, he is more optimistic
about a socialist future, partly because he is more hopeful about the prospects
for a popular democracy, one in which ordinary citizens play a substantial
role in society's governing process. While for Weber socialism would mean
greater bureaucracy and thus less individual freedom, for Marx socialism
would mean greater democracy and thus more individual freedom. We thus
see a fundamental difference between the two: is the practice of a participatory democracy compatible with the requirements of a modern industrial society? Marx says yes; Weber says no. While Marx envisions a democratic

socialism, Weber foresees no possibility other than a bureaucratic state socialism.

Second, Marx recognizes that even with the abolition of private ownership, any system of large-scale production will still require the presence of some "directing authority." On this point, drawing attention to the distinction between ownership and control, Marx and Weber are in agreement. But Marx rejects the supposition that the exercise of any such authority entails a relationship of domination. Under capitalism, to be sure, because it is a forced labor system whose "driving motive" is "the greatest possible exploitation of labour-power by the capitalist," workplace despotism and the oppression of the working class are inevitable. But under socialism, Marx argues, things are (or can be) different. Where the process of production is carried out under the "joint control of the producers"—that is, by workers themselves—the labor of "supervision and management" assumes a non-antagonistic form. In a cooperative system of production, where the primary goal is the fulfillment of human needs rather than the maximization of profit, the directing authority will function not like a capitalist overseer, squeezing every last drop of labor out of a resistant working class, but more like "the conductor of an orchestra." In large-scale production, Marx acknowledges, a controlling function— a conductor—is necessary to "secure the harmonious co-operation of the activities of individuals," but in contrast to Weber he does not believe that such control necessarily translates into bureaucratic domination or oligarchic rule. Marx's vision of socialism presupposes a possibility rejected by Weber, namely, the democratic organization of society and the cooperative organization of production.[80]

* * *

Marx foresees a future far preferable to the capitalist present, but possible only through a socialist revolution. Durkheim too anticipates a much improved world down the road, but he does not believe a revolution is required to achieve it. For Weber, a revolution might occur, but whether it does or not, the future will not be dramatically better than the present, and if socialism supplants capitalism, it will likely be worse. We might say that Marx envisions fundamental change but only through political struggle, Durkheim envisions fundamental change without political struggle, and Weber envisions political struggle but no fundamental change.

Chapter Nine

Conclusion

Marx, Durkheim, and Weber lived during an era now more than a century in the past. The modern western world of today—"late" (or "post-") modernity as it is sometimes called—is significantly different from the modern western world they wrote about. Among the many new twentieth- and twenty-first-century developments occurring, to a greater or lesser extent, in the countries of North America and Western Europe are the following: the shift from a manufacturing-based industrial economy to a post-industrial service economy; the decline of the blue-collar working class and the growth of a low-wage class of service workers, mostly female and disproportionately people of color; the establishment and expansion of the welfare state; the digital revolution, computerization, and the rapid spread of information technology; the emergence of new social media, including Facebook and Twitter, and new forms of interpersonal relationships; and the rise of new social movements—beyond the labor movement—organized around issues of race/ethnicity, gender, sexuality, the environment, and so forth. In many other respects too, the world of today is different from the world of the classical sociologists. But there are continuities as well. Most importantly, perhaps, the society we live in is still—more than ever, in fact—a *capitalist* society, and it has many of the same problems as the capitalism of the nineteenth century, including class inequality, economic crises, unemployment, poverty, and exploitive labor conditions.

The times have changed, certainly. But they haven't changed completely, and in some fundamental ways they haven't changed much at all. While we might be tempted to dismiss Marx, Durkheim, and Weber as dead white

European males, many of the problems they grappled with are still with us today, and their ideas as well continue to possess a great deal of life. Even in the new millennium, as I hope this book has shown, their writings are exceptionally stimulating—due not only to their acuity and foresight, but also to their thought-provoking failings and their often mistaken though intriguing predictions about the future. It is illuminating to read the classical sociologists because they got many things right, but it is no less enlightening to consider how they were led to get many things wrong. In either case, whether we turn to Marx, Durkheim, and Weber in search of new insights or as targets of criticism, their work remains well worth reading.

For contemporary sociologists, other social scientists, and even many scholars in the humanities, classical social theory is a valuable intellectual resource—a springboard for research and reflection, analysis and interpretation, argument and debate. Some sociologists study Marx, Durkheim, and Weber to discover general theoretical principles that might yield encompassing explanations for a wide range of empirical findings. Others mine their work with particular research interests in mind. They might, for example, seek to elucidate some empirical reality by refurbishing and applying Marx's concept of alienation, or Durkheim's concept of anomie, or Weber's concept of charisma. For others, C. Wright Mills for example, the "classical tradition" is valuable less for its testable propositions and specific empirical content than for its broad capacity to orient our thinking and help us "make sense of what is happening in the world." Scholars find value in Marx, Durkheim, and Weber for other reasons as well: they raise big questions still worth pursuing, furnish a useful vocabulary for talking about social life, provide a critical lens for interpreting the problems of modern society, and offer a seemingly infinite supply of research topics.[1]

The enduring vitality of the writings of Marx, Durkheim, and Weber is suggested also by the presence of their work in the curriculum of nearly every sociology department in the United States and in many other countries as well. Sociology students, at both the undergraduate and graduate levels, are expected to study the classics. The purposes of this requirement are varied: to impart the sociological tradition by familiarizing students with the origins and history of the discipline; to equip them with a common conceptual tool kit, a shared language, and a stockpile of venerable questions and conjectures; to instruct students in the practical skills necessary for theory construction and for carrying out theoretically informed research projects; to challenge students' taken-for-granted assumptions and open their minds to new ways of thinking and perceiving; to develop their ability to critically evaluate the social world; and to ensure that students possess the intellectual background needed for understanding contemporary intellectual currents and comprehending recent developments and controversies in the social sciences. Which of these (or other) purposes are prioritized depends on the department and the instructor. Nevertheless, it is difficult to imagine anyone with a degree in sociology who does not have at least a basic knowledge of the "holy trinity."

The trio of Marx, Durkheim, and Weber is an indispensable resource in the education of sociology students, the training of social scientists, and the practice of social research. This is one good reason for continuing to read their work. But it is not the only reason or even the most important reason. Indeed, much would be lost if the writings of these three were confined to the academic world or utilized solely for scholarly purposes. At present, of course, there does not appear to be a huge popular demand for books on social theory, but this does not deny the value such work might have for a broader non-academic public. This lay public, incidentally—this population of people with no particular professional stake in the discipline of sociology but who might nevertheless benefit from studying Marx, Durkheim, and Weber—includes the vast majority of sociology majors and the vast majority of students enrolled in undergraduate courses in sociological theory. For instructors in such courses, accordingly, it is worth keeping in mind that for the most part we are teaching soon-to-become citizens, not soon-to-become sociologists.

This takes us to what is, fortunately, another good reason that Marx, Durkheim, and Weber are still worth reading—and not just by sociology insiders, but by thoughtful citizens as well. What the writings of these three have to offer more generally is the power to deepen our understanding of modern society, enlighten us about our social surroundings, and shake up our ingrained ideas about the world. Those of us who teach classical sociological theory see this happening all the time. Though students sometimes have to be dragged to the water, getting them to drink is not all that difficult, and sometimes they even discover they are thirsty. This is not surprising. After all, Marx, Durkheim, and Weber addressed numerous topics that nearly everyone today thinks about or talks about on occasion: class, inequality, politics, conflict, business, ideology, power, education, science, the state, culture, bureaucracy, social change, work, specialization, religion, human nature, and many others. Though their language is sometimes obscure and their arguments often complicated, their writings do speak to enduring problems of general interest. We should not expect the classical sociologists to give us definite conclusions or final answers of course, but they do supply us with a useful if not invaluable point of departure and they provide us with plenty of nourishing food for thought.

The work of Marx, Durkheim, and Weber has value not only because it fuels the sociological enterprise, but also because it encourages us as citizens—compels us even—to reflect on our own political identities and worldviews, to think about who we are and where we stand. The thematic chapters in particular are intended precisely to serve this end. By placing Marx, Durkheim, and Weber in dialogue with one another, these chapters give us a chance to wrestle with the conflicting ideas of three preeminent classical sociologists. And as we now know, these three figures differ revealingly on important issues that even today are likely to be of interest to a broad public audience. (1) What are the defining features of the modern condition, what are the chief pathologies of modern life, what are their causes, and how might they be remedied? (2) What is the fate of the individual in the modern world, what are the characteristics of a worthy individualism, what social conditions endanger individualism, and what changes are necessary to enhance human freedom and autonomy? (3) What is the meaning of democracy, what are the prospects for increasing democratization, what purposes does democracy serve, and why is it desirable? (4) What are the relative merits of socialism versus capitalism, on what grounds might we choose between them, what would a socialist society look like, and how might a socialist future differ from the capitalist present?

These four sets of questions, in turn, as should be clear from reading the thematic chapters, raise a host of additional issues. With these too, we find significant disagreement in the theories of Marx, Durkheim, and Weber. Is capitalism the ultimate source of modern society's ailments? If not, how do we interpret the pathologies of modern life, and to what do we attribute these? What are the driving forces of social change in the modern world? Where are we headed? What reasons are there for being either optimistic or pessimistic about the future? What are the prospects for the development of a qualitatively different type of modern society or a qualitative better version of today's modern society? What possibilities exist for the expansion of democracy, the creation of less alienating working conditions, an increase in the opportunities for individual self-realization, and the establishment of a more just and equal society—and through what means might such ends be achieved?

Besides being an inevitable source of contention, these issues, and many others like them, are ones concerning which we can hardly avoid forming an opinion. On any particular question, we might find ourselves agreeing more with Marx, or with Durkheim, or with Weber. Or we might gravitate toward a position that somehow synthesizes the views of two of them or maybe all three. Or we might reject their thinking in its entirety on one or more issues and adopt a standpoint that differs significantly from all three of them. Wherever we end up, however, it is exceedingly helpful to have three distinct and well-defined perspectives to serve as a jumping-off point in our own individual deliberations and in our exchanges with other people also struggling to clarify their values and beliefs.

Precisely because Marx, Durkheim, and Weber are at odds with each other on big issues of lasting importance, treating them together and comparing their divergent perspectives on modern society gives us a unique opportunity for self-examination—for scrutinizing our ideas about the world, sorting through our opinions on the key problems of the day, taking stock of our political convictions, and appraising our conduct as moral agents and responsible citizens. The work of Marx, Durkheim, and Weber is still worth reading for this reason alone.

Notes

1. INTRODUCTION

1. On the "classical tradition" of sociological theory, see C. Wright Mills, "Introduction: The Classical Tradition," in *Images of Man: The Classical Tradition in Sociological Thinking*, ed. C. Wright Mills (New York: George Braziller, 1960), 1–17. For two valuable surveys of classical sociology that discuss the contributions of theorists beyond the "holy trinity," see Kenneth H. Tucker, Jr., *Classical Social Theory: A Contemporary Approach* (Malden, MA: Blackwell, 2002) and John Bratton, David Denham, and Linda Deutschmann, *Capitalism and Classical Sociological Theory* (Toronto: University of Toronto Press, 2009).

2. Karl Polanyi, *The Great Transformation: The Political and Economic Origins of Our Time* (Boston: Beacon Press, 1957); Raymond Williams, *Culture and Society, 1780–1950* (New York: Harper Torchbooks, 1958), xv; E. J. Hobsbawm, *The Age of Revolution, 1789–1848* (New York: Mentor, 1962), 17.

3. Peter Gay, "Introduction," in *The Enlightenment: A Comprehensive Anthology*, ed. Peter Gay (New York: Simon & Schuster, 1973), 20, 17; Immanuel Kant, "Preface to the First Edition," in *Critique of Pure Reason*, trans. Norman Kemp Smith (New York: St. Martin's, 1965), 9. For useful overviews of the Enlightenment, see Peter Gay, *The Enlightenment: An Interpretation*, vol. 2, *The Science of Freedom* (New York: Norton, 1969); Norman Hampson, *The Enlightenment* (New York: Penguin, 1982). On the division between the more moderate and more radical wings of Enlightenment thought, see Jonathan I. Israel, *Democratic Enlightenment: Philosophy, Revolution, and Human Rights 1750–1790* (Oxford: Oxford University Press, 2011). On the influence of the Enlightenment on the development of sociology, see Larry J. Ray, *Theorizing Classical Sociology* (Philadelphia, PA: Open University Press, 1999); Peter Hamilton, "The Enlightenment and the Birth of Social Science," in *Modernity: An Introduction to Modern Societies*, ed. Stuart Hall, David Held, Don Humbert, and Kenneth Thompson (Cambridge, MA: Blackwell, 1996), 19–54.

4. Gay, "Introduction," 17; Peter Gay, *The Party of Humanity: Essays in the French Enlightenment* (New York: Norton, 1959), 270; Hamilton, "The Enlightenment," 28, 30–31, 36.

5. Gay, *Party of Humanity*, 201, 270–74; Gay, "Introduction," 19; Hamilton, "The Enlightenment," 37–38; Gay, *The Enlightenment*, 98–122.

6. Hampson, *The Enlightenment*, 150; Hamilton, "The Enlightenment," 31–33; Gay, *The Enlightenment*, 92. On the revolutionary nature of the Enlightenment, see Israel, *Democratic Enlightenment*, 1–35.

7. Jack R. Censer and Lynn Hunt, *Liberty, Equality, Fraternity: Exploring the French Revolution* (University Park: Pennsylvania State University Press, 2001), 4.

8. Hobsbawm, *Age of Revolution*, 83; William Doyle, *The French Revolution: A Very Short Introduction* (Oxford: Oxford University Press, 2001), 40.

9. Doyle, *French Revolution*, 65–66, 12–15; Censer and Hunt, *Liberty, Equality, Fraternity*, 55; on the less than fully democratic substance of the Declaration, see Hobsbawm, *Age of Revolution*, 81.

10. Censer and Hunt, *Liberty, Equality, Fraternity*, 13, 17; Doyle, *French Revolution*, 32–33, 74–75, 80; Robert Darnton, "What Was Revolutionary about the French Revolution?" *New York Review of Books*, January 19, 1989, 3.

11. Censer and Hunt, *Liberty, Equality, Fraternity*, 144; Doyle, *French Revolution*, 81.

12. For a useful overview of the Industrial Revolution, see Phyllis Deane, *The First Industrial Revolution*, 2nd ed. (Cambridge: Cambridge University Press, 1979); and for two valuable assessments of the scholarly controversies surrounding the Industrial Revolution, see Maxine Berg and Pat Hudson, "Rehabilitating the Industrial Revolution," *Economic History Review* 45, no. 1 (1992): 24–50; Joel Mokyr, "Editor's Introduction: The New Economic History and the Industrial Revolution," in *The British Industrial Revolution: An Economic Perspective*, ed. Joel Mokyr (Boulder, CO: Westview, 1993), 1–131.

13. Hobsbawm, *Age of Revolution*, 46.

14. Polanyi, *The Great Transformation*, 33; on the process of urbanization, see Krishan Kumar, *Prophecy and Progress: The Sociology of Industrial and Post-Industrial Society* (New York: Penguin, 1978), 66–74; and on the "human results" of the Industrial Revolution, see E. J. Hobsbawm, *Industry and Empire* (Baltimore, MD: Penguin, 1968), 79–96.

15. Hobsbawm, *Industry and Empire*, 85; Hobsbawm, *Age of Revolution*, 77; Berg and Hudson, "Rehabilitating the Industrial Revolution," 42.

16. Hobsbawm, *Industry and Empire*, 94; for a landmark study, see E. P. Thompson, *The Making of the English Working Class* (New York: Vintage, 1966); on the rise of the "first socialists," during the period from 1800 to 1848, see Albert S. Lindemann, *A History of European Socialism* (New Haven, CT: Yale University Press, 1983), 37–85.

17. Anthony Giddens and Christopher Pierson, *Conversations with Anthony Giddens: Making Sense of Modernity* (Stanford, CA: Stanford University Press, 1998), 94; see also Anthony Giddens, *The Consequences of Modernity* (Stanford, CA: Stanford University Press, 1990); Rob Stones, "Introduction: Continuity and Change in the Preoccupations of Key Sociological Thinkers," in *Key Sociological Thinkers*, ed. Rob Stones, 2nd ed. (New York: Palgrave, 2008), 5–8.

18. Gerard Delanty, "The Foundations of Social Theory: Origins and Trajectories," in *The Blackwell Companion to Social Theory*, ed. Bryan S. Turner, 2nd ed. (Oxford: Blackwell, 2000), 21.

19. Michel Foucault, *Power*, ed. James D. Faubion, trans. Robert Hurley and others (New York: New Press, 2000), 352; John A. Hughes, Wes W. Sharrock, and Peter J. Martin, *Understanding Classical Sociology: Marx, Weber, Durkheim*, 2nd ed. (London: Sage, 2003), 10, 13.

20. Peter Wagner, *A Sociology of Modernity: Liberty and Discipline* (New York: Routledge, 1994), x; Philip Abrams, "The Sense of the Past and the Origins of Sociology," *Past and Present* 55 (May 1972): 22; Randall Collins, "The European Sociological Tradition and Twen-

ty-First Century World Sociology," in *Sociology for the Twenty-First Century: Continuities and Cutting Edges*, ed. Janet L. Abu-Lughod (Chicago: University of Chicago Press, 1999), 28.

21. Karl Marx, *Grundrisse: Foundations of the Critique of Political Economy*, trans. Martin Nicolaus (New York: Vintage, 1973), 701, 409–10; Karl Marx, *Capital: A Critique of Political Economy*, vol. 1, trans. Ben Fowkes (New York: Penguin Classics, 1990), 617; Karl Marx, *Capital: A Critique of Political Economy*, vol. 3, trans. David Fernbach (New York: Penguin Classics, 1991), 371; Karl Marx and Friedrich Engels, *Manifesto of the Communist Party*, in *The Marx-Engels Reader*, ed. Robert C. Tucker, 2nd ed. (New York: Norton, 1978), 476–77; Karl Marx, "Montesquieu LVI," in Karl Marx and Frederick Engels, *Collected Works*, vol. 8 (New York: International Publishers, 1975–), 266.

22. Marcel Fournier, *Emile Durkheim: A Biography*, trans. David Macey (New York: Polity, 2013), 730–31; Emile Durkheim, *Socialism*, trans. Charlotte Sattler (New York: Collier, 1962), 168.

23. Max Weber, "Suffrage and Democracy in Germany," in *Weber: Political Writings*, ed. Peter Lassman and Ronald Speirs (New York: Cambridge University Press, 1994), 84–87; on Weber's pro-modern outlook, see Alan Scott, "Capitalism, Weber, and Democracy," *Max Weber Studies* 1, no. 1 (2000): 33–55.

24. On Marx, Durkheim, and Weber as critics of modernity and as thinkers reflecting on the crisis of modern society, see Peter Wagner, *Modernity: Understanding the Present* (Cambridge: Polity, 2012), 17–20; Gerard Delanty, *Modernity and Postmodernity: Knowledge, Power and the Self* (London: Sage, 2000), 16–20, 25–29.

25. Russell Jacoby, *The Last Intellectuals: American Culture in the Age of Academe* (New York: Basic Books, 2000); Michael Burawoy, "For Public Sociology," *American Sociological Review* 70, no. 1 (February 2005): 4–28; Sheldon S. Wolin, "Political Theory as a Vocation," *American Political Science Review* 63, no. 4 (December 1969): 1078–80.

26. Wolin, "Political Theory as a Vocation," 1080.

27. Craig Calhoun et al., "Introduction," in *Classical Sociological Theory* (Malden, MA: Blackwell, 2002), 3.

2. KARL MARX (1818–1883)

1. Karl Marx, "Letters from the Deutsch-Französische Jahrbücher," in Karl Marx and Frederick Engels, *Collected Works*, vol. 3 (New York: International Publishers, 1975–), 142 [hereafter *MECW*]; see also "Marx to Friedrich Adolph Sorge," in *MECW*, vol. 45, 282–84. On Marx's sometimes misunderstood view of utopian socialism, see Eric J. Hobsbawm, "Marx, Engels and Pre-Marxian Socialism," in *The History of Marxism*, vol. 1, *Marxism in Marx's Day*, ed. Eric J. Hobsbawm (Bloomington: Indiana University Press, 1982), 1–27; Hal Draper, *Karl Marx's Theory of Revolution*, vol. 4, *Critique of Other Socialisms* (New York: Monthly Review Press, 1990), 1–21; David Leopold, "The Structure of Marx and Engels' Considered Account of Utopian Socialism," *History of Political Thought* 26, no. 3 (Autumn 2005): 445–66.

2. Karl Marx and Frederick Engels, *The German Ideology*, in *MECW*, vol. 5, 52; Karl Marx, "Critique of the Gotha Programme," in *MECW*, vol. 24, 87. See also Peter Hudis, *Marx's Concept of the Alternative to Capitalism* (Chicago, IL: Haymarket Books, 2012).

3. Karl Marx, *Capital: A Critique of Political Economy*, vol. 1, trans. Ben Fowkes (New York: Penguin Classics, 1990), 286n6.

4. Marx and Engels, *German Ideology*, 27, 236, 31.

5. In the interest of clarity I differentiate and treat separately what I call his theory of society from his theory of history, but Marx himself makes no such distinction.

6. For three valuable efforts to clarify and systematize the technical concepts Marx uses here, see John McMurtry, *The Structure of Marx's World-View* (Princeton, NJ: Princeton University Press, 1978); S. H. Rigby, *Marxism and History: A Critical Introduction*, 2nd ed. (Manchester, UK: Manchester University Press, 1998); G. A. Cohen, *Karl Marx's Theory of History: A Defence*, expanded ed. (Princeton, NJ: Princeton University Press, 2000).

7. Karl Marx, *Capital: A Critique of Political Economy*, vol. 3, trans. David Fernbach (New York: Penguin Classics, 1991), 927; Karl Marx and Friedrich Engels, *Manifesto of the Communist Party*, in *The Marx-Engels Reader*, ed. Robert C. Tucker, 2nd ed. (New York: Norton, 1978), 473.

8. Marx and Engels, *German Ideology*, 31–32; Marx, *Capital*, vol. 1, 283; Karl Marx, *Grundrisse: Foundations of the Critique of Political Economy*, trans. Martin Nicolaus (New York: Vintage, 1973), 494.

9. Karl Marx, "Preface," in *Contribution to a Critique of Political Economy* (New York: International Publishers, 1970), 20. For an illuminating discussion of the formation and role of the superstructure in Marx's theory, see McMurtry, *Marx's World-View*, 157–71; see also Eric Olin Wright, Andrew Levine, and Elliott Sober, *Reconstructing Marxism: Essays on Explanation and the Theory of History* (London: Verso, 1992): 95–96, 231–32.

10. Marx, "Preface," 20–21; Marx and Engels, *German Ideology*, 46–47.

11. Marx and Engels, *German Ideology*, 44, 37; Karl Marx, *The Eighteenth Brumaire of Louis Bonaparte* (New York: International Publishers, 1969), 47; Karl Marx, "Marx to Pavel Vasilyevich Annenkov," in *MECW*, vol. 38, 102; see also Karl Marx, *The Poverty of Philosophy* (New York: International Publishers, 1971), 109.

12. On the issue of "economic determinism" in Marx, see McMurtry, *Marx's World-View*, 157–87; Paul Wetherly, "Marxism and Economic Determination: Clarification and Defence of an 'Old-Fashioned' Principle," *Review of Radical Political Economics* 33, no. 3 (Fall 2001): 273–79.

13. Marx and Engels, *German Ideology*, 31, 55, 50; see also ibid., 39–40, 42–45, 50–54; Marx, "Marx to Annenkov." For a useful analysis of the logic of Marx's historical materialism and the sense in which it is a theory of history, see Wright et al., *Reconstructing Marxism*, 47–60. They make the point that Marx's theory of history purports to explain "major historical trends," not "particular events" (ibid., 54).

14. Arthur M. Prinz, "Background and Ulterior Motives of Marx's 'Preface' of 1859," *Journal of the History of Ideas* 30, no. 3 (July–September 1969): 437–50.

15. Marx, "Marx to Annenkov," 96.

16. Karl Marx, *Wage Labour and Capital*, in *MECW*, vol. 9, 212; Marx, *The Poverty of Philosophy*, 109; see also Marx, *Capital*, vol. 1, 286.

17. Marx, "Preface," 21; Karl Marx, "Speech at the Anniversary of the *People's Paper*," in *MECW*, vol. 14, 656; Marx, *Grundrisse*, 749.

18. Marx, "Preface," 21; Cohen, *Karl Marx's Theory of History*, x.

19. Marx and Engels, *German Ideology*, 30–31, 38–39, 58, 100–101, 126; Karl Marx and Frederick Engels, *The Holy Family or Critique of Critical Criticism*, in *MECW*, vol. 4, 53.

20. Karl Marx, "Contribution to the Critique of Hegel's Philosophy of Right: Introduction," in *Marx-Engels Reader*, 53–54, 60; Marx and Engels, *The Holy Family*, 153; see also Karl Marx, "To Arnold Ruge," in *MECW*, vol. 1, 394–95.

21. Karl Marx, "Meeting of the Central Authority," in *MECW*, vol. 10, 626; Marx, *Eighteenth Brumaire*, 15; Karl Marx, "Notes on Bakunin's Book *Statehood and Anarchy*," in *MECW*, vol. 24, 518; Marx and Engels, *German Ideology*, 38, 48–49, 54.

22. In the following pages I cite mostly primary sources, but my understanding of Marx's analysis of capitalism is heavily indebted to a number of secondary sources. I want to single out in particular four useful guides to reading Marx, including one classic in the field and three more recent additions to the literature: Paul M. Sweezy, *The Theory of Capitalist Development: Principles of Marxian Political Economy* (New York: Monthly Review, 1970 [1942]); Michael Henrich, *An Introduction to the Three Volumes of Karl Marx's* Capital, trans. Alexander Locascio (New York: Monthly Review, 2004); Ben Fine and Alfredo Saad-Filho, *Marx's* Capital, 5th ed. (New York: Pluto Press, 2010); David Harvey, *A Companion to Marx's* Capital (London: Verso, 2010).

23. Karl Marx, *Contribution to a Critique of Political Economy* (New York: International Publishers, 1970), 27–28; Marx, *Capital*, vol. 1, 125–27.

24. Marx, *Capital*, vol. 1, 247–57.

25. Ibid., 247–48, 253–55.

26. Ibid., 733, 739; Marx, *Grundrisse*, 487–88; see also Marx, *Capital*, vol. 3, 1019; Karl Marx, *Capital: A Critique of Political Economy*, vol. 2, trans. David Fernbach (New York: Vintage, 1981), 120; Karl Marx, *Theories of Surplus-Value, Part I* (Moscow: Progress Publishers, 1963), 270.

27. Marx, *Capital*, vol. 1, 135–37, 296; Karl Marx, *Wages, Price and Profit* (Peking: Foreign Languages Press, 1975), 34–35.

28. Marx, *Capital*, vol. 1, 129–30, 293–95; Marx, *Wages, Price and Profit*, 36–37. For a more detailed examination of Marx's theory of value, see Heinrich, *Karl Marx's* Capital, 39–79.

29. Marx, *Wages, Price and Profit*, 26–27, 41; Marx, *Wage Labour and Capital*, 208; Marx, *Capital*, vol. 1, 135.

30. Marx, *Capital*, vol. 1, 273, 873–940; Marx, *Wages, Price and Profit*, 44–45; Marx, *Grundrisse*, 459–514.

31. Marx, *Capital*, vol. 1, 874–75, 928–29.

32. Ibid., 874, 885–86, 896, 899.

33. Ibid., 270–74, 874, 899; Marx, *Wage Labour and Capital*, 203.

34. Marx, *Grundrisse*, 460.

35. Marx, *Wage Labour and Capital*, 201.

36. Marx, *Capital*, vol. 1, 274–76, 675–82; Marx, *Wages, Price and Profit*, 46.

37. Marx, *Capital*, vol. 1, 275; Marx, *Wages, Price and Profit*, 72–73.

38. Marx, *Capital*, vol. 1, 781–802, 935; Marx, *Capital*, vol. 2, 487.

39. Marx, *Capital*, vol. 1, 279; see also ibid., 415–16.

40. Ibid., 279–80.

41. Marx, *Theories of Surplus-Value, Part I*, 406–7; Marx, *Capital*, vol. 1, 449, 730, 291–92.

42. Marx, *Capital*, vol. 3, 127; Marx, *Capital*, vol. 1, 258–69, 325; Marx, *Capital*, vol. 2, 196–97; Marx, *Grundrisse*, 424, 433.

43. Marx, *Capital*, vol. 1, 266, 317, 315.

44. Ibid., 301; on Marx's theory of surplus value, see also ibid., 292, 730–31; Marx, *Theories of Surplus-Value, Part I*, 314–16.

45. Marx, *Capital*, vol. 1, 324–25, 672; see also Marx, *Wages, Price and Profit*, 48–49; Marx, *Grundrisse*, 322–25.

46. Marx, *Capital*, vol. 3, 958. For this interpretation of Marx's concept of exploitation, see Jeffrey Reiman, "Exploitation, Force, and the Moral Assessment of Capitalism: Thoughts on Roemer and Cohen," *Philosophy and Public Affairs* 16, no. 1 (Winter 1987): 3–41.

47. Marx, *Capital*, vol. 1, 449, 326.

48. Ibid., 432–38, 645–46.

49. Ibid., 450, 546, 549–60.

50. Ibid., 533–34, 375–76, 425.

51. Ibid., 723.

52. Ibid., 433; Marx, *Capital*, vol. 3, 373–74, 319.

53. Marx, *Capital*, vol. 1, 580–82; Marx, *Grundrisse*, 749; see also Marx, *Capital*, vol. 3, 214, 357–59, 362–64; Marx, *Wage Labour and Capital*, 228.

54. Marx, *Capital*, vol. 3, 352–53; Marx, *Grundrisse*, 287, 420.

55. Marx, *Capital*, vol. 1, 742; Marx, *Capital*, vol. 3, 615; Marx and Engels, *Manifesto*, 478.

56. Karl Marx, *Theories of Surplus-Value, Part II* (Moscow: Progress Publishers, 1968), 527; Marx, *Capital*, vol. 3, 365–66.

57. Marx and Engels, *Manifesto*, 474.

58. Marx, *Capital*, vol. 3, 182; Marx, *Capital*, vol. 1, 799; Marx and Engels, *Manifesto*, 483.

59. I discuss Marx's conception of socialism and socialist revolution more fully in chapter 8.

60. Marx and Engels, *Manifesto*, 474, 475, 479; Marx, *Capital*, vol. 1, 616; Marx, *Grundrisse*, 585–86; Marx and Engels, *German Ideology*, 73.

61. Marx and Engels, *Manifesto*, 477; Marx and Engels, *German Ideology*, 73.

62. Marx, *Capital*, vol. 1, 617–18; Marx, *Capital*, vol. 2, 120; Marx and Engels, *Manifesto*, 476. For an interpretation of Marx's analysis of the dynamic spirit of capitalist modernity, see Marshall Berman, *All That Is Solid Melts into Air: The Experience of Modernity* (New York: Simon & Schuster, 1982), 87–129.

63. Marx, *Grundrisse*, 409–10; Marx, *Capital*, vol. 3, 958, 371; Marx and Engels, *Manifesto*, 477.

64. See Marx, Capital, vol. 1, 667; Cohen, *Karl Marx's Theory of History*, 305.

65. Marx, *Capital*, vol. 1, 739; Marx, *Grundrisse*, 710; Marx, *Capital*, vol. 3, 958–59; Karl Marx, *The Economic and Philosophic Manuscripts of 1844*, trans. Martin Milligan (New York: International Publishers, 1964), 133–34; Marx and Engels, *German Ideology*, 49; Karl Marx, "Letter to the Labour Parliament," in *MECW*, vol. 13, 56–57.

66. Marx, *Capital*, vol. 1, 929.

67. Marx and Engels, *Manifesto*, 483; Marx, *Capital*, vol. 1, 799, 929.

68. Marx and Engels, *Manifesto*, 480–81, 483; Marx, *Poverty of Philosophy*, 172–73.

69. Eric Hobsbawm, *How to Change the World: Marx and Marxism 1840–2011* (London: Little, Brown, 2011), 14–15, 116–17. For a useful overview of the recent Marxian efforts to address the apparent weaknesses in Marx's theory of class, see John F. Sitton, *Recent Marxian Theory: Class Formation and Social Conflict in Contemporary Capitalism* (Albany: State University of New York Press, 1996).

3. EMILE DURKHEIM (1858–1917)

1. Robert Alun Jones, *Emile Durkheim: An Introduction to Four Major Works* (Beverly Hills, CA: Sage, 1986), 81. For the characterization of Durkheim's *Rules* as a "manifesto," see Kenneth Thompson, *Emile Durkheim* (London: Tavistock, 1982), 92; Gianfranco Poggi, *Durkheim* (Oxford: Oxford University Press, 2000), 14. On the political dimension of Durkheim's work, see also Marcel Fournier, *Emile Durkheim: A Biography*, trans. David Macey (New York: Polity, 2013).

2. E. J. Hobsbawm, *The Age of Revolution: 1789–1848* (New York: Mentor Books, 1962).

3. Emile Durkheim, *Socialism*, trans. Charlotte Sattler (New York: Collier, 1962), 159.

4. Robert Bellah, "Introduction," in *Emile Durkheim on Morality and Society*, ed. Robert N. Bellah (Chicago: University of Chicago Press, 1973), x, xvi. On the historical context of Durkheim's writings, see Bellah, "Introduction," ix–lv; Lewis A. Coser, *Masters of Sociological Thought: Ideas in Historical and Social Context*, 2nd ed. (Long Grove, IL: Waveland Press, 2003), 128–74; Richard Bellamy, *Liberalism and Modern Society* (University Park: Pennsylvania State University Press, 1992), 58–104.

5. Emile Durkheim, *On Suicide*, trans. Robin Buss (New York: Penguin, 2006), 344; Fournier, *Emile Durkheim*, 69.

6. Emile Durkheim, "Sociology and Its Scientific Field," in *Essays on Sociology and Philosophy by Emile Durkheim et al.*, ed. Kurt Wolfe (New York: Harper Torchbooks, 1960), 354; Emile Durkheim, *Montesquieu and Rousseau: Forerunners of Sociology* (Ann Arbor, MI: Ann Arbor Paperbacks, 1965), 3; Emile Durkheim, "Sociology in France in the Nineteenth Century," in *Emile Durkheim on Morality and Society*, 16–18.

7. Durkheim, "Sociology and Its Scientific Field," 363.

8. Emile Durkheim, *The Rules of Sociological Method*, ed. Steven Lukes, trans. W. D. Halls (New York: Free Press, 1982), 51, 37.

9. Durkheim, *Rules*, 51, 70, 53–54, 47n4; Emile Durkheim, *The Elementary Forms of Religious Life*, trans. Karen E. Fields (New York: Free Press, 1995), 209–11; Emile Durkheim, *Sociology and Philosophy*, trans. D. F. Pocock (New York: Free Press, 1974), 25; Durkheim, "Sociology and Its Scientific Field," 364–67. On the multiple meanings and ambiguities in Durkheim's usage of the term "constraint," see Steven Lukes, *Emile Durkheim: His Life and Work; A Historical and Critical Study* (Stanford, CA: Stanford University Press, 1985), 12–14.

10. Durkheim, *Rules*, 56; see Durkheim, "Sociology and Its Scientific Field," 368–69.

11. Durkheim, *Elementary Forms*, 15; Durkheim, *Rules*, 52.

12. Durkheim, *Suicide*, 344; Durkheim, "Sociology in France," 16; Durkheim, *Rules*, 129. See also Durkheim, *Sociology and Philosophy*, 24–26; Emile Durkheim, *The Division of Labor in Society*, trans. W. D. Halls (New York: Free Press, 1984), 288n16; Emile Durkheim, *Moral Education: A Study in the Theory and Application of the Sociology of Education*, trans. Everett K. Wilson and Herman Schnurer (New York: Free Press, 1961), 61–63.

13. Durkheim, *Sociology and Philosophy*, 2; Durkheim, *Rules*, 40–41; Durkheim, *Elementary Forms*, 15; Durkheim, *Division of Labor*, 220–21, 286–87.

14. Durkheim, *Rules*, 35–36, 60.

15. Durkheim, "Sociology in France," 5; Emile Durkheim, "Sociology and the Social Sciences," in *Rules*, 177; Durkheim, *Rules*, 36–38; Durkheim, "Sociology and the Social Sciences," 86–87.

16. Durkheim, *Rules*, 60–62, 31.

17. Durkheim, *Division of Labor*, xxix; Durkheim, *Rules*, 36, 31, 81, 60; see also Durkheim, *Elementary Forms*, 21–22.

18. Durkheim, *Elementary Forms*, 4; Durkheim, "Sociology in France," 3; Durkheim, *Montesquieu and Rousseau*, 50–55.

19. Durkheim, *Montesquieu and Rousseau*, 4; Durkheim, "Sociology and the Social Sciences," in *Emile Durkheim on Institutional Analysis*, ed. and trans. Mark Traugott (Chicago: University of Chicago Press, 1978), 71.

20. Emile Durkheim, "Course in Sociology: Opening Lectures," in *Emile Durkheim on Institutional Analysis*, 44–47; Durkheim, "Sociology," 376; Durkheim, *Elementary Forms*, 25; Durkheim, *Moral Education*, 258.

21. Durkheim, "Course in Sociology," 52, 56–57; Durkheim, *Rules*, 38, 63–66.

22. Durkheim, "Preface," in Emile Durkheim, *Suicide: A Study in Sociology*, trans. John A. Spaulding and George Simpson (New York: Free Press, 1951), 35–36 (this preface is not included in the more recent translation of *Suicide*); Emile Durkheim, "Prefaces to L'Annee Sociologique," in *Essays on Sociology and Philosophy*, 341, 347.

23. Durkheim, "Course in Sociology," 62, 66; Durkheim, "Sociology in France," 15; Durkheim, "Sociology," 380; Durkheim, "Preface," in *Suicide*, 36.

24. Durkheim, *Rules*, 162, 119–46.

25. Emile Durkheim, *Education and Sociology*, trans. Sherwood D. Fox (New York: Free Press, 1956), 98–99; Durkheim, *Rules*, 119–20, 123; see also Emile Durkheim, "Two Laws of Penal Evolution," *Economy and Society* 3 (1973): 297.

26. Durkheim, *Rules*, 37, 45, 121; Emile Durkheim, "Review of A. Labriola: *Essais sur la Conception Materialiste de l'Histoire*," in *Durkheim on Politics and the State*, ed. Anthony Giddens, trans. W. D. Hall (Stanford, CA: Stanford University Press, 1986), 129–30.

27. Durkheim, *Rules*, 40, 129, 135, 134.

28. Durkheim, "Sociology and Its Scientific Field," 373, 360; Durkheim, "Review of A. Labriola," 132.

29. Durkheim, *Division of Labor*, xxvi; Durkheim, *Rules*, 85, 160–61.

30. Durkheim, *Rules*, 85–87; Durkheim, *Division of Labor*, xxvii.

31. Durkheim, *Rules*, 94–97. I will discuss the specific case of inheritance more fully in chapter 5.

32. Durkheim, *Sociology and Philosophy*, 59–62; Durkheim, *Rules*, 87, 104.

33. For a detailed reconstruction of Durkheim's evolutionary argument, see Ernest Wallwork, "Religion and Social Structure in *The Division of Labor*," *American Anthropologist* 86, no. 1 (March 1984): 43–64.

34. Poggi, *Durkheim*, 39–42; Durkheim, *Division of Labor*, 126–27; Emile Durkheim, "Introduction to the Sociology of the Family," in *Emile Durkheim on Institutional Analysis*, 205–6.

35. Durkheim, *Division of Labor*, 132.

36. Ibid., 180, 195.

37. Ibid., 200–203.

38. Ibid., 208–13, 276.

39. Durkheim, *Division of Labor*, 38–39, 142, 105–6; see also Anthony Giddens, "Introduction: Durkheim's Writings in Sociology and Social Philosophy," in *Emile Durkheim: Selected Writings*, ed. Anthony Giddens (New York: Cambridge University Press, 1972), 5–6.

40. Durkheim, *Division of Labor*, 85, 106, 117–18, 229–30.

41. Ibid., 226–30, 232–33; see also Durkheim, *Moral Education*, 95–126.

42. Durkheim, *Division of Labor*, 122, 332–33. I will discuss Durkheim's thinking about the individual and individualism more fully in chapter 6.

43. Durkheim, *Division of Labor*, 24, 29, 34–35, 68–72, 77–83.

44. Ibid., 61–63.

45. Ibid., 82–83.

46. Ibid., 101, 153.

47. Ibid., xxvi, 84–85, 141.

48. Ibid., 84–85, 174.

49. Ibid., 103–5.

50. Ibid., 16–17, 337–38, 21, 331.

51. Ibid., xxx.

52. Ibid., 291.

53. Durkheim, "Preface," in *Suicide*, 37.

54. Durkheim, *Suicide*, 411–12; see Anthony Giddens, "The Suicide Problem in French Sociology," in *Studies in Social and Political Theory*, ed. Anthony Giddens (London: Hutchinson, 1977), 322–32.

55. Durkheim, *Suicide*, 24.

56. Ibid., 24, 28, 331–32.

57. Ibid., 155, 332, 340–44, 359–60.

58. On the dubious nature of Durkheim's procedure, which essentially assumes the validity of his types of suicide rather than discovering them empirically, see Lukes, *Emile Durkheim*, 201–2.

59. Integration and regulation correspond to what Durkheim elsewhere refers to as two "elements of morality": "attachment to social groups" and the "spirit of discipline." For a more detailed discussion of these two elements, along with a third, "autonomy," see Durkheim, *Moral Education*.

60. Durkheim, *Suicide*, 317, 332.

61. Ibid., 235–36, 238–39.

62. Ibid., 239–41; see also Durkheim, *Division of Labor*, 191.

63. Durkheim, *Suicide*, 246.

64. Ibid., 305.

65. Ibid., 396, 225, 231–32.

66. Ibid., 224, 163, 165.

67. Ibid., 217.

68. Ibid., 217–24. See also Emile Durkheim, "The Politics of the Future," trans. W. Watts Miller and J. Mergy, *Durkheimian Studies* 15 (2009): 3–6. In this article, purportedly his last publication, Durkheim writes about the unifying effects of the First World War on the French nation, an experience that had the positive result of affirming the "sense of the social" and causing individuals to "subordinate their interests to the interests of society" (ibid., 5).

69. Durkheim, *Suicide*, 270–73; on the idea that a healthy existence requires reachable aspirations, see also Durkheim, *Moral Education*, 38–40.

70. Durkheim, *Suicide*, 315.

71. Ibid., 303, 291, 300.

72. Durkheim, *Suicide*, 317–18; Lukes, *Emile Durkheim*, 206–7.

73. Durkheim, *Education and Sociology*, 84–85; Durkheim, *Montesquieu and Rousseau*, 18; Emile Durkheim, *The Evolution of Educational Thought*, trans. Peter Collins (London: Routledge & Kegan Paul, 1977), 329, 324.

74. Durkheim, *Elementary Forms*, 351; Emile Durkheim, "The Dualism of Human Nature," in *Emile Durkheim on Morality and Society*, 150; Lukes, *Emile Durkheim*, 499.

75. Durkheim, *Elementary Forms*, 351, 214; Durkheim, *Education and Sociology*, 76–77.

76. Durkheim, *Elementary Forms*, 66, 226, 420–21, 2; Emile Durkheim, *Professional Ethics and Civic Morals*, trans. Cornelia Brookfield (London: Routledge, 1992), 172.

77. Durkheim, *Elementary Forms*, 421, 208, 226–27, 422–25, 230.

78. Ibid., 265–66, 283, 271. On the evolution of Durkheim's thinking about human nature and the development of the homo duplex model, see M. J. Hawkins, "A Re-Examination of Durkheim's Theory of Human Nature," *Sociological Review* 25, no 2 (1977): 429–46.

79. Durkheim, *Elementary Forms*, 15, 266; Durkheim, *Suicide*, 354.

80. Durkheim "The Dualism of Human Nature," 151–52; Durkheim, *Elementary Forms*, 15, 421, 440.

81. Durkheim, *Professional Ethics*, 14–15.

82. Durkheim, *Education and Sociology*, 73, 124–25; the term "second gestation" comes from Guy van de Walle, "Durkheim and Socialization," *Durkheimian Studies* 14 (2008): 40.

83. Durkheim, *Moral Education*, 42, 133–34; Durkheim, *Education and Sociology*, 115–16, 72, 124–25, 122.
84. Durkheim, "Sociology and Its Scientific Field," 367–68; Durkheim, *Rules*, 47n6; Durkheim, *Elementary Forms*, 273, 425; Durkheim, *Sociology and Philosophy*, 40.
85. Durkheim, "The Dualism of Human Nature," 161.

4. MAX WEBER (1864–1920)

1. Wolfgang J. Mommsen, *The Political and Social Theory of Max Weber: Collected Essays* (Chicago: University of Chicago Press, 1989), 7.
2. Max Weber, *The Protestant Ethic and the Spirit of Capitalism*, trans. Talcott Parsons (London: Counterpoint, 1985), 54; David J. Chalcraft and Austin Harrington, eds., *The Protestant Ethic Debate: Max Weber's Replies to His Critics, 1907–1910*, trans. Austin Harrington and Mary Shields (Cambridge: Liverpool University Press, 2001), 106.
3. Max Weber, "Author's Introduction," in *The Protestant Ethic*, 26; Max Weber, "The Social Psychology of the World Religions," in *From Max Weber: Essays in Sociology*, trans. and ed. H. H. Gerth and C. Wright Mills (New York: Oxford University Press, 1946), 292–93; Max Weber, "The Meaning of 'Ethical Neutrality' in Sociology and Economics," in *The Methodology of the Social Sciences*, trans. Edward A. Shils and Henry A. Finch (New York: Free Press, 1949), 34. On Weber's central themes, see Wilhelm Hennis, *Max Weber's Central Question*, 2nd ed., trans. Keith Tribe (Newbury, UK: 2000); Friedrich H. Tenbruck, "The Problem of Thematic Unity in the Works of Max Weber," trans. M. S. Whimster, *British Journal of Sociology* 31, no. 3 (September 1980): 316–51; Stephen Kalberg, "The Search for Thematic Orientations in a Fragmented Oeuvre; The Discussion of Max Weber in Recent German Sociological Literature," *Sociology* 13, no. 1 (January 1979): 127–39; Steven Seidman, "The Main Aims and Thematic Structures of Max Weber's Sociology," *Canadian Journal of Sociology* 9, no. 4 (1984): 381–404.
4. Gianfranco Poggi, *Weber: A Short Introduction* (Cambridge: Polity, 2006), 52; Max Weber, *Economy and Society: An Outline of Interpretive Sociology*, trans. Ephraim Fischoff et al. (Berkeley: University of California Press, 1978), 30, 998; Weber, *Protestant Ethic*, 77–78, 194; Weber, "Author's Introduction," 13–17, 26–27; Marianne Weber, *Max Weber: A Biography*, trans. Harry Zohn (New York: Wiley, 1975), 333. For two particularly useful overviews of Weber's concept of rationality, see Stephen Kalberg, "Max Weber's Types of Rationality: Cornerstone for the Analysis of Rationalization Processes in History," *American Journal of Sociology* 85, no. 5 (March 1980): 1145–79; Donald N. Levine, *The Flight from Ambiguity: Essays in Social and Cultural Theory* (Chicago: University of Chicago Press, 1985), 142–78.
5. Weber, "Social Psychology," 280–81, 293–94; George Ritzer, *The McDonaldization of Society*, Revised New Century Edition (Thousand Oaks, CA: Pine Forge, 2004); Michel Foucault, *Discipline and Punish: The Birth of the Prison*, trans. Alan Sheridan (New York: Vintage, 1991), 228, 233.
6. Max Weber, "Religious Rejections of the World and Their Directions," in *From Max Weber*, 356.
7. Weber, *Economy and Society*, 1116.
8. Ibid., 4, 24–26. On some of the limitations of Weber's typology of social action, see Donald N. Levine, "The Continuing Challenge of Weber's Theory of Rational Action," in *Max Weber's* Economy and Society: *A Critical Companion*, ed. Charles Camic, Philip S. Gorski,

and David M. Trubek (Stanford, CA: Stanford University Press, 2005), 112–14; and Mustafa Emirbayer, "Beyond Weberian Action Theory," in ibid., 185–203.

9. Weber, *Economy and Society*, 25–26.

10. Weber, *Economy and Society*, 30; Jeffrey C. Alexander, *Theoretical Logic in Sociology*, vol. 3, *The Classical Attempt at Theoretical Synthesis: Max Weber* (Berkeley: University of California Press, 1983), 26.

11. Weber, *Economy and Society*, 30; Max Weber, "Marginal Utility Theory and 'The Fundamental Law of Psychophysics,'" trans. Louis Schneider, *Social Science Quarterly* 56, no. 1 (June 1975): 33; Karl Marx and Friedrich Engels, *Manifesto of the Communist Party*, in *The Marx-Engels Reader*, ed. Robert C. Tucker, 2nd ed. (New York: Norton, 1978), 475.

12. Rogers Brubaker, *The Limits of Rationality: An Essay on the Social and Moral Thought of Max Weber* (London: Allen & Unwin, 1984), 10; Weber, *Economy and Society*, 63, 85. I will discuss the conflict between formal and substantive rationality more fully in the following chapter.

13. Weber, "Author's Introduction," 19–21, 24; Weber, *Protestant Ethic*, 76, 166; Weber, *Economy and Society*, 164–66, 1118; Max Weber, *General Economic History* (New Brunswick, NJ: Transaction, 1981), 334; Max Weber, "Suffrage and Democracy in Germany," in *Weber: Political Writings*, ed. Peter Lassman and Ronald Speirs (Cambridge: Cambridge University Press, 1994), 89–90; see also Richard Swedberg, *Max Weber and the Idea of Economic Sociology* (Princeton, NJ: Princeton University Press, 1998), 45–50.

14. Weber, "Author's Introduction," 17; Weber, *Protestant Ethic*, 56–58; Weber, *General Economic History*, 355–56; Chalcraft and Harrington, *The Protestant Ethic Debate*, 71–74.

15. Weber, *Economy and Society*, 165–66; Weber, *General Economic History*, 275–78; Weber, "Author's Introduction," 17–22, 24; Weber, *Protestant Ethic*, 76.

16. Weber, *General Economic History*, 277, 312; see also Swedberg, *Max Weber and the Idea of Economic Sociology*, 17–21; Randall Collins, "Weber's Last Theory of Capitalism: A Systematization," *American Sociological Review* 45, no. 6 (December 1980): 925–42.

17. Weber, *General Economic History*, 276, 302; Weber, *Economy and Society*, 137–38, 147–48.

18. Weber, *General Economic History*, 277; Weber, *Economy and Society*, 162, 137, 1156; Weber, "Author's Introduction," 22.

19. Weber, *General Economic History*, 276; Weber, *Economy and Society*, 975, 636.

20. Weber, *General Economic History*, 275; Weber, "Author's Introduction," 19; Weber, *Economy and Society*, 68–87, 91–94, 108.

21. Weber, *General Economic History*, 277; Weber, *Economy and Society*, 148, 162.

22. Weber, *General Economic History*, 277; Weber, "Author's Introduction," 25; Weber, *Economy and Society*, 162, 1095; Max Weber, "Parliament and Government in a Reconstructed Germany," in ibid., 30, 998.

23. Weber, *General Economic History*, 279.

24. Weber, "Author's Introduction," 21–22; Weber, *Economy and Society*, 162; see also Wolfgang Schluchter, *Paradoxes of Modernity: Culture and Conduct in the Theory of Max Weber*, trans. Neil Solomon (Stanford, CA: Stanford University Press, 1996), 200–202.

25. Weber, *Economy and Society*, 165, 161, 1156.

26. Weber, *General Economic History*, 354, 313–14; Weber, *Economy and Society*, 480; Weber, "Author's Introduction," 26.

27. For two useful book-length overviews of Weber's argument, see Gianfranco Poggi, *Calvinism and the Capitalist Spirit: Max Weber's* Protestant Ethic (Amherst: University of Massachusetts Press, 1983); Gordon Marshall, *In Search of the Spirit of Capitalism: An Essay on Max Weber's Protestant Ethic Thesis* (New York: Columbia University Press, 1982).

28. Weber, *Protestant Ethic*, 166, 91–92; Chalcraft and Harrington, *The Protestant Ethic Debate*, 107.

29. Weber, *Protestant Ethic*, 48–53, 55–56; Chalcraft and Harrington, *The Protestant Ethic Debate*, 71, 75–76.

30. Weber, *Protestant Ethic*, 48, 51–52, 62.

31. Ibid., 58–67.

32. Ibid., 53, 70–73, 78.

33. Ibid., 60, 90, 180.

34. Ibid., 36, 79–80, 83–85, 160; Weber, *Economy and Society*, 1196–98.

35. Weber, *Protestant Ethic*, 98–105; Weber, *Economy and Society*, 1198–200; Max Weber, "Science as a Vocation," in *From Max Weber*, 139, 155; Max Weber, *The Religion of China*, trans. Hans H. Gerth (New York: Free Press, 1951), 226–27.

36. Weber, *Economy and Society*, 1199; Weber, *Protestant Ethic*, 104, 111–10, 113–14, 232n66; Weber, *Religion of China*, 240.

37. Weber, *Protestant Ethic*, 36, 117–19, 126, 153–54, 235n79; Weber, *General Economic History*, 366; Weber, *Economy and Society*, 544–51, 1200.

38. Marshall, *In Search of the Spirit of Capitalism*, 71, 75–76; Weber, *Protestant Ethic*, 157–58, 161–63, 172, 261n14.

39. Weber, *Protestant Ethic*, 180.

40. Ibid., 166; see also Harvey Goldman, *Max Weber and Thomas Mann: Calling and the Shaping of the Self* (Berkeley: University of California Press, 1988), 45–49.

41. Weber, *Protestant Ethic*, 176, 171–72.

42. Ibid., 177–78, 163.

43. Ibid., 163, 169.

44. *Economy and Society*, 575; Weber, *Protestant Ethic*, 174, 181, 89–90; Weber, *Religion of China*, 238.

45. Weber, *Protestant Ethic*, 90, 277–78n84; Max Weber, "'Objectivity' in Social Science and Social Policy," in *The Methodology of the Social Sciences*, 68–71.

46. Weber, *Protestant Ethic*, 54–55, 62, 68, 72, 181–82, 282n108.

47. Weber, *Economy and Society*, 214, 946, 953–54; Weber, "Parliament and Government," 1407–8. The German term Weber employs, *Herrschaft*, has no precise English equivalent. It is typically translated as "domination" or "authority," which I use interchangeably. For a discussion of this issue, see Melvin Richter, *The History of Political and Social Concepts: A Critical Introduction* (New York: Oxford University Press, 1995), 58–78.

48. Max Weber, "Politics as a Vocation," in *From Max Weber*, 79; Weber, *Economy and Society*, 262, 1133; the parenthetical quotes come from Frank Parkin, *Max Weber* (New York: Tavistock, 1982), 77.

49. Weber, "Social Psychology," 296–97; Weber, "Politics as a Vocation," 78; Weber, *Economy and Society*, 226–27, 36, 216, 231.

50. Max Weber, "The Three Pure Types of Legitimate Rule," in *The Essential Weber: A Reader*, ed. Sam Whimster (New York: Routledge, 2004), 135–36; Weber, "Social Psychology," 296; Weber, *Economy and Society*, 226–41, 956, 958.

51. Weber, "Social Psychology," 295; Weber, "The Three Pure Types," 138–45; Weber, "Politics as a Vocation," 79; Weber, *Economy and Society*, 241–45, 1111–14.

52. Weber, "The Three Pure Types," 139; Weber, "Social Psychology," 296; Weber, *Economy and Society*, 241–45, 1115–17, 1119.

53. Weber, *Economy and Society*, 244, 246–54, 1114–15, 121–27, 1148–49; Weber, "Social Psychology," 297–98.

54. Weber, "The Three Pure Types," 133; Weber, "Politics as a Vocation," 79; Weber, "Social Psychology," 294–95; Weber, *Economy and Society*, 215–16, 954.

55. Weber, "The Three Pure Types," 133–34; Weber, "Social Psychology," 299; Weber, "Politics as a Vocation," 79; Weber, *Economy and Society*, 217–26, 959.

56. Weber, *Economy and Society*, 1133.

57. Weber, "Politics as a Vocation," 80; Weber, *Economy and Society*, 1132–33, 1148–49, 1156.

58. Weber, *Economy and Society*, 220–21, 956, 971, 1002, 1116; Weber, "Parliament and Government," 1393–94; Weber, "Social Psychology," 299; Weber, "The Three Pure Types," 134–35.

59. Weber, "Parliament and Government," 1400–1401.

60. Weber, *Economy and Society*, 218, 225–26, 956–58, 983.

61. Ibid., 225, 975.

62. Ibid., 223, 974.

63. Ibid., 225, 959–60, 991, 1000, 1002; Weber, "Parliament and Government," 1418; Weber, "Author's Introduction," 16.

64. Weber, *Economy and Society*, 223, 957, 973–74, 987; Max Weber, "Max Weber on Bureaucratization in 1909," in J. P. Mayer, *Max Weber and German Politics* (New York: Arno Press, 1979), 125; Jukka Gronow, "The Element of Irrationality: Max Weber's Diagnosis of Modern Culture," *Acta Sociologica* 31, no. 4 (1988): 327.

65. Weber, *Economy and Society*, 223, 987; Weber, "Parliament and Government," 1401; Weber, "Socialism," in *Weber: Political Writings*, 279.

66. See Sheldon S. Wolin, "Max Weber: Legitimation, Methods, and the Politics of Theory," *Political Theory* 9, no. 3 (August 1981): 415–16.

67. Weber, "Science as a Vocation," 155.

68. Ibid., 143, 152; Max Weber, "The Nation State and Economic Policy," in *Weber: Political Writings*, 14–15. On the controversy regarding the status of academic intellectuals in Weber's Germany, see Fritz K. Ringer, *The Decline of the German Mandarins: The German Academic Community, 1890–1933* (Cambridge, MA: Harvard University Press, 1969).

69. Weber, *Economy and Society*, 1002; Weber, "Science as a Vocation," 134–35, 137; Weber, "The Meaning of 'Ethical Neutrality,'" 5–6; Weber, *Protestant Ethic*, 180.

70. Weber, "Science as a Vocation," 137–38.

71. Weber, "'Objectivity' in Social Science," 72, 76–78, 81–82, 110–11; Weber, "The Meaning of 'Ethical Neutrality,'" 22; Weber, "Science as a Vocation," 143.

72. Weber, "'Objectivity' in Social Science," 72, 81.

73. Ibid., 84, 104, 112; Marianne Weber, *Max Weber*, 314; Weber, "Science as a Vocation," 138.

74. Weber, "Religious Rejections," 350–51; Weber, *Economy and Society*, 506; Weber, "Science as a Vocation," 139.

75. Weber, "Religious Rejections," 351, 355–57; Weber, "'Objectivity' in Social Science," 57.

76. Weber, "'Objectivity' in Social Science," 51, 53, 59; Weber, *Economy and Society*, 1381.

77. Weber, "Science as a Vocation," 143, 153; Weber, "'Objectivity' in Social Science," 54.

78. Marianne Weber, *Max Weber*, 418; Weber, "The Meaning of 'Ethical Neutrality,'" 3.

79. Weber, "Politics as a Vocation," 122–23; Weber, "Social Psychology," 275; see also Steven Seidman, "Modernity, Meaning, and Cultural Pessimism in Max Weber," *Sociological Analysis* 44, no. 4 (1983): 267–78.

80. Weber, "The Meaning of 'Ethical Neutrality,'" 17–18; Weber, "'Objectivity' in Social Science," 56; Max Weber, "Between Two Laws," in *Weber: Political Writings*, 79.

81. Weber, "Religious Rejections," 331, 335; see also Brubaker, *The Limits of Rationality*, 61–90; Lawrence A. Schaff, *Fleeing the Iron Cage: Culture, Politics, and Modernity in the Thought of Max Weber* (Berkeley: University of California Press, 1989), 93–97. On Weber's conception of modern culture more generally, see Nicholas Gane, *Max Weber and Postmodern Theory: Rationalization versus Re-enchantment* (New York: Palgrave, 2002) and Ralph Schroeder, *Max Weber and the Sociology of Culture* (London: Sage, 1992).

82. Weber, "Science as a Vocation," 152–53, 156; Max Weber, "Between Two Laws," 78–79.

83. Weber, "Science as a Vocation," 150–51.

84. Ibid., 151–52; Weber, "The Meaning of "Ethical Neutrality,'" 18–23; Weber, "'Objectivity' in Social Science," 52–54. For a stimulating overview and critique of Weber's theory of "practical political judgment," see Peter Breiner, *Max Weber and Democratic Politics* (Ithaca, NY: Cornell University Press, 1996).

85. Weber, "'Objectivity' in Social Science," 53–54, 58; Weber, "Science as a Vocation," 147, 152.

86. Weber, "Parliament and Government," 1402; Weber, *Economy and Society*, 998; Dennis Wrong, "Introduction," in *Max Weber*, ed. Dennis Wrong (Englewood Cliffs, NJ: Prentice-Hall, 1970), 26; Brubaker, *Limits of Rationality*, 2.

87. Weber, "Science as a Vocation," 155.

5. THE MODERN CONDITION

1. Frederick Engels, "Karl Marx's Funeral," in Karl Marx and Frederick Engels, *Collected Works*, vol. 24 (New York: International Publishers, 1975–), 468 [hereafter *MECW*]; Karl Marx, *Capital: A Critique of Political Economy*, vol. 1, trans. Ben Fowkes (New York: Penguin Classics, 1990), 762.

2. Karl Marx, *Wages, Price and Profit* (Peking: Foreign Languages Press, 1975), 42; Karl Marx and Frederick Engels, *Manifesto of the Communist Party*, in *The Marx-Engels Reader*, ed. Robert C. Tucker, 2nd ed. (New York: Norton, 1978), 474; Karl Marx, *Capital: A Critique of Political Economy*, vol. 3, trans. David Fernbach (New York: Penguin Classics, 1991), 1020; Marx, *Capital*, vol. 1, 999.

3. Marx, *Capital*, vol. 1, 93.

4. Karl Marx, *Grundrisse: Foundations of the Critique of Political Economy*, trans. Martin Nicolaus (New York: Vintage, 1973), 325, 552; Karl Marx, *Wage Labour and Capital*, in *MECW*, vol. 9, 224–27; Marx, *Capital*, vol. 1, 433, 617, 799.

5. Marx, *Capital*, vol. 1, 449.

6. Marx, *Capital*, vol. 3, 961; Marx, *Capital*, vol. 1, 342, 486; Marx, *Grundrisse*, 409.

7. Marx, *Capital*, vol. 1, 358, 424–25, 448, 450, 1010–11, 1020–31; see also Marx, *Grundrisse*, 585–89. For two excellent articles on Marx's analysis of the rise of modern capitalist industry, see Donald MacKenzie, "Marx and the Machine," *Technology and Culture* 25, no. 3 (July 1984): 473–502; Joseph Fracchia, "The Capitalist Labour-Process and the Body in Pain: The Corporeal Depths of Marx's Concept of Immiseration," *Historical Materialism* 16, no. 4 (2008): 35–66.

8. Marx, *Capital*, vol. 1, 455–58, 461–63, 469, 480, 486.

9. Ibid., 590, 526, 547–48, 534, 542, 645–46; Marx and Engels, *Manifesto*, 479; Marx, *Grundrisse*, 693. See also Marx, *Capital*, vol. 1, 1020–25, 1034–38.

10. Karl Marx, "Inaugural Address of the Working Men's International Association," in *MECW*, vol. 20, 216; see also Marx, *Wages, Price and Profit*, 64–65. For a brief report on the contemporary relevance of the concept of immiseration, see A. Kent MacDougall, "Pandemic Immiseration," *Monthly Review* 49, no. 2 (June 1997): 31–34.

11. Fracchia, "The Capitalist Labour-Process and the Body in Pain," 41n19.

12. Marx, *Capital*, vol. 1, 1037, 764n1, 483, 799 (italics added); Marx, *Grundrisse*, 308.

13. Marx, *Capital*, vol. 1, 618, 553, 482–83, 548, 638, 375, 1061–64, 532, 799.

14. For a now classic study of Marx's theory of alienation, see Bertell Ollman, *Alienation: Marx's Conception of Man in Capitalist Society*, 2nd ed. (Cambridge: Cambridge University Press, 1976).

15. Marx, *Capital*, vol. 1, 292; Karl Marx, *The Economic and Philosophic Manuscripts of 1844*, trans. Martin Milligan (New York: International Publishers, 1964), 108–10; Marx, *Grundrisse*, 308, 455, 831.

16. Marx, *Manuscripts*, 110–11; Marx, *Wage Labour and Capital*, 202–3; Karl Marx, "Comments on James Mill, *Élémens D'Économie Politique*," in *MECW*, vol. 3, 219–20, 227–28.

17. Marx, *Capital*, vol. 1, 284; Marx, *Manuscripts*, 112–13; Marx, *Grundrisse*, 243.

18. Marx, *Manuscripts*, 114–15; Marx, "Comments on James Mill," 217, 227–28; Marx, *Capital*, vol. 1, 280; for a somewhat differently stated analysis of alienated social relations, see Marx, *Grundrisse*, 157, 162, 196–97, 470, 585–86.

19. Marx, *Grundrisse*, 470; Marx, "Comments on James Mill," 217, 220, 228.

20. Marx, *Capital*, vol. 1, 96.

21. Emile Durkheim, *On Suicide*, trans. Robin Buss (New York: Penguin, 2006), 436–37, 432, 349; Emile Durkheim, "The Intellectual Elite and Democracy," in *Emile Durkheim on Morality and Society*, ed. Robert N. Bellah (Chicago: University of Chicago Press, 1973), 59; Emile Durkheim, *The Elementary Forms of Religious Life*, trans. Karen E. Fields (New York: Free Press, 1995), 429.

22. Emile Durkheim, *Socialism*, trans. Charlotte Sattler (New York: Collier, 1962), 168, 40.

23. Emile Durkheim, *Professional Ethics and Civic Morals*, trans. Cornelia Brookfield (London: Routledge, 1992), 11; Durkheim, *Suicide*, 412, 280–81; Emile Durkheim, *The Division of Labor in Society*, trans. W. D. Halls (New York: Free Press, 1984), 339.

24. Durkheim, *Elementary Forms*, 429; Durkheim, *Socialism*, 167, 179; Durkheim, *Suicide*, 412.

25. Ibid., 291–322, xlvi.

26. Durkheim, *Suicide*, 225–26, 234.

27. Emile Durkheim, *Moral Education: A Study in the Theory and Application of the Sociology of Education*, trans. Everett K. Wilson and Herman Schnurer (New York: Free Press, 1961), 233–35, 65, 102; Emile Durkheim, "Belot and Socialism," in *Durkheim on Politics and the State*, ed. Anthony Giddens, trans. W. D. Halls (Stanford, CA: Stanford University Press, 1986), 119.

28. Durkheim, *Division of Labor*, 292, 305; Durkheim, *Professional Ethics*, 16, 35–36; see also the discussion of Sismondi in Durkheim, *Socialism*, 106–18.

29. Durkheim, *Division of Labor*, 292–93, 305–6.

30. Ibid., 294, 306–8.

31. On the ambiguity in Durkheim's concept of anomie and its shifting meanings in his work, see Donald N. Levine, *The Flight from Ambiguity: Essays in Social and Cultural Theory* (Chicago: University of Chicago Press, 1985), 55–72.

32. Durkheim, *Professional Ethics*, 6–8; Durkheim, *Division of Labor*, xxxii.

33. Durkheim, *Division of Labor*, xxxi–xxxii; Durkheim, *Professional Ethics*, 9–10, 29; Durkheim, *Socialism*, 239; on his critique of the "classical economists," see also Emile Durkheim, "The Politics of the Future," trans. W. Watts Miller and J. Mergy, *Durkheimian Studies* 15 (2009): 4.

34. Durkheim, *Division of Labor*, xxxiii–xxxiv, 132; Durkheim, *Professional Ethics*, 11–12.

35. On Durkheim's analysis of economic inequality and his conception of justice, see J.-C. Filloux, "Inequalities and Social Stratification in Durkheim's Sociology," in *Emile Durkheim, Sociologist and Moralist*, ed. Stephen P. Turner (London: Routledge), 211–28; Carmen J. Sirianni, "Justice and the Division of Labour: A Reconsideration of Durkheim's *Division of Labour in Society*," *Socialist Review* 32, no. 3 (August 1984): 449–70; S. J. D. Green, "Emile Durkheim on Human Talents and Two Traditions of Social Justice," *British Journal of Sociology* 40, no. 1 (March 1989): 97–117; Anne Rawls, "Conflict as a Foundation for Consensus: Contradictions of Industrial Capitalism in Book III of Durkheim's *Division of Labor*," *Critical Sociology* 29, no. 3 (2003): 295–335.

36. Durkheim, *Division of Labor*, 313; Durkheim, *Professional Ethics*, 213.

37. Durkheim, *Division of Labor*, 312–13.

38. Ibid., 312–14; Durkheim, *Professional Ethics*, 219.

39. Durkheim, *Division of Labor*, 316–18; Durkheim, *Professional Ethics*, 203–4, 206–13.

40. Durkheim, *Division of Labor*, 319–20; Durkheim, *Socialism*, 59; Durkheim, *Professional Ethics*, 174–75, 216–17, 213–14.

41. Durkheim, *Moral Education*, 12, 20; Durkheim, *Division of Labor*, 320–22; Durkheim, *Professional Ethics*, 207, 209.

42. Durkheim, *Division of Labor*, xxvi, xliv–xlv, liv; Durkheim, *Suicide*, 417–18, 423–24; Durkheim, *Professional Ethics*, 36, 63. For his argument in support of a "corporative system," see Durkheim, *Division of Labor*, xxxi–lix ("Preface to the Second Edition"); Durkheim, *Suicide*, 422–37; Durkheim, *Professional Ethics*, 28–41. For useful secondary sources on Durkheim's corporatism, see M. J. Hawkins, "Durkheim on Occupational Corporations: An Exegesis and Interpretation," *Journal of the History of Ideas* 55, no. 3 (July 1994): 461–81; Frank Hearn, "Durkheim's Political Sociology: Corporatism, State Autonomy, and Democracy," *Social Research* 52, no. 1 (Spring 1985): 151–77; Dominick LaCapra, *Emile Durkheim: Sociologist and Philosopher* (Chicago: University of Chicago Press, 1985), 211–24. I focus here on the moral and economic functions of corporate organizations as conceived by Durkheim; in chapter 7 I discuss the political role he sees these playing.

43. Durkheim, *Division of Labor*, xxxvi, l–li; Durkheim, *Suicide*, 426–27, 429; Durkheim, *Professional Ethics*, 20, 37–39.

44. Durkheim, *Suicide*, 423, 428; Durkheim, *Moral Education*, 234; Durkheim, *Professional Ethics*, 29; Emile Durkheim, "Review of Antonio Labriola, *Essais sur la Conception Materialiste de l'Histoire*," in *Emile Durkheim on Institutional Analysis*, ed. and trans. Mark Traugott (Chicago: University of Chicago Press, 1978), 128; Durkheim, *Division of Labor*, xxxix.

45. Durkheim, *Division of Labor*, xxxvi–xxxix, 165; Durkheim, *Professional Ethics*, 16–19; Durkheim, *Socialism*, 147; LaCapra, *Emile Durkheim*, 21.

46. Max Weber, "Science as a Vocation," in *From Max Weber: Essays in Sociology*, trans. and ed. H. H. Gerth and C. Wright Mills (New York: Oxford University Press, 1946), 155.

47. Peter Baehr, "The 'Iron Cage' and the 'Shell as Hard as Steel': Parsons, Weber, and the *Stahlhartes Gehäuse* Metaphor in the *Protestant Ethic and the Spirit of Capitalism*," *History and Theory* 40, no. 2 (May 2001): 153–69; David Chalcraft, "Bringing the Text Back In: On Ways of Reading the Iron Cage Metaphor in the Two Editions of the *Protestant Ethic*," in

Organizing Modernity: New Weberian Perspectives on Work, Organization and Society, ed. Larry J. Ray and Michael Reed (London: Routledge, 1994), 16–45.

48. Max Weber, *The Protestant Ethic and the Spirit of Capitalism*, trans. Talcott Parsons (London: Counterpoint, 1985), 181; Max Weber, *Economy and Society: An Outline of Interpretive Sociology*, trans. Ephraim Fischoff et al. (Berkeley: University of California Press, 1978), 1148–49, 1155–56, 941, 302–7, 980–83; Max Weber, "Parliament and Government in a Reconstructed Germany," in *Economy and Society*, 1394; Max Weber, "Suffrage and Democracy in Germany," in *Weber: Political Writings*, ed. Peter Lassman and Ronald Speirs (Cambridge: Cambridge University Press, 1994), 103; Max Weber, "Socialism," in *Weber: Political Writings*, 279–81.

49. Weber, *Economy and Society*, 585, 600, 731, 1186; Weber, "Socialism," 284; Max Weber, "Author's Introduction," in *The Protestant Ethic*, 17; Wolfgang J. Mommsen, *The Age of Bureaucracy: Perspectives on the Political Sociology of Max Weber* (Oxford: Basil Blackwell, 1974), 55.

50. Weber, *Protestant Ethic*, 182, 62, 72, 54–55; H. H. Gerth and C. Wright Mills, "Introduction: The Man and His Work," in *From Max Weber*, 73; Max Weber, *The Russian Revolution*, trans. and ed. Gordon C. Wells and Peter Baehr (Ithaca, NY: Cornell University Press, 1995), 109; see also Max Weber, *Roscher and Knies: The Logical Problems of Historical Economics*, trans. Guy Oaks (New York: Free Press, 1975), 193–94.

51. Weber, *Economy and Society*, 729–30, 1155–56, 1010, 110; Max Weber, *Critique of Stammler*, trans. Guy Oakes (New York: Free Press, 1977), 101; Weber, "Socialism," 283; Weber, "Parliament and Government," 1402; Weber, *Protestant Ethic*, 282n108; J. E. T. Eldridge, ed., *Max Weber: The Interpretation of Social Reality* (New York: Scribner, 1971), 154–55.

52. Weber, *Economy and Society*, 998, 990–91; Weber, "Parliament and Government," 1402–3 (italics added).

53. Weber, *Economy and Society*, 223–25, 987; Weber, "Parliament and Government," 1403.

54. Weber, "Parliament and Government," 1403; Weber, *Economy and Society*, 987–88; Max Weber, "Max Weber on Bureaucratization in 1909," in J. P. Mayer, *Max Weber and German Politics* (New York: Arno Press, 1979), 127. On the imprecision in Weber's concept of freedom, see Claus Offe, *Reflections on America: Tocqueville, Weber and Adorno in the United States*, trans. Patrick Camiller (Malden, MA: Polity Press, 2004), 52–53; see also Kari Palonen, "Max Weber's Reconceptualization of Freedom," *Political Theory* 27, no. 4 (August 1999): 523–44.

55. Weber, "Parliament and Government," 1401, 1403; Weber, *Economy and Society*, 224–25, 959–60, 987, 1000.

56. Harvey Goldman, *Politics, Death, and the Devil: Self and Power in Max Weber and Thomas Mann* (Berkeley: University of California Press, 1992), 168–73; Max Weber, "The Meaning of 'Ethical Neutrality' in Sociology and Economics," in *The Methodology of the Social Sciences*, trans. Edward A. Shils and Henry A. Finch (New York: Free Press, 1949), 26; Weber, "Max Weber on Bureaucratization," 127–28.

57. Weber, "Parliament and Government," 1403–4, 1438, 1448. See also Wolfgang Schluchter, "Value-Neutrality and the Ethic of Responsibility," in Guenther Roth and Wolfgang Schluchter, *Max Weber's Vision of History: Ethics and Methods* (Berkeley: University of California Press, 1979), 97–100.

58. David Beetham, *Bureaucracy* (Minneapolis: University of Minnesota Press, 1987), 57; Max Weber, *The Agrarian Sociology of Ancient Civilizations*, trans. R. I. Frank (London: New

Left Books, 1976), 365; Weber, "Suffrage and Democracy," 90; Weber, "Max Weber on Bureaucratization," 126–27; Weber, *Economy and Society*, 1117.

59. Weber, "Parliament and Government," 1403; Weber, "Max Weber on Bureaucratization," 128.

60. Max Weber, "The Social Psychology of the World Religions," in *From Max Weber*, 293–94. In the following pages I draw on the useful discussion of the contrast between formal and substantive rationality in Rogers Brubaker, *The Limits of Rationality: An Essay on the Social and Moral Thought of Max Weber* (London: Allen & Unwin, 1984), 35–43.

61. Weber, *Economy and Society*, 85–86, 94.

62. Weber, *Economy and Society*, 85, 107–11; Max Weber, "Religious Rejections of the World and Their Directions," in *From Max Weber*, 331; see also Brubaker, *The Limits of Rationality*, 41–42.

63. Weber, *Economy and Society*, 636–37, 584–85.

64. Ibid., 927, 110, 138.

65. Ibid., 975; see also 979–80.

66. Ibid., 811–13, 656–57, 893. On the conflict between "formal justice" and "substantive justice," see Anthony T. Kronman, *Max Weber* (Stanford, CA: Stanford University Press, 1983), 92–95.

67. Max Weber, "'Objectivity' in Social Science and Social Policy," in *Methodology of the Social Sciences*, 58.

68. See Alvin W. Gouldner, "Introduction" in Durkheim, *Socialism*, 23; LaCapra, *Emile Durkheim*, 24.

69. Karl Löwith, *Max Weber and Karl Marx* (London: Allen & Unwin, 1982), 25; Weber, "'Objectivity' in Social Science," 58.

70. Jeffrey C. Alexander, *Theoretical Logic in Sociology*, vol. 3, *The Classical Attempt at Theoretical Synthesis: Max Weber* (Berkeley: University of California Press, 1983), 123; Wilhelm Hennis, *Max Weber's Central Question*, 2nd ed., trans. Keith Tribe (Newbury, UK: Threshold Press, 2000), 180–97.

71. Marx, *Grundrisse*, 487–88; Karl Marx, "Preface," in *Contribution to a Critique of Political Economy* (New York: International Publishers, 1970), 21–22.

72. Stephen Kalberg, "The Modern World as a Monolithic Iron Cage? Utilizing Max Weber to Define the Internal Dynamics of the American Political Culture Today," *Max Weber Studies* 1, no. 2 (May 2001): 178–95.

73. Marx, *Capital*, vol. 1, 739.

6. THE FATE OF THE INDIVIDUAL

1. Koenraad W. Swart, "'Individualism' in the Mid-Nineteenth Century (1826–1860)," *Journal of the History of Ideas* 23, no. 1 (January–March 1962): 77–90; Steven Lukes, *Individualism* (New York: Harper Torchbooks, 1973).

2. Karl Marx, *Capital: A Critique of Political Economy*, vol. 1, trans. Ben Fowkes (New York: Penguin Classics, 1990), 739; Emile Durkheim, "Individualism and the Intellectuals," in *Emile Durkheim on Morality and Society*, ed. Robert N. Bellah (Chicago: University of Chicago Press, 1973), 48; Max Weber, *The Protestant Ethic and the Spirit of Capitalism*, trans. Talcott Parsons (London: Unwin, 1985), 181.

3. Ian Forbes, *Marx and the New Individual* (London: Unwin Hyman, 1990), xix; Karl Marx and Frederick Engels, *The German Ideology*, in Karl Marx and Frederick Engels, *Collected Works*, vol. 5 (New York: International Publishers, 1975–), 37 [hereafter *MECW*]; Marx, *Capital*, vol. 1, 283–84; Karl Marx, *Grundrisse: Foundations of the Critique of Political Economy*, trans. Martin Nicolaus (New York: Vintage, 1973), 494.

4. Marx, *Grundrisse*, 84, 496. On Marx's theory of individuality, see Forbes, *Marx and the New Individual*; Carol C. Gould, *Marx's Social Ontology: Individuality and Community in Marx's Theory of Social Reality* (Cambridge, MA: MIT Press, 1978); Derek Sayer, *Capitalism and Modernity: An Excursus on Marx and Weber* (London: Routledge, 1991), 2–3, 13–20, 56–66.

5. Marx, *Grundrisse*, 84, 158, 163; Marx, *Capital*, vol. 1, 170; Gould, *Marx's Social Ontology*, 11.

6. Karl Marx and Frederick Engels, *Manifesto of the Communist Party*, in *The Marx-Engels Reader*, ed. Robert C. Tucker, 2nd ed. (New York: Norton, 1978), 475, 478; Marx, *Grundrisse*, 409–10, 163, 325.

7. Marx, *Grundrisse*, 84, 157–58, 161–64, 196–97; Marx and Engels, *German Ideology*, 78–79.

8. Marx, *Grundrisse*, 158; Marx and Engels, *German Ideology*, 78; David Archard, "The Marxist Ethic of Self-Realization: Individuality and Community," in *Moral Philosophy and Contemporary Problems*, ed. J. D. G. Evans (Cambridge: Cambridge University Press, 1987), 19–34; Gould, *Marx's Social Ontology*, 21–26.

9. Marx, *Grundrisse*, 158, 162; Marx and Engels, *German Ideology*, 81; Karl Marx, "Preface," in *Contribution to a Critique of Political Economy* (New York: International Publishers, 1970), 22.

10. Karl Marx and Frederick Engels, *The Holy Family or Critique of Critical Criticism*, in *MECW*, vol. 4, 131; Marx, *Grundrisse*, 611; see also Karl Marx, *The Economic and Philosophic Manuscripts of 1844*, trans. Martin Milligan (New York: International Publishers, 1964), 144. For some useful sources on Marx's concept of freedom, see Gould, *Marx's Social Ontology*, 101–28; Steven Lukes, *Marxism and Morality* (New York: Oxford University Press, 1987), 71–99; Ernesto Screpanti, *Libertarian Communism: Marx, Engels and the Political Economy of Freedom* (New York: Palgrave Macmillan, 2007); R. G. Peffer, *Marxism, Morality, and Social Justice* (Princeton, NJ: Princeton University Press, 1990), 115–65.

11. Karl Marx, *Wage Labour and Capital*, in *MECW*, vol. 9, 198, 203; Karl Marx, *Capital: A Critique of Political Economy*, vol. 3, trans. David Fernbach (New York: Penguin Classics, 1991), 926–27, 958; Marx, *Capital*, vol. 1, 761, 875, 899, 1027–28; Marx, *Grundrisse*, 611. On capitalism as a system of forced labor, see Jairus Banaji, "The Fictions of Free Labour: Contract, Coercion, and So-Called Unfree Labour," *Historical Materialism* 11, no. 3 (2003): 66–95. My discussion of Marx here is limited to the economic dimension of human freedom; I consider the political dimension in the next chapter.

12. Marx, *Capital*, vol. 1, 280; see also Marx, *Grundrisse*, 239–50.

13. Marx, *Grundrisse*, 163–64, 464–65, 509; Marx, *Capital*, vol. 1, 382, 724; Marx, *Wage Labour and Capital*, 202–3. On Marx's analysis of the element of force in "free" wage labor, see G. A. Cohen, "The Structure of Proletarian Unfreedom," *Philosophy & Public Affairs* 12, no. 1 (Winter 1983): 3–33; Jeffrey Reiman, "Exploitation, Force, and the Moral Assessment of Capitalism: Thoughts on Roemer and Cohen," *Philosophy & Public Affairs* 16, no. 1 (Winter 1987): 3–41.

14. Marx, *Capital*, vol. 1, 1079, 719, 1064; Marx, *Wage Labour and Capital*, 203.

15. Marx, *Capital*, vol. 1, 280, 415–16, 382; Banaji, "The Fictions of Free Labour," 70; Marx and Engels, *German Ideology*, 262; Marx, *Grundrisse*, 307.

16. Marx, *Grundrisse*, 712, 172–73; Karl Marx, *Wages, Price and Profit* (Peking: Foreign Languages Press, 1975), 67–68; Karl Marx, *Theories of Surplus Value*, part 3 (Moscow: Progress Publishers, 1971), 256–57. On the relationship between freedom and time, see Julia Maskivker, "Employment as a Limitation on Self-Ownership," *Human Rights Review* 12, no. 1 (2011): 27–45.

17. Marx, *Grundrisse*, 634; Marx, *Capital*, vol. 1, 667, 375–76; Karl Marx, *Economic Manuscript of 1861–63*, in *MECW*, vol. 30, 191; see also Marx and Engels, *German Ideology*, 431–32.

18. Marx, *Capital*, vol. 3, 958; Marx, *Grundrisse*, 701, 706, 708; Marx, *Capital*, vol. 1, 437–38. See also G. A. Cohen, *Karl Marx's Theory of History: A Defence*, expanded ed. (Princeton, NJ: Princeton University Press, 2000), 302–25.

19. William James Booth, "Gone Fishing: Making Sense of Marx's Concept of Communism," *Political Theory* 17, no. 2 (May 1989): 211; Marx, *Grundrisse*, 158; Marx, *Capital*, vol. 3, 958–59. See also James C. Klagge, "Marx's Realms of 'Freedom' and 'Necessity,'" *Canadian Journal of Philosophy* 16, no. 4 (December 1986): 769–78; Moishe Postone, *Time, Labor, and Social Domination: A Reinterpretation of Marx's Critical Theory* (New York: Cambridge University Press, 1993), 373–84.

20. Klagge, "Marx's Realms of 'Freedom' and 'Necessity,'" 771, 774; Marx, *Capital*, vol. 3, 958–59; Marx, *Theories of Surplus Value*, part 3, 257; Marx and Engels, *German Ideology*, 47; Marx, *Capital*, vol. 1, 667.

21. Marx, *Grundrisse*, 158, 409, 488, 611. For two different perspectives on Marx's concept of self-realization, see Jon Elster, *Making Sense of Marx* (Cambridge: Cambridge University Press, 1985), 82–92, 521–27; Nilou Mobasser, "Marx and Self-Realization," *New Left Review* 161 (January–February 1987): 119–28. Also useful is Jon Elster, "Self-Realization in Work and Politics: The Marxist Conception of the Good Life," *Philosophy & Policy* 3, no. 2 (Spring 1986): 97–126.

22. Marx, *Grundrisse*, 84, 158, 242–44; Karl Marx, "Comments on James Mill, *Élémens d'Économie Politique*," in *MECW*, vol. 3, 217, 227–28; Marx, *Economic and Philosophic Manuscripts*, 137–38; Marx and Engels, *German Ideology*, 78; Marx and Engels, *Manifesto*, 491; see also Archard, "The Marxist Ethic of Self-Realization."

23. Emile Durkheim, "Course in Sociology: Opening Lectures," in *Emile Durkheim on Institutional Analysis*, ed. and trans. Mark Traugott (Chicago: University of Chicago Press, 1978), 69; Emile Durkheim, *Moral Education: A Study in the Theory and Application of the Sociology of Education*, trans. Everett K. Wilson and Herman Schnurer (New York: Free Press, 1961), 104–5, 233–34, 246, 251, 260, 277–78.

24. Emile Durkheim, *The Elementary Forms of Religious Life*, trans. Karen E. Fields (New York: Free Press, 1995), 215; Emile Durkheim, *On Suicide*, trans. Robin Buss (New York: Penguin, 2006), 163–64; Emile Durkheim, "Individualism and the Intellectuals," in *Emile Durkheim on Morality and Society*, ed. Robert N. Bellah (Chicago: University of Chicago Press, 1973), 49; Emile Durkheim, *Education and Sociology*, trans. Sherwood D. Fox (New York: Free Press, 1956), 64, 120.

25. Durkheim, "Individualism and the Intellectuals," 231n4; Emile Durkheim, *The Division of Labor in Society*, trans. W. D. Halls (New York: Free Press, 1984), xxx; Durkheim, *Moral Education*, 67–68; see also Emile Durkheim, *Sociology and Philosophy*, trans. D. F. Pocock (New York: Free Press, 1974), 53–55. On Durkheim's unique mix of communitarianism and liberalism, see Mark S. Cladis, *A Communitarian Defense of Liberalism: Emile Durkheim and Contemporary Social Theory* (Stanford, CA: Stanford University Press, 1992).

26. Durkheim, *Division of Labor*, 143, 84; Emile Durkheim, *Professional Ethics and Civic Morals*, trans. Cornelia Brookfield (London: Routledge, 1992), 56; Durkheim, *Suicide*, 373.

27. Durkheim, *Suicide*, 373; Durkheim, *Division of Labor*, 85, 105–6, 117–18, 141, 174, 285, 333, 335; Durkheim, "Individualism and the Intellectuals," 51–52.

28. Durkheim, *Division of Labor*, 142–43, 146, 106; Durkheim, *Suicide*, 176.

29. Durkheim, *Division of Labor*, 3–4, 329–30, 333–34; Durkheim, *Sociology and Philosophy*, 72; see also Durkheim, *Education and Sociology*, 117–19.

30. Durkheim, *Moral Education*, 17–94, 96.

31. On the Dreyfus affair and the political context of Durkheim's article on individualism, see Chad R. Farrell, "Durkheim, Moral Individualism and the Dreyfus Affair," *Current Perspectives in Social Theory* 17 (1997): 313–30; Peter Jelavich, "Republican Ethics as Social Science: The Case of Emile Durkheim," in *Critical Issues in Social Thought*, ed. Murray Milgate and Cheryl B. Welch (London: Academic Press, 1989), 139–57; Pierre Birnbaum, "French Jewish Sociologists between Reason and Faith: The Impact of the Dreyfus Affair," *Jewish Social Studies* 2, no. 1 (1995): 1–35; Marcel Fournier, *Emile Durkheim: A Biography*, trans. David Macey (New York: Polity, 2013), 285–308.

32. Durkheim, "Individualism and the Intellectuals," 44, 56.

33. Ibid., 44.

34. Ibid., 44–45; Durkheim, *Sociology and Philosophy*, 72.

35. Emile Durkheim, "Two Laws of Penal Evolution," *Economy and Society* 3 (1973): 302; Durkheim, *Suicide*, 374; Durkheim, *Sociology and Philosophy*, 53; Durkheim, "Individualism and the Intellectuals," 45.

36. Durkheim, *Moral Education*, 214, 223; Durkheim, "Two Laws," 302; Durkheim, "Individualism and the Intellectuals," 48–49.

37. Durkheim, "Individualism and the Intellectuals," 56, 48; Durkheim, *Sociology and Philosophy*, 92.

38. Durkheim, "Individualism and the Intellectuals," 49–50, 55–56; Durkheim, *Moral Education*, 111–26.

39. Durkheim, *Division of Labor*, 141, 333; Durkheim, *Professional Ethics*, 68.

40. Durkheim, *Suicide*, 370–71; Durkheim, *Division of Labor*, 122; Durkheim, *Moral Education*, 107; Durkheim, "Individualism and the Intellectuals," 46–48; see also Durkheim, *Sociology and Philosophy*, 37.

41. Durkheim, *Suicide*, 374; Durkheim, "Individualism and the Intellectuals," 50, 53–54.

42. Durkheim, *Professional Ethics*, 60.

43. Durkheim, *Education and Sociology*, 134, 89; Emile Durkheim, "Social Property and Democracy: Review of Alfred Fouillee, *La Propriete Sociale et la Democratie*," in *Durkheim on Politics and the State*, ed. Anthony Giddens, trans. W. D. Halls (Stanford, CA: Stanford University Press, 1986), 91; Emile Durkheim, *The Evolution of Educational Thought*, trans. Peter Collins (London: Routledge & Kegan Paul, 1977), 320, 336. On the relationship between moral education and moral individualism, see Cladis, *A Communitarian Defense of Liberalism*, 185–225.

44. Durkheim, *Moral Education*, 12, 94, 115–17, 120; Durkheim, *Education and Sociology*, 120, 64, 74.

45. Durkheim, *Sociology and Philosophy*, 91; Durkheim, *Professional Ethics*, 56; Durkheim, "The Intellectual Elite and Democracy," 60; Durkheim, *Elementary Forms*, 212–13, 352, 357, 375, 390, 421, 424, 429; Emile Durkheim, "The Dualism of Human Nature," in *Emile Durkheim on Morality and Society*, 161.

46. Jeffrey C. Alexander, *Theoretical Logic in Sociology*, vol. 3, *The Classical Attempt at Theoretical Synthesis: Max Weber* (Berkeley: University of California Press, 1983), 123.

47. Donald N. Levine, *The Flight from Ambiguity: Essays in Social and Cultural Theory* (Chicago: University of Chicago Press, 1985), 162–73; Weber, *Protestant Ethic*, 54–55; Max

Weber, *Economy and Society: An Outline of Interpretive Sociology*, trans. Ephraim Fischoff et al. (Berkeley: University of California Press, 1978), 1156.

48. Max Weber, "Critical Studies in the Logic of the Cultural Sciences," in *The Methodology of the Social Sciences*, trans. Edward A. Shils and Henry A. Finch (New York: Free Press, 1949), 124–25; Max Weber, *Roscher and Knies: The Logical Problems of Historical Economics*, trans. Guy Oaks (New York: Free Press, 1975), 191; see also Rogers Brubaker, *The Limits of Rationality: An Essay on the Social and Moral Thought of Max Weber* (London: Allen & Unwin, 1984), 92–94.

49. Max Weber, "The Meaning of 'Ethical Neutrality' in Sociology and Economics," in *The Methodology of the Social Sciences*, 17; Weber, *Economy and Society*, 21–22; Wolfgang J. Mommsen, *The Age of Bureaucracy: Perspectives on the Political Sociology of Max Weber* (Oxford: Basil Blackwell, 1974), 20.

50. Max Weber, "The Social Psychology of the World Religions," in *From Max Weber: Essays in Sociology*, trans. and ed. H. H. Gerth and C. Wright Mills (New York: Oxford University Press, 1946), 293; Weber, *The Protestant Ethic*, 77; Stephen Kalberg, "General Introduction: Max Weber and the Modern West," in The Protestant Ethic and the Spirit of Capitalism *with Other Writings on the Rise of the West*, ed. Stephen Kalberg, 4th ed. (New York: Oxford University Press, 2009), x–xi; Stephen Kalberg, "Max Weber's Types of Rationality: Cornerstones for the Analysis of Rationalization Processes in History," *American Journal of Sociology* 85, no. 2 (March 1980): 1151–52.

51. Weber, "The Meaning of 'Ethical Neutrality,'" 17–18; Max Weber, "'Objectivity' in Social Science and Social Policy," in *The Methodology of the Social Sciences*, 54.

52. Weber, "The Meaning of 'Ethical Neutrality,'" 24; Weber, *Economy and Society*, 30, 1148–49; Wolfgang J. Mommsen, *The Political and Social Theory of Max Weber* (Chicago: University of Chicago Press, 1989), 150–53; Max Weber, "Marginal Utility Theory and 'The Fundamental Law of Psychophysics,'" trans. Louis Schneider, *Social Science Quarterly* 56, no. 1 (June 1975): 33.

53. Brubaker, *The Limits of Rationality*, 92–96; Weber, "The Meaning of 'Ethical Neutrality,'" 18; Weber, *Roscher and Knies*, 192; Max Weber, *The Religion of China: Confucianism and Taoism*, trans. Hans H. Gerth (New York: Free Press, 1951), 235.

54. Weber, *Economy and Society*, 30; Weber, "'Objectivity' in Social Science," 55; Weber, *Religion of China*, 235; Harvey Goldman, *Max Weber and Thomas Mann: Calling and the Shaping of the Self* (Berkeley: University of California Press, 1988), 165.

55. Max Weber, "Science as a Vocation," in *From Max Weber*, 151–53, 156; Weber, "'Objectivity' in Social Science," 55; Max Weber, "Between Two Laws," in *Weber: Political Writings*, ed. Peter Lassman and Ronald Speirs (Cambridge: Cambridge University Press, 1994), 79; Weber, *Protestant Ethic*, 118–19.

56. Weber, *Roscher and Knies*, 192; Goldman, *Max Weber and Thomas Mann*, 144.

57. Weber, *Protestant Ethic*, 79.

58. Weber, *Protestant Ethic*, 54; Weber, "The Meaning of 'Ethical Neutrality,'" 5–6; Harvey Goldman, *Politics, Death, and the Devil: Self and Power in Max Weber and Thomas Mann* (Berkeley: University of California Press, 1992), 72–73.

59. Weber, "The Meaning of 'Ethical Neutrality,'" 18; Weber, *Roscher and Knies*, 192–94; Weber, "Critical Studies in the Logic of the Cultural Sciences," 124–25; Brubaker, *The Limits of Rationality*, 93.

60. Stephen P. Turner, "Bunyan's Cage and Weber's Calling," *Sociological Inquiry* 52, no. 1 (Winter 1982): 85; Karl Löwith, *Max Weber and Karl Marx*, trans. Hans Fantel (London: Allen & Unwin, 1982), 57.

61. Max Weber, *The Religion of India: The Sociology of Hinduism and Buddhism*, trans. Hans H. Gerth and Don Martindale (New York: Free Press, 1958), 342.

62. Weber, "Science as a Vocation," 151–52; Weber, "'Objectivity' in Social Science," 50–57.

63. Cited in Sung Ho Kim, *Max Weber's Politics of Civil Society* (New York: Cambridge University Press, 2004), 7; Max Weber, "Voluntary Associational Life (*Vereinswesen*)," *Max Weber Studies* 2, no. 2 (2002): 199–209; Max Weber, "The Protestant Sects and the Spirit of Capitalism," in *From Max Weber*, 302–22; Max Weber, "'Churches' and 'Sects' in North America: An Ecclesiastical Socio-Political Sketch," *Sociological Theory* 3, no. 1 (Spring 1985): 7–13.

64. Marianne Weber, *Max Weber: A Biography*, trans. Harry Zohn (New York: Wiley, 1975), 378; see also Brubaker, *The Limits of Rationality*, 98; Jürgen Habermas, *The Postnational Constellation: Political Essays*, trans. Max Pensky (Cambridge, MA: MIT Press, 2001), 140; Steven Seidman, "Modernity, Meaning, and Cultural Pessimism in Max Weber," *Sociological Analysis* 44, no. 4 (1983): 274.

65. Jeffrey Prager, "Moral Integration and Political Inclusion: A Comparison of Durkheim's and Weber's Theories of Democracy," *Social Forces* 59, no. 4 (June 1981): 919.

66. Lukes, *Individualism*, 73–78, 86, 148–52; Marx, *A Contribution to the Critique of Political Economy*, 188; Durkheim, "The Dualism of Human Nature," 150; on Weber, see Wilhelm Hennis, *Max Weber's Central Question*, 2nd ed., trans. Keith Tribe (England: Threshold Press, 2000), 3–101.

67. Karl Marx, "Speech at the Anniversary of the People's Paper," in *MECW*, vol. 14, 656; David J. Chalcraft and Austin Harrington, eds., *The Protestant Ethic Debate: Max Weber's Replies to His Critics, 1907–1910*, trans. Austin Harrington and Mary Shields (Cambridge: Liverpool University Press, 2001), 106.

68. Marx and Engels, *Manifesto*, 475–76; Durkheim, "Individualism and the Intellectuals," 44.

69. Lukes, *Individualism*, 129–30, 32.

70. Marx, *Capital*, vol. 1, 990.

71. Durkheim, *Suicide*, 305n; Durkheim, *Division of Labor*, 306–7, 312–14; Durkheim, *Professional Ethics*, 213.

72. Max Weber, "Parliament and Government in a Reconstructed Germany," in *Economy and Society*, 1402–3; Wolfgang J. Mommsen, "Capitalism and Socialism: Weber's Dialogue with Marx," trans. David Herr, in *A Weber-Marx Dialogue*, ed. Robert J. Antonio and Ronald M. Glassman (Lawrence: University of Kansas Press, 1985), 243.

73. Marx, *Capital*, vol. 1, 899; Marx and Engels, *German Ideology*, 214, 53. See also Michael A. Lebowitz, *The Contradictions of Real Socialism: The Conductor and the Conducted* (New York: Monthly Review, 2012).

74. Durkheim, *Division of Labor*, 334.

75. Weber, "The Meaning of Ethical Neutrality," 5–6; Weber, "Science as a Vocation," 137.

76. Bryan S. Turner, *Classical Sociology* (London: Sage, 1999), 65.

7. THE STATE AND DEMOCRACY

1. John Keane, *The Life and Death of Democracy* (New York: Norton, 2009), 473; David Held, *Models of Democracy*, 3rd ed. (Stanford, CA: Stanford University Press, 2006).

2. Karl Marx, *Critique of Hegel's "Philosophy of Right,"* trans. Annette Jolin and Joseph O'Malley (Cambridge: Cambridge University Press, 1977), 5, 32–33, 41–42, 72–73, 77, 80–81; Karl Marx, "On the Jewish Question," in Karl Marx and Frederick Engels, *Collected Works*, vol. 3 (New York: International Publishers, 1975), 154 [hereafter *MECW*]. See also David Leopold, *The Young Marx: German Philosophy, Modern Politics, and Human Flourishing* (Cambridge: Cambridge University Press, 2007), 62–69.

3. Marx, *Critique*, 26, 72; Joseph O'Malley, "Editor's Introduction," in Marx, *Critique*, xlviii–lii, li; Richard N. Hunt, *The Political Ideas of Marx and Engels*, vol. 1, *Marxism and Totalitarian Democracy, 1818–1850* (Pittsburgh, PA: University of Pittsburgh Press, 1974), 54–56.

4. Marx, *Critique*, 14, 18, 19.

5. Marx, "On the Jewish Question," 152–55, 166; Marx, *Critique*, 80.

6. Karl Marx, "Critical Marginal Notes on the Article 'The King of Prussia and Social Reform by a Prussian,'" in *MECW*, vol. 3, 197, 199, 204–6.

7. Karl Marx, "Preface," in *Contribution to a Critique of Political Economy* (New York: International Publishers, 1970), 20–21; Karl Marx and Frederick Engels, *The Holy Family or Critique of Critical Criticism*, in *MECW*, vol. 4, 121; Karl Marx, "Critique of the Gotha Programme," in *MECW*, vol. 24, 94; Karl Marx, *Capital: A Critique of Political Economy*, vol. 3, trans. David Fernbach (New York: Penguin Classics, 1991), 972.

8. Karl Marx, *The Eighteenth Brumaire of Louis Bonaparte* (New York: International Publishers, 1969), 121. On Marx's two theories of the capitalist state, see Held, *Models of Democracy*, 117–21; Richard N. Hunt, *The Political Ideas of Marx and Engels*, vol. 2, *Classical Marxism, 1850–1895* (Pittsburgh, PA: University of Pittsburgh Press, 1984), 27–98; Paul Thomas, *Alien Politics: Marxist State Theory Retrieved* (New York: Routledge, 1994).

9. Karl Marx and Frederick Engels, *The German Ideology*, in *MECW*, vol. 5, 90; Karl Marx and Frederick Engels, *Manifesto of the Communist Party*, in *The Marx-Engels Reader*, ed. Robert C. Tucker, 2nd ed. (New York: Norton, 1978), 475; Karl Marx, "The Chartists," in *MECW*, vol. 11, 334; Karl Marx, "Moralising Criticism and Critical Morality," in *MECW*, vol. 6, 319.

10. Marx and Engels, *Manifesto*, 490; Hal Draper, *Karl Marx's Theory of Revolution*, vol. 1, *State and Bureaucracy* (New York: Monthly Review, 1977), 587; Marx, *Eighteenth Brumaire*, 131, 120–21; Karl Marx, *The Civil War in France* (Peking: Foreign Languages Press, 1970), 71, 164–65.

11. Marx, *Critique*, 29–33, 118–21; Marx, *Civil War in France*, 168; Marx, "Gotha Programme," 94; Marx, "On the Jewish Question," 168.

12. Maximilien Rubel, "Notes on Marx's Conception of Democracy," *New Politics* 16 (Winter 1962): 86; Draper, *Karl Marx's Theory of Revolution*, 31–59, 282.

13. Karl Marx, "Comments on the Latest Prussian Censorship Instruction," in *MECW*, vol. 1, 122, 130. See also Karl Marx, "Debates on Freedom of the Press and Publication of the Proceedings of the Assembly of the Estates," in *MECW*, vol. 1, 132–81.

14. Marx, *Critique*, 46–48, 50, 72.

15. Hunt, *The Political Ideas of Marx and Engels*, vol. 2, xi, 365; Marx, *Civil War in France*, 78.

16. Karl Marx, *The Poverty of Philosophy* (New York: International Publishers, 1971), 174; Karl Marx, "Notes on Bakunin's Book *Statehood and Anarchy*," in *MECW*, vol. 24, 519; Marx and Engels, *Manifesto*, 490; Marx, "Gotha Programme," 96; Marx, *The Civil War in France*, 69, 167, 170. On Marx's concept of the abolition of the state, see Hunt, *The Political Ideas of Marx and Engels*, vol. 2, 231–65; Leopold, *The Young Marx*, 254–62.

17. Marx, "Gotha Programme," 95; Marx, "Notes on Bakunin," 517, 519, 521; Karl Marx, "Marx to Joseph Weydemeyer," in *MECW*, vol. 39, 65. For two detailed examinations of Marx's use of this term, see Hunt, *The Political Ideas of Marx and Engels*, vol. 1, 284–336; Hal Draper, *The Dictatorship of the Proletariat: From Marx to Lenin* (New York: Monthly Review, 1987), 11–41.

18. Marx, *The Civil War in France*, 63, 72, 99; See Hunt, *The Political Ideas of Marx and Engels*, vol. 2, 99–161; Monty Johnstone, "The Commune and Marx's Conception of the Dictatorship of the Proletariat and the Role of the Party," in *Images of the Commune*, ed. James J. Keith (Montreal: McGill Queens University Press, 1978), 201–24; Mehmet Tabak, "Marx's Theory of Proletarian Dictatorship Revisited," *Science & Society* 64, no. 3 (Fall 2000): 333–56.

19. Marx, *Civil War in France*, 64, 228, 69, 166.

20. Ibid., 64, 67–68; see also 171, 227.

21. Ibid., 232, 141, 68–70, 74, 167.

22. Draper, *Karl Marx's Theory of Revolution*, 283, 59.

23. Richard Bellamy, *Liberalism and Modern Society* (University Park: Pennsylvania State University Press, 1992), 93; Hans-Peter Müller, "Durkheim's Political Sociology," in *Emile Durkheim, Sociologist and Moralist*, ed. Stephen P. Turner (London: Routledge), 95; Gianfranco Poggi, *Durkheim* (Oxford: Oxford University Press, 2000), 123–24, 139–40.

24. Emile Durkheim, *Professional Ethics and Civic Morals*, trans. Cornelia Brookfield (London: Routledge, 1992), 48, 50–51; Emile Durkheim, *Socialism*, trans. Charlotte Sattler (New York: Collier, 1962), 53; Emile Durkheim, "The State," in *Durkheim on Politics and the State*, ed. Anthony Giddens, trans. W. D. Halls (Stanford, CA: Stanford University Press, 1986), 45, 47.

25. Durkheim, "The State," 45.

26. Durkheim, *Professional Ethics*, 79–80.

27. Ibid., 50–51, 79–80; Durkheim, "The State," 45–47.

28. Durkheim, *Professional Ethics*, 56–57; Durkheim, "The State," 48–49; Emile Durkheim, *The Division of Labor in Society*, trans. W. D. Halls (New York: Free Press, 1984), 166–68. See also Anthony Giddens, "Introduction," in *Durkheim on Politics and the State*, 2–3.

29. Emile Durkheim, "Review of Saverio Merlino, *Formes et Essence du Socialisme*," in *Durkheim on Politics and the State*, 144; Durkheim, "The State," 50; Durkheim, *Socialism*, 102.

30. Durkheim, "Review of Saverio Merlino," 144; Durkheim, *Professional Ethics*, 57, 60, 65, 69; Durkheim, "The State," 50.

31. Durkheim, *Professional Ethics*, 62–66, 69.

32. Durkheim, *Division of Labor*, 42–43; Durkheim, *Professional Ethics*, 60, 68–69, 71.

33. Durkheim, *Professional Ethics*, 74–75; Durkheim, "The State," 47–50.

34. Durkheim, *Professional Ethics*, 71–72, 74–75; Durkheim, *Division of Labor*, 339; Emile Durkheim, *Moral Education: A Study in the Theory and Application of the Sociology of Education*, trans. Everett K. Wilson and Herman Schnurer (New York: Free Press, 1961), 77. See also Antonino Palumbo and Alan Scott, "Weber, Durkheim and the Sociology of the Modern State," in *The Cambridge History of Twentieth-Century Political Thought*, ed. Terence Ball and Richard Bellamy (Cambridge: Cambridge University Press, 2003), 385–86.

35. Durkheim, *Professional Ethics*, 213; Durkheim, "The State," 49–50; Durkheim, *Socialism*, 59–60; Durkheim, *Moral Education*, 77; Emile Durkheim, "Social Property and Democracy: Review of Alfred Fouillee, *La Propriete Sociale et la Democratie*," in *Durkheim on Politics and the State*, 88; Durkheim, *Division of Labor*, 321.

36. Durkheim, *Professional Ethics*, 76–79.

37. Ibid., 49, 92.

38. On Durkheim's conception of democracy, see Mark S. Cladis, *A Communitarian Defense of Liberalism: Emile Durkheim and Contemporary Social Theory* (Stanford, CA: Stanford University Press, 1992), 149–65.

39. Durkheim, *Professional Ethics*, 81–82.

40. Ibid., 85–86; Emile Durkheim, *Education and Sociology*, trans. Sherwood D. Fox (New York: Free Press, 1956), 81; Durkheim, "Social Property and Democracy," 90–91; Giddens, "Introduction," 7–9. I borrow the phrase "two-way" communication from Anthony Giddens, *Capitalism and Modern Social Theory* (Cambridge: Cambridge University Press, 1971), 102.

41. Durkheim, *Professional Ethics*, 84, 88–90; Durkheim, *Education and Sociology*, 106; Durkheim, *Division of Labor*, 167–68.

42. Emile Durkheim, *On Suicide*, trans. Robin Buss (New York: Penguin, 2006), 422–23, 426, 434; Durkheim, *Division of Labor*, xxxiii–xxxiv, liv; Durkheim, *Professional Ethics*, 96, 100.

43. Durkheim, "Review of Saverio Merlino," 144–45; Durkheim, *Professional Ethics*, 63, 101; Emile Durkheim, "Two Laws of Penal Evolution," *Economy and Society* 3 (1973): 286–87.

44. Durkheim, *Professional Ethics*, 96, 103–6; Durkheim, *Suicide*, 436; Durkheim, *Division of Labor*, liii–liv, 139.

45. Durkheim, *Professional Ethics*, 89.

46. Ibid., 89–90.

47. Ibid., 89–90; Durkheim, "Social Property and Democracy," 90.

48. Max Weber, "On the Situation of Constitutional Democracy in Russia," in *Weber: Political Writings*, ed. Peter Lassman and Ronald Spiers (New York: Cambridge University Press, 1994), 69.

49. Lawrence A. Scaff, "Max Weber's Politics and Political Education," *American Political Science Review* 67, no. 1 (March 1973): 128–29, 140; David Beetham, *Max Weber and the Theory of Modern Politics* (Cambridge: Polity Press, 1985), 13; Max Weber, "The Nation State and Economic Policy," in *Weber: Political Writings*, 23; Max Weber, "'Objectivity' in Social Science and Social Policy," in *The Methodology of the Social Sciences*, trans. Edward A. Shils and Henry A. Finch (New York: Free Press, 1949), 58.

50. Max Weber, "Between Two Laws," in *Weber: Political Writings*, 78; Weber, "'Objectivity' in Social Science and Social Policy," 50; Weber, "The Nation State and Economic Policy," 27; Peter Breiner, *Max Weber and Democratic Politics* (Ithaca, NY: Cornell University Press, 1996), 2.

51. Weber, "The Nation State and Economic Policy," 16–17. On Weber's sometimes tendentious use of the criteria of feasibility, applying it more stringently to political programs he opposes and less stringently to those he favors, see Breiner, *Max Weber and Democratic Politics*, esp. 1, 10, 17–18.

52. Max Weber, "Politics as a Vocation," in *From Max Weber: Essays in Sociology*, trans. and ed. H. H. Gerth and C. Wright Mills (New York: Oxford University Press, 1946), 78, 82–83; Max Weber, *Economy and Society: An Outline of Interpretive Sociology*, trans. Ephraim Fischoff et al. (Berkeley: University of California Press, 1978), 54–56, 901–4; Max Weber, "Religious Rejections of the World and Their Directions," in *From Max Weber*, 334; Max Weber, "The Meaning of 'Ethical Neutrality' in Sociology and Economics," in *The Methodology of the Social Sciences*, 46.

53. Weber, "The Meaning of 'Ethical Neutrality,'" 47, 17–18, 26–27; Weber, "Politics as a Vocation," 78; Weber, *Economy and Society*, 38, 941; Max Weber, "Parliament and Government in a Reconstructed Germany," in *Economy and Society*, 1399; Max Weber, "Science as a Vocation," in *From Max Weber*, 153; Weber cited in Wolfgang J. Mommsen, *Max Weber and*

German Politics, 1890–1920, trans. Michael S. Steinberg (Chicago: University of Chicago Press, 1984), 41; Weber, "The Nation State and Economic Policy," 15.

54. Weber, "Politics as a Vocation," 120–28; Weber, "The Meaning of 'Ethical Neutrality,'" 17; see also Mark Warren, "Max Weber's Liberalism for a Nietzschean World," *American Political Science Review* 82, no. 1 (March 1988): 31–50.

55. Max Weber, "Capitalism and Rural Society in Germany," in *From Max Weber*, 370; Weber, "Parliament and Government," 1403; Max Weber, *The Russian Revolution*, trans. Gordon C. Wells and Peter Baehr (Ithaca, NY: Cornell University Press, 1995), 108–9; Max Weber, "Suffrage and Democracy in Germany," in *Weber: Political Writings*, 103–4, 129; Max Weber, "The President of the Reich," in *Weber: Political Writings*, 304–8.

56. Sven Eliaeson, "Constitutional Caesarism: Weber's Politics in Their German Context," in *The Cambridge Companion to Weber*, ed. Stephen Turner (Cambridge: Cambridge University Press, 2000), 132; Sven Eliaeson, "Max Weber and Plebiscitary Democracy," in *Max Weber, Democracy and Modernization*, ed. Ralph Schroeder (New York: St. Martin's, 1998), 47–48; Marianne Weber, *Max Weber: A Biography*, trans. Harry Zohn (New York: Wiley, 1975), 223; David Beetham, "Max Weber and the Liberal Political Tradition," *European Journal of Sociology* 30 (1989): 312.

57. Weber, *Economy and Society*, 289–92, 948–52, 1128; see also J. J. R. Thomas, "Weber and Direct Democracy," *British Journal of Sociology* 35, no. 2 (June 1984): 216–40; Stefan Breuer, "The Concept of Democracy in Weber's Political Sociology," in *Max Weber, Democracy and Modernization*, 1–13.

58. Political theorists typically define "direct" democracy in opposition to "representative" democracy. Weber's critique, however, applies not only to pure direct democracy, where the people themselves govern without the intermediary of representatives, but also to representative institutions where the discretionary power of elected officials is limited—that is, where they are required to act in accordance with the dictates of the electorate. Citizens in this type of representative democracy, both through their direct participation in the political process and through their indirect participation as voters, exercise a considerable degree of political power. This is sometimes called "popular" or "participatory" democracy, to set it apart from the elite or leadership democracy that Weber advocates. In what follows then, since he criticizes both simultaneously, I present Weber as an opponent of "direct" and "participatory" democracy, using these terms more or less interchangeably.

59. Weber, *Economy and Society*, 290–92, 949–50.

60. Max Weber, "Author's Introduction," in *The Protestant Ethic and the Spirit of Capitalism*, trans. Talcott Parsons (London: Counterpoint, 1985), 16; Weber, "Parliament and Government," 1453; Weber, *Economy and Society*, 948–52, 971–73; Weber, "Suffrage and Democracy," 126–29.

61. Weber, *Economy and Society*, 289, 948–52, 1128; Weber, "Parliament and Government," 1455–56; Weber, "Suffrage and Democracy," 128–29.

62. Weber, *Economy and Society*, 284–88, 952, 1131; Weber, "Parliament and Government," 1414, 1445; Weber, "Politics as a Vocation," 99.

63. Weber, "Parliament and Government," 1459–60; Weber, "Suffrage and Democracy," 108, 113, 125; Weber, "Politics as a Vocation," 86. For analysis and critique of Weber's view of the masses, see also Peter Baehr, "The 'Masses' in Weber's Political Sociology," *Economy and Society* 19, no. 2 (May 1990): 242–65; Catherine Brennan, *Max Weber on Power and Social Stratification: An Interpretation and Critique* (Brookfield, VT: Ashgate, 1997), esp. 243–49.

64. Weber, *Economy and Society*, 302–5, 941; Weber, "Suffrage and Democracy," 103; Weber, cited in Mommsen, *Max Weber and German Politics*, 394.

65. Weber, *Economy and Society*, 985; on Weber's conception of leadership democracy, see Beetham, *Max Weber and the Theory of Modern Politics*, 264–69; Breiner, *Max Weber and Democratic Politics*, 158–67.

66. Anthony Giddens, *Politics and Sociology in the Thought of Max Weber* (London: Macmillan, 1972), 55; Weber, cited in Hans Henrik Bruun, *Science, Values and Politics in Max Weber's Methodology*, new expanded ed. (Burlington, VT: Ashgate, 2007), 267; Weber, "Parliament and Government," 1383–84; see also Mommsen, *Max Weber and German Politics*, 395–96.

67. Weber, "Parliament and Government," 1392, 1403–4, 1419, 1438; Weber, "Politics as a Vocation," 90, 95.

68. Weber, "Parliament and Government," 1392, 1416, 1408, 1411, 1459.

69. Ibid., 1414, 1416, 1419–20, 1450.

70. Ibid., 1409–14, 1427; Weber, "Politics as a Vocation," 111.

71. Weber, "Parliament and Government," 1417–19.

72. Beetham, *Max Weber and the Theory of Modern Politics*, 113–16; Weber, "Parliament and Government," 1450. For a provocative reinterpretation of popular power and elite accountability in Weber's theory of democracy, see Jeffrey Edward Green, "Max Weber and the Reinvention of Popular Power," *Max Weber Studies* 8, no. 2 (2008): 187–224.

73. Mommsen, *Max Weber and German Politics*, 184.

74. Weber, *Economy and Society*, 268–69; Weber, "Parliament and Government," 1451–59; Weber, "The President of the Reich," 304; see also Weber, "Politics as a Vocation," 106–7.

75. Max Weber, "The Three Pure Types of Legitimate Rule," in *The Essential Weber: A Reader*, ed. Sam Whimster (New York: Routledge, 2004), 144–45; Marianne Weber, *Max Weber: A Biography*, 653; Weber, *Economy and Society*, 985; Weber, "The President of the Reich," 308; see also Mommsen, *Max Weber and German Politics*, 187.

76. Steven Pfaff, "Nationalism, Charisma, and Plebiscitary Leadership: The Problem of Democratization in Max Weber's Political Sociology," *Sociological Inquiry* 72, no. 1 (Winter 2002): 82; Mommsen, *Max Weber and German Politics*, 407–8; Mommsen, *The Age of Bureaucracy: Perspectives on the Political Sociology of Max Weber* (Oxford: Basil Blackwell, 1974), 93; Scaff, "Max Weber's Politics," 139.

77. Beetham, *Max Weber and the Theory of Modern Politics*, 102, 239, 266.

78. Durkheim, *Professional Ethics*, 64.

79. Weber, "The Nation State and Economic Policy," 16; Durkheim, *Professional Ethics*, 71–72, 75; Palumbo and Scott, "Weber, Durkheim and the Sociology of the Modern State," 282–91; Bryan S. Turner, *Classical Sociology* (London: Sage, 1999), 65; Mommsen, *Max Weber and German Politics*, 79.

80. Marx, *Civil War in France*, 167. For a valuable discussion of Weber on these issues, see Wolfgang J. Mommsen, "Max Weber as a Critic of Marxism," *Canadian Journal of Sociology* 2, no. 4 (Autumn 1977): 389–90; for a Marxist critique of Durkheim's theory of the state, see Tom Bottomore, "A Marxist Consideration of Durkheim," *Social Forces* 59, no. 4 (June 1981): 902–17.

81. Wolfgang J. Mommsen, *The Political and Social Theory of Max Weber* (Chicago: University of Chicago Press, 1989), 25.

82. Jeffrey Prager, "Moral Integration and Political Inclusion: A Comparison of Durkheim's and Weber's Theories of Democracy," *Social Forces* 59, no. 4 (June 1981): 937–38.

83. Marx, *Civil War in France*, 78.

84. See Ira J. Cohen, "The Underemphasis on Democracy in Marx and Weber," *A Weber-Marx Dialogue*, ed. Robert J. Antonio and Ronald M. Glassman (Lawrence: University of Kansas Press, 1985), 274–99.

85. On the "Theories of Bureaucratic Power" in Marx and Weber, see David Beetham, *Bureaucracy* (Minneapolis: University of Minnesota Press, 1987), 56–96, quote 57.

86. Ibid., 57.

87. Warren, "Max Weber's Liberalism," 45; see also Cohen, "The Underemphasis on Democracy in Marx and Weber," 289–95; Breiner, *Max Weber and Democratic Politics*, 202–32.

88. Weber, "The Meaning of 'Ethical Neutrality,'" 24.

8. SOCIALISM AND CAPITALISM

1. Pew Research Center for People & the Press, "Little Change in Public's Response to 'Capitalism,' 'Socialism'" (December 28, 2011), http://www.people-press.org/2011/12/28/little-change-in-publics-response-to-capitalism-socialism (accessed September 15, 2013).

2. On the variety of socialism before and after Marx, see Eric J. Hobsbawm, "Marx, Engels and Pre-Marxian Socialism," in *The History of Marxism*, vol. 1, *Marxism in Marx's Day*, ed. Eric J. Hobsbawm (Bloomington: Indiana University Press, 1982), 1–28; Alan Ryan, *On Politics, Book Two: Hobbes to the Present* (New York: Norton, 2012), 878–910.

3. Karl Marx, "Preface," in *Contribution to a Critique of Political Economy* (New York: International Publishers, 1970), 20; Karl Marx, "Debates on the Law on Thefts of Wood," in Karl Marx and Frederick Engels, *Collected Works*, vol. 1 (New York: International Publishers, 1975), 224–63 [hereafter *MECW*]; Karl Marx, "Justification of the Correspondent from the Mosel," in *MECW*, vol. 1, 332–58; Engels, cited in David McLellan, *Karl Marx: His Life and Thought* (New York: Harper & Row, 1973), 57; Hal Draper, *Karl Marx's Theory of Revolution*, vol. 1, *State and Bureaucracy* (New York: Monthly Review, 1977), 64.

4. Richard N. Hunt, *The Political Ideas of Marx and Engels*, vol. 1, *Marxism and Totalitarian Democracy, 1818–1850* (Pittsburgh, PA: University of Pittsburgh Press, 1974), 50–52.

5. See especially Karl Marx, *Critique of Hegel's "Philosophy of Right,"* trans. Annette Jolin and Joseph O'Malley (Cambridge: Cambridge University Press, 1977); Karl Marx, "On the Jewish Question," in *MECW*, vol. 3, 146–74; Karl Marx, "Critical Marginal Notes on the Article 'The King of Prussia and Social Reform by a Prussian,'" in *MECW*, vol. 3, 189–206.

6. Karl Marx, "Contribution to the Critique of Hegel's *Philosophy of Right*: Introduction," in *The Marx-Engels Reader*, ed. Robert C. Tucker, 2nd ed. (New York: Norton, 1978), 64–65; W. A. Suchting, *Marx: An Introduction* (New York: New York University Press, 1983), 34.

7. Karl Marx, "Letters from the Deutsch-Französische Jahrbücher," in *MECW*, vol. 3, 142; Draper, *Marx's Theory of Revolution*, vol. 1, 136–38, 174–81; Marx, "Critical Marginal Notes," 201. See also Michael Löwy, *The Theory of Revolution in the Young Marx* (Chicago: Haymarket Books, 2005), 49–51, 64–86; August Nimtz, "Marx and Engels—The Unsung Heroes of the Democratic Breakthrough," *Science & Society* 63, no. 2 (Summer 1999): 205–7.

8. Karl Marx, *The Economic and Philosophic Manuscripts of 1844*, trans. Martin Milligan (New York: International Publishers, 1972). My analysis in this paragraph draws on two valuable sources: Draper, *Marx's Theory of Revolution*, vol. 1, 162–67; Suchting, *Marx: An Introduction*, 36–37. On how Marx's time in Paris contributed to his evolution as a socialist, see also Marcello Musto, "Marx in Paris: Manuscripts and Notebooks of 1844," trans. Patrick Camiller, *Science & Society* 73, no. 3 (July 2009): 386–402; Jonathan Sperber, *Karl Marx: A Nineteenth Century Life* (New York: Liveright, 2013), 116–19.

9. Karl Marx and Frederick Engels, *The German Ideology*, in *MECW*, vol. 5, 49; Karl Marx, "Theses on Feuerbach," in *MECW*, vol. 5, 3–5; Löwy, *The Theory of Revolution*, 109–36.

10. Marx and Engels, *German Ideology*, 215.

11. Karl Marx, *Capital: A Critique of Political Economy*, vol. 1, trans. Ben Fowkes (New York: Penguin Classics, 1990), 96. For what Marx might say to today's proponents of the "there is no alternative" thesis, see Charles Derber, *Marx's Ghost: Midnight Conversations on Changing the World* (Boulder, CO: Paradigm, 2011).

12. Karl Marx, *Grundrisse: Foundations of the Critique of Political Economy*, trans. Martin Nicolaus (New York: Vintage, 1973), 159; Karl Marx, *Capital: A Critique of Political Economy*, vol. 3, trans. David Fernbach (New York: Penguin Classics, 1991), 371, 958–59; Karl Marx, "Letter to the Labour Parliament," in *MECW*, vol. 13, 58; Karl Marx and Frederick Engels, *Manifesto of the Communist Party*, in *The Marx-Engels Reader*, ed. Robert C. Tucker, 2nd ed. (New York: Norton, 1978), 483, 478; Karl Marx, "Critique of the Gotha Programme," in *MECW*, vol. 24, 83.

13. Karl Marx, "Provisional Rules of the Association," in *MECW*, vol. 20, 14; Marx and Engels, *Manifesto*, 496–97; Karl Marx, "Instructions for the Delegates of the Provisional General Council," in *MECW*, vol. 20, 191–92; Karl Marx and Frederick Engels, "Address of the Central Authority to the League," in *MECW*, vol. 10, 281; see also Karl Marx, *The Eighteenth Brumaire of Louis Bonaparte* (New York: International Publishers, 1969), 50.

14. Karl Marx, "Inaugural Address of the Working Men's International Association," in *MECW*, vol. 20, 11; Karl Marx, *Wages, Price and Profit* (Peking: Foreign Languages Press, 1975), 78–79; Marx, *Capital*, vol. 1, 769; Marx, *Economic and Philosophic Manuscripts*, 118.

15. Karl Marx and Frederick Engels, "Marx and Engels to August Bebel, Wilhelm Liebknecht, Wilhelm Bracke and Others (Circular Letter)," in *MECW*, vol. 45, 408; Marx, "Critical Marginal Notes," 202; Karl Marx, "Marx to Johann Baptist Von Schweitzer," in *MECW*, vol. 43, 133; Marx, "Letters from the Deutsch-Französische Jahrbücher," 144; Karl Marx, "Marx to Engels," in *MECW*, vol. 42, 287; Karl Marx, "Marx to Ferdinand Domela Nieuwenhuis," in *MECW*, vol. 46, 67.

16. Marx, "Provisional Rules of the Association," 14; Karl Marx, *The Civil War in France* (Peking: Foreign Languages Press, 1970), 73; Marx and Engels, *Manifesto*, 482. See also Draper, *Marx's Theory of Revolution*, vol. 1, 213–34; Hal Draper, *Karl Marx's Theory of Revolution*, vol. 2, *The Politics of Social Classes* (New York: Monthly Review, 1978), 147–65.

17. Karl Marx, "Political Indifferentism," in *MECW*, vol. 23, 392–97; Karl Marx, "Marx to Ludwig Kugelman," in *MECW*, vol. 42, 326; Marx and Engels, "Circular Letter," 406–8; Marx and Engels, *Manifesto*, 497–98.

18. Karl Marx, "Marx to Friedrich Adolph Sorge," in *MECW*, vol. 45, 284; Marx and Engels, "Circular Letter," 408; Marx, "Contribution to the Critique of Hegel's *Philosophy of Right*: Introduction," 60; Karl Marx, "The Chartists," in *MECW*, vol. 11, 335–36; Karl Marx, "La Liberté Speech," at http://www.marxist.org/archive/marx/works/1872/09/08/htm. On Marx's thinking about the issue of peaceful versus violent revolution, see Hunt, *The Political Ideas of Marx and Engels*, 133–47, 258; Steven Seidman, *Liberalism and the Origins of European Social Theory* (Berkeley: University of California Press, 1983), 112–14.

19. Draper, *Karl Marx's Theory of Revolution*, vol. 2, 29–32; Marx, *Wages, Price and Profit*, 74; Marx, "Instructions for the Delegates of the Provisional General Council," 191.

20. Karl Marx and Frederick Engels, "Resolution of the Conference of Delegates of the International Working Men's Association," in *MECW*, vol. 20, 426–27; Marx, "Inaugural Address of the Working Men's International Association," 12; Marx and Engels, *Manifesto*, 484, 490; Karl Marx, "Notes on Bakunin's Book *Statehood and Anarchy*," in *MECW*, vol. 24,

517, 521; Marx, "Gotha Programme," 95; Karl Marx, "Marx to Joseph Weydemeyer," in *MECW*, vol. 39, 65.

21. Marx, *Capital*, vol. 1, 99; for a useful analysis of Marx's conception of the socialist future, see Bertell Ollman, "Marx's Vision of Communism: A Reconstruction," *Critique* 8 (Summer 1977): 5–41.

22. Richard N. Hunt, *The Political Ideas of Marx and Engels*, vol. 2, *Classical Marxism, 1850–1895* (Pittsburgh, PA: University of Pittsburgh Press, 1984), 365; Marx, "Letter to the Labour Parliament," 56; Marx and Engels, *German Ideology*, 47; Marx, "Gotha Programme," 87.

23. Marx, "Preface," 22.

24. Cited in Steven Lukes, *Emile Durkheim: His Life and Work: A Historical and Critical Study* (Stanford, CA: Stanford University Press, 1985), 321; see also Marcel Fournier, *Emile Durkheim: A Biography*, trans. David Macey (New York: Polity, 2013), 707–8.

25. Lukes, *Emile Durkheim*, 546, 321; Emile Durkheim, *Socialism*, trans. Charlotte Sattler (New York: Collier, 1962), 40–41; Emile Durkheim, "Review of Antonio Labriola, *Essais sur la Conception Matérialiste de l'Histoire*," in *Emile Durkheim on Institutional Analysis*, ed. and trans. Mark Traugott (Chicago: University of Chicago Press, 1978), 128. On Durkheim as a "liberal socialist," see also Fournier, *Emile Durkheim*, 6, 80–82, 161–62, 209–14, 345, 350–53, 489–93.

26. Durkheim, *Socialism*, 39–40, 183–84; Emile Durkheim, "The Definition of Socialism," in *Durkheim on Politics and the State*, ed. Anthony Giddens, trans. W. D. Hall (Stanford, CA: Stanford University Press, 1986), 97–98; Dick Pels, "A Fellow-Traveller's Dilemma: Sociology and Socialism in the Writings of Durkheim," *Acta Politica* 19, no. 3 (1984): 309–29.

27. Durkheim, "The Definition of Socialism," 98–100; Durkheim, *Socialism*, 41–42, 44; see also Emile Durkheim, "Review of Gaston Richard, *Le Socialisme et la Science Sociale*," in *Durkheim on Politics and the State*, 127–28.

28. Durkheim, *Socialism*, 87, 41; Emile Durkheim, "Review of Saverio Merlino, *Formes et Essence du Socialisme*," in *Durkheim on Politics and the State*, 137.

29. Durkheim, *Socialism*, 42–43.

30. Ibid., 45–51; Durkheim, "The Definition of Socialism," 103–9.

31. Durkheim, "Belot and Socialism," in *Durkheim on Politics and the State*, 116–17; Durkheim, *Socialism*, 53; Emile Durkheim, *The Division of Labor in Society*, trans. W. D. Halls (New York: Free Press, 1984), xxxi–xxxii.

32. Durkheim, *Socialism*, 54–58; Durkheim, "Definition of Socialism," 109–12; Durkheim, "Belot and Socialism," 115–20; see also Emile Durkheim, "The Politics of the Future," trans. W. Watts Miller and J. Mergy, *Durkheimian Studies* 15 (2009): 3–4.

33. Pels, "A Fellow-Traveller's Dilemma," 318. For a useful discussion of some of the differences between Durkheim and Marx, see Tom Bottomore, "A Marxist Consideration of Durkheim," *Social Forces* 59, no. 4 (June 1981): 902–17.

34. Marx and Engels, *Manifesto*, 498; Fournier, *Emile Durkheim*, 161; Marcel Mauss, "Introduction to the First Edition," in Durkheim, *Socialism*, 34.

35. Emile Durkheim, "Review of Saverio Merlino," 142–43, 145; Durkheim, "Definition of Socialism," 107–8; Durkheim, *Socialism*, 245–46, 50, 61.

36. Mauss, "Introduction," 34; Durkheim, "Review of Saverio Merlino," 143; Emile Durkheim, "The Intellectual Elite and Democracy," in *Emile Durkheim on Morality and Society*, ed. Robert N. Bellah (Chicago: University of Chicago Press, 1973), 59.

37. Lukes, *Durkheim*, 330; Mauss, "Introduction," 34.

38. Fournier, *Emile Durkheim*, 491–92.

39. Durkheim, *Socialism*, 40, 171; Emile Durkheim, *Education and Sociology*, trans. Sherwood D. Fox (New York: Free Press, 1956), 151.

40. Emile Durkheim, *Professional Ethics and Civic Morals*, trans. Cornelia Brookfield (London: Routledge, 1992), 94; Durkheim, *Socialism*, 246; Durkheim, "Review of Saverio Merlino," 138; Fournier, *Emile Durkheim*, 491–92.

41. Durkheim, "Review of Saverio Merlino," 140.

42. Durkheim, *Professional Ethics*, 30–31; Durkheim, *Division of Labor*, lv–lvi.

43. Durkheim, *Division of Labor*, 313; Durkheim, *Professional Ethics*, 69, 71; Emile Durkheim, "Individualism and the Intellectuals," in *Emile Durkheim on Morality and Society*, 56.

44. Durkheim, *Socialism*, 239–43, 274–75; Emile Durkheim, *Moral Education: A Study in the Theory and Application of the Sociology of Education*, trans. Everett K. Wilson and Herman Schnurer (New York: Free Press, 1961), 40, 54.

45. Durkheim, *Socialism*, 274, 247, 285; Raymond Aron, *Main Currents in Sociological Thought II: Durkheim, Pareto, Weber*, trans. Richard Howard and Helen Weaver (Garden City, NY: Anchor, 1970), 85, 89.

46. Durkheim, *Socialism*, 61, 239; Durkheim, "Review of Saverio Merlino," 143.

47. Max Weber, *The Protestant Ethic and the Spirit of Capitalism*, trans. Talcott Parsons (London: Counterpoint, 1985), 54–55; Max Weber, *Economy and Society: An Outline of Interpretive Sociology*, trans. Ephraim Fischoff et al. (Berkeley: University of California Press, 1978), 1186; Max Weber, *The Russian Revolution*, trans. and ed. Gordon C. Wells and Peter Baehr (Ithaca, NY: Cornell University Press, 1995), 109.

48. For a valuable discussion of these issues, written from a perspective sympathetic to Weber's position, see Wolfgang J. Mommsen, "Capitalism and Socialism: Weber's Dialogue with Marx," trans. David Herr, in *A Weber-Marx Dialogue*, ed. Robert J. Antonio and Ronald M. Glassman (Lawrence: University of Kansas Press, 1985), 234–61.

49. Weber, *Economy and Society*, 302–7, 926–40; Max Weber, "Socialism," in *Weber: Political Writings*, ed. Peter Lassman and Ronald Speirs (Cambridge: Cambridge University Press, 1994), 277, 290, 292–94.

50. Weber, "Socialism," 290, 292–94.

51. Weber, *Economy and Society*, 203, 305, 928–29, 931; Weber, "Socialism," 293; see also Erik Olin Wright, "The Shadow of Exploitation in Weber's Class Analysis," in *Max Weber's Economy and Society: A Critical Companion*, ed. Charles Camic, Philip S. Gorski, and David M. Trubek (Stanford, CA: Stanford University Press, 2005), 212–14.

52. Max Weber, "Suffrage and Democracy in Germany," in *Weber: Political Writings*, 84, 86–87; Max Weber, "The Nation State and Economic Policy," in *Weber: Political Writings*, 16; Marianne Weber, *Max Weber: A Biography*, trans. Harry Zohn (New York: Wiley, 1975), 135, 221; Wolfgang J. Mommsen, *Max Weber and German Politics, 1890–1920*, trans. Michael S. Steinberg (Chicago: University of Chicago Press, 1984), 68–84.

53. Weber, "Suffrage and Democracy," 87–88.

54. Weber, "Socialism," 296–97.

55. Ibid., 289, 291.

56. Weber, "Parliament and Government in a Reconstructed Germany," in *Economy and Society*, 1401; Weber, "Socialism," 288.

57. Weber, "Parliament and Government," 1393–94, 1400–1401; Weber, *Economy and Society*, 223.

58. Weber, "Socialism," 286; Weber, "Suffrage and Democracy," 90; Weber, "Parliament and Government," 1401–2.

59. Weber, "Parliament and Government," 1402; Weber, "Socialism," 292.

60. Weber, "Parliament and Government," 1394; Weber, *Economy and Society*, 1002; Weber, "Suffrage and Democracy," 90.

61. Guenther Roth, "Max Weber, Scion of the Cosmopolitan Bourgeoisie: Historical Context and Present-Day Relevance," in *Max Weber's* Economy and Society, 39–40.

62. Weber, *Economy and Society*, 85–86, 108–9.

63. Ibid., 81, 85–86, 107–13.

64. Weber, "Parliament and Government," 1403–4; Weber, "Suffrage and Democracy," 84; Max Weber, *The Agrarian Sociology of Ancient Civilizations*, trans. R. I. Frank (London: NLB, 1976), 365; see also David Beetham, *Max Weber and the Theory of Modern Politics* (Cambridge: Polity Press, 1985), 82–83.

65. Beetham, *Max Weber and the Theory of Modern Politics*, 84; Robert J. Antonio and Ronald M. Glassman, "Introduction," in *A Weber-Marx Dialogue*, xv; Fritz Ringer, *Max Weber: An Intellectual Biography* (Chicago: University of Chicago Press, 2004), 217–18.

66. Weber, "Socialism," 279–81; Weber, *Economy and Society*, 137–40, 218–19, 980–83; Weber, "Parliament and Government," 1394.

67. Weber, "Socialism," 281; Weber, *Economy and Society*, 137–38.

68. Weber, *Economy and Society*, 110.

69. Max Weber, "A Research Strategy for the Study of Occupational Careers and Mobility Patterns," in *Max Weber: The Interpretation of Social Reality*, ed. J. E. T. Eldridge (New York: Scribner, 1971), 154–55; Weber, *Economy and Society*, 151; Weber, "Parliament and Government," 1401–2, Weber, "Socialism," 286.

70. Weber, "Socialism," 288.

71. Durkheim, cited in Mark S. Cladis, *A Communitarian Defense of Liberalism: Emile Durkheim and Contemporary Social Theory* (Stanford, CA: Stanford University Press, 1992), 299n2; Weber, *Economy and Society*, 600, 729–30, 1186; Durkheim, *Division of Labor*, 306–7.

72. Durkheim, *Socialism*, 247; Marx, *Capital*, vol. 1, 433; Durkheim, *Division of Labor*, xxxi.

73. Weber, *Protestant Ethic*, 282n108. On Weber's thoughts regarding the struggles of the working class, see Weber, "Socialism," 274–75; Mommsen, *Max Weber and German Politics*, 114–15, 120–21; Richard Bellamy, *Liberalism and Modern Society: A Historical Argument* (University Park: Pennsylvania State University Press, 1992), 172–73.

74. Marx, *Capital*, vol. 1, 449. On the concept of exploitation in Marx and Durkheim, see J.-C. Filloux, "Inequalities and Social Stratification in Durkheim's Sociology," in *Emile Durkheim, Sociologist and Moralist*, ed. Stephen P. Turner (London: Routledge, 1993), 211–28; and on the concept of exploitation in Marx and Weber, see Wright, "The Shadow of Exploitation in Weber's Class Analysis," 204–36.

75. Marx and Engels, *German Ideology*, 49.

76. Marx, "Preface," 22; Durkheim, *Division of Labor*, 321.

77. Durkheim, *Socialism*, 54–58.

78. See Anthony Giddens, *The Class Structure of the Advanced Societies* (New York: Harper Torchbooks, 1973), 46–47, 51; Anthony Giddens, "Marx and Weber: A Reply to Mr. Walton," *Sociology* 5 (1971): 396.

79. Weber, "Socialism," 279, 292, 288; see also Gert H. Mueller, "Socialism and Capitalism in the Work of Max Weber," *British Journal of Sociology* 33, no. 2 (June 1982): 151–71.

80. Marx, *Capital*, vol. 1, 448–49; Marx, *Capital*, vol. 3, 507, 959; Marx, "Letter to the Labour Parliament," 58; see also Michael A. Lebowitz, *The Contradictions of Real Socialism: The Conductor and the Conducted* (New York: Monthly Review Press, 2012).

9. CONCLUSION

1. C. Wright Mills, "Introduction: The Classical Tradition," in *Images of Man: The Classical Tradition in Sociological Thinking*, ed. C. Wright Mills (New York: George Braziller, 1960), 2–3.

Selected Bibliography

Abend, Gabriel. "The Meaning of 'Theory.'" *Sociological Theory* 26, no. 2 (June 2008): 173–99.

Abrahms, Philip. "The Sense of the Past and the Origins of Sociology." *Past and Present* 55 (May 1972): 18–32.

Alexander, Jeffrey C. *Theoretical Logic in Sociology.* Vol. 3, *The Classical Attempt at Theoretical Synthesis: Max Weber.* Berkeley: University of California Press, 1983.

Antonio, Robert J., and Ronald M. Glassman. "Introduction." In *A Weber-Marx Dialogue,* edited by Robert J. Antonio and Ronald M. Glassman, xi–xxi. Lawrence: University Press of Kansas, 1985.

Archard, David. "The Marxist Ethic of Self-Realization: Individuality and Community." In *Moral Philosophy and Contemporary Problems,* edited by J. D. G. Evans, 19–34. Cambridge: Cambridge University Press, 1987.

Aron, Raymond. *Main Currents in Sociological Thought II: Durkheim, Pareto, Weber.* Translated by Richard Howard and Helen Weaver. Garden City, NY: Anchor, 1970.

Baehr, Peter. "The 'Masses' in Weber's Political Sociology." *Economy and Society* 19, no. 2 (May 1990): 242–65.

———. "The 'Iron Cage' and the 'Shell as Hard as Steel': Parsons, Weber, and the *Stahlhartes Gehäuse* Metaphor in the *Protestant Ethic and the Spirit of Capitalism.*" *History and Theory* 40, no. 2 (May 2001): 153–69.

Banaji, Jairus. "The Fictions of Free Labour: Contract, Coercion, and So-Called Unfree Labour." *Historical Materialism* 11, no. 3 (2003): 66–95.

Barbalet, Jack. *Weber, Passion and Profits: "The Protestant Ethic and the Spirit of Capitalism" in Context.* Cambridge: Cambridge University Press, 2008.

Beetham, David. *Max Weber and the Theory of Modern Politics.* New York: Polity Press, 1985.

———. *Bureaucracy.* Minneapolis: University of Minnesota Press, 1987.

———. "Max Weber and the Liberal Political Tradition." *European Journal of Sociology* 30 (1989): 311–23.

Bellah, Robert H., ed. *Emile Durkheim on Morality and Society: Selected Writings.* Chicago, IL: University of Chicago Press, 1973.

Bellamy, Richard. *Liberalism and Modern Society: A Historical Argument.* University Park: Pennsylvania State University Press, 1992.

Bendix, Reinhard. *Max Weber: An Intellectual Portrait.* Berkeley: University of California Press, 1977.

Berg, Maxine, and Pat Hudson. "Rehabilitating the Industrial Revolution." *Economic History Review* 45, no. 1 (1992): 24–50.

Berman, Marshall. *All That Is Solid Melts into Air: The Experience of Modernity.* New York: Simon & Schuster, 1982.

Besnard, Philippe. "Anomie and Fatalism in Durkheim's Theory of Regulation." In *Emile Durkheim: Sociologist and Moralist,* edited by Stephen Turner, 169–90. London: Routledge, 1993.

Birnbaum, Pierre. "French Jewish Sociologists between Reason and Faith: The Impact of the Dreyfus Affair." *Jewish Social Studies* 2, no. 1 (1995): 1–35.

Booth, William James. "Gone Fishing: Making Sense of Marx's Concept of Communism." *Political Theory* 17, no. 2 (May 1989): 205–22.

Bottomore, Tom. "A Marxist Consideration of Durkheim." *Social Forces* 59, no. 4 (June 1981): 902–17.

Bratton, John, David Denham, and Linda Deutschmann. *Capitalism and Classical Sociological Theory.* Toronto: University of Toronto Press, 2009.

Breiner, Peter. *Max Weber and Democratic Politics.* Ithaca, NY: Cornell University Press, 1996.

Brennan, Catherine. *Max Weber on Power and Social Stratification: An Interpretation and Critique.* Brookfield, VT: Ashgate, 1997.

Breuer, Stefan. "The Concept of Democracy in Weber's Political Sociology." In *Max Weber, Democracy and Modernization,* edited by Ralph Schroeder, 1–13. New York: St. Martin's, 1998.

Brubaker, Rogers. *The Limits of Rationality: An Essay on the Social and Moral Thought of Max Weber.* London: Allen & Unwin, 1984.

Bruun, H. H. *Science, Values and Politics in Max Weber's Methodology.* New expanded edition. Burlington, VT: Ashgate, 2007.

Calhoun, Craig, Joseph Gerteis, James Moody, Steven Pfaff, Kathryn Schmidt, and Indermohan Virk. "Introduction." In *Classical Sociological Theory,* edited by Craig Calhoun et al., 1–15. Malden, MA: Blackwell, 2002.

Camic, Charles, Philip S. Gorski, and David M. Trubek, eds. *Max Weber's Economy and Society: A Critical Companion.* Stanford, CA: Stanford University Press, 2005.

Censer, Jack R., and Lynn Hunt. *Liberty, Equality, Fraternity: Exploring the French Revolution.* University Park: Pennsylvania State University Press, 2001.

Chalcraft, David J. "Bringing the Text Back In: On Ways of Reading the Iron Cage Metaphor in the Two Editions of the *Protestant Ethic.*" In *Organizing Modernity: New Weberian Perspectives on Work, Organization and Society,* edited by Larry J. Ray and Michael Reed, 16–45. London: Routledge, 1994.

Chalcraft, David J., and Austin Harrington, eds. *The Protestant Ethic Debate: Max Weber's Replies to His Critics, 1907–1910.* Translated by Austin Harrington and Mary Shields. Cambridge: Liverpool University Press, 2001.

Cladis, Mark S. *A Communitarian Defense of Liberalism: Emile Durkheim and Contemporary Social Theory.* Stanford, CA: Stanford University Press, 1992.

———. "Durkheim's Individual in Society: A Sacred Marriage?" *Journal of the History of Ideas* 53, no. 1 (January–March 1992): 71–90.

Cohen, G. A. "The Structure of Proletarian Unfreedom." *Philosophy & Public Affairs* 12, no. 1 (Winter 1983): 3–33.

———. *Karl Marx's Theory of History: A Defence.* Expanded edition. Princeton, NJ: Princeton University Press, 2000.

Cohen, Ira J. "The Underemphasis on Democracy in Marx and Weber." In *A Weber-Marx Dialogue,* edited by Robert J. Antonio and Ronald M. Glassman, 274–99. Lawrence: University Press of Kansas, 1985.

Collins, Randall. "Weber's Last Theory of Capitalism: A Systematization." *American Sociological Review* 45, no. 6 (December 1980): 925–42.

———. "The European Sociological Tradition and Twenty-First-Century World Sociology." In *Sociology for the Twenty-First Century: Continuities and Cutting Edges,* edited by Janet L. Abu-Lughod, 26–42. Chicago, IL: University of Chicago Press, 1999.

Coser, Lewis A. *Masters of Sociological Thought: Ideas in Historical and Social Context.* 2nd ed. Long Grove, IL: Waveland Press, 2003.

Darnton, Robert. "What Was Revolutionary about the French Revolution?" *New York Review of Books,* January 19, 1989, 3–10.

Deane, Phyllis. *The First Industrial Revolution.* 2nd ed. Cambridge: Cambridge University Press, 1979.

Delanty, Gerard. "The Foundations of Social Theory: Origins and Trajectories." In *The Blackwell Companion to Social Theory,* edited by Bryan S. Turner, 2nd ed., 21–46. Oxford: Blackwell, 2000.

———. *Modernity and Postmodernity: Knowledge, Power and the Self.* London: Sage, 2000.

Derber, Charles. *Marx's Ghost: Midnight Conversations on Changing the World.* Boulder, CO: Paradigm, 2011.

Doyle, William. *The French Revolution: A Very Short Introduction.* Oxford: Oxford University Press, 2001.

Draper, Hal. *Karl Marx's Theory of Revolution.* Vol. 1, *State and Bureaucracy.* New York: Monthly Review, 1977.

———. *Karl Marx's Theory of Revolution.* Vol. 2, *The Politics of Social Classes.* New York: Monthly Review, 1978.

———. *Karl Marx's Theory of Revolution.* Vol. 3, *The "Dictatorship of the Proletariat."* New York: Monthly Review, 1986.

———. *The Dictatorship of the Proletariat: From Marx to Lenin.* New York: Monthly Review, 1987.

———. *Karl Marx's Theory of Revolution.* Vol. 4, *Critique of Other Socialisms.* New York: Monthly Review Press, 1990.

Durkheim, Emile. *Suicide: A Study in Sociology.* Translated by John A. Spaulding and George Simpson. New York: Free Press, 1951.

———. *Education and Sociology.* Translated by Sherwood D. Fox. New York: Free Press, 1956.

———. *Moral Education: A Study in the Theory and Application of the Sociology of Education.* Translated by Everett K. Wilson and Herman Schnurer. New York: Free Press, 1961.

———. *Socialism.* Translated by Charlotte Sattler. New York: Collier, 1962.

———. *Montesquieu and Rousseau: Forerunners of Sociology.* Ann Arbor, MI: Ann Arbor Paperbacks, 1965.

———. "Two Laws of Penal Evolution." Translated by T. Anthony Jones. *Economy and Society* 3 (1973): 285–308.

———. *Sociology and Philosophy.* Translated by D. F. Pocock. New York: Free Press, 1974.

————. *The Evolution of Educational Thought.* Translated by Peter Collins. London: Routledge & Kegan Paul, 1977.

————. *The Rules of Sociological Method and Selected Texts on Sociology and Its Method.*
Translated by W. D. Halls. Edited by Steven Lukes. New York: Free Press, 1982.

————. *The Division of Labor in Society.* Translated by W. D. Halls. New York: Free Press,
1984.

————. *Professional Ethics and Civic Morals.* Translated by Cornelia Brookfield. London:
Routledge, 1992.

————. *The Elementary Forms of Religious Life.* Translated by Karen E. Fields. New York:
Free Press, 1995.

————. *On Suicide.* Translated by Robin Buss. New York: Penguin, 2006.

————. "Anti-Semitism and Social Crisis." Translated by Chad Alan Goldberg. *Sociological
Theory* 26, no. 4 (December 2008): 321–23.

————. "The Politics of the Future." Translated by W. Watts Miller and J. Mergy. *Durkheimian Studies* 15 (2009): 3–6.

Eldridge, J. E. T., ed. *Max Weber: The Interpretation of Social Reality.* New York: Scribner,
1971.

Eliaeson, Sven. "Max Weber and Plebiscitary Democracy." In *Max Weber, Democracy and
Modernization,* edited by Ralph Schroeder, 47–60. New York: St. Martin's, 1998.

————. "Constitutional Caesarism: Weber's Politics in Their German Context." In *The Cambridge Companion to Weber,* edited by Stephen Turner, 131–48. Cambridge: Cambridge
University Press, 2000.

Elster, Jon. *Making Sense of Marx.* Cambridge: Cambridge University Press, 1985.

————. "Self-Realization in Work and Politics: The Marxist Conception of the Good Life."
Philosophy & Policy 3, no. 2 (Spring 1986): 97–126.

Emirbayer, Mustafa. "Beyond Weberian Action Theory." In *Max Weber's* Economy and Society: *A Critical Companion,* edited by Charles Camic, Philip S. Gorski, and David M.
Trubek, 185–203. Stanford, CA: Stanford University Press, 2005.

Farrell, Chad R. "Durkheim, Moral Individualism and the Dreyfus Affair." *Current Perspectives in Social Theory* 17 (1997): 313–30.

Filloux, J.-C. "Inequalities and Social Stratification in Durkheim's Sociology." In *Emile Durkheim: Sociologist and Moralist,* edited by Stephen Turner, 211–28. London: Routledge,
1993.

Fine, Ben, and Alfredo Saad-Filho. *Marx's* Capital. 5th ed. New York: Pluto Press, 2010.

Forbes, Ian. *Marx and the New Individual.* London: Unwin Hyman, 1990.

Foucault, Michel. *Discipline and Punish: The Birth of the Prison.* Translated by Alan Sheridan.
New York: Vintage, 1991.

Fournier, Marcel. *Emile Durkheim: A Biography.* Translated by David Macey. New York:
Polity, 2013.

Fracchia, Joseph. "The Capitalist Labour Process and the Body in Pain: The Corporeal Depths
of Marx's Concept of Immiseration." *Historical Materialism* 16, no. 4 (2008): 35–66.

Gane, Nicholas. *Max Weber and Postmodern Theory: Rationalization versus Re-Enchantment.*
New York: Palgrave, 2002.

Gay, Peter. *The Party of Humanity: Essays in the French Enlightenment.* New York: Norton,
1959.

————. *The Enlightenment: An Interpretation.* Vol. 2, *The Science of Freedom.* New York:
Norton, 1969.

————. "Introduction." In *The Enlightenment: A Comprehensive Anthology,* edited by Peter
Gay, 13–26. New York: Simon & Schuster, 1973.

Gerth, H. H., and C. Wright Mills. *From Max Weber: Essays in Sociology.* Translated and edited by H. H. Gerth and C. Wright Mills. New York: Oxford University Press, 1946.

Giddens, Anthony. *Capitalism and Modern Social Theory: An Analysis of the Writings of Marx, Durkheim and Max Weber.* Cambridge: Cambridge University Press, 1971.

————. "Marx and Weber: A Reply to Mr. Walton." *Sociology* 5 (1971): 395–97.

————. *Politics and Sociology in the Thought of Max Weber.* London: Macmillan, 1972.

————, ed. *Emile Durkheim: Selected Writings.* New York: Cambridge University Press, 1972.

————. *The Class Structure of the Advanced Societies.* New York: Harper Torchbooks, 1973.

————. *Studies in Social and Political Theory.* London: Hutchinson, 1977.

————, ed. *Durkheim on Politics and the State.* Translated by W. D. Hall. Stanford, CA: Stanford University Press, 1986.

————. "Introduction." In *Durkheim on Politics and the State*, edited by Anthony Giddens, 1–31. Stanford, CA: Stanford University Press, 1986.

————. *The Consequence of Modernity.* Stanford, CA: Stanford University Press, 1990.

————, and Christopher Pierson. *Conversations with Anthony Giddens: Making Sense of Modernity.* Stanford, CA: Stanford University Press, 1998.

Goldman, Harvey. *Max Weber and Thomas Mann: Calling and the Shaping of the Self.* Berkeley: University of California Press, 1988.

————. *Politics, Death, and the Devil: Self and Power in Max Weber and Thomas Mann.* Berkeley: University of California Press, 1992.

————. "*Economy and Society* and the Revision of Weber's Ethics." In *Max Weber's* Economy and Society: *A Critical Companion*, edited by Charles Camic, Philip S. Gorski, and David M. Trubek, 47–69. Stanford, CA: Stanford University Press, 2005.

Gould, Carol C. *Marx's Social Ontology: Individuality and Community in Marx's Theory of Social Reality.* Cambridge, MA: MIT Press, 1978.

Green, Jeffrey Edward. "Max Weber and the Reinvention of Popular Power." *Max Weber Studies* 8, no. 2 (2008): 187–224.

Green, S. J. D. "Emile Durkheim on Human Talents and Two Traditions of Social Justice." *British Journal of Sociology* 40, no. 1 (March 1989): 97–117.

Gronow, Jukka. "The Element of Irrationality: Max Weber's Diagnosis of Modern Culture." *Acta Sociologica* 31, no. 4 (1988): 319–31.

Habermas, Jürgen. *The Theory of Communicative Action.* Vol. 1, *Reason and the Rationalization of Society.* Translated by Thomas McCarthy. Boston, MA: Beacon Press, 1981.

————. *The Postnational Constellation: Political Essays.* Translated by Max Pensky. Cambridge, MA: MIT Press, 2001.

Hamilton, Peter, "The Enlightenment and the Birth of Social Science." In *Modernity: An Introduction to Modern Societies*, edited by Stuart Hall, David Held, Don Humbert, and Kenneth Thompson, 19–54. Cambridge, MA: Blackwell, 1969.

Hampson, Norman. *The Enlightenment.* New York: Penguin, 1982.

Harvey, David. *Companion to Marx's* Capital. London: Verso, 2010.

Hawkins, M. J. "A Re-Examination of Durkheim's Theory of Human Nature." *Sociological Review* 25, no. 2 (1977): 429–46.

————. "Continuity and Change in Durkheim's Theory of Social Solidarity." *Sociological Quarterly* 20, no. 1 (Winter 1979): 155–64.

————. "Traditionalism and Organicism in Durkheim's Early Writings, 1885–1893." *Journal of the History of the Behavioral Sciences* 16 (1980): 31–44.

————. "Durkheim on Occupational Corporations: An Exegesis and Interpretation." *Journal of the History of Ideas* 55, no. 3 (July 1994): 461–81.

Hearn, Frank. "Durkheim's Political Sociology: Corporatism, State Autonomy, and Democracy." *Social Research* 52, no. 1 (Spring 1985): 211–24.

Held, David. *Models of Democracy*. 3rd ed. Stanford, CA: Stanford University Press, 2006.

Hennis, Wilhelm. *Max Weber's Central Question*. 2nd ed. Translated by Keith Tribe. Newbury, UK: Threshold Press, 2000.

———. *Max Weber's Science of Man: New Studies for a Biography of the Work*. Translated by Keith Tribe. Newbury, UK: Threshold Press, 2000.

Henrich, Michael. *An Introduction to the Three Volumes of Karl Marx's Capital*. Translated by Alexander Locascio. New York: Monthly Review, 2004.

Hobsbawm, E. J. *The Age of Revolution, 1789–1848*. New York: New American Library, 1962.

———. *Industry and Empire*. Baltimore, MD: Penguin, 1968.

———. "Marx, Engels and Pre-Marxian Socialism." In *The History of Marxism*, vol. 1, *Marxism in Marx's Day*, edited by Eric J. Hobsbawm, 1–27. Bloomington: Indiana University Press, 1982.

———. *How to Change the World: Marx and Marxism 1840–2011*. London: Little, Brown, 2011.

Holmstrom, Nancy. "Exploitation." *Canadian Journal of Philosophy* 7, no. 2 (June 1977): 353–69.

Hudis, Peter. *Marx's Concept of the Alternative to Capitalism*. Chicago, IL: Haymarket Books, 2012.

Hughes, H. Stuart. *Consciousness and Society: The Reorientation of European Social Thought, 1890–1930*. Rev. ed. New York: Vintage, 1977.

Hughes, John A., Wes W. Sharrock, and Peter J. Martin. *Understanding Classical Sociology: Marx, Weber, Durkheim*. 2nd ed. London: Sage, 2003.

Hunt, Richard N. *The Political Ideas of Marx and Engels I: Marxism and Totalitarian Democracy, 1818–1850*. Pittsburgh, PA: University of Pittsburgh Press, 1974.

———. *The Political Ideas of Marx and Engels II: Classical Marxism, 1850–1895*. Pittsburgh, PA: University of Pittsburgh Press, 1984.

Isambert, François-Andre. "Durkheim's Sociology of Moral Facts." In *Emile Durkheim: Sociologist and Moralist*, edited by Stephen Turner, 193–210. London: Routledge, 1993.

Israel, Jonathan I. *Democratic Enlightenment: Philosophy, Revolution, and Human Rights 1750–1790*. Oxford: Oxford University Press, 2011.

Jelavich, Peter. "Republican Ethics as Social Science: The Case of Emile Durkheim." In *Critical Issues in Social Thought*, edited by Murray Milgate and Cheryl B. Welch, 139–57. London: Academic Press, 1989.

Joas, Hans. "Durkheim's Intellectual Development: The Problem of the Emergence of a New Morality and New Institutions as a Leitmotif in Durkheim's Oeuvre." In *Emile Durkheim: Sociologist and Moralist*, edited by Stephen Turner, 229–45. London: Routledge, 1993.

Johnstone, Monty. "The Commune and Marx's Conception of the Dictatorship of the Proletariat and the Role of the Party." In *Images of the Commune*, edited by James J. Keith, 201–24. Montreal: McGill Queens University Press, 1978.

Jones, Robert Alun. *Emile Durkheim: An Introduction to Four Major Works*. Beverly Hills, CA: Sage, 1986.

Jones, Susan Stedman. *Durkheim Reconsidered*. Cambridge: Polity, 2001.

Kalberg, Stephen. "The Search for Thematic Orientations in a Fragmented Oeuvre: The Discussion of Max Weber in Recent German Sociological Literature." *Sociology* 13, no. 1 (January 1979): 127–39.

———. "Max Weber's Types of Rationality: Cornerstone for the Analysis of Rationalization Processes in History." *American Journal of Sociology* 85, no. 5 (March 1980): 1145–79.

———. "The Modern World as a Monolithic Iron Cage? Utilizing Max Weber to Define the Internal Dynamics of the American Political Culture Today." *Max Weber Studies* 1, no. 2 (May 2001): 178–95.

———. "General Introduction: Max Weber and the Modern West." In The Protestant Ethic and the Spirit of Capitalism *with Other Writings on the Rise of the West*, edited by Stephen Kalberg, 4th ed., vii–xviii. New York: Oxford University Press, 2009.

Käsler, Dirk. *Max Weber: An Introduction to His Life and Work*. Chicago, IL: University of Chicago Press, 1988.

Kaufman-Osborn, Timothy V. "Emile Durkheim and the Science of Corporatism." *Political Theory* 14, no. 4 (November 1986): 638–59.

Keane, John. *The Life and Death of Democracy*. New York: Norton, 2009.

Kim, Sung Ho. *Max Weber's Politics of Civil Society*. Cambridge: Cambridge University Press, 2004.

Klagge, James C. "Marx's Realms of 'Freedom' and 'Necessity.'" *Canadian Journal of Philosophy* 16, no. 4 (December 1986): 769–78.

Koch, Andrew M. "Rationality, Romanticism and the Individual: Max Weber's 'Modernism' and the Confrontation with 'Modernity.'" *Canadian Journal of Political Science* 26, no. 1 (March 1993): 123–44.

———. *Romance and Reason: Ontological and Social Sources of Alienation in the Writings of Max Weber*. Lanham, MD: Lexington Books, 2006.

Kronman, Anthony T. *Max Weber*. Stanford, CA: Stanford University Press, 1983.

Kumar, Krishan. *Prophecy and Progress: The Sociology of Industrial and Post-Industrial Society*. New York: Penguin, 1978.

LaCapra, Dominick. *Emile Durkheim: Sociologist and Philosopher*. Chicago, IL: University of Chicago Press, 1985.

Lassman, Peter, and Ronald Speirs, eds. *Weber: Political Writings*. Cambridge: Cambridge University Press, 1994.

Lebowitz, Michael A. *The Contradictions of Real Socialism: The Conductor and the Conducted*. New York: Monthly Review, 2012.

Leopold, David. "The Structure of Marx and Engels' Considered Account of Utopian Socialism." *History of Political Thought* 26, no. 3 (Autumn 2005): 445–66.

———. *The Young Marx: German Philosophy, Modern Politics, and Human Flourishing*. Cambridge: Cambridge University Press, 2007.

Levine, Donald N. *The Flight from Ambiguity: Essays in Social and Cultural Theory*. Chicago, IL: University of Chicago Press, 1985.

———. "The Continuing Challenge of Weber's Theory of Rational Action." In *Max Weber's Economy and Society: A Critical Companion*, edited by Charles Camic, Philip S. Gorski, and David M. Trubek, 101–26. Stanford, CA: Stanford University Press, 2005.

Löwith, Karl. *Max Weber and Karl Marx*. London: Allen & Unwin, 1982.

Löwy, Michael. *The Theory of Revolution in the Young Marx*. Chicago, IL: Haymarket Books, 2005.

Lukes, Steven. *Individualism*. New York: Harper Torchbooks, 1973.

———. *Emile Durkheim: His Life and Work; A Historical and Critical Study*. Stanford, CA: Stanford University Press, 1985.

———. *Marxism and Morality*. New York: Oxford University Press, 1987.

MacKenzie, Donald. "Marx and the Machine." *Technology and Culture* 25, no. 3 (July 1984): 473–502.

Mackinnon, Malcolm H. "Max Weber's Disenchantment: Lineages of Kant and Channing." *Journal of Classical Sociology* 1, no. 3 (December 2001): 329–51.

Marshall, Gordon. *In Search of the Spirit of Capitalism: An Essay on Max Weber's Protestant Ethic Thesis.* New York: Columbia University Press, 1982.

Marske, Charles E. "Durkheim's 'Cult of the Individual' and the Moral Reconstitution of Society." *Sociological Theory* 5, no. 1 (Spring 1987): 1–14.

Marx, Karl. *Theories of Surplus Value.* Part 1. Moscow: Progress Publishers, 1963.

———. *The Economic and Philosophic Manuscripts of 1844.* Translated by Martin Milligan. New York: International Publishers, 1964.

———. *Theories of Surplus Value.* Part 2. Moscow: Progress Publishers, 1968.

———. *The Eighteenth Brumaire of Louis Bonaparte.* New York: International Publishers, 1969.

———. *The Civil War in France.* Peking: Foreign Languages Press, 1970.

———. *Contribution to a Critique of Political Economy.* New York: International Publishers, 1970.

———. *The Poverty of Philosophy.* New York: International Publishers, 1971.

———. *Theories of Surplus Value.* Part 3. Moscow: Progress Publishers, 1971.

———. *Grundrisse: Foundations of the Critique of Political Economy.* Translated by Martin Nicolaus. New York: Vintage, 1973.

———. *Wages, Price and Profit.* Peking: Foreign Languages Press, 1975.

———. *Critique of Hegel's "Philosophy of Right."* Translated by Annette Jolin and Joseph O'Malley. Cambridge: Cambridge University Press, 1977.

———. "Contribution to a Critique of Hegel's *Philosophy of Right*: Introduction." In *The Marx-Engels Reader*, edited by Robert C. Tucker, 2nd ed., 53–63. New York: Norton, 1978.

———. *Capital: A Critique of Political Economy.* Vol. 2. Translated by David Fernbach. New York: Vintage, 1981.

———. *Capital: A Critique of Political Economy.* Vol. 1. Translated by Ben Fowkes. New York: Penguin Classics, 1990.

———. *Capital: A Critique of Political Economy.* Vol. 3. Translated by David Fernback. New York: Penguin Classics, 1991.

Marx, Karl, and Frederick Engels. *Manifesto of the Communist Party.* In *The Marx-Engels Reader*, 2nd ed. Edited by Robert C. Tucker, 469–500. New York: Norton, 1978.

———. *Collected Works.* 50 vols. New York: International Publishers, 1975–2004.

Maskivker, Julia. "Employment as a Limitation on Self-Ownership." *Human Rights Review* 12, no. 1 (2011): 27–45.

Mauss, Marcel. "Introduction to the First Edition." In Emile Durkheim, *Socialism*, 32–36. Translated by Charlotte Sattler. New York: Collier, 1962.

McLellan, David. *Karl Marx: His Life and Thought.* New York: Harper & Row, 1973.

McMurtry, John. *The Structure of Marx's World-View.* Princeton, NJ: Princeton University Press, 1978.

Meštrović, Stjepan G. *Emile Durkheim and the Reformation of Sociology.* Totowa, NJ: Rowman & Littlefield, 1988.

Mills, C. Wright, "Introduction: The Classical Tradition." In *Images of Man: The Classical Tradition in Sociological Thinking*, edited by C. Wright Mills, 1–17. New York: George Braziller, 1960.

Mobasser, Nilou. "Marx and Self-Realization." *New Left Review* 161 (January–February 1987): 119–28.

Mokyr, Joel. "Editor's Introduction: The New Economic History and the Industrial Revolution." In *The British Industrial Revolution: An Economic Perspective*, edited by Joel Mokyr, 1–131. Boulder, CO: Westview, 1993.

Mommsen, Wolfgang J. *The Age of Bureaucracy: Perspectives on the Political Sociology of Max Weber.* Oxford: Basil Blackwell, 1974.

———. "Max Weber as a Critic of Marxism." *Canadian Journal of Sociology* 2, no. 4 (Autumn 1977): 373–98.

———. *Max Weber and German Politics, 1890–1920.* Translated by Michael S. Steinberg. Chicago, IL: University of Chicago Press, 1984.

———. "Capitalism and Socialism: Weber's Dialogue with Marx." Translated by David Herr. In *A Weber-Marx Dialogue*, edited by Robert J. Antonio and Ronald M. Glassman, 234–61. Lawrence: University Press of Kansas, 1985.

———. *The Political and Social Theory of Max Weber: Collected Essays.* Chicago, IL: University of Chicago Press, 1989.

Morrison, Ken. *Marx, Durkheim, Weber: Formations of Modern Social Thought.* 2nd ed. London: Sage, 2006.

Mueller, Gert H. "Socialism and Capitalism in the Work of Max Weber." *British Journal of Sociology* 33, no. 2 (June 1982): 151–71.

Müller, Hans-Peter. "Durkheim's Political Sociology." In *Emile Durkheim: Sociologist and Moralist*, edited by Stephen Turner, 95–110. London: Routledge, 1993.

Musto, Marcello. "Marx in Paris: Manuscripts and Notebooks of 1844." Translated by Patrick Camiller. *Science & Society* 73, no. 3 (July 2009): 386–402.

Nimtz, August. "Marx and Engels—The Unsung Heroes of the Democratic Breakthrough." *Science & Society* 63, no. 2 (Summer 1999): 203–31.

Offe, Claus. *Reflections on America: Tocqueville, Weber and Adorno in the United States.* Translated by Patrick Camiller. Malden, MA: Polity Press, 2004.

Ollman, Bertell. *Alienation: Marx's Conception of Man in Capitalist Society.* 2nd ed. Cambridge: Cambridge University Press, 1976.

———. "Marx's Vision of Communism: A Reconstruction." *Critique* 8 (Summer 1977): 5–41.

O'Malley, Joseph. "Editor's Introduction." In *Critique of Hegel's 'Philosophy of Right' by Karl Marx*, edited and translated by Joseph O'Malley, 1x–lxvii. Cambridge: Cambridge University Press, 1977.

Palonen, Kari. "Max Weber's Reconceptualization of Freedom." *Political Theory* 27, no. 4 (August 1999): 523–44.

Palumbo, Antonino, and Alan Scott. "Weber, Durkheim and the Sociology of the Modern State." In *The Cambridge History of Twentieth-Century Political Thought*, edited by Terence Ball and Richard Bellamy, 368–91. Cambridge: Cambridge University Press, 2003.

Parkin, Frank. *Max Weber.* New York: Tavistock, 1982.

Pearce, Frank. *The Radical Durkheim.* London: Unwin & Hyman, 1989.

Peffer, R. G. *Marxism, Morality, and Social Justice.* Princeton, NJ: Princeton University Press, 1990.

Pels, Dick. "A Fellow-Traveller's Dilemma: Sociology and Socialism in the Writings of Durkheim." *Acta Politica* 19, no. 3 (1984): 309–29.

Pfaff, Steven. "Nationalism, Charisma, and Plebiscitary Leadership: The Problem of Democratization in Max Weber's Political Sociology." *Sociological Inquiry* 72, no. 1 (Winter 2002): 81–107.

Pickering, W. S. F., ed. *Durkheim: Essays on Moral and Education.* Translated by H. L. Sutcliffe. London: Routledge & Kegan Paul, 1979.

Poggi, Gianfranco. "The Chronic Trauma: The Great Transformation, Restoration Thought and the Sociological Tradition." *British Journal of Sociology* 19, no. 1 (March 1968): 89–95.

———. *Calvinism and the Capitalist Spirit: Max Weber's Protestant Ethic.* Amherst: University of Massachusetts Press, 1983.

————. *Durkheim*. Oxford: Oxford University Press, 2000.

————. *Weber: A Short Introduction*. Cambridge: Polity, 2006.

Polanyi, Karl. *The Great Transformation: The Political and Economic Origins of Our Time*. Boston, MA: Beacon Press, 1957.

Portis, E. B. "Max Weber's Theory of Personality." *Sociological Inquiry* 48, no. 2 (1978): 113–20.

Postone, Moishe. *Time, Labor, and Social Domination: A Reinterpretation of Marx's Critical Theory*. New York: Cambridge University Press, 1993.

Prager, Jeffrey. "Moral Integration and Political Inclusion: A Comparison of Durkheim's and Weber's Theories of Democracy." *Social Forces* 59, no. 4 (June 1981): 918–50.

Prinz, Arthur M. "Background and Ulterior Motives of Marx's 'Preface' of 1859." *Journal of the History of Ideas* 30, no. 3 (July–September 1969): 437–50.

Rawls, Anne. "Conflict as a Foundation for Consensus: Contradictions of Industrial Capitalism in Book III of Durkheim's *Division of Labor*." *Critical Sociology* 29, no. 3 (2003): 295–335.

Ray, Larry J. *Theorizing Classical Sociology*. Buckingham: Open University Press, 1999.

Reiman, Jeffrey. "Exploitation, Force, and the Moral Assessment of Capitalism: Thoughts on Roemer and Cohen." *Philosophy & Public Affairs* 16, no. 1 (Winter 1987): 3–41.

Richter, Melvin. *The History of Political and Social Concepts: A Critical Introduction*. New York: Oxford University Press, 1995.

Rigby, S. H. *Marxism and History: A Critical Introduction*. 2nd ed. Manchester, UK: Manchester University Press, 1998.

Ringer, Fritz. *The Decline of the German Mandarins: The German Academic Community, 1890–1933*. Cambridge, MA: Harvard University Press, 1969.

————. *Max Weber: An Intellectual Biography*. Chicago, IL: University of Chicago Press, 2004.

Ritzer, George. *The McDonaldization of Society*. Revised New Century Edition. Thousand Oaks, CA: Pine Forge, 2004.

Roth, Guenther, and Wolfgang Schluchter. *Max Weber's Vision of History: Ethics and Methods*. Berkeley: University of California Press, 1979.

Rubel, Maximilien. "Notes on Marx's Conception of Democracy." *New Politics* 16 (Winter 1962): 78–90.

Ryan, Alan. *On Politics. Book Two: Hobbes to the Present*. New York: Norton, 2012.

Sayer, Derek. *Capitalism and Modernity: An Excursus on Marx and Weber*. London: Routledge, 1991.

Scaff, Lawrence A. "Max Weber's Politics and Political Education." *American Political Science Review* 67, no. 1 (March 1973): 128–41.

————. *Fleeing the Iron Cage: Culture, Politics, and Modernity in the Thought of Max Weber*. Berkeley: University of California Press, 1989.

————. "Weber before Weberian Sociology." In *Reading Weber*, edited by Keith Tribe, 15–41. London: Routledge, 1989.

————. "Weber on the Cultural Situation of the Modern Age." In *The Cambridge Companion to Weber*, edited by Stephen Turner, 99–116. Cambridge: Cambridge University Press, 2000.

————. *Max Weber in America*. Princeton, NJ: Princeton University Press, 2011.

Schluchter, Wolfgang. *Paradoxes of Modernity: Culture and Conduct in the Theory of Max Weber*. Translated by Neil Solomon. Stanford, CA: Stanford University Press, 1996.

Schoenfeld, Eugen, and Stjepan G. Meštrović. "Durkheim's Concept of Justice and Its Relationship to Social Solidarity." *Sociological Analysis* 50, no. 2 (Summer 1989): 111–27.

Schroeder, Ralph. "Nietzsche and Weber: Two 'Prophets' of the Modern World." In *Max Weber, Rationality and Modernity*, edited by Sam Whimster and Scott Lash, 207–21. London: Allen & Unwin, 1987.

―――. "'Personality' and 'Inner Distance': The Conception of the Individual in Max Weber's Sociology." *History of the Human Sciences* 4, no. 1 (1991): 61–78.

―――. *Max Weber and the Sociology of Culture*. London: Sage, 1992.

Scott, Alan. "Capitalism, Weber and Democracy." *Max Weber Studies* 1, no. 1 (November 2000): 33–55.

Screpanti, Ernesto. *Libertarian Communism: Marx, Engels and the Political Economy of Freedom*. New York: Palgrave Macmillan, 2007.

Seidman, Steven. "Modernity, Meaning and Cultural Pessimism in Max Weber." *Sociological Analysis* 44, no. 4 (1983): 267–78.

―――. *Liberalism and the Origins of European Social Theory*. Berkeley: University of California Press, 1983.

―――. "The Main Aims and Thematic Structures of Max Weber's Sociology." *Canadian Journal of Sociology* 9, no. 4 (1984): 381–404.

―――. "Modernity and the Problem of Meaning: The Durkheimian Tradition." *Sociological Analysis* 46, no. 2 (1985): 109–30.

Shafir, Gershon. "The Incongruity between Destiny and Merit: Max Weber on Meaningful Existence and Modernity." *British Journal of Sociology* 36, no. 4 (December 1985): 516–30.

Sirianni, Carmen J. "Justice and the Division of Labour: A Reconsideration of Durkheim's *Division of Labour in Society*." *Sociological Review* 32, no. 3 (August 1984): 450–70.

Sitton, John F. *Recent Marxian Theory: Class Formation and Social Conflict in Contemporary Capitalism*. Albany: State University of New York Press, 1996.

Sperber, Jonathan. *Karl Marx: A Nineteenth Century Life*. New York: Liveright, 2013.

Stones, Rob. "Introduction: Continuity and Change in the Preoccupations of Key Sociological Thinkers." In *Key Sociological Thinkers*, edited by Rob Stones, 2nd ed., 1–42. New York: Palgrave, 2008.

Suchting, W. A. *Marx: An Introduction*. New York: New York University Press, 1983.

Swart, Koenraad W. "'Individualism' in the Mid-Nineteenth Century (1826–1860)." *Journal of the History of Ideas* 23, no. 1 (January–March 1962): 77–90.

Swedberg, Richard. *Max Weber and the Idea of Economic Sociology*. Princeton, NJ: Princeton University Press, 1998.

―――. *The Max Weber Dictionary: Key Words and Central Concepts*. Stanford, CA: Stanford University Press, 2005.

Sweezy, Paul. *The Theory of Capitalist Development: Principles of Marxian Political Economy*. New York: Monthly Review, 1970.

Tabak, Mehmet. "Marx's Theory of Proletarian Dictatorship Revisited." *Science & Society* 64, no. 3 (Fall 2000): 333–56.

Tenbruck, Friedrich H. "The Problem of Thematic Unity in the Works of Max Weber." *British Journal of Sociology* 31, no. 3 (September 1980): 316–51.

Thomas, J. J. R. "Weber and Direct Democracy." *British Journal of Sociology* 35, no. 2 (June 1984): 216–40.

Thomas, Paul. *Alien Politics: Marxist State Theory Retrieved*. New York: Routledge, 1994.

Thompson, Kenneth. *Emile Durkheim*. London: Tavistock, 1982.

Titunik, Regina F. "Status, Vanity and Equal Dignity in Max Weber's Political Thought." *Economy and Society* 24, no. 1 (February 1995): 101–21.

―――. "The Continuation of History: Max Weber and the Advent of a New Aristocracy." *Journal of Politics* 59, no. 3 (August 1997): 680–700.

———. "Democracy, Domination, and Legitimacy in Max Weber's Political Thought." In *Max Weber's* Economy and Society*: A Critical Companion*, edited by Charles Camic, Philip S. Gorski, and David M. Trubek, 143–63. Stanford, CA: Stanford University Press, 2005.

Traugott, Mark, ed. *Emile Durkheim on Institutional Analysis*. Translated by Mark Traugott. Chicago, IL: University of Chicago Press, 1978.

Tribe, Keith, ed. *Reading Weber*. London: Routledge, 1989.

Tucker, Kenneth H., Jr. *Classical Social Theory: A Contemporary Approach*. Malden, MA: Blackwell, 2002.

Turner, Bryan S. *Classical Sociology*. London: Sage, 1999.

Turner, Stephen P. "Bunyan's Cage and Weber's Calling." *Sociological Inquiry* 52, no. 1 (Winter 1982): 84–87.

———, ed. *Emile Durkheim: Sociologist and Moralist*. London: Routledge, 1993.

———, ed. *The Cambridge Companion to Weber*. Cambridge: Cambridge University Press, 2000.

Vogt, W. Paul. "Durkheim's Sociology of Law: Morality and the Cult of the Individual." In *Emile Durkheim: Sociologist and Moralist*, edited by Stephen Turner, 71–94. London: Routledge, 1993.

Wagner, Peter. *A Sociology of Modernity: Liberty and Discipline*. New York: Routledge, 1994.

———. *Modernity: Understanding the Present*. Cambridge, MA: Polity, 2012.

Wallwork, Ernest. "Religion and Social Structure in *The Division of Labor*." *American Anthropologist* 86, no. 1 (March 1984): 43–64.

Warren, Mark. "Max Weber's Liberalism for a Nietzschean World." *American Political Science Review* 82, no. 1 (March 1988): 31–50.

Weaver, Mark. "Weber's Critique of Advocacy in the Classroom: Critical Thinking and Civic Education." *PS: Political Science and Politics* 31, no. 4 (December 1998): 799–801.

Weber, Marianne. *Max Weber: A Biography*. Translated by Harry Zohn. New York: Wiley, 1975.

Weber, Max. *The Methodology of the Social Sciences*. Translated by Edward A. Shils and Henry A. Finch. New York: Free Press, 1949.

———. *The Religion of China: Confucianism and Taoism*. Translated by Hans H. Gerth. New York: Free Press, 1951.

———. *The Religion of India: The Sociology of Hinduism and Buddhism*. Translated by Hans H. Gerth and Don Martindale. New York: Free Press, 1958.

———. "Marginal Utility Theory and 'The Fundamental Law of Psychophysics.'" Translated by Louis Schneider. *Social Science Quarterly* 56, no. 1 (June 1975): 21–36.

———. *Roscher and Knies: The Logical Problems of Historical Economics*. Translated by Guy Oaks. New York: Free Press, 1975.

———. *The Agrarian Sociology of Ancient Civilizations*. Translated by R. I. Frank. London: New Left Books, 1976.

———. *Critique of Stammler*. Translated by Guy Oaks. New York: Free Press, 1977.

———. *Economy and Society: An Outline of Interpretive Sociology*. Translated by Ephraim Fischoff et al. Berkeley: University of California Press, 1978.

———. "Max Weber on Bureaucratization in 1909." In J. P. Mayer, *Max Weber and German Politics*. New York: Arno Press, 1979.

———. *General Economic History*. New Brunswick, NJ: Transaction, 1981.

———. *The Protestant Ethic and the Spirit of Capitalism*. Translated by Talcott Parsons. London: Unwin, 1985.

———. "'Churches' and 'Sects' in North America: An Ecclesiastical Socio-Political Sketch." *Sociological Theory* 3, no. 1 (Spring 1985): 7–13.

———. *The Russian Revolution*. Translated and Edited by Gordon C. Wells and Peter Baehr. Ithaca, NY: Cornell University Press, 1995.

———. "Voluntary Associational Life (*Vereinswesen*)." *Max Weber Studies* 2, no. 2 (2002): 199–209.

Wellen, Richard. "The Politics of Intellectual Integrity." *Max Weber Studies* 2, no. 1 (November 2001): 81–101.

Wetherly, Paul. "Marxism and Economic Determination: Clarification and Defence of an 'Old-Fashioned' Principle." *Review of Radical Political Economics* 33, no. 3 (Fall 2001): 273–79.

Whimster, Sam. "Translator's Note on Weber's 'Introduction to the Economic Ethics of the World Religions.'" *Max Weber Studies* 3, no. 1 (November 2002): 74–98.

———, ed. *The Essential Weber: A Reader*. New York: Routledge, 2004.

Whimster, Sam, and Scott Lash, eds. *Max Weber, Rationality and Modernity*. London: Allen & Unwin, 1987.

Williams, Raymond. *Culture and Society, 1780–1950*. New York: Harper Torchbooks, 1958.

Wolfe, Kurt, ed. *Essays on Sociology and Philosophy by Emile Durkheim et al*. New York: Harper Torchbooks, 1960.

Wolin, Sheldon S. "Political Theory as a Vocation." *American Political Science Review* 63, no 4 (December 1969): 1062–82.

———. "Max Weber: Legitimation, Method, and the Politics of Theory." *Political Theory* 9, no. 3 (August 1981): 401–24.

Wright, Erik Olin. "The Shadow of Exploitation in Weber's Class Analysis." In *Max Weber's Economy and Society: A Critical Companion*, edited by Charles Camic, Philip S. Gorski, and David M. Trubek, 204–36. Stanford, CA: Stanford University Press, 2005.

Wright, Erik Olin, Andrew Levine, and Elliott Sober. *Reconstructing Marxism: Essays on Explanation and the Theory of History*. London: Verso, 1992.

Wrong, Dennis, ed. *Max Weber*. Englewood Cliffs, NJ: Prentice-Hall, 1970.

Index

Abrahms, Philip, 11
accounting, and modern rational
   capitalism, 99
accumulation: continuous, 28, 46; Franklin
   on, 101–102; Marx on, 28, 46, 132;
   primitive, 34–36
adaptation: Durkheim on, 222; Weber on,
   153, 188
administration, Weber on, 157, 227
affectual action, 94, 95
Alexander, Jeffrey, 163
alienation, Marx on, 40, 136–138
altruism, Durkheim on, 181
altruistic suicide, 79, 80–81
anomic suicide, 79, 80, 83–84
anomie, Durkheim on, 140, 141–143, 179
Aristotle, 63
ascetic Protestantism, Weber on, 103–106
authority: rationalization and, 108–112;
   types of, 108–109. *See also* power

Beetham, David, 154, 226, 231, 233
Berg, Maxine, 9
Bonaparte, Louis Napoleon, 208
Bonaparte, Napoleon, 7
Breiner, Peter, 224
Brubaker, Rogers, 124, 191, 194
bureaucracy: Hegel on, 205, 210; Marx on,
   210, 239; Paris Commune and, 212;
   Weber on, 112–115, 152–155, 157,
   192–194, 227, 239, 264, 268

business enterprise, capitalist, Weber on,
   156
business-household separation, and
   modern rational capitalism, 100

calculation, Weber on, 95
Calvinism, 104–105, 107
capital, Industrial Revolution and, 9
capitalism, 241–242; current state of, 53,
   279; development of, 34–36, 131–132;
   Durkheim on, 251–260; and freedom,
   171–177; and individualism, 169–171;
   Marx on, 21, 22, 34–36, 44–47, 48,
   49–50, 131–132, 169–177, 207–209,
   242–251; as modernizing force, 49–50,
   246; as precondition of socialism,
   246–247; problems with, 44–47, 48,
   138, 263–264, 270–273; rise of, 2;
   versus slavery, 43; and state, 207–209;
   types of, 97; Weber on, 96–101,
   150–152, 260–270
capitalist business enterprise, Weber on,
   156
capitalist circuit, 32, 41
capitalist development: Marx on, 48–53;
   Weber on, 261–264
capitalist mode of production, Marx on,
   31–47
Catholicism, and suicide, 82
causal explanations, 65–66
Censor, Jack, 6

subjective freedom, 198–200; Weber on, 186–187, 191–192
substantive rationality, 155–158
suffrage: Marx on, 209; Paris Commune and, 213. *See also* democracy
suicide: Durkheim on, 78–85, 197; social rate of, 78–79; social types of, 79–84
surplus labor-time, Marx on, 42–43, 174
surplus value: Marx on, 41; relative, 43

technology: Industrial Revolution and, 7; information, 279; Marx on, 28, 133; and modern rational capitalism, 99
time, Marx on, 42–183, 44, 173–176
Tolstoy, Leo, 120
trade, Industrial Revolution and, 7
trade unions: Marx on, 247; Weber on, 263
traditional action, 94, 95
traditional authority, 109, 112
traditionalism, Weber on, 102
transformation: Durkheim on, 256–257; Marx on, 49. *See also* great transformation
transparency, in government, Durkheim on, 219–220
Turgot, Anne Robert Jacques, 3
Turner, Stephen, 191

ultimate values, Weber on, 188, 189–190
unemployment, 38
urbanization, 8; Marx on, 49; and proletariat, 52
use-value, 31

valorization, Marx on, 132, 133

value judgments, 119–120
value pluralism, 121–122
value-rational action, 94
values, Weber on, 188, 189–190
variable capital, Marx on, 42
Voltaire, 3
voluntary organizations, Weber on, 193

wages, 46; decline in, 134
Warren, Mark, 240
Weber, Max, 91–124; on capitalism, 260–270; on democracy, 223–234, 234–235, 236, 236–237, 238–240; versus Durkheim, 161–162; on evaluation, 67; on future, 277; on history, 163–164; on individualism, 185–193, 197–198, 198–200, 201; versus Marx, 275–277; on modernity, 10–13, 148–158, 160–161, 194–196, 267–270; on progress, 163, 185; as public intellectual, 13–14; on socialism, 271, 272–273, 275–277; study of, rationale for, 1, 10–11, 279–283
Wolin, Sheldon, 14
working class, 270–273; Durkheim on, 254–255; immiseration of, 134–136; Marx on, 21, 47, 130–138, 242–251; and Paris Commune, 211–213; revolutionary, formation of, 51–53; self-emancipation of, 248; term, 245; Weber on, 152, 228, 269–270
workplace: conditions in, 135; discipline of, 44; Marx on, 39, 40, 47, 135, 173; specialization in, Durkheim on, 141–142; Weber on, 156–157

About the Author

Edward Royce is professor emeritus of sociology at Rollins College. In addition to *Classical Social Theory and Modern Society: Marx, Durkheim, Weber*, he is also the author of *The Origins of Southern Sharecropping* (1993) and *Poverty and Power: The Problem of Structural Inequality* (2015). He currently lives in Northampton, Massachusetts.